Emotion, Imagination, and the Limits of Reason

The emotions pose many philosophical questions. We don't choose them; they come over us spontaneously. Sometimes emotions seem to get it wrong: we experience wrongdoing but do not feel anger, feel fear but recognize there is no danger. Yet often we expect emotions to be reasonable, intelligible and appropriate responses to certain situations. How do we explain these apparent contradictions?

Emotion, Imagination, and the Limits of Reason presents a bold new picture of the emotions that challenges prevailing philosophical orthodoxy. Talia Morag argues that too much emphasis has been placed on the "reasonableness" of emotions and far too little on two neglected areas: the imagination and the unconscious. She uses these to propose a new philosophical and psychoanalytic conception of the emotions that challenges the perceived rationality of emotions; views the emotions as fundamental to determining one's self-image; and bases therapy on the ability to "listen" to one's emotional episode as it occurs.

Emotion, Imagination, and the Limits of Reason is one of the first books to connect philosophical research on the emotions to psychoanalysis. It will be essential reading for those studying ethics, the emotions, moral psychology and philosophy of psychology, as well as those interested in psychoanalysis.

Talia Morag teaches Philosophy and Psychoanalysis at the University of Sydney and is an adjunct fellow at Western Sydney University, Australia. She is the director of *Psyche + Society*, which brings discussions about social psychology to the wider public.

Emotion, Imagination, and the Limits of Reason

Talia Morag

Routledge
Taylor & Francis Group
LONDON AND NEW YORK

First published 2016 by Routledge

2 Park Square, Milton Park, Abingdon, Oxfordshire OX14 4RN
711 Third Avenue, New York, NY 10017

Routledge is an imprint of the Taylor & Francis Group, an informa business

First issued in paperback 2017

British Library Cataloguing in Publication Data
A catalogue record for this book is available from the British Library

Library of Congress Cataloging in Publication Data
Names: Morag, Talia, author.
Title: Emotion, imagination, and the limits of reason / by Talia Morag.
Description: 1 [edition]. | New York : Routledge, 2016. | Includes bibliographical references and index.
Identifiers: LCCN 2015050447 | ISBN 9781138656949 (hardback : alk. paper) | ISBN 9781315621616 (e-book)
Subjects: LCSH: Emotions (Philosophy) | Emotions. | Reason. | Imagination. | Imagination (Philosophy) | Subconsciousness. | Psychoanalysis.
Classification: LCC B105.E46 M66 2016 | DDC 128/.37—dc23LC record available at http://lccn.loc.gov/2015050447

ISBN: 978-1-138-65694-9 (hbk)
ISBN: 978-1-138-55952-3 (pbk)

Typeset in Sabon
by FiSH Books Ltd, Enfield

To my grandparents, Yona and Ben (Bunio) Abish

Contents

Acknowledgments

I thank David Macarthur for the many eye-opening conversations we have had throughout the writing and reworking of this book, which helped me to clarify crucial conceptual issues. I also thank him for his teachings of Wittgenstein's metaphysical quietism and of pragmatist epistemology, and especially for introducing me to his Liberal Naturalism, which provided me with important methodological tools for the inquiry I conduct in this book. I also thank Paul Redding and Robert Dunn for their detailed comments on the first draft of this book. I would also like to acknowledge Russell Grigg for our stimulating and enriching correspondence about psychoanalysis before, during and after the writing of this book. I am also grateful to my PhD thesis examiners, who provided valuable comments for the first version of this book: Jim Hopkins, Ronald de Sousa, and especially Stephen White. Stephen's remarks, in particular, have sharpened and broadened the ambitions of this book. I thank my students in the philosophy and psychoanalysis course I have taught at the University of Sydney since 2010, especially Jack Cassidy, whose questions pressed on particularly important matters. I wholeheartedly thank Noa Salamon for being an inspiring example of a psychotherapist. I thank my beloved husband David for his relentless help and support and my daughter Thea for being so patient and understanding, especially during the writing of the first version of this book. I am deeply grateful to my loving parents Varda and Michael Morag for their belief, encouragement and endless generosity. I especially thank my grandparents, Yona and Ben Abish, for their love and financial support, thanks to which I was able to pursue my university studies and my passion for philosophy. And finally I would also like to thank Badde Manors, Clipper Café, and especially Sonoma Bakery Café in Glebe, Sydney, for having me spend hours on end on the premises and for the great coffee.

Introduction

What is an emotion? As with most contemporary philosophical engagements with this question, this book focuses on occurrent emotions, on emotional episodes, bouts of affect that strike us or come over us, which have a passionate, embodied, expressive, experiential aspect, an experience of a certain temporal duration. The first part of this book shows that existing philosophical accounts of emotions fail to fit the phenomenon, that is, that they fail to capture the *emotionality* of emotions. In a sense, the conception of emotional episodes proposed in the second part of this book emerges as a response to existing philosophical conceptions that do not have the resources to do justice to two crucial aspects of our ordinary experience of emotions.

(1) The very same situation or circumstances may arouse a certain emotion-type in one person and a different emotion-type in another person and leave yet another person emotionally indifferent. Imagine three friends waiting for another fourth friend, who is a bit late. One person may begin to feel angry that the friend is late. Another may worry that something might have happened to the late friend. And the third person may not feel anything at all. Indeed, the very same person may emotionally react in different ways or remain emotionally indifferent to the same circumstances on different occasions. Today the rude waiter "pushed my buttons," as we say, and irritated me, yesterday I was amused by his rudeness, and tomorrow his rudeness may leave me completely indifferent. What changes from one day to the next? What makes me emote while you stay indifferent? I call this question *the singularity question*. The difference between my patterns of emotional reaction and your patterns is often spoken of in terms of difference in character. But saying that we have different characters is just another way to describe this question rather than answering it. And in any case, sometimes we emote out of character.[1] And although people's emotional patterns may be quite stable, these patterns are not written in stone. At least some of them can come and go or change over time.

1 Cf. Cheshire Calhoun, "Subjectivity and Emotion," in *Thinking about Feeling*, ed. Robert Solomon (New York, NY: Oxford University Press, 2004), 119.

The singularity question as such is rarely mentioned in the philosophical literature, although some exceptions can be found. Jenefer Robinson, for example, whose account of emotion is discussed in Chapter 2, asks, "Why am I emotional about something on some occasions and on other occasions not? Or why does the very same event make me emotional and not you?"[2] But another version of this issue is so familiar that it has almost become a cliché. The cliché is about the possibility of a divergence of what one thinks and how one emotes. That is, I can think or judge or see that a situation merits anger and yet not get angry.[3] Thinking or judging does not entail emoting. Philosophers of emotion repeatedly make this conceptual point and then set it aside.[4] Yet, this consideration implies a fact about our experience of emotions that none of these philosophers care to articulate or explain, namely that we may remain indifferent in circumstances that fit a certain emotional reaction, whether or not we explicitly judge that these circumstances justify a certain emotional reaction.

(2) Another aspect of our ordinary experience of emotions, which is insufficiently explained in the contemporary literature, has to do with their unreliable responsiveness to reason. Although emotions come over us spontaneously and are not experiences we somehow decide or choose to undergo, we often expect emotions to be reasonable, to be intelligible and appropriate responses to the situation in which they arose. Indeed, often, when we judge emotional reactions to be unreasonable or inappropriate, we expect people to be able to control them and dim them down. Sometimes, people may control or dim down their emotions once they recognize their inappropriateness. Other times, such attempts to control one's emotions through rational criticism fail. Although all philosophers have noticed the phenomenon of emotions that are recalcitrant to reason, this phenomenon remains largely under-described and unexplained.

The phenomenon is under-described since the philosophical literature acknowledges only a very limited family of cases of recalcitrance, represented by very few examples, such as phobias or persistent prejudiced emotions, e.g. disgust of homosexuals or contempt of women. In Chapter 1, I provide paradigms for further types of recalcitrance that are largely ignored in the literature, even if they are familiar from everyday experience. Perhaps the main reason for this gap in the literature has to do with the insufficient discussion of the various notions of appropriateness in reference to which we

2 Jenefer Robinson, *Deeper than Reason: Emotion and its Role in Literature, Music and Art* (Oxford: Clarendon Press, 2005), 95.

3 E.g. Paul E. Griffiths, "The Degeneration of the Cognitive Theory of Emotions," *Philosophical Psychology* 2, no. 3 (1989): 300; Jerome A. Shaffer, "An Assessment of Emotion," *American Philosophical Quarterly* 20, no. 2 (1983): 163; Robinson, *Deeper than Reason*, 14.

4 Robert Solomon also remarks that this point is a "now standard ... though it is rarely spelled out in sufficient detail." Robert Solomon, "On Emotions as Judgments," in *Not Passion's Slaves: Emotions and Choice* (New York: Oxford University Press, 2003), 94.

judge our emotions. In Chapters 1 and 2, I explore the available notions of emotion appropriateness and add another hitherto neglected notion. I claim that recalcitrance is much more widespread than is currently acknowledged, which treats recalcitrance as a marginal and relatively rare occurrence.

I further claim that the phenomenon of recalcitrance goes unexplained in the philosophical literature, and only because certain types of recalcitrance are not even considered in contemporary debates. Any viable account of emotion should allow for both success and failure of attempts to rationally control emotions, but current accounts do not allow for such variability, familiar from everyday experience. How is it that our emotions sometimes alter and align with our normative judgments about them and sometimes not? I call this *the question of reason-sensitivity.*

The main goal of this book is to answer these two interrelated questions about the formation and subsidence of emotional episodes. In other words, the book aims to clarify the very episodic nature of emotions, entailed in the concept of emotion that philosophers aim to clarify, a conceptual clarification with an empirical dimension. Indeed, as will become evident in the first part of this book, almost all current philosophical accounts of emotion presuppose a causal story and some of them explicitly provide one, and all these accounts fail to answer the singularity question and the question of reason-sensitivity. In the second part of the book I propose a new account for the formation and subsidence of emotional episodes and clarify the extent to which reasons partake in them.

My methodology in this inquiry consists in bringing to bear on one another three relatively isolated domains of philosophy: the philosophy of emotion, the philosophy of practical rationality, and the philosophy of psychoanalysis. Each of these philosophical domains focuses on certain phenomena: emotions, reasons and reasoning, and psychological symptoms. Bringing those domains to bear on one another involves conceptual difficulties to do with the distinct terminologies and focus of each field. Indeed, the areas of overlap require the formulation of some new concepts to help articulate their bearing upon each other.

The question of the relation of emotions to reason becomes difficult once we give up – as most philosophers presume to have done – on the "judgmentalist" idea that emotions are formed through a judgment that a certain situation merits or fits an emotional reaction of a certain type. Although most agree that emotions are not judgments, emotional reactions, once verbally expressed, *appear* to embed reasons. If I am able to report that I am angry that John stole my car, then effectively I am not only describing the emotionally salient features of the situation but I may appear or take myself to be claiming that John's stealing my car is the (normative) reason for my anger. This is precisely why emotions become candidates for rational criticism in the first place. Once a reason is given for a certain reaction, that reason can be judged to be good or bad in reference to norms of emotion appropriateness. But if emotions are not rationally formed through a judgment, then what kind of a "reason" is this? The emotion literature does not deal with this issue, whose clarification is necessary for a better understanding of the complex relation between emotions and reasons.

Philosophers of practical rationality that talk about emotions, here represented by Tim Scanlon and Richard Moran, do not distinguish emotions from other attitudes. Indeed, they are rationalistic about emotions, in the sense that they claim that all attitudes normally are (or should be) judgment sensitive.[5] Moran further claims that emotion formation and subsidence may occur through the grasp of reasons in explicit rational deliberation. In a sense, philosophers of practical rationality may be considered judgmentalists about emotions. But given their elaborate discussion about the nature of reasons and reason-sensitivity, which goes far beyond the discussion of any judgmentalist in the philosophy of emotion, their terminology and taxonomy of reasons is most helpful, by way of comparison and opposition, for the formulation of the relevant terminology of "reasons" for the special case of emotions.

Through a comparative study of what Tim Scanlon calls "reasons in the standard normative sense," I formulate in Chapter 1 a new notion of a reason look-alike, which is not a reason in the standard normative sense. An emotion *appears* to embed this look-alike reason only *after* it has been described in words, but it is in fact a merely retroactive rationalization. I claim that it is verbal expression and report that makes people treat emotions as rationally assessable in reference to norms of emotion appropriateness. Rationally formed attitudes that embed reasons in the standard normative sense (such as many beliefs) are reason-sensitive, as Moran says. That is, when such reasons are revoked, the attitude is thereby revoked, due to the constitutive relation between the reason and the attitude in question. In contrast, verbally expressed emotions are not reason-sensitive in Moran's sense but are rather susceptible to what I call normative pressure, a kind of peer-group pressure that can be more or less effective in controlling emotions, in ways that I discuss in Chapter 5.

Philosophers of emotion talk about the "motivational force"[6] of

5 That Moran models emotional attitudes on the case of belief is evident throughout his recent book: Richard Moran, *Authority and Estrangement: An Essay on Self-Knowledge* (Princeton: Princeton University Press, 2001). Similarly, for Scanlon: T. M. Scanlon, *What We Owe to Each Other* (Cambridge, MA: Harvard University Press, 1998). Matthew Boyle and Pamela Hieronymi also treat emotions as analogous to beliefs as is evident in Matthew Boyle, "Active Belief," *Canadian Journal of Philosophy*, Supplementary Volume 35, "Belief and Agency" (2009): 131; Pamela Hieronmymi, "Responsibility for believing," *Synthese* 161 (2008): 367.

6 E.g. Michael S. Brady, "The Irrationality of Recalcitrant Emotions", *Philosophical Studies* 145, no. 3 (2009): 417, 425–426; Aaron Ben Ze'ev, "Emotion Are Not Mere Judgments," *Philosophy and Phenomenological Research* 68, no. 2 (2004): 451; Patricia Greenspan, "A Case of Mixed Feelings: Ambivalence and the Logic of Emotion," in *Explaining Emotions*, ed. Amélie O. Rorty (Berkeley: University of California Press, 1980).

emotions or more recently about their "action tendencies,"[7] such as lashing out in anger or running away in fear. Such actions are not intentional actions that are guided by reasons, in the way that buying groceries according to a shopping list is intentional. And yet we are able to, and often do, retroactively rationalize such actions. The relation between emotionally expressive actions and reason has been widely neglected in the literature. In Chapter 3, I make comparative use of the philosophy of Elizabeth Anscombe on intentional action and propose a new way to understand such behaviors as neither rational nor sub-personal. Although I focus on a very particular kind of an action tendency, I suggest that my treatment of this topic can prove fruitful for the understanding of emotionally expressive actions in general.

Perhaps the most difficult methodological challenge of this book consists in turning to Freud's original texts in order to extract insights that are relevant to the question of emotion formation. The general attitude toward Freud today consists in an admiring skepticism that renders him essentially irrelevant. Philosophy, psychology, common culture and even contemporary psychoanalysis regard Freud as an important historical figure whose relevant insights have been assimilated and whose theories and case studies have no credence in terms of scientific evidence. "Freud bashing" by figures such Adolf Grünbaum, Frank Cioffi and, more recently, Frederic Crews, is widely accepted and there are good reasons to accept all those criticisms, given their presuppositions, the most important of which is psychoanalysis' pretention to qualify as (experimental) science.[8]

Freud famously conceived of himself as a scientist and of psychoanalysis as a developing natural science. He declared that "the intellect and the mind are objects for scientific research in exactly the same way as any non-human things. Psycho-analysis has a special right to speak for the scientific *Weltanschauung*."[9] In light of Freud's self-conception, he has been declared a failed scientist and his psychoanalysis a pseudo-science, and not without justification. This situation is a result of a chronic confusion about the status of psychoanalysis – one shared by Freud himself – that has done significant damage to the possibility of taking it seriously as an intellectual and therapeutic discipline. Crews is representative of many in remarking of psychoanalysis:

7 E.g. Jesse J. Prinz, *Gut Reactions: A Perceptual Theory of Emotion* (New York: Oxford University Press, 2004), in particular Chapter 8.

8 Adolf Grünbaum, *The Foundations of Psychoanalysis: A Philosophical Critique* (Berkeley: University of California Press, 1984); Frank Cioffi, *Freud and the Question of Pseudoscience* (Chicago: Open Court, 1998); Frederick Crews, ed., *The Memory Wars: Freud's Legacy in Dispute* (London UK: Granta Books, 1997 [1995]).

9 Sigmund Freud, *New Introductory Lectures on Psycho-Analysis* (1933 [1932]), in *The Standard Edition of the Complete Psychological Works of Sigmund Freud*, trans. James Strachey (London: The Hogarth Press, 1995 [1966]), 22, 159. Hereafter all references will use the standard abbreviation of S.E., followed by volume number.

> Its false therapeutic claims, its indefiniteness, its circular demonstrations, its revolutionary tone, its pretension to limitless insight, and its recourse to bluffing and slander in place of evidence all pointed to a break with the scientific ethos and a surrender to grandiosity on Freud's part.[10]

I turn to Freud's texts then, in the wake of these criticisms and their aftermath. I do not use Freud as an authority or as the pioneer of a new science. Rather, I read Freud's texts in order to recover fundamental insights that have been hitherto unappreciated and hence underexplored in this climate of Freud-skepticism. I agree that Freud's psychoanalysis is not a science, not even a social science and indeed it is replete with unilluminating metaphor. Like Thomas Nagel (and Jim Hopkins, Richard Wollheim, Sebastian Gardner) I agree that the psychoanalytic explanation for certain behaviors consists in or rather has the potential to consist in an extension of common-sense psychology. As Nagel says: "Psychoanalysis makes use of a complex network of interpretations, just as common-sense psychology does when it allows us to understand someone's reactions by referring to an interconnected network of desires, beliefs, emotions, memories, obsessions, inhibitions, values and identifications."[11]

But the task of articulating how psychoanalysis relates to common-sense psychology has not yet been embarked upon, since the literature still retains questionable and obscure Freudian terminology without translating it into the language of common-sense psychology. The main explanatory concept of psychoanalysis, which is in desperate need of reconstruction or re-articulation, is the concept of the unconscious. Even philosophers of emotion who do not engage with psychoanalysis, accept without objection the existence of "unconscious emotions."[12] But what is this strange quality of certain mental states of being unavailable to consciousness, and how do certain mental states, including emotions, become "unconscious"? As long as psychoanalytic explanations speak of the unconscious by taking recourse to equally obscure concepts, such as "repression," "regression," the "Id,"

10 Frederick Crews, "The Freud Question: An Exchange," *The New York Review of Books*, December 8, 2011. See also Ken Taylor's recent blog, where he says that Freud was wrong about everything: Ken Taylor, "The Legacy of Freud," www.philosophytalk.org/community/blog/ken-taylor/2014/02/legacy-freud.

11 Thomas Nagel, "Freud's Permanent Revolution," *The New York Review of Books* 41: 9, May 12, 1994; Jim Hopkins, "Psychoanalytic and Scientific Reasoning," *British Journal of Psychotherapy* 13, no. 1 (1996); Richard Wollheim, *The Mind and Its Depth* (Cambridge, MA: Harvard University Press, 1993); Sebastian Gardner, *Irrationality and the Philosophy of Psychoanalysis* (Cambridge: Cambridge University Press, 2006 [1993]).

12 See Prinz's overview: Prinz, *Gut Reactions*, 198–205. See also Amélie O. Rorty, "Freud on Unconscious Affects, Mourning and the Erotic Mind," in *The Analytic Freud: Philosophy and Psychoanalysis*, ed. Michael P. Levine (London: Routledge, 2000); Paul Redding, "Freud's Theory of Consciousness," in *The Analytic Freud: Philosophy and Psychoanalysis*, ed. Michael P. Levine (London: Routledge, 2000).

or "forces" or "drives" without explaining those in ordinary terms, such explanations will continue to occupy only the margins of psychological studies. Even Jonathan Lear, probably the leading philosopher of psychoanalysis to engage with the philosophy of practical rationality (and implicitly with the philosophy of emotion) in recent years, uses all these murky terms without explaining away their obscurity.

Another pervasive problem with psychoanalytic explanations, whether of Freud himself or of philosophers who take recourse to some of his ideas, consists in the unlikely supposition that very few past events or memories condition one's later emotional difficulties in life. Although people often tell stories about themselves where they explain their faults and weaknesses in terms of past mental wounds, such stories suffer from implausibility. Unless one is a rape victim, a survivor of war, torture or natural disaster or some other extreme traumatic event, it is hard to see how a single (or even a few) moderately unpleasant events in one's distant past would be somehow so much more important than the many other moderately unpleasant events spread throughout one's life so as to determine one's future emotional challenges.

This book is not the first to turn to Freudian psychoanalysis in the context of the philosophy of emotion, and Chapter 3 presents the accounts of Amélie Rorty and Ronald de Sousa, who more or less explicitly use certain Freudian ideas to explain pathological emotional patterns such as recalcitrance. But their accounts, as I show, take recourse to the concept of the unconscious without describing exactly what it entails and further ascribe to one or a few past events or memories an implausibly deterministic role in one's emotional life. One of the main innovations of my account consists in the liberation of the concept of the Freudian unconscious from its current confusion and obscurity, which also shows how and why the past may causally influence the present without determining it.

I thus introduce a new conception of the unconscious, which can be used to explain emotional reactions, whether pathological or not. Given this explanatory aim, I do not engage in Freud scholarship in this book. That is, I do not provide a close reading of the sections of Freud's texts on which this new conception of the unconscious is based, nor do I engage in a comparative study about the various conceptions of the unconscious that are available in Freud's texts and in the philosophy of psychoanalysis today. Although I believe that my conception of the unconscious can be used to produce a radically new reading of Freud, I do not embark on this project here. The force of my conception of the Freudian unconscious, as I show in the book, is its use in a causal account of emotional reactions that overcomes the outstanding explanatory challenges in the philosophy of emotion.

In order to navigate among these three fields of philosophy, to critically assess and compare the available accounts of emotions, and formulate my own terminology with which I construct a new causal account for emotions,

I adhere to a pragmatic methodology, which grounds my inquiry in our ordinary experiences and explanatory practices of emotions. That is, I try as much as possible to use everyday language, the language we ordinarily use to describe our psychological states of mind to one another. I also insist on the consideration of aspects of our ordinary experience of emotions that remain largely overlooked in the current literature. As I show in the first four chapters, the emotion literature suffers from a limited variety of examples, which circumscribe the data that current accounts can, or aim to, explain. I use examples from the philosophical literature, as well as from Freud's case studies and from stories I have heard from psychotherapists and friends as well as from my own experience, to demonstrate the explanatory force of my account as well as the lack of explanatory resources of other contemporary accounts.

As said above, the book's main line of inquiry into emotions examines their formation: What causes specific individuals to undergo an emotional episode or to be emotional when they do? Since the object of inquiry, emotions, will take the whole book to clarify, I begin with a very minimal and uncontroversial notion for occurent emotions: they have an episodic nature, that is, they are formed, they last to variable degrees and then subside; they involve prototypical physiological and often also behavioral manifestations; and they typically render certain people and things in the here-and-now emotionally salient, people and things who are often (but not always) also the trigger of the emotional episode.

The physiological and behavioral manifestations of emotional episodes can be said to be of a certain type, labeled "anger," fear," "joy," and so forth. That is, we associate certain prototypical physiological and behavioral manifestations with emotion-types. Each emotion-type is associated with prototypical facial expressions, such as smiles for joy and frowns for anger. Emotion-types often involve typical physiological feelings, such as a racing heart when afraid or excited, or a heat sensation when embarrassed or angry. Emotions can be expressed through typical "action tendencies" such as fight, flight, or freeze for fear, revenge or shouting for anger, and crying for sadness or joy. Some emotion-types can also be characterized by activity of certain areas of the brain, such as fear and the amygdala.[13]

A specific emotional episode thus has an expressive or *affective aspect*, that is the aspect of the emotion as an experience we suffer as patients. We may and often do express our emotions verbally, whether out loud or by talking to ourselves via inner speech. When people express their emotion in words, they also effectively describe it. Emotions, in other words, also have a *describable aspect*. For example, as I feel my heart racing, my cheeks burning, and my fists clenching, I am often able to say that I am angry and

13 Paul Griffiths, "Towards a Machiavellian Theory of Emotional Appraisal," in *Emotion, Evolution and Rationality*, ed. Dylan Evans and Pierre Cruse (Oxford: Oxford University Press, 2004), 92.

I am also able to specify the person or thing in the here-and-now situation that is emotionally salient to me. And, usually, I can also specify particular aspects of that person or thing that are emotionally salient. For example, I can say that I am angry with John, that I am angry he stole my car.

As will be explained in Chapter 1, many philosophers speak of the emotionally salient features in the here-and-now situation as the emotion's intentional object or as the emotion's target. I shall continue speaking in terms of emotionally salient features since I do not want to presuppose intentionality or targeting. What I call the describable aspect of an emotion thus includes the emotion-type and the here-and-now emotionally salient features.

This book attempts to explain only those emotions that subjects can easily describe in this manner. I thus leave aside, at least for the moment, the question of moods, those emotional states that do not make particular people and things affectively salient but that color everything in one's surroundings. In order to examine the causation of emotional episodes, I turn to their description in ordinary language, the one provided by the emoting subject, as a principle of their individuation. That verbal description is also often expressive.

This method of individuation may seem strange to those who want to know what emotions *really* are, no matter how we talk about them. Philosophers that are scientifically oriented may object to the use of ordinary language to individuate any phenomenon that is to be studied scientifically, since it is too vague and cannot provide well-regimented categories worthy of scientific inquiry. However, individuation through description in ordinary language is actually not at all controversial and is implicitly used by most researchers, whether they acknowledge it or not. In particular, empirical psychologists who conduct experiments on humans, experiments to which scientifically oriented philosophers constantly refer, usually rely on the subjects' reports of their emotions in order to individuate their object of inquiry, even if they do not necessarily trust the report to be accurate.[14]

In some cases, experimenters may individuate an emotional reaction through the subject's behavior, classifying it as an instantiation of this or that emotion type and specifying the here-and-now person or thing that the subject is emotionally attending to. But in those cases too, the episode is individuated by a description in ordinary language – the observer's description. This interpretative description is very likely to match the subject self-report when it comes to the specified emotion-type, unless the subject denies altogether that she is being emotional. The interpretative description may diverge from the subject's self-report when it comes to the specification

14 The many experiments surveyed in Prinz's book, all include subject's reports and some also physiological and behavioral responses. Just a few examples: Prinz, *Gut Reactions*, 30, 31, 56, 57, 70, 73, 94, 175.

of the emotionally salient features of the situation. But even in those cases, we cannot deny the subject the right to say what is emotionally salient to her at the moment of her self-report. Salience is a feature of people's self-aware experience. The interpreter may still be correct in the sense that she has identified the trigger of the emotional reaction, a trigger that in such cases differs from the emotionally salient features of the situation. No matter how we end up making sense of such cases, the point of departure for any investigation into emotional salience, whatever its causes may be, is the subject's self-report.

Finally, some experimenters may directly refer to brain activity. But even in those cases, the emotional state should not be understood as individuated by brain activity measurements. Such measurements are taken to mean that a certain subject is in an emotional state of a certain type due to previously established correlations with verbal descriptions of emotional states through self-report or observer interpretation. As Martha Nussbaum explains:

> We do not withdraw emotion-ascriptions otherwise grounded if we discover that the subject is not in a certain brain state. (Indeed, the only way that the brain-state assumed apparent importance was through putative correlation with instances of emotion identified on other grounds.)[15]

Although I do not believe that emotions can be reduced to brain-states or to some other well-regimented scientific category, I need not defend this view here. Individuation through description in ordinary language effectively comprises the point of departure of emotion researchers in general. I make this principle of individuation explicit not just in order to avoid controversy or disagreement regarding the reducibility or irreducibility of emotions to the language of neuroscience or physics. As I show throughout the book, verbally describing emotions does not merely provide epistemic access to emotions or a way to refer to them. Rather, emotions and their verbal description intimately and deeply connect, a connection that comprises one of the main themes of this book.

I have thus introduced what I mean by "emotions" and how I individuate them in order to ask about their formation. But when I say I propose a causal account for emotional episodes, what do I mean by "causation"? Traditional accounts of causation go hand in hand with physicalism. According to physicalism, everything that exists is a posit of a physical theory and obeys causal laws. Everything else, including the objects and causes studied in other sciences or the objects and causes we talk about in

15 Martha Nussbaum, "Emotions as Judgments of Value and Importance," in *Thinking about Feeling*, ed. Robert Solomon (New York, NY: Oxford University Press, 2004) 195.

ordinary language – is ontologically reducible to the objects and causes of physics, even if ordinary language cannot be translated into the language of physics.[16]

Everyday language, on this view, does not pick out the relevant causal factor in the right way. It may be difficult or even impossible to articulate the causal occurrences of everyday life in the language of physics, but properly speaking, causation belongs only to the level describable by physics. Physicalism thus goes hand in hand with what has been called "causal fundamentalism," the idea that there is a unique causal order in nature that is the task of physics to articulate. Physicalism and causal fundamentalism were once orthodoxy, and are still common today. And until recently, it seemed that the only way to avoid these commitments was to propound some form of supernaturalism.

My allegiance is not to physicalism or a causal fundamentalism but to naturalism. The most plausible form of naturalism, "Liberal Naturalism," takes seriously the plurality of explanations within the various sciences and ordinary discourse, as well as the plurality of kinds of objects to which they are committed. Once we acknowledge the plurality of explanatory practices, we can also acknowledge causal pluralism. As David Macarthur says:

> Some of the most exciting recent work on causation suggests that we see causation as having close conceptual ties to explanation and explanatory contexts. Such an account of causation poses a significant challenge to causal fundamentalism by lending strong support to the doctrine of causal pluralism. If causal talk is always understood relative to background explanatory context the fact that there are different levels of explanation implies that there can be a plurality of complete causal explanations for the same event.[17]

In other words, liberal naturalism does not privilege causation at the physical level, as if physical causes are the only "real" causes. The same event may be causally explained by various explanatory practices, each of which would account for an aspect of the event that is describable in terms of that specific practice.

Questions about the causation of emotions include questions that are asked at various levels of explanation with which I am not concerned in this book: Why do we, qua organisms, have emotions at all? Why do we have the emotion-types that we do, with their typical behavioral and physiological characteristics? How do we develop from infants with a small range of possible emotional reactions to adults with a rich repertoire of emotion-

16 Donald Davidson, "Mental Events," [1970] in *Essays on Actions and Events*, 2nd edn, (Oxford: Oxford University Press, 2001 [1980]).

17 David Macarthur, "Taking the Human Sciences Seriously," in *Naturalism and Normativity*, ed. Mario De Caro and David Macarthur (New York: Columbia University Press, 2010), 130.

types? Questions about the sources of the repertoire of emotion-types of a typical human adult in a certain social and linguistic niche are asked and may be researched at the biological, evolutionary, neurological and social levels of explanation. None of these questions concerns me in this book.

My question can now be articulated as follows: Given that a certain person of a certain culture and linguistic community has the capacity to emote in a way that is at least roughly identifiable by an emotion-type word, what causes a specific person to *spontaneously* emote in a specific describable way in certain specific circumstances? I emphasize the term "spontaneously" in order to exclude cases where emotions are primarily caused by physiological intervention such as stimulating certain areas of the brain, taking certain drugs or substances, or by lack of sleep or illness. *This* question, about a singular spontaneous emotional reaction is asked at the psychological level of causation.

Furthermore, I do not assume that causation must be nomological. In this book, I rely on the account of causal explanation advocated by James Woodward, which makes allowance for causal pluralism and singular causation. Woodward talks about the singular "why-explanation" for the occurrence of a particular event.[18] When providing such an explanation, we focus on a certain description of the event or a certain aspect of that description, which we aim to explain. What we identify as a cause for that aspect is something that "made a difference for" the occurrence of the event.[19] Without that identified cause, the event would either have not occurred at all or would have been different in some specified respect. As Woodward says:

> Singular causal explanations wear the source of their explanatory efficacy on their face – they explain not because they tacitly invoke a "hidden" law or statement of sufficient conditions, but because they identify conditions such that changes in these conditions would make a difference for whether the explanandum-phenomenon or some specified alternatives to it would ensue.[20]

This is an interventionist account of causation. Namely, whenever one can ask about a particular condition the "what-if-things-had-been-different" question, one can talk about causation. And that question can be asked within a plurality of our explanatory practices using different vocabularies. As Woodward shows, this interventionist account of singular causation suits natural scientific explanations, where we find a "generalized analogue of the explanation-making features which we attribute … to singular causal

18 James Woodward, "A Theory of Singular Causal Explanation," *Erkenntnis* 21 (1984): 231–232.
19 Ibid., 236.
20 Ibid., 237.

explanations."[21] But it also fits explanations of the social sciences, where there are localized generalizations rather than nomological laws.[22]

Woodward's account of singular causation, as I show in the book, also applies to psychological explanation at the level of commonsense everyday language. There too, we can ask and answer the "what-if-things-had-been-different" question. However, psychological events such as emotional reactions occur as a result of many factors, social and individual, that may include many details of the person's singular biography. The causes for each such reaction are singular in the sense that they are usually not reproducible, and do not lend themselves to laws or generalizations that can serve to reliably predict how a specific person will emote in specified circumstances. Although we can ascribe to people emotional patterns and although those patterns may be quite stable, these patterns are not laws. They may evolve over time, they may come and go, and their interruption is a common source of drama and suspense in our lives, as well as in fiction.

If science is a practice, which studies law-like causal relations between kinds of objects or causal generalizations (whether local or global) over classes of objects, then singular psychological causal explanations are non-scientific. This does not make them supernatural. In contrast to the orthodox view of causal fundamentalism and physicalism, contemporary liberal naturalism admits that everyday language can pick out relevant causes just as our ordinary practices assume (for example, when we explain to one another how our emotions could have been different if some other causal factor were in place).

My terrain is of singular causation, a form of non-scientific explanation. When it comes to human emotional life, the singular occurrences that we can and do explain in our ordinary social practices are too subjective, too idiosyncratic, too dependent on the particular subject's biography and self-image – to be generalizable across many people in a law-like manner. As said above, even the same person may emotionally react differently to similar circumstances at various points in time. This is not to deny that many of us emotionally respond similarly in various circumstances. Science may be able to explain or even predict statistical distributions of emotional reactions across certain classes of people, but it cannot answer the question that is the focus of this book, namely, *what makes this particular individual emote in a certain way in a certain specific situation.*

The affective processes that cause emotions, on my account, which I present in Chapter 5, are processes of the imagination. The imaginative capacities I propose operate independently of reason. I do not thereby revive the old-fashioned facultative psychology, which treats reason and imagination as two distinct faculties. Today, reason and imagination are

21 Ibid., 239.

22 See James Woodward, "Explanations and Invariance in the Special Sciences," *The British Journal for the Philosophy of Science* 51, no. 2 (2000).

often considered as intertwined in their operation.[23] Drawing on Freud's texts, I introduce two additional imaginative capacities that I call the connective and the synthetic imagination, which I claim to be distinctively non-rational. These are associative imaginative capacities that operate below the level of awareness and that in regard to which one is passive (unlike the imaginative capacity that is involved in conscious fantasizing or day-dreaming).

The notion of causal non-rational associations of the imagination is familiar from the philosophical enterprise of David Hume.[24] Hume writes:

> Reason can never shew us the connexion of one object with another, tho' aided by experience, and the observation of their constant conjunction in all past instances. When the mind, therefore, passes from the idea or impression of one object to the idea or belief of another, it is not determin'd by reason, but by certain principles, which associate together the ideas of these objects, and unite them in the imagination.[25]

Hume's associations, which are a basic explanatory tool in his philosophy, are universal and are governed by principles common to all human subjects. Hume's associations, which connect images or rather fragments of images to one another, are meant to explain the operations of the mind in general, including perception.

Hegel mocked Hume's laws of associations on the grounds that imaginative associations are too capricious to follow any law:

> The so-called *laws of the association of ideas* ... are not *laws*, just for the reason that there are so many laws about the same thing, as to suggest a caprice and contingency opposed to the very nature of law.[26]

And also:

> The train of images and representations suggested by association is the sport of vacant-minded ideation.[27]

The existence of distinctively imaginative and lawless associations was thus

23 Tamar Gendler, "Imagination," *The Stanford Encyclopedia of Philosophy*, (Fall 2011 Edition), ed. Edward N. Zalta, http://plato.stanford.edu/archives/fall2011/entries/imagination.

24 David Hume, *A Treatise of Human Nature* (London: Everyman's Library Press, 1911), Book 1, Part 1, Sect. iv: "Of the Connection or Association of Ideas".

25 Hume, *Treatise*, Book 1, Part 3, Sect 6.

26 G. W. F Hegel, *Hegel's Philosophy of Mind: Part Three of the Encyclopaedia of the Philosophical Sciences (1830)*, trans. W. Wallace (Oxford: Clarendon Press, 1971), §455. Emphasis in original.

27 Ibid.

acknowledged but also expelled from philosophical discussion whose proper realm is the realm of reason – its nature, scope and limits. Frege, too, argued that private associations have no place in rational inquiry, which aims for objective truth. But philosophy is also concerned with the limits of reasons. And this limitation has been encountered in the contemporary philosophy of emotions, with its outstanding difficulty being to explain recalcitrant emotions and to answer the question of the causal formation of singular emotional reactions.

Jerry Fodor sums up the main concern about associationism, which made it fall out of philosophical fashion: "associationism ... made an utter mystery of the coherence of mental life."[28] Rational capacities for inference and the construction of theories are indeed characterized by such coherence, and it would be wrong, to think as Hume did, that associationism can explain *all* mental phenomena. But as claimed in this book, our emotional lives are not always stable nor are they very coherent. Associations do justice to this inconsistency and incoherence.

I claim that Freud's most brilliant and revolutionary move was to take the private and lawless imaginative associations that philosophy threw away and put it at the center of inquiry into our emotional lives. In that respect, by mocking Hume's laws of associations, Hegel inadvertently discovered the lawless imaginative associations that are at the heart of psychoanalytic explanations. Similarly, Frege, who deliberately articulated his principles of inquiry into logical inference so as to exclude private associations, inadvertently provided the framework that can articulate the principles of inquiry into non-rational imaginative associations.

The Freudian imaginative associations I propose, albeit Humean in spirit, nevertheless significantly differ from Hume's concept of associations. Unlike Hume's associations, the imaginative associations I propose are not meant to explain or account for the mind's operations as a whole. The Freudian associations are hypothesized in order to explain only a restricted class of mental phenomena. These are mental occurrences roughly characterized as embodied mental states that come over us and in regard to which we feel passive, but that unlike the operations of the digestive system, they strike as inchoately meaningful, as revealing something about us as socially interactive persons, and which invite verbal expression and explanation in terms of something within us of which we can become aware. These are phenomena such as slips of the tongue, laughing at jokes, the appreciation of art works, dreams, sexual desires, and emotional episodes, on which I focus in this book.

Furthermore, unlike Hume's associations, the associations I propose do not presuppose a universal human nature. Although they also depend on one's language and cultural references that are widely shared, they are

28 Jerry Fodor, "Meaningful Words without Sense and Other Revolutions," *3AM Magazine*, October 19, 2012.

highly subjective and depend on the idiosyncratic imagination of each individual, as well as on one's particular and irreproducible biography. Imaginative associations thus do not obey any laws of associations, as Hume's associations are meant to obey. Although, as I claim in Chapter 5, people have certain habits of association in such a way that their emotional lives lend themselves to the identification of patterns of emotional reactions, the idiosyncrasy of the imagination and the relative unreliability of associative habits, render singular emotional reactions of specific individuals unfit for scientific study. As Hegel says: "Science ... everyone admits, is compelled by its form to busy itself with thought which abstracts from the mass of particulars. For this reason ...imagination with its contingency and caprice ... is of necessity excluded from science."[29]

In other words, although imaginative associations have causal effects on one's psychological state of mind and thus qualify as empirical phenomena, their "contingency and caprice" excludes them from scientific inquiry. The terrain of the inquiry of singular emotional reactions, therefore, belongs to the hitherto unacknowledged category of the non-scientific empirical. Yet this does not mean that singular emotional episodes are empirically inaccessible. As I show in Chapter 6, imaginative associations are, albeit to a limited extent, available to introspective self-awareness.

Although introspection cannot tell us much about external reality, it is, as I show in Chapter 6, a valid method of inquiry into some of one's own psychological states. Whereas Hume's preferred metaphor regarding introspection involved some kind of an "inner eye," my preferred metaphor is the audible rather than the visual. We are all able to "listen" to our own passing thoughts and inner speech. It is this metaphorical "listening" that makes imaginative associations empirically but non-scientifically accessible. As I explain in Chapter 6, "listening" to oneself is a skill one may refine through the method of inquiry invented by Freud known as "free association," which captures his revolutionary emphasis on what we may call the passive or associative imagination.

Most people today who experience emotional challenges usually turn either to medication or to cognitive behavioral therapy, which emphasizes the power of reasoning to change or to make up one's mind. This dichotomy between physiological causes and reasons is also evident in contemporary philosophy of emotion. The philosophical landscape is divided between the rationalists who speak of emotions as the behavioral expressions of rational agents and the sub-personalists who speak of emotions as products of a law-like causal mechanism, which operate below the person level. This book aims to propose a *third* way, by bringing back to center stage the associative imagination in the philosophy of psychology.

29 G. W. F. Hegel, *Introductory Lectures on Aesthetics*, trans. Bernard Bosanquet, ed. Michael Inwood (London: Penguin, 1993), 7–8.

Somewhere between rational agency on the one hand and sub-personal brain functions on the other hand, there is the non-rational person who is nonetheless intelligible to other persons, and whose emotional behavior expresses her cares and concerns qua a socially-interactive member of a linguistic community.

Part I

1 Emotions as judgments or as modes of "seeing-as"

The explanatory challenges toward a causal account for emotional episodes

> When a man is said to express emotion, what is being said about him comes to this. At first, he is conscious of having an emotion, but not conscious of what this emotion is. All he is conscious of is a perturbation or excitement, which he feels going on within him, but of whose nature he is ignorant. While in this state, all he can say about his emotion is: "I feel ... I don't know what I feel." From this helpless and oppressed condition he extricates himself by doing something which we call expressing himself. This is an activity which has something to do with the thing we call language: he expresses himself by speaking.[1]

It is often the case that we are able to describe what we are feeling and to express our emotion in words more easily than Collingwood seems to suggest. Nevertheless, the claim that we feel "perturbation or excitement" before we describe it or are able to describe it seems correct. An emotional episode of the sort we feel and proceed to describe is an affective state that differs from mere sensation precisely since it feels that there is something to say and understand about it, that we can become aware of what explains it.

An emotional episode typically directs our attention to certain features of the here-and-now situation, certain people and things that become emotionally salient to us. And whether or not these emotionally salient features are also what triggered our emotional episode, we see those people and things as the cause of our emotion.[2] In addition, we can usually describe the physiological and behavioral particularities of the perturbation and excitement we feel in terms of emotion-types.

It is perhaps a question whether or not a subject can identify or describe correctly what she feels. It stands to reason that if one can report at all about an emotional episode one can provide a rough-and-ready characterization of the emotion-type one is experiencing. Perhaps one cannot decide in the first instance whether one feels contentment or gratification or

1 R. G. Collingwood, *The Principles of Art* (Oxford: Clarendon Press, 1938), 109–110.
2 Robert Solomon, "Emotions and Choice," [1973] in *Explaining Emotions*, ed. Amélie Rorty (Berkeley: University of California Press, 1980), 260.

whether one feels glee or pride or joy. But one would be in the ballpark, as it were, since these emotions' affective or expressive aspects are typically similar.

What about emotions whose action tendencies overlap? Perhaps one could confuse attacking in fear with attacking in anger? There is no need to assume that one must be feeling only one emotion-type at each moment. There are cases of mixed feelings where two emotion-types of different typical affect are experienced more or less together, such as disgust and compassion, contempt and admiration, gratitude and resentment and so forth. Such cases are discussed in the second part of this book. For now, it seems reasonable to accept that even in such cases, if one can report at all about the ambivalent episode, one is likely to be able to provide at least one out of the two relevant emotion-type terms that may be suitable to describe the experience.

Altogether, we experience the emotional episode as a reaction to someone else's behavior or to something that is happening in the here-and-now situation, as an attitude that we have toward the people and things that we see as having caused our emotional episode. We are thus usually able to describe ourselves as emotionally relating to someone or something: "I am angry with John," or "I am afraid of Carol." An emotional episode can also be described in terms of a relation to imagined or remembered people and things, but for the sake of simplicity I focus on present people and things, a discussion that can easily be generalized to include emotionally salient features of remembered or imagined situations.

The emotionally salient features of the situation are often other people that become affected by the emotional reaction. Being marked as the cause of someone else's emotion raises questions about their responsibility for the emoter's perturbation and excitation: What have they done to cause someone else's anger or fear? Have they done something wrong? Are they posing a risk? Should their self-image be affected by it? Furthermore, people who have become emotionally salient for someone who is undergoing an emotional episode are often subjected to action tendencies such as aggression in anger, fear or jealousy, imitation in the case of admiration and envy, and so forth. Being seen as emotion-provoking affects one's social position, and emotional relations often further implicate other people in the emoter's social niche. The emoting subject is also affected by her own emotional episode, even if nobody else knows about it. Her fear makes her feel small and vulnerable, her pride makes her feel that she is above other people or at least above her own previous self, her guilt may come with a tendency to punish herself, her shame or embarrassment might cause her to hide at home and not want to see anyone, and so forth. Even joy can make one want to get clear on its cause for the sake of repeating it in the future.

This ethical dimension of emotions, their impact on the well-being and on the social position of the people involved, puts the emoting subject under normative pressure to describe the kind of emotional relation she is in.

Sometimes people will find it acceptable that someone just "gives me the creeps" in the case of fear,[3] or that "I'm just so into him" in the case of admiration, or that "Sorry, I just can't stand her," in the case of contempt. But usually the emoting subject, as well as others around her, want to have a more clear understanding of the emotional relation that is affecting the social position of those involved. What did the person who has been marked as emotion-provoking do? Did something happen to that person? What behavior or occurrence is the emotional relation calling attention to?

This normative demand for a verbal description comes hand in hand with a demand for justification. If people are going to be affected in this manner, then the emotionally salient person or thing should merit this emotional salience. Is the emotionally salient person merely a causal trigger for an emotional relation she has nothing to do with, or can she be regarded as responsible for this emotionally expressive behavior? In other words, seeing a person or a thing as emotion-provoking is normatively taken to be an evaluative attitude. The emoting subject faces the demand to rationally justify her emotionally expressive behavior. The emotionally salient people and things must be more than mere causal triggers for shame or fear to be socially acceptable – they should be evaluable as shameful or fearful.

This demand for emotional salience to correspond to a rationally justifiable evaluation is usually spoken in terms of judging the emotional episode to be "appropriate" or "inappropriate." I shall articulate a few notions of appropriateness or inappropriateness in this chapter as well as in Chapter 3, but for now I want to note the two most widely acknowledged conceptions of emotion appropriateness: fittingness of the emotion type and intensity to the situation at hand.

Judgments of emotion-type fittingness are made in reference to what Justin D'Arms and Daniel Jacobson call "norms of fittingness,"[4] norms that match emotion-type words with roughly described circumstances: fear fits danger or people and things that can be evaluated as dangerous, anger fits wrongs or people that can be evaluated as having wronged the emoting subject, guilt fits circumstances where the subject has committed a wrong, disgust fits contamination or the unpalatable, shame a failing, pride an achievement, joy – benefit, and so forth. What exactly counts as a wrong, an achievement, a benefit, and even danger further depends on various other social, moral and prudential norms, which may vary from culture to culture and from one social niche to another within the same culture. This

3 Ronald de Sousa, "The Rationality of Emotions," in *Explaining Emotions*, ed. Amélie Rorty (Berkeley: University of California Press, 1980), 139.

4 Justin D'Arms and Daniel Jacobson, "The Significance of Recalcitrant Emotion (or, Anti-quasijudgmentalism)," in *Philosophy and the Emotions*, ed. Anthony Hatzimoysis (Cambridge: Cambridge University Press, 2003), 132; Justin D'Arms and Daniel Jacobson, "The Moralistic Fallacy: On the 'Appropriateness' of Emotions," *Philosophy and Phenomenological Research* 61, no. 1 (2000): 74.

is why norms of fit "cannot be settled by conceptual analysis or linguistic fiat," their specific articulation is "provisional, open to revision,"[5] and cannot be read in a strict or literal sense. And the same can be said for norms of fit for emotion intensity. Intensity could only be described vaguely as "very angry" or "just a little angry," and here too people should be allowed difference of opinion as to the appropriate degree of an emotional response to a certain situation.

I think it is fair to say that many philosophers, especially those that do not define themselves as philosophers of emotion but that work in ethics, moral psychology, and aesthetics, belong to what we may call the conceptualist camp. Those who belong to this camp do not only speak of emotionally salient people and things in the here-and-now situation but further claim these people and things are the "intentional objects" of the emotion. When it comes to the specific features of these people and things – those that the emoting subject describes as the relevant emotionally salient aspects – the philosophers of this camp do not only speak of them as the description of what one takes to be the causal trigger of the emotion or as a response to the normative pressure to justify one's emotion, but they further describe those aspects as the "intentional content" of the emotional attitude. According to the conceptualist, then, when one describes one's emotion, one specifies the intentional object of the emotion and the aspect under which that object is the object of the emotion. For example, I am angry with John under the aspect that he stole my car.[6] And this general schema can also be formulated as a propositional attitude "I am angry that John stole my car," or generally as:

I E that P

This does not mean that conceptualists must claim that the proposition P is the object of the emotion or that the emotional attitude is toward an abstract object such as a proposition.[7] The proposition "John stole my car" is the intentional content of the attitude. The intentional object of the emotion is still John, and I am angry with him under the aspect that he stole my car. It is true that we often describe our emotions in the form "I E that P." In fact, this could be seen as a general schema for the verbal description of an emotional episode, what I call in the introduction the describable

5 D'Arms and Jacobson, "The Significance of Recalcitrant Emotion," 132. See also Paul Griffiths' argument against conceptual analysis of formal object in Paul Griffiths, *What Emotions Really Are: The Problem of Psychological Categories* (Chicago: Chicago University Press, 1998), 23–24.
6 Solomon, "Emotions and Choice," 253.
7 Some conceptualists do make this claim, e.g. Solomon: ibid., 258. See also Prinz, *Gut Reactions*, 22–23; Ronald de Sousa, conversely, takes the line I present: Ronald de Sousa, *The Rationality of Emotion*, (Cambridge MA: MIT Press, 1990 [1987]), Chapter 5, especially his discussion of Nissenbaum at 113.

aspect of an emotion. But according to most conceptualists, this is not just a way to verbally describe or express one's emotion but the conceptual bedding of the emotion itself.

In other words, according to the conceptualist, emotions are rationally assessable states of mind. Either E fits P in reference to the relevant norms or it does not. That is, according to the conceptualist, rational assessment of emotions as fitting or unfitting is not just an ethical dimension that is placed above, as it were, the causal dimension of emotions. Rational assessibility, according to the conceptualist, is part and parcel of emotional states. This also means that philosophers of the conceptualist camp speak of emotions as inherently evaluative states of mind, and not merely as states that are regarded as evaluations in our social interactions, in the manner described above.

When it comes to philosophers who define themselves as philosophers of emotion, conceptualist accounts go into further detail. That is, they specify in what way emotions embed conceptuality. The first section of this chapter presents the account known as "judgmentalism," according to which emotions are normative judgments of fit, namely judgments that the here-and-now situation calls for a certain emotional response. The first section makes explicit the kind of causal account for the formation of emotional episodes that is implicit in judgmentalism. The critical examination of judgmentalism, presented in the second section, leads to abandoning it in favor of an alternative approach, which basically corresponds to the preliminary definition of emotions presented in the introduction, that is, that emotions are ways of seeing or rather of experiencing certain features of the situation as emotionally salient. The third section of this chapter is largely dedicated to presenting a minimalist conception of the "seeing as" alternative, which could be agreed upon by all the contemporary accounts discussed throughout this book that do not subscribe to judgmentalism. The third section also describes and criticizes the conceptualist version of the seeing-as accounts.[8]

I think it is fair to say that this conceptualist seeing-as view is the one held by most conceptualists, within the philosophy of emotion as well as in other fields of philosophy that adhere to the view that emotions are rationally assessable attitudes with intentional content. I nevertheless begin with and dedicate a large part of this chapter to judgmentalism since it serves to delineate the general way to understand the describable aspect of an emotional episode, as well as to identify the explanatory questions about the formation and subsidence of emotional episodes. These questions or challenges are inherited, as it were, from the widely accepted criticisms of

8 E.g. Richard Moran, *Authority and Estrangement*; Robert Solomon, "Emotions and Choice"; Ronald de Sousa "The Rationality of Emotions"; Patricia Greenspan, "Emotions, Rationality, and Mind/Body," in *Thinking about Feeling*, ed. Robert Solomon (New York, NY: Oxford University Press, 2004), 125–134.

judgmentalism, and that against which any causal account of emotional reactions should be assessed.

1. The judgmentalist view

Many nuanced versions of "judgmentalism" can be found in the literature, and I will not provide a survey of them here. In what follows, I describe a synthesized version of "judgmentalism" which I find the most plausible and that incorporates various critical insights that can be found in the literature.[9] According to the judgmentalist, as Robert Solomon says, an emotional reaction is a normative judgment.[10] In other words, the emotional attitude is an evaluative judgment that the situation fits a certain emotional response. For the sake of discussion, I shall talk about emotions as having intentional content, as presupposed by judgmentalists.

As evaluative judgments, emotions can be correct or incorrect, as strange as it may sound to talk about "correctness" of emotions. An emotional attitude gets it right if the content of the attitude, namely P, fits the emotion-type E, in reference to the relevant norms. This means that for the judgmentalist, norms of fit are not just norms of justification in reference to which we criticize or defend emotional attitudes. Norms of fit, on the judgmentalist view, are also implicitly operative when one experiences an emotional episode, since emotions are normative judgments.

The judgmentalist claim is that even before we reassess whether our emotional reaction is fitting, our very reaction, articulable as "I E that P," entails a belief that P fits E in reference to the relevant norm of fit. Or otherwise put, the emotional reaction implicitly entails the belief that the situation under the description P instantiates the typical circumstances that roughly fit E. As Solomon says: "If I do not find my situation awkward, I cannot be ashamed or embarrassed. If I do not judge that I have suffered a loss, I cannot be sad or jealous."[11] The "correctness" of emotions then, is the correction of the belief that E fits P, which is entailed in the emotional attitude.

In other words, P in the attitude "I E that P", the intentional content of the emotional attitude, can be considered as the description of what the emotion is about, the description of what in the situation the subject perceives as the cause for her emotional attitude, and – if emotions entail the

9 In fact, various authors who list today's judgmentalists provide slightly different lists of philosophers. I will not attempt here to decide exactly who is a judgmentalist and who is not. The paradigm judgmentalists are probably Robert Solomon, Martha Nussbaum (Martha Nussbaum, *Upheavals of Thought: The Intelligence of Emotions*, (New York: Cambridge University Press, 2001)) and the psychologist Richard Lazarus (Richard S. Lazarus, *Emotion and Adaptation* (New York: Oxford University Press, 1991)). For a discussion of several versions of judgmentalism, see Robinson, *Deeper than Reason*, Chapter 1.

10 Solomon, "Emotions and Choice," 257.

11 Ibid., 258.

belief that E fits P as the judgmentalist claims – then P is also the description of that object that the subject takes to be a consideration in favor of the emotional attitude, namely a reason of fit. Although judgmentalists do not talk about emotions as embedding reasons of fit, they are nonetheless committed to that claim. What kind of reason is this meant to be?

Tim Scanlon speaks of two basic kinds of reasons. The first kind is the most familiar one in philosophy. These are "objective reasons," namely reasons that stand in an objectively valid inferential relation to other reasons or true propositions. These are good reasons, considerations in favor of this or that intentional mental state (intentions, beliefs, desires, and emotions), that stand rational scrutiny in reference to norms of inference and justification.[12]

The second kind of reason is subjective or "operative." These are the considerations a specific subject takes to be in favor of this or that intentional state of mind. Such considerations are reasons by virtue of the subject grasping them as such. Operative reasons, which affect one's psychological state of mind, may or may not be objectively good reasons. As Scanlon explains:

> There is a difference between asking what reason there is for believing that P and asking what a given person's reason for believing it was. (I will refer to the latter as the person's operative reason.) Both of these questions have to do with what I am calling "reasons in the standard normative sense." The first asks for an assessment of the grounds for taking P to be the case, while the second asks what, as a matter of biographical fact, Jones took to be a reason for believing it.[13]

According to judgmentalism, then, the reason that is embedded in one's implicit evaluation that the situation fits or calls for an emotional reason is an operative reason. It can turn out to be a good reason or a bad reason on further scrutiny.

Judgmentalism, which sees emotions as intertwined with their respective beliefs, does justice to certain aspects of our ordinary experience with emotions. Often, when one is afraid, one also believes that the situation is dangerous. Often, when one is angry, one also believes that one has suffered a wrong.[14] Furthermore, a verbally described emotional episode looks like a

12 Scanlon often talks of beliefs and intentions rather than emotions. But he explicitly says that his account of reasons and reasoning is not just for belief and intentions but also for hopes, fears, and other emotional attitudes like respect, anger, admiration, contempt, and indignation. He calls them all "judgment-sensitive attitudes". See for example, T. M. Scanlon, *What We Owe to Each Other*, (Cambridge, MA: Harvard University Press, 1998), 18, 19, 20, 23.

13 Ibid., 19.

14 In fact, D'Arms and Jacobson think that this is the "standard case," D'Arms and Jacobson, "The Significance of Recalcitrant Emotion," 132.

judgment of fit. Consider the statement that describes and expresses my emotional state: "I am angry that John stole my car." "John stole my car" can be regarded as a consideration in favor of my anger in reference to the norm of fit that anger is a fitting response to a wrong, and to the moral norm that stealing is wrong.

In fact, such statements not only look like a judgment of fit but are occasionally treated by others as if they were judgments in context of emotion criticism. We expect people to be able to give reasons for and justify their emotional reaction as we would for any judgment. Just as we expect people to change their minds if they find their own judgment wrong or unjustified, we expect people to renounce their emotional reaction and dim it down if they find it unjustified or unfitting to the situation in which it arose. That is, we treat emotions as evaluative and our practices of criticism in reference to norms of fit involve an expectation that one can reassess the evaluation that is supposedly implicit in one's emotion and that one's emotional state would alter according to or align with one's reflective judgment of fit.

In *Authority and Estrangement*, Richard Moran carefully describes how one can "step back" from various attitudes, including emotions, and deliberate about whether one should have those attitudes, whether they are indeed called for or justified by the situation to which they are directed. That is, Moran describes a situation where we bracket our mental state and deliberate about what to believe or want, about how to act and also about how to feel about a certain situation.[15] Moran's discussion is detailed and subtle as he shows why and how such deliberation is distinctively first-personal, involving commitments and responsibilities only the subject can take when that subject exercises her capacity to change her own state of mind. I will here focus only on fragments of Moran's account of rational deliberation, which are relevant to the purposes of this section.

When I deliberate about what I should feel, I look to the situation at hand in order to understand "how things are out there," an understanding from which I draw reasons or considerations for or against a certain emotional attitude.[16] Perhaps since Moran uses belief as his model for emotions, he does not explicitly mention norms of emotion fittingness. Unlike beliefs, which refer to norms of rationality that are universally held by all rational agents, norms of fit are more culture and subject dependent. Nevertheless, the reasons of fit one weighs in deliberation in reference to one's endorsed norms of fittingness, come from one's own description of the situation at hand.

As Moran says, when I engage in reasoning, I take it that my state of mind will change according to the conclusion I reach. That is, when I deliberate whether or how I should emotionally react to a certain situation, I do not merely expect to reach a decision or a resolution with the hope that I

15 Moran, *Authority and Estrangement*, Chapters 2 and 4. See also Christine M. Korsgaard, *The Sources of Normativity* (Cambridge: Cambridge University Press, 1996), 93.

16 Moran, *Authority and Estrangement*, 150.

shall manage to comply with that resolution. Deliberation is an activity of an agency that takes her rational reflection to be *constitutive* of her state of mind. In other words, the conceptual and rational connection between one's conclusion and one's mental state is also meant to be a causal connection. As Moran says:

> To take oneself to be in a position to ask and answer this [deliberative] question about one's belief or intention [or emotional attitude][17] is to take oneself to be in a position to *make* something true in one's answering it ... [R]eflective (deliberative) questioning takes upon itself the capacity to play a constituting role in determining the psychological facts themselves.[18]

I think Moran is right that we sometimes deliberate whether an emotion is fitting and take our explicit process of evaluation, of rational inference in reference to norms of fit, to be what shall determine whether or not our emotion subsides. By "subside" I mean that the emotional episode is cut short. One stops thinking or expressing the now revoked describable aspect of the emotion and the physiological and behavioral aspect of the episode calms down gradually, perhaps more quickly than it would if the emotion were allowed to run its course without interruption.

Furthermore, when we revoke our emotion and the emotion indeed subsides, we implicitly ascribe this subsidence to our rational agency. This is also our expectation of other people. We expect them to be able to make our criticism about the fittingness of their emotional reaction into their own self-criticism, and we expect their activity of reasoning and their reflectively endorsed conclusion to have a constitutive effect on their emotions. In particular, we expect them not to have the emotion any more if they revoke it as unfitting to the circumstances.

But Moran goes further when he virtually claims that characterizing the relation between one's deliberative conclusion and one's state of mind as constitutive is more than an expectation or an after-the-fact description – it is the way the mind actually works.[19] In fact, Moran even allows for cases where one is unsure what to feel and is not yet experiencing any emotion and engages in a "deliberative inquiry about how to feel, how to respond."[20]

17 I added "or emotional attitude" since, as mentioned above, Moran's account on emotions is modeled on his account of beliefs.

18 Moran, *Authority and Estrangement*, 146.

19 On the constitutive role of deliberation in formation of a state of mind see: ibid., 55–60. See also T. M. Scanlon, "Metaphysics and Morals," in *Naturalism and Normativity*, ed. Mario De Caro and David Macarthur; Pamela Hieronymi, "Controlling Attitudes," *Pacific Philosophical Quarterly* 87 (2006); Pamela Hieronymi, "The Wrong Kind of Reason," *The Journal of Philosophy* 102, no. 9 (2005); and Boyle, "Active Belief."

20 Moran, *Authority and Estrangement*, 59. The formation of emotion by deliberation in the case of emotional uncertainty is discussed in 57–60.

Does this mean that Moran thinks we can argue or reason ourselves into an emotional episode by evaluating the situation in reference to norms of fit? I will return to this issue shortly.

The judgmentalist seems to share Moran's view about dimming down emotional episodes through a deliberative judgment against them. As Solomon says, if I discover that John actually did not steal my car I *can* no longer be angry with him.[21] That is, it is by virtue of looking "out there" and coming to the conclusion that the situation does not merit anger, that my anger subsides. In this example, the attitude "I E that P" is revoked on the grounds that P is false. Presumably a judgmentalist should also allow for circumstances where P is true, say that you are five minutes late, but where P does not fit E, say my anger or my concern. I can reflectively judge that the situation does not fit my reaction or that I am over-reacting and thereby allay my anger or concern.

Whether or not an emotion subsides as a result of a constitutive relation, emotions are sometimes responsive to after-the-fact fittingness judgments in the right way, indeed often the expected way. It may thus be tempting to say that if emotional reactions are appropriately responsive or sensitive to fittingness judgments, and they often are, then the original emotional reaction is also a normative judgment.

It is consistent with a judgmentalist view that emotions will result from a reflective normative judgment, but this does not mean that emotions must all be formed deliberatively. If the notion of judgment invoked by judgmentalist always involved "critically endorsed thoughts,"[22] as critics sometimes say, then judgmentalism would be an implausible view. Emotions are something we go through, something that happens to us. Their phenomenology includes passivity.[23] We do not normally argue ourselves into having an emotion (even if we sometimes do "work ourselves up" into an emotional episode).

However, as Robert Solomon explains, this is not the notion the judgmentalist presupposes when claiming that emotions are judgments. Solomon speaks of emotion-judgments as pre-reflective and spontaneous. Indeed, most of our judgments are not preceded by explicit deliberation, but are made spontaneously as part of our normal comportment. They are "in the midst of and an essential part of our engagements."[24]

Solomon gives the example of judgments in ethics, most of which we make unreflectively through spontaneous action, when we do the right thing without thinking too much. Judgments of taste are also often made

21 Solomon, *Choice*, 254.
22 D'Arms and Jacobson, "The Moralistic Fallacy," 67.
23 See for example Cheshire Calhoun, "Cognitive Emotions?" in *What Is an Emotion? Classical Readings in Philosophical Psychology*, ed. Cheshire Calhoun and Robert Solomon (New York: Oxford University Press, 1984), 330.
24 Solomon, "On Emotions as Judgments," 96.

spontaneously, when we are taken by a work of art, or fascinated by someone's beauty, or enjoy a glass of wine. These ethical and aesthetic judgments are spontaneous, but are also the result of education, experience, and refinement. "So too, an emotion, though spontaneous, may be the product of a lifetime of cultivation."[25]

One need not explicitly reflect or deliberate in order to judge. When it comes to the case of beliefs, Moran claims, their rational formation and revision often occurs on auto-pilot, as it were, without self-awareness or explicit deliberation. He says:

> [T]he concept of belief is of something systematic and normatively controlled, so that having a belief involves having a network of other beliefs, which are mutually rationally supportive ... It may be true, even trivially true, that *I* myself cannot revise my beliefs unless I am aware of them. But my beliefs, like the flow of perceptions, interact and undergo revisions all the time without any intervention on my part. Their general rationality does not need my constant supervision.[26]

A judgmentalist may then say that verbally described emotions can be considered judgments, spontaneous evaluations of the situation as provoking this or that emotion. Emotions, like beliefs, may be rationally formed, through an auto-pilot inference in reference to one's norms of fittingness, without one's explicit involvement or awareness. In other words, a judgmentalist may take recourse to a notion of spontaneity of auto-pilot yet articulable inferential processes governed by norms of fit.

Another notion of spontaneity that involves rational agency to a greater extent is the one implied by Elizabeth Anscombe in her book *Intention.*[27] Actions may be considered intentional even when one is not explicitly engaged in practical reasoning prior to or during their execution. Actions are done intentionally when one can describe what one is doing and explain why one is doing it. That is, an action is intentional if the agent can state or articulate reasons for the action – in terms of their desires, interests, goals and purposes – while the action is taking place. As Anscombe shows, when we answer why-questions about our intentional actions – that is questions to be answered in terms of means-end reasoning – we effectively provide further descriptions of what we are doing. Consider Anscombe's famous example, which I here paraphrase in the form of a dialogue between the agent who is performing the action and someone else.[28]

25 Ibid., 97.
26 Moran, *Authority and Estrangement*, 110–111.
27 G. E. M. Anscombe, *Intention*, 2nd edn (Oxford: Basil Blackwell, 1985 [1963]).
28 Ibid., §23.

- What are you doing?
- I am moving my arm up and down.
- Why are you moving your arm up and down?
- I am pumping.
- Why are you pumping?
- I'm replenishing the water supply for the house.
- Why are you replenishing the water supply?
- I am poisoning the inhabitants of that house.
- Why are you poisoning these people?
- To end the war.

The answers of the agent describe what he is doing and why. According to Anscombe, all the answers that the agent gives are descriptions of what he is doing, except for the last one, since we cannot say *now* that he is ending the war.

Although we can state or articulate reasons for our action in a manner that appears to trace a means-ends practical reasoning, this does not mean that we articulate those descriptions to ourselves while we act or that we engage in explicit reasoning via inner speech. We nevertheless act "under description" inasmuch as that description or descriptions are readily articulable, that is, inasmuch as we are aware of our goals and purposes that guide our activity.[29]

As in the case of Anscombian action, many emotional reactions, those that we can verbally describe and that are the focus of this book, are readily describable and once they are verbally expressed, they appear to embed a reason of fit. In fact, we can regard the describable aspect of a verbally expressed emotion as an answer to a why-question, analogical to the Anscombian one. That is a why-question that enquires about the subject's reasons to emotionally react and that implicitly ascribes to the subject some kind of responsibility for the emotion, a certain agential involvement. We can even imagine John surprised that I burst into his office in anger (just before I accuse him of stealing my car) asking, "Why are you angry?", expecting me not just to describe my emotional state of mind but to *justify* it, to take responsibility for it by providing reasons of fit. Verbally described emotions can perhaps be considered as judgments inasmuch as we can provide reasons of fit for them during the emotional episode.

But even a notion of a spontaneous and pre-reflective judgment cannot survive the objections presented in the next section. These objections against judgmentalism will also present the two main explanatory challenges for any theory of emotion.

29 Ibid., §19.

2. Objections to judgmentalism

There are many objections to judgmentalism in the literature and I will not provide a full survey of them here.[30] In what follows I present the two objections I find most convincing, on the ground of which judgmentalism should be abandoned. These objections also raise problems and questions that continue to haunt all existing accounts of emotions, as will be demonstrated in this chapter and the following three chapters of this book.

A. The emotionality problem

The first objection is known as *the problem of unemotional judgments*.[31] That is, one can judge that a certain emotion-type fits the situation under the description P, and yet fail to experience the relevant emotion. One can find a situation anger-provoking, for example, and yet fail to care, remain indifferent.

There are some cases of an extreme nature where we would expect anyone to emote in a fitting manner. If someone loses a loved one and feels no grief or if someone injures people while drunk-driving and fails to feel guilty – we would think there is something not quite right about such a person. We will say that such a person is unaware of her feelings due to shock or otherwise that such a person lacks normal emotional capacities. We consider such cases as pathologies, not the norm.[32]

However, it is possible to imagine cases where one person would emotionally react to a situation and another would not, without there being a disagreement on the fittingness of the situation to the emotion in question. Say I am walking down the street with a friend and a drunk insults us or says something rude about the way we are dressed. I feel insulted and angry whereas my friend does not. She can understand why I feel angry and insulted and she too makes the same fittingness judgment. But she just does not get emotional.

An emotion thus cannot be merely a fittingness judgment. If one wants to be a judgmentalist, then something has to be added to such a judgment in order for it to become the respective emotion. Judgmentalists recognize this difficulty and they all add what we may call a "care-factor" to the

30 For a review of the objections to judgmentalism see Robinson, *Deeper than Reason*, Chapter 1.

31 For example, Griffiths, *What Emotions Really Are*, 29; Robert Roberts, "What an Emotion is: A Sketch," *The Philosophical Review* 97, no. 2 (1988), 197–198; Robinson, *Deeper than Reason*, 14; Jerome Shaffer, "An Assessment of Emotion," *American Philosophical Quarterly* 20, no. 2 (1983): 163; Bennett Helm, *Emotional Reason: Deliberation, Motivation, and the Nature of Value* (Cambridge: Cambridge University Press, 2001), 38–41.

32 Solomon, "On Emotions as Judgments," 109.

fittingness judgment. That is, emotions are not just evaluative judgments that we can agree or disagree upon; they include a personal involvement of the subject as a caring individual. Robert Solomon says in this connection:

> to have an emotion requires not only a specifiable set of judgments but certain desires as well. One might make a judgment ... in an impersonal and uninvolved way, without caring one way or the other. But an emotional [judgment] is necessarily personal and involved. Compare "What he said to me was offensive" (but I don't care what he thinks) and "He offended me!" Only the latter is constitutive of anger.[33]

Elsewhere, Solomon characterizes this "personal and involved" way of judging as "taking personally" the relevant evaluative judgment of emotion-fittingness. "Taking something personally," Solomon explains, "means experiencing it as particularly important to oneself, as personally 'meaningful,' perhaps concerning a matter in which we have deep personal 'investments.'"[34]

But how can we spell out exactly what such personal investments mean? What is the care-factor? If a term such as "care" is used simply to indicate the passionate aspect of an emotion or the additional "ingredient" that makes a fittingness judgment into an emotion, then all we have done is say that emotions are emotional fittingness judgments. Even if we do not look for a reductive definition that would describe emotions in terms that are different to "emotion," this kind of description does not elucidate anything. It adds nothing to our understanding of the difference between dispassionate evaluative judgments and the emotional ones.[35]

The other option is to consider the care-factor to be a desire or a care for what we may call one's core-values. Say I make the fittingness judgment that my student's rudeness is irritating, even anger-provoking. In addition to that, that situation also bears on my desire to be a respected teacher and my valuing a professional distance between students and teachers. A care-factor that has content, that is valuing of or a desire to something or someone, is thus another evaluation, namely that one's fittingness judgment about the situation at hand bears on certain cares or concerns. According to this contentful understanding of the care-factor, a fittingness judgment

33 Solomon, "Emotions and Choice," 276.

34 Solomon, "On Emotions as Judgments," 104. See also Solomon's discussion about how taking personally an offensive remark is required to make the fittingness judgment emotional in ibid., 110–113.

35 This kind of understanding of the care-factor will make phrases such as "taking personally" into "tired metaphors" as Griffiths claims: Paul E. Griffiths, "The Degeneration of the Cognitive Theory of Emotions," 306. See also Bennett Helm's criticism about Nussbaum's metaphorical and non-explanatory notion of acceptance of a judgment "with the core of my being" that is meant to make a judgment emotional: Helm, *Emotional Reason*, 39–40.

becomes emotional when it is paired with an additional judgment about one's core-value and its relevance to the situation.

This picture may be appealing when we consider some of our practices of emotion justification and criticism, in which we explicitly engage in eliciting care-factor reasons for our emotional reaction. Examine first cases of mixed feelings or emotional ambivalence, where we feel two apparently contradictory emotions toward the same object under the same description. To take Patricia Greenspan's famous example, we may experience both joy and envy when a friend achieves something that we wanted for ourselves. Each emotional attitude on this ambivalent occasion can be justified not just through fittingness to the same object under the same description, but also by making explicit a certain care-factor judgment, which is different for each emotion. As Greenspan says:

> Where I am in competition with a close friend, happiness at his winning might be adequately justified by my identification with him, and unhappiness by my concern for my own interests, even though each of these reasons would seem to count as reason *against* exhibiting the contrary emotion. Ambivalence is possible, then, in a basically rational person.[36]

In other words, my "positive" joy is justified by my care for my friend and his happiness, and my "negative" envy is justified by my care for myself and my interests.[37] In contexts of justification of mixed feelings, one passes explicit care-factor judgments. And it may be tempting to regard those explicit judgments as tracing spontaneous judgments that are implicitly involved in the initial emotional reaction.

We also make explicit care-factor judgments in response to a certain kind of criticism, which is rarely discussed in the literature even if it is quite common. These are criticisms of the form: "Why are you taking this so personally?"; "Why do you care?"; "It's not like you to respond like this … you usually take such things much more lightly." Say I am jealous that my husband is having a flirtatious conversation with another woman. You may agree that I have (temporarily) lost my husband's attention while he is talking to a woman who is obviously being flirtatious and that my jealousy is

36 Greenspan, "A Case of Mixed Feelings," 236.

37 Greenspan uses this example to claim that emotions are not all-things-considered judgments, since they can be justified only in reference to a limited portion of one's relevant background cares and concerns, rather than by the "total background," ibid., 237. Greenspan then claims that emotions cannot be judgments since they are not justified all-things-considered. But this claim seems dogmatic and strange. Dogmatic, since there is no *a priori* reason to claim that judgments *must* be justified all-things-considered. Strange, since, as Greenspan basically demonstrates through her example, I can explicitly pass the judgment that my envy of my friend fits the situation, and justify this judgment by eliciting the further judgment about my own interests, without considering the care for my friend.

fitting. And yet you may still think that it is possible and preferable not to take this situation personally, not care about it.

You may remind me that I deeply believe in personal freedom and that I care about my husband's being desirable to other women. I may even enjoy a bit of pretend-competition from a position of confidence in my husband's love and desire for me. The person who is criticizing the emoter is referring not to norms of fittingness but to the emoter's character. As Chashire Calhoun says: "In daily life, we sometimes sense that even though an emotion is right for the situation, it is wrong for the person; it is out of character."[38]

This notion of appropriateness, namely fittingness to character, has received little attention in the emotion literature. What has gone completely unnoticed is the shift such criticisms go through when they become self-criticisms. If I identify with what you say and if these values are indeed important to me I can come to see that I actually do not care about this harmless and short flirtation in the relevant way to be jealous. This kind of deliberation is done in reference to one's endorsed or endorsable cares and concerns. In other words, when others criticize me, they refer to what they see as my character, to my cares and concerns as they can be seen from my patterns of behavior, emotional and intentional. But when I criticize myself, I re-examine my cares as concerns as mine – as cares and concerns that I endorse. That is, when I criticize myself, I question whether or not it is the kind of reaction that suits me, that is, that suits how I see myself, that suits who I want to be or become. Is this the kind of reaction that fits a person like me, with my values, virtues, cares and concerns – cares and concerns that I endorse? This kind of criticism takes recourse to another notion of emotion appropriateness, namely fittingness to one's self-image, to the way one sees oneself as having and cultivating certain cares and concerns.[39] It is worthwhile noting, however, that it is not clear whether this appropriateness is normative. On the one hand, my self-image is what I say it is, this is just part of the concept "self-image." If that is the case then I cannot be wrong about my self-image. On the other hand, perhaps I can be wrong, inasmuch as an interlocutor may identify inconsistencies within my thoughts about myself. I leave the question of the normativity of self-image open.

Reasoning about my endorsed cares and concerns and their relevance to the situation at hand and reaching the conclusion that I actually lack the relevant care to have the emotion that is now under criticism can sometimes help assuage my emotional reaction. I can cut short my jealousy episode, or my irritation with a rude student, when I realize through reasoning that I actually do not endorse the relevant care and that I need not have this

38 Cheshire Calhoun, "Subjectivity and Emotion," 119.

39 There is another notion of emotion appropriateness to do with social propriety, recently brought into the emotion literature by D'Arms and Jacobson. I discuss that notion of moralistic appropriateness and its connection to the notion proposed here of fittingness to one's self-image in Chapter 3.4.A.

otherwise fitting emotion. I think it is fair to say that at least sometimes, we take ourselves to have some kind of constitutive effect on our emotional reaction when we judge against it in this manner. Indeed, sometimes our emotions seem responsive in the right way or sensitive to such deliberation in reference to one's self-image as having certain cares and concerns. It may thus be tempting to talk of a constitutive relation between endorsed cares and emotions and to claim that an emotion is comprised of two spontaneous judgments – a judgment of fit and a care-factor judgment.

However, if we regard the care-factor as an additional judgment, then we encounter the same problem of unemotional judgments. For example, I can judge that I have wronged my colleague and deeply care about being morally upstanding and still not feel guilty.[40] I can judge my student to be rude and even anger-provoking and care about maintaining my respect with the students, I can even be more firm with this student and put him in his place, but I need not actually get irritated or angry about the situation. Values and desires play an important role in our practical reasoning and affect our decisions to act. But valuing and desiring are distinct from emoting.

Using terms like "care" or "taking personally" or "great importance for the person's own flourishing"[41] may be misleading. One may mistakenly think such terms both designate something informative such as the articulation of a desire or a core-value, as well as color those desires and values as emotional. This kind of slide from one meaning of the term to another is typical of philosophers who speak of emotions as evaluations. See for example how Charles Taylor characterizes what makes an object emotionally relevant or as he calls it as having an emotional "import."

> By "import" I mean a way in which something can be relevant or of importance to the desires or purposes or aspirations or feelings of a subject; or otherwise put, a property of something whereby it is a matter of non-indifference to a subject.[42]

But these two possible meanings of the word "care," passion or the opposite of emotional indifference on the one hand and core-value on the other hand, should not be confused. Adding a care to a fittingness judgment is either an uninformative synonym to the term "emotional" or it is an additional judgment that may be itself dispassionate. Insisting that by adding a care-factor we add both emotionality and additional information amounts to saying that we are emotional about the relevant values or desires. But this strategy would be just as unhelpful as saying that we are emotional about

40 See Schaffer, "An Assessment," 163; and Roberts, "What an Emotion is," 197–198.

41 Nussbaum, *Upheavals of Thought*, 4.

42 Charles Taylor, "Self-Interpreting Animals," in *Human Agency and Language: Philosophical Papers 1* (Cambridge: Cambridge University Press, 1985), 48–49.

fittingness judgments. Why would we be emotional about fittingness judgments or about care-factor judgments? Adding a care-factor is not going to salvage judgmentalism from the problem of unemotional judgments. And this is not just a conceptual problem, namely that judging, valuing and desiring do not entail emoting. Judgmentalism does not do justice to an important aspect of our ordinary experience of emotions. If emotions were indeed rationally formed through an auto-pilot process of evaluation in reference to norms of fit and to one's self-image, then all such evaluations would be emotional, and yet they are not.[43] The emotionality problem for judgmentalism is strongly related to the incapacity of judgmentalism to answer or even accommodate the singularity of emotional response outlined in the Introduction, namely the variation of response among people (with similar norms of fit and similar endorsed values) as well as the variation of response of the same person on different occasions of very similar circumstances.

B. The problem of recalcitrant emotions

Normally, as explained above, when a subject describes an emotion as an attitude such that it appears to embed a reason of fit, that reason can then be assessed in reference to norms of fit. If the subject revokes the stated reason for her emotion and judges it to be a bad reason, namely if the description of the situation (P) is false, or if it is true but fails to fit the relevant emotion-type (E) or its intensity (I) in reference to the relevant social norms – then we expect the emotional episode to subside or its intensity to dim down.

There are some cases, however, where the explicit and reflective disavowal of the evaluation implicit in the emotion fails to have the right effect. These emotions are recalcitrant to reason. But, if emotions were judgments, one would expect them to always subside in case the emoting subject has disavowed the judgment. The existence of recalcitrant emotions thus comprises a strong objection against judgmentalism.

The examples of recalcitrant emotions found in the philosophical literature are of what D'Arms and Jacobson call stable emotional recalcitrance, namely "a standing disposition to have recalcitrant bouts of a particular emotion."[44] In other words, these are dispositions to experience a certain emotion-type E in typical circumstances that do not fit the emotion E. On each such occasion, the subject herself is aware that she is having (again) an emotion that is unfitting to the situation, but that she can't help it.

The most common examples found in the literature are specific phobias,

43 For a similar line of argument see: Griffiths' discussion on the two possible meanings of "desire," in his criticism of Joal Marks' account of emotion: Griffiths, *What Emotions Really Are*, 32.

44 D'Arms and Jacobson, "The Significance of Recalcitrant Emotion," 140.

such as fear of snakes and fear of flying. Other examples are of emotions that reflect prejudices such as contempt to or fear of people of a certain race or sex, or feelings of disgust and revulsion toward homosexuals, prejudices that the subject disavows. I was unable to find in the philosophical literature an example of what we may call "occasional recalcitrance" that is limited to a certain period of time or to a specific relationship.[45]

Stable recalcitrance matches an emotion-type to typical circumstances, and so saying that the subject disavows their emotion can be spoken of in terms of disavowing a generalized belief about those typical circumstances. Such beliefs would be: Homosexuals are immoral, abnormal and disgusting (and are thus fear-, disgust-, and contempt-provoking); Women are stupid (contempt-provoking); or flying is terribly dangerous (fear-provoking). These beliefs, according to a judgmentalist, are implicitly embedded in such emotional reactions. How can a judgmentalist account for occasions where emotions remain unaffected by the disavowal such beliefs? Cheshire Calhoun surveys the ways in which the judgmentalist tries to deal with such cases and convincingly shows that the judgmentalist solutions are unsatisfactory. I here present her strongest points (with some elaborations).

The first route a judgmentalist may take regards what we may call emotional prejudices such as the contempt toward women or disgust toward homosexuals. These emotions embed, according to the judgmentalist, a prejudiced judgment of fittingness. If a subject disavows the prejudiced beliefs that are implicit in those emotional judgments, and yet their emotion is recalcitrant to their avowal of the inverse "enlightened" belief, then the subject is self-deceived. In other words, the judgmentalist can regard the subjects that can't help but having sexist, racist and homophobic emotions as actually holding those sexist, racist and homophobic beliefs despite their avid disavowal of those beliefs. People may like to think of themselves as not having such beliefs and yet their emotions expose what they really think. If they continue to wonder how come they can emote in this way despite their enlightened views, they are simply refusing to acknowledge their actual views.

Calhoun concedes that self-deception is a common practice and yet such an interpretation requires justification. When a subject claims to hold a (non-prejudiced) belief and is able to justify that belief, and when she has held that belief for a long time, one would need some evidence to claim that she is self-deceived. If the subject indeed has prejudiced beliefs, these should be evident in her practices and actions. But if the subject manages not to give her prejudiced emotions motivational force in her actions, if her

45 I found only one such example of a woman who resents her partner even if she does not believe he is using her, in Cheshire Calhoun, "Cognitive Emotions?" However, I found this example not convincing, since its details show that this woman resents her partner for taking her for granted and for being indulgent. Indeed, the details throughout Calhoun's paper indicate that this woman has good reason to resent her partner, only that "using her" is not the right description for the reasons of resentment.

behavior indicates that she holds "enlightened" beliefs, then she is "innocent of self-deception or pretense until proven guilty."[46] Simply stating that prejudiced recalcitrance must be an indication of self-deception would be a dogmatic explanation aimed at justifying judgmentalism at all costs.

The second route a judgmentalist may take in order to deal with cases of prejudiced recalcitrance is to suppose that such emotions reflect a belief that the subject held in her distant past due perhaps to prejudiced parents or educational environment. The emotion thus embeds a judgment or a belief that the subject used to endorse. In other words, the subject's "emotional responses have failed to keep pace with her revised beliefs."[47] But why is the subject unable to alter her emotional reaction as quickly as she can remind herself of her avowed beliefs? It begins to be unclear why one would continue to say that emotions embed beliefs in the first place. A judgmentalist that advocates such an argument has sold out.

The third option, which could be used both for cases of prejudiced emotions and for phobias (and perhaps also for recalcitrance that is limited to a certain relationship or situation), is to claim that the emoting subject holds both the avowed and disavowed beliefs. "Neither counts as her only real belief. Thus, an unresolved tension pervades her belief system."[48] If the subject indeed fluctuates in her avowed beliefs or if the subject acts in ways that demonstrate an implicit fluctuation in her avowed beliefs, then we could say she holds two conflicting beliefs. But without such evidence there is no good reason for this claim. Continual emotional avowals of what the subject dispassionately disavows in her "cold" judgments does not count as evidence. At best, it would be compatible with an otherwise dogmatic claim about that subject's holding two conflicting beliefs.[49]

The judgmentalist cannot provide a good description of recalcitrant emotions. Can the judgmentalist concede that some emotions, the recalcitrant ones, are not judgments? Such an option seems like an *ad hoc* concession and a premature despair from finding a unified account for emotions. Maybe this would not be so bad if all we had to exclude from the judgmentalist account were some phobias and prejudiced emotions. Indeed, some stable recalcitrance, such as fear of flying may be "normalized," managed and forgiven.[50]

46 Calhoun, "Cognitive Emotions?," 332. Amélie Rorty argues against that option on similar grounds, further noting that there are typical ways to be "proven guilty." She writes: "Characteristically, self-deception involves quite distinctive behavior: signs of facial malaise, frozen features, certain sorts of systematic failure in action." Amélie Rorty, "Explaining Emotions," in *Explaining Emotions*, ed. Amélie Rorty (Berkeley: University of California Press, 1980), 115.

47 Calhoun, "Cognitive Emotions?" 333.

48 Ibid., 334.

49 Claiming that the subject holds the contrary belief unconsciously would be subject to the same criticism. See Brady, "The Irrationality of Recalcitrant Emotions," 415.

50 Taylor Carman, "First Persons: On Richard Moran's Authority and Estrangement," *Inquiry: An Interdisciplinary Journal of Philosophy* 43, no.3 (2003): 401–402.

But recalcitrance is actually a much more widespread phenomenon than is currently acknowledged in the literature for it to be marginalized as an exception to the rule. Occasional recalcitrance, individuated by a relationship or limited to a certain period of time, happens quite often. Take for example the guilt some feel after a divorce, even when that divorce was not preceded by an affair or some other form of betrayal. Some people may feel guilty for years after a breakup, even when they firmly believe that love is not a promise, that love may sometimes run its course and end, and that they have the right to pursue their own romantic happiness. This can happen to a person that never felt such guilt after any other breakup beforehand. Such recalcitrant guilt need not be some general disposition or traceable to a pattern of breakups. It can be specific to this particular breakup.

Or take another example, of a person who is normally self-confident and outgoing. And yet that person has one friend next to whom he feels insecure and fearful to speak his mind. He does not even think his friend is very intimidating or critical or that he is much smarter than himself. Despite his avowed views, he cannot help but feel afraid that if he says what he thinks he will make a fool of himself. I think it is fair to say that such occasional recalcitrance is no rare affair. Indeed, who does not have some recalcitrant emotional issues with one person or other in their lives – a parent, a sibling, a friend, a partner, or a colleague?

Recalcitrance becomes an even more serious challenge to the judgmentalist when we consider the judgment about one's cares and concerns or core-values that is supposed to be paired with the relevant fittingness judgment. If emotional episodes required a care-factor judgment for their occurrence, then we would expect them to subside when one judges that one does not care in the relevant way to have that emotion. And yet, some emotions can be recalcitrant to such deliberative care factor judgments in reference to the subject's self-image.

Say a drunk on the street has insulted me. The comment was indeed insulting and when I tell the story to a friend she says: "yes, I can see why you were offended, and yet – why are you taking this so personally? Who cares about this drunk anyway?" I know that my friend is right. I actually have no relations with that person, I am unlikely to ever see him again and the comment, in itself, does not straightforwardly bear on any of my cares and concerns. I realize I should not care about this, that I am not the kind of person that would be angry in these (fitting) circumstances, that this emotion is unfitting to me, to my self-image. And yet my anger does not subside. Indeed, a few days pass and I still think about it in anger, and I keep imagining to myself various comebacks I should have said to him at the time.

The existence and prevalence of recalcitrant emotions, as well as the problem of unemotional judgments, make judgmentalism an untenable position. This also means that the processes that give rise to emotions are not rationally inferential processes of evaluation that operate in a normative space of various notions of emotion appropriateness. As said in the beginning of this chapter, we indeed treat our emotions as evaluative, especially in contexts of criticisms, but supposing that this means they are indeed evaluative attitudes, as the conceptualist camp does, is an additional claim that requires justification. But even if emotions are evaluative attitudes, this evaluation does not amount to a normative judgment.

3. The "seeing-as" approach

Motivated by the objections discussed in the previous section (and by other objections), philosophers have proposed a different way to understand the describable aspect of emotional reactions. Call this the seeing-as view of emotions, according to which emotions are modes of *seeing* the situation *as* anger-provoking or guilt-provoking and so forth. The subject experiencing the emotion, in other words, attends to certain aspects of her situation, *seeing* them *as* emotion-provoking. This alternative basically corresponds to the preliminary definition of emotional episodes given in the beginning of this chapter. But what exactly does seeing-as mean? This section aims to clarify the seeing-as approach, to examine its promise and to identify its explanatory challenges.

A. The analogy with the visual case of "seeing-as"

The term "seeing-as" comes from an analogy between describable emotional episodes and certain visual experiences. Robert Roberts explains:

> Wittgenstein discusses a kind of visual experience which is not a visual sensation. He says, "I contemplate a face, and then suddenly notice its likeness to another. I *see* that it has not changed; and yet I see it differently. I call this experience 'noticing an aspect'"(p. 193). One "sees an aspect" of a face by construing it "in terms of" another face, is something like an act of imagination. The analogy with feeling awkward is instructive: Just as one *experiences* something about the face by letting the other face "inform" it, so in feeling awkward one experiences oneself in certain terms, or in a certain connection (perhaps in connection with some paradigm of awkwardness).[51]

Seeing-as involves attending to or focusing on something – in terms of something else. The salience in question is of an aspect of something that is brought to attention through its comparison with something else. This comparison is not intentional or deliberate, but rather strikes one's

51 Roberts, "What an Emotion is," 187.

awareness as one "suddenly notices" the similarity between the two things. Roberts insightfully remarks that this is "an act of imagination." The capacity to compare two things, or rather to see a similarity between two things, is an imaginative capacity. And imagining, although distinct from mere sensation, nevertheless relates to sensation. Seeing something in terms of something else involves a kind of structuring of sensation.

We can specify what feature of this face is similar to what feature in the other face. For example, we can point to the noses, the facial expressions and the hair color in each face and say that they are similar to one another. But in order for others to agree with us they too have to see the faces in question and identify for themselves the specified similarities.

After we list the specifications that show how one face is similar to another, our interlocutors may still not agree that the faces are similar. They know that the faces can be seen as similar since we see them as similar. And yet they will still not see that face as similar to the other face. We will not charge a person who cannot see the similarity that we do with irrationality or with making false inferences or holding onto questionable norms. All we can say in reply to such an interlocutor is: "can't you *see*?"

The specifications we can give, the individual similarities between respective parts in the two faces that together comprise their overall similarity, cannot in turn be judged as good or bad, valid or invalid similarities. They are simply seen and they can be seen by others, even if not necessarily by everyone. If a judgment is a result of reasoning, whether reflective or autopilot, if a judgment is the sort of mental state that can be revoked by assessing reasons for or against it in reference to the relevant norms, then seeing-as does not qualify as a judgment.

Roberts emphasizes the experiential aspect of seeing-as and the notion of salience such experiences involve, by referring to another example of Wittgenstein, the duck-rabbit drawing that can be seen either as a duck or as a rabbit:

> Just as seeing the duck-rabbit as a duck is not merely knowing that it can be seen as a duck, nor merely judging that it can be so seen, but is construing it as such, so the person who feels triumphant is not merely judging that he is triumphant, but is construing himself as such. Construing seems to involve dwelling on or attending to, or at a minimum holding onto, some aspect, for example, the duckiness of the duck-rabbit or one's triumph. It seems to mean bringing some perceived paradigm, or some concept or image or thought, *to bear*. In the case of seeing the duck-rabbit as a duck, or of feeling triumphant, it is to bring some such thing *experientially* to bear.[52]

52 Roberts, "What an Emotion is," 187.

There is an important difference between the duck-rabbit example and the one about being struck by the similarity of two faces. In the duck-rabbit example we see a drawing in terms of a concept (of a duck or a rabbit), and in the faces example we see an image in terms of another image. This issue will become important in this book. What are emotions like? A conceptual or an imagistic seeing-as? In any case, both kinds of seeing-as have an experiential aspect that cannot be reduced to an interpretation or an understanding.

The analogy between this kind of visual experience and emotional episodes seems promising. Just as the same drawing can be seen as two different things so can the same situation be seen as emotionally salient in different ways. For example, I can feel compassion toward an arrogant person as she rants about how successful she is: "poor woman, she clearly has low self-esteem." Or I can resent her: "who cares what her hidden insecurities are? Her arrogance is aggressive and comes at my expense." Or I can feel contempt towards her: "pathetic woman, can she really not see how deluded her arrogance is? Do her anxiety attacks communicate nothing?"

An apparent dis-analogy from the visual case has to do with the capacity of having a few emotional perspectives at once. When it comes to the duck-rabbit drawing, we will see it either as a duck or as a rabbit. We cannot see the drawing as both duck and rabbit at the same moment. But when it comes to emotions, as in the case of mixed feelings, we can experience more than one emotion toward the same object at the same time. But do we? I am not sure how the physiological aspects of two different emotions may "blend" in the case of mixed feelings and I do not want to make any claims in this connection. But when one feels two emotions toward the same object and is able to describe them to oneself, one's attention may fluctuate between one emotional attitude and the other, perhaps in analogy to one's fluctuating perspectives seeing the duck at one moment and the rabbit at the following moment. The imagistic seeing-as seems to overcome this dis-analogy. For example, I can see that a certain child looks like both his parents. I may fluctuate my attention between the mother-like and the father-like features, or I can see them both at once.

Even if the analogy between the visual seeing-as and emotions may be imperfect, the seeing-as approach to emotions comprises an alternative to judgmentalism that is worth exploring. The suggestion here is of a notion of emotional salience that results from bringing two things to (imaginatively) bear on one another. In other words, certain terms are brought to bear on the here and now situation, making certain aspects of it emotionally salient. The question is what are the terms in which we see a situation as provoking this or that emotion. And the specified notion of salience will also procure the causal processes that give rise to emotions, here conceived as caused by this bringing to bear certain terms on the here-and-now situation.

Philosophers differ in the way they describe the terms in which the situation is construed as having the relevant emotional import. The differences are certainly major and thus give rise to very different descriptions of what emotions are. But before I begin to discuss the various seeing-as accounts available in the literature, I want to first discuss the promise of any seeing-as approach to emotions, namely that it allows for the possibility of both sensitivity and insensitivity of described emotional episodes to reason.

B. Emotions as modes of "seeing-as" and their relation to reasons

Whatever the terms in which we construe a situation emotionally end up being, the result of bringing them to bear on the here-and-now situation is the emotional salience of certain people and things in that situation. In other words, some objects in the current situation stand out as emotionally pertinent, and in the cases this book aims to explain, the subject who undergoes the emotional episode can label her affective state with an emotion-type word and can describe the emotionally salient features of the here-and-now situation.

As explicated in the beginning of this chapter, emotional salience can be verbally described in the form of a propositional attitude, where the proposition can be regarded as a reason of fit. This is partly why a described emotion looks like a judgment. But, as agreed by many today and as argued in the first part of this chapter, emotions are not judgments. If emotional episodes are not rationally formed, how should we understand the "reasons" that described emotions appear to embed? In what sense are they reasons at all?

The look-alike reasons that appear to be embedded in described emotional episodes are certainly not objective reasons. They have not yet faced deliberation in reference to one's endorsed norms of emotion fittingness and to one's self-image as having and cultivating certain cares and concerns. The subject may *later* endorse these look-alike reasons as good reasons and then they can count as objective reasons, but they are not objective reasons in the first instance.

Neither are these look-alike reasons operative reasons. They were not considerations taken by the subject to be in favor of this or that emotional reaction. If they were, emotions would be inferential judgments. Revoking those reasons would then ensure that the emotion would subside. The phenomenon of recalcitrance shows that this is not the case and that emotions are not judgments, and hence are not caused by the subject's grasping an operative reason, no matter how swiftly or spontaneously.

Unlike objective or operative reasons, look-alike reasons are not, in the first instance, considerations at all. They were not considered in connection to any question or on the way to any conclusion and are therefore not reasons in the standard normative sense. They are descriptions of the emotionally salient features of the situation at hand, a salience which is in turn the manifestation of the "bringing to bear" of certain terms on the situation.

Now whether these look-alike reasons can or should be rationally assessable, and how or in what way they can or should be responsive to reasoning against them, depends on whether we hold a conceptual or an imagistic seeing-as account. If the seeing-as account we hold is a conceptual seeing-as, where the emotional salience is brought about through the bringing to bear of a certain concept on the situation at hand, then what I have called the describable aspect of an emotional episode is in fact the intentional content of an emotional attitude. That content was not rationally formed, but any attitude with conceptual content is rationally assessable and sensitive to reason. That is, the attitude is meant to be responsive to reasoning against it by virtue of a conceptual and constitutive connection between the attitude and the deliberative conclusion that the attitude is not rationally justified. In other words, even if the attitude conceptually embeds only a look-alike and not an operative reason, it is now submitted to the rational norms (of fit) just as any other attitude with intentional content is.

Nevertheless, reason-sensitivity for the seeing-as conceptualist is not as demanding as the one presupposed by judgmentalists. According to the judgmentalist, the intentional content of the emotional attitude is rationally formed through the grasp on an operative reason. Reasoning against that attitude therefore takes away its principal cause. The emotional attitude is thereby meant to subside. But according to the seeing-as conceptualist, the emotional attitude was not rationally formed. The attitude's subsidence as a response to reasoning against it thereby depends on the degree of the rationality of the subject. A very rational subject would have a reliable disposition to respond in the right way and to change her attitudes (including beliefs, intentions, desires and emotions) according to her rational deliberations. But not all subjects need to be so rational. Practically speaking, the disposition to respond in the right way to rational deliberation may work more or less well. Some people might not be able to dim down any particular emotional reaction, but with repeated reasoning against a certain emotional reaction to certain typical circumstances they can eliminate the emotional pattern over time.[53] This means that a conceptualist seeing-as account can allow for quite a bit of recalcitrance as well as for many cases where emotions do respond to reasoning in the expected or demanded way.

What if one holds an imagistic seeing-as account? On such an account, the terms that are brought to bear on certain people or things in the here-and-now situation are imagistic rather than conceptual, and so look-alike reasons, the verbal descriptions of the emotionally salient features of the situation, do not constitute the emotion's intentional content. Indeed, according to such a view, emotions do not have intentional content, and they are not reason-sensitive. The description of the emotionally salient

53 See for example Patricia Greenspan, "Learning Emotions and Ethics," in *The Oxford Handbook of Philosophy of Emotion*, ed. Peter Goldie (Oxford: Oxford University Press, 2009): 554.

features of the here-and-now situation is just that – a description, and if it looks like a reason, or is given as a reason, it is merely a retroactive rationalization. Nevertheless, looking like reasons is enough to treat these descriptions as if they were reasons and put them under normative pressure to be good reasons.

Even if the description of the emotionally salient features of the situation is not in the first instance considered inferentially, the question about the fittingness of an emotional reaction often hovers above described emotional reactions, since they often involve or implicate other people. There is, in other words, normative pressure that is akin to peer group pressure to treat the description P embedded in the described emotional attitude as a consideration that bears on the question: Is this emotion justified or fitting?[54] Just like operative reasons, retroactive rationalizations are up for scrutiny and criticism. Otherwise put, there is normative pressure for the described emotional attitude to cohere with the subject's endorsed norms of emotion-fittingness. It is in that sense that we treat emotions as we treat judgments, even if they are not judgments in the first place.

This notion of "normative pressure" should not be understood in terms of Moran's ideal of rationality that states of mind should bear a constitutive relation to one's explicit reasoning about them.[55] Rather, the demand that our emotions be aligned with our normative judgments is, once more, akin to peer-group pressure on the individual to be coherent and consistent in their social interactions and to conform to norms of appropriateness. In other words, it is not reason itself that should work well, produce the right conclusions and have the right influence on one's psychology. Rather, it is the person who is expected to control her emotions in a way that fits with her self-conception as a rational or moral person with certain norms of fit, cares and concerns. This normative peer-group pressure to align one's emotional state with one's deliberative judgment may or may not have the desired effect. The imagistic seeing-as approach, then, which denies that there is a rationally constitutive relation between one's deliberative judgment and one's emotion, allows them to sometimes converge and other times diverge.

The seeing-as approach to emotions, whether it is conceptualist or imagistic, therefore promises to do justice to the complicated and often unpredictable relation between emotions and one's judgments about their fittingness or appropriateness. Any specific seeing-as account would have to deliver on this promise. Saying that some emotions are recalcitrant since one cannot help *seeing* the situation *as* provoking this or that emotion while

54 This is how I think we should understand de Sousa's claim that "paying attention to certain things is a source of reasons, but comes before them." De Sousa, "The Rationality of Emotions," 139.

55 Richard Moran, "Replies to Heal, Reginster, Wilson and Lear," *Philosophy and Phenomenological Research* 69, no. 2 (2004): 472.

judging to the contrary is a description of recalcitrance, not its explanation. That is, any specific notion of salience should have the resources to explain why it is that deliberation in reference to various normative notions of emotion appropriateness sometimes seems to have a relevant effect on a person's psychology, if it is not by virtue of intrinsic or constitutive emotion control. And any seeing-as account should also explain how the various kinds of stable and occasional emotional recalcitrance occur.

I divide the seeing-as views that are available in the contemporary philosophical literature into four main groups that correspond roughly to the kinds of terms involved in the notion of salience proposed by each account. That is, since this book aims to conceptually clarify the emotionality of emotions, namely their episodic nature including their formation and subsidence, then the various accounts are grouped according to the causal stories they provide or presuppose. And a seeing-as account of emotion comes with such a story, whether implicit or explicit, since bringing to bear certain terms on the situation at hand is precisely the process that gives rise to emotional episodes.

There is inevitable crudity in grouping together a plurality of different accounts into one category. Many of the differences among these accounts, some of which are considerable, get lost in the process. And some possible categorizations of accounts of emotions become irrelevant in the categorization that this book offers. In particular, I leave aside one way to categorize accounts of emotion, namely the accounts that use a perceptual model for emotions. A perceptualist about emotions could be a judgmentalist, as in the case of Martha Nussbaum, or can hold a seeing-as account. Furthermore, a perceptualist may be a conceptualist about perception and emotions and assume causal processes that involve conceptuality, or she may be a non-conceptualist, as are most perceptualists about emotions.[56] The rest of this part of the book, then, is dedicated to the critical discussion of the seeing-as accounts available in the literature, whether or not the philosophers who hold them emphasize or explicitly rely on an analogy between emotions and perception. In the next section, I critically examine the first group that holds a conceptualist seeing-as account. I show that this view should be rejected, since it also faces the emotionality problem described in the second section of this chapter. I conclude the chapter by

56 Perceptualists about emotions include: Aristotle, *Rhetoric*; Louis Charland, "Feeling and Representing: Computational Theory and the Modularity of Affect," *Synthese* 105, no. 3 (1995); Michael Brady, "Recalcitrant Emotions and Visual Illusions," *American Philosophical Quarterly* 44, no. 3, (2007); Christine Tappolet, "Emotions, Perceptions, and Emotional Illusions," in *Perceptual Illusions: Philosophical and Psychological Essays*, ed. Clotilde Calabi (London: Palgrave Macmillan, 2012); Sabine Döring, "Why Be Emotional?" in *The Oxford Handbook of Philosophy of Emotion*, ed. Peter Goldie (Clarendon: Oxford University Press, 2009), 283–302; Prinz, *Gut Reactions*; Remy Debes, "Neither Here nor There: The Cognitive Nature of Emotion", *Philosophical Studies* 146, no. 1 (2009).

formulating the explanatory challenges that any seeing-as account of emotion should answer. These will serve as terms of criticism when discussing the other seeing-as accounts over the next three chapters.

C. *Propositionally structured construals and the care-factor objection*

The first seeing-as group of accounts speaks of propositions as the terms in which a situation is experienced emotionally. Some, such as Patricia Greenspan, talk about these propositions as actual thoughts that the emoting subject explicitly entertains.[57] These are evaluative thoughts that are short of belief. For example, when I am afraid that a dog will bite me I think to myself "the dog is dangerous." But the proposition is only a thought; it is not assented to, it is not a judgment of fit. The situation is seen in terms of that entertained thought, which nevertheless appears to refer to norms of fit or rather to the themes with which norms of fit characterize objects of emotions such as danger for fear and achievement for pride.

On Roberts' account, we may but need not explicitly entertain a propositionally structured thought. He also speaks of entertaining a concept on its own, detached from a proposition, such as "danger" for the case of fear. Roberts also allows for the entertaining of an image, but I was unable to find an example for the image case in Robert's work.[58] Crucially, however, even if a subject need not explicitly entertain thoughts on Roberts' account, the subject nevertheless perceives the situation as propositionally structured. For example, "fear presents X as an aversive possibility of a significant degree of probability; May X or its aversive consequences be avoided."[59] I think it is fair to say that Roberts ends up speaking of the situation as being seen in terms of propositionally structured paradigms of the relevant emotion-types. An even more implicit use of conceptuality can be found in Calhoun's account, which allows for a few concepts to be the terms in which a situation is seen without the subject being aware of those concepts.[60]

57 Patricia Greenspan, *Emotions and Reasons* (London: Routledge, 1988).

58 Calhoun calls those concepts "cognitive sets": Calhoun, "Cognitive Emotions?" Tamar Gendler's notion of "alief" is very similar to Calhoun's "cognitive set," only that she also allows the set to include images: Tamar Gendler, "Alief and Belief," *Journal of Philosophy* 105, no.10 (2008): 634–663. Gendler's "alief" is not presented as an account of emotion, but rather only of recalcitrant emotions, included in what she labels "belief-discordant behaviour." Both Calhoun and Gendler use the term "associations" to articulate their accounts, but their use of the term is very different to the one suggested in Chapter 5.

59 Robert Roberts, "Emotions and the Cannons of Evaluation," in *The Oxford Handbook of Philosophy of Emotion*, ed. Peter Goldie (New York: Oxford University Press, 2010), 561–584, 570.

60 In that sense, her account bears similarity to Ronald de Sousa's account of paradigm scenarios, discussed in Chapter 3.3.

These accounts rely on conceptuality, whether playing a role in explicit thoughts that cross one's mind or only in the implicit structure of one's sensible experience. Either way, the emotional episode is assumed to come over us in the first instance not only as articulable but already in an articulated form as Taylor says,[61] as if with a ready-made description, or with "subtitles."[62] But concepts or propositions need not themselves carry any affective or emotional weight. And so, these conceptualist seeing-as accounts inevitably face what I have called in the previous section the emotionality problem.

Jenefer Robinson remarks, regarding Greenspan's claim that emotions involve explicit entertainment of thoughts: "On the face of things, it would seem that I can think about danger all day long without ever becoming afraid or acting to avoid it."[63] Judgmentalism faces the problem of unemotional judgments, and here we have an analogous problem of unemotional thoughts.

As explained in the second part of this chapter (1.2.A), adding a care-factor such as a desire, or talking about emotionally significant objects or importance to our well-being, will not solve the emotionality problem. And this is the case whether we speak of judgments or thoughts. Insofar as terms such as "care" or "importance" are meant to carry affective significance, then they remain uninformatively synonymous to "being emotional." Saying that thoughts are emotional since we "live" them or "take them seriously" elucidates nothing about the emotionality of such thoughts.[64]

But when we turn to spell out such cares in terms of specific core-values or desires, the added care-factor amounts to a further judgment or thought, with its own conceptual content. And such judgments or thoughts regarding what we care about and its relevance to the situation at hand, may be held unemotionally as any other judgment or thought. As explained before (1.2.A), adding a care-factor to an evaluative proposition (whether merely a thought or assented to in judgment), will not provide the missing emotionality.

Roberts' construals, even if they need not involve explicit entertainment of thoughts or concept-words, also face the emotionality problem, as Roberts acknowledges and explains:

61 Taylor, "Self-Interpreting Animals," 64.

62 The term "subtitles" in this connection is borrowed from Collins' criticism of Mcdowell's view that perception comes in propositional form: John McDowell, *Mind and World* (Cambridge, MA: Harvard University Press, 2004). Collins' criticism is in: Arthur W. Collins, "Beastly Experience", *Philosophy and Phenomenological Research* 58, no. 2 (1998).

63 Robinson, *Deeper than Reason*, 22.

64 See Griffiths' criticism of Michael Stocker's use of such terms: Griffiths, "The Degeneration of the Cognitive Theory of Emotions," 306.

> But construing oneself as triumphant or awkward is not sufficient for *feeling* triumphant or awkward. Such a construal seems to be necessary to the feeling, but it is not the whole story. If I am very philosophical about my awkwardness in a French conversation – that is, if I have no great stake in speaking graceful French – I may be vividly aware of my awkwardness without feeling awkward. Similarly with triumph: Imagine a jaded old senator ... He runs once again, this time more out of habit and a mild distaste for the prospect of retirement than out of enthusiasm for his work or the contest ... Upon hearing of his victory he construes himself as triumphant – without feeling triumphant. Lacking in these two cases is a *concern* about being in the condition one construes oneself to be in. To feel self-righteous one must want to be (or to be thought to be) morally superior. To feel guilty one must dislike being guilty.[65]

Roberts thus adds a care-factor to his construals by taking recourse to a notion of concern. A concern would be one of the terms in which the situation is seen-as.[66] Concerns, for Roberts, are "desires and aversions, and the attachments and interests from which many of our desires and aversions derive."[67] These terms qualify as adding to our understanding of emotions since they designate intentional states that are about something and thus have conceptual content. They do not just amount to "being emotional." The question is whether these terms can carry the kind of affective significance that would make a construal emotional.

Are any of those terms distinct from the core-values and desires discussed in the second part of this chapter (1.2.A)? "Attachment" is probably the most seductive notion here, since it does not merely imply "closeness." We think of attachment as inherently affective. In fact, according to Jesse Prinz, attachment is an emotion, a basic emotion.[68] But as an emotional episode, attachment on its own manifests itself mainly in infancy through the action tendency of physically clinging to a parent or to some other object, or through the anxiety the infant feels when the attached-to object is taken away. Roberts does not speak of attachment episodes but of attachments as general dispositions to emote in the relevant way when the object one is attached to is involved. Love, for Roberts, is such an attachment, the kind "that lovers have for one another, and parents for their children and children for their parents, and good friends for one another."[69] He says:

65 Roberts, "What an Emotion is," 188.
66 Ibid., 192.
67 Ibid., 202.
68 Prinz, *Gut Reactions*, 157.
69 Roberts, "What an Emotion is," 203.

> The responses characteristic of such attachment are too various and conflicting for it to be an emotion. They can be joy when the beloved is flourishing, indignation when she is insulted, gratitude when she is benefited, fear when she is threatened, hope when her prospects are good, grief when she dies, and much more. Love in this sense is not an emotion, but a disposition to a range of emotions. Which emotion occurs is a function of how the beloved in construed.[70]

Plausibly we will all experience grief when a loved one dies. But this is an extreme event after which one's life radically changes. We would all be afraid if our loved one's life was threatened. But do we always experience an episode of fear when our loved one is in any sort of danger? Say my friend's job is threatened. Must I be afraid? I may respond with fear or compassion, I may secretly gloat that now she is in a situation similar to the one I was in a year ago, when she mocked me for being afraid. Or I may fail to feel anything at all and just offer my advice or other practical assistance.

In other words, I may construe certain aspects of the here-and-now situation as emotion-provoking, as characterized by themes that fit certain emotional reactions such as dangers, achievements, loss, benefit, and I may also love and be attached to the construed object (my friend, my parent) and yet I need not respond emotionally. The kind of love or attachment Roberts has in mind cannot be the "secret ingredient" or the care-factor that makes a construal emotional. In other words, saying generally "I love my daughter" or "I love my friend," does not denote a reliable disposition to have fitting emotions, as Roberts here seems to claim. These general statements seem more like a summary description of a complex emotional relationship (including perhaps occasional episodes of love-emotion or separation anxiety).

The "positive" care or concern terms Roberts uses: desires, interests, and attachments, need not involve emotionality. And aversion or "negative" cares or concerns also suffer from the same problem. Turning to likes and dislikes will not help either. If by "like" we merely mean "positively emotional" and by "dislike" we mean "negatively emotional" then turning to likes and dislikes adds nothing to our understanding of the term "emotional." But when we specify the objects of the likes and dislikes and thereby give those preferences content, we face the emotionality problem again. Consider my disappointment that the airing of a TV series was cancelled in favor of a football game. Am I emotional because I like that TV show? "I like that TV show" is a judgment, and I can say it or act on it dispassionately. In fact, on another very similar occasion I may not get emotional, even if I like that TV show just the same.

70 Ibid., 203.

The emotionality problem will reappear whenever we use evaluative terms to be those that are brought to bear on the situation at hand. Construing a situation in evaluative terms, just like evaluations, may or may not be emotional. Indeed, when we use evaluative terms to make explicit the notion of salience involved in emotions, it begins to be hard to specify the difference between a construal and an evaluative judgment. What is the difference between seeing an object as a dislikable object and evaluating it to be dislikable? Merely restating that the first has an experiential or sensible dimension that the second may lack will not do. What we need is an understanding of seeing-as that would illuminate why seeing-as has this ineliminable experiential dimension in the first place.

Robinson acknowledges that likes and dislikes are evaluations. But, as will be discussed in detail in the next chapter, she understands them to be non-rational and automatic evaluations called "affective appraisals." Robinson criticizes the view that the situation is seen as emotionally salient when the subject sees the situation in terms of like/dislike affective appraisals. I will not present here her arguments against this view.[71] Instead, I want to draw attention to the way in which Robinson presents this view, that likes and dislikes, or aversions and preferences, as she calls them, could give content to the care-factor:

> So one way to conceptualize an affective appraisal is as "saying" **I like it!** or **I don't like it!** I use semi-bold letters to render these non-cognitive evaluations, because what I am talking about is not just some dispassionate evaluation of the form "I like this all right, although I've seen better" or "I do not like this, but I can live with it," but rather a fast, automatic, "hot" evaluation of what is important to me and my wants and values, and which *because of this* leads to physiological activity and action tendencies.[72]

Robinson's appeal to semi-bold letters is meant to signify the difference between "hot" and "cold" evaluations. "Hotness," however, is a metaphor or just another way of saying "emotional." Cares and concerns, "what is important to me and my wants and values," and their evaluation as relevant to the situation at hand need not be "hot" or passionate. Cares, concerns, likes and dislikes were meant to explain emotionality, but the only way to stress that this valuing or wanting, liking or disliking is affective consists in saying so or in writing it in semi-bold letters.

The appeal to a care-factor is meant to account for the selectiveness of our emotional life. We are not emotional about all the situations that may fit or be construed through this or that emotion-type term. Roberts'

71 Robinson, *Deeper than Reason*, 64–65.
72 Robinson, *Deeper than Reason*, 64.

concerns, however, cannot provide the kind of discrimination we are looking for. In fact, the very same concern can be involved in both an emotional and an unemotional reaction to the same situation.

For example, I see someone throwing rubbish on the lawn in the park. I care deeply about the environment; I am attached to this particular park and have an interest in its cleanliness. I construe that person as having committed a wrong, indeed an offense to everyone else that enjoys this park including myself. Some people would get angry with that person in such situations or feel contempt toward that person. They may shout at them with a red face or otherwise demonstrate reproach. Others will not even get irritated. Their concerns will not make them emotional even if it can be a reason for them to act. They will calmly approach the person with a smile and say "look, there's a bin right there." They may even throw the litter to the rubbish bin themselves. They will go on with their day and forget about the incident shortly after.

It is true that we often expect people to emote about issues they care about. As explained above, the care-factor, just like emotion-type or intensity fittingness, is certainly relevant to emotions as a term of criticism. In other words, we see emotions as reflecting a person's cares and concerns and we may be surprised to see someone we know well emotionally express themselves in a way that does not fit with the cares and concerns we normally ascribe to them. And we also expect our own emotions to fit with our endorsed cares and concerns, to be appropriate to who we are, what we are committed to and to how we see ourselves. In fact, this notion of emotion appropriateness, the fittingness of the attitude to one's self-image, may also be involved in criticism in reference to emotion-type or intensity fittingness. If I find that I have an unfitting emotion or that I am over-reacting, I may be able to dim down my emotion by virtue of my self-image as a reasonable person.

But cares and concerns, desires, interests or core-values will not explain or account for emotionality. Whatever the terms in which we see the situation as shame- or resentment-provoking, care-factor terms will not do the required job. This first group of seeing-as accounts that relies on a conceptually structured construal, represented here by Roberts and Greenspan, thus does not provide the notion of emotional salience we are looking for. That is to say, whatever are the terms in which we see a situation as emotion-provoking, they are not propositions or concepts that are effectively descriptions of the situation at hand.

D. The explanatory challenges for any "seeing-as" account of emotion

As argued in the first part of this chapter, emotional reactions are not judgments. Emotional reactions are not rationally formed, no matter how spontaneously or in an auto-pilot mode of reasoning. Judgmentalism cannot account for the divergence of one's emotionally expressive behavior and one's implicit or explicit views about the appropriateness of certain emotional responses to the situation at hand (under a certain description). We need not and do not always experience a certain emotion type when we find the circumstances fitting an emotional reaction. And sometimes we emotionally react in ways we then judge to be inappropriate, and our emotional reaction may or may not subside and align with our normative judgment. The causal processes that give rise to emotional reactions are therefore not inferential processes of evaluation in reference to various norms of emotion appropriateness, no matter how spontaneous and pre-reflective.

The seeing-as approach to emotional reaction, described in minimal terms in the third section of this chapter (1.3.A–B), promises to overcome the difficulties encountered by judgmentalism. Experiencing a describable emotional salience may converge or diverge from one's judgment about the fittingness of the verbally expressed emotions. Any seeing-as account should specify the terms in which the situation is seen as emotion-provoking. Such an account will thereby describe the process that gives rise to a describable emotional reaction, namely the "bringing to bear" of those terms on the here-and-now situation.

I conclude this chapter with the formulation of the explanatory challenges any seeing-as account faces, in light of the criticism of judgmentalism (as well as of the seeing-as philosophers who conceive of emotional salience as propositionally structured). Any account of emotional salience, in other words, that thereby suggests certain affective processes that cause emotions, should comply with the two following conditions, or settle the following two long standing questions:

1. Whatever are the terms whose bringing to bear on the situation trigger an emotional episode, whatever are the affective processes that cause emotions, they should account for the emotionality of the episode. That is, the affective processes should have the resources to answer what I called in the Introduction the singularity question, namely why is this specific person having this specific emotional episode with its describable and expressive aspects? Why is this specific person emotional in this describable way here-and-now? If an account needs to take recourse to an additional "spice" or ingredient that would make the proposed processes affective or their produced mental states emotional, then appealing to a care-factor will not help.
2. Whatever affective processes an account of emotional salience proposes, the emotional reaction they yield can be described in the form of an attitude embedding look-alike reasons. Any seeing-as account should have the resources to explain the partial responsiveness of emotions to the subject's explicit judgments that revoke those look-alike reasons as bad reasons. In other words, any account should allow

for and explain both responsiveness and recalcitrance (whether stable or occasional) to reason in reference to various normative notions of emotion appropriateness.

Chapters 2, 3 and 4 include critical discussions of three more seeing-as accounts for emotions that are available in the literature, even if strictly speaking the account presented in Chapter 3 and in particular in Chapter 4 focus on the causal explanation of patterns of emotional reactions we call pathological, such as recalcitrant emotions. A critical examination will show that the available accounts fail to answer the singularity question and that they do not have the resources to explain both responsiveness and the various kinds of unresponsiveness to reason. Nevertheless, each such seeing-as account provides new insights and poses further constraints on what affective processes can be. In the second part of this book (Chapter 5) I aim to propose a seeing-as account that complies with all the constraints and conditions accumulated in the critiques of the first four chapters.

2 The sub-personalist accounts

The criticism of judgmentalism in the previous chapter led to the conclusion that emotional reactions are modes of seeing-as, where certain aspects of the situation at hand are experienced as emotionally salient. A seeing-as account for emotional reactions should include the specification of the terms in which we see a situation as provoking this or that emotion. That same account would also procure the causal explanation for emotional reactions. Bringing certain terms to bear on the situation so that it is experienced as having emotionally salient features is precisely the process that gives rise to emotions. If we know what these terms are and how they are brought to bear on the situation, then we have a causal account for the formation of an emotional reaction. The criticism of judgmentalism demonstrates that whatever these terms are, they are not reasons in the standard normative sense and that whatever affective processes are, they are not rational processes, that is, they are not inferential processes done in reference to norms of fit.

In this chapter I examine the "sub-personalist" view, where "sub-personalist" designates the proposed kind of non-rational processes that cause emotional reactions. I take the accounts of Paul Griffiths, Jesse Prinz, Jenefer Robinson, Justin D'Arm, and Daniel Jacobson, to be the main representatives of this view. Although the accounts of these philosophers are far from identical, and indeed they criticize one another in print, they all share the same foundation, which is the topic of this chapter.

I begin by articulating the foundation of this view and proceed to examine whether it fulfills the conditions a seeing-as account has to fulfill, as stated in the end of Chapter 1. I will conclude that these accounts fail to provide the notion of salience required for the explanation of emotional reactions. And yet, they contain insights that pose further constraints on any account of the processes that cause emotional reactions.

1. Characterizing affective processes

Any account that proposes a notion of emotional salience (together with the causal processes that bring this salience about) should do justice to the phenomenology of emotions, in particular their "passivity." As noted in the last chapter, emotional episodes are experienced as something that happens to us rather than something that we intentionally do. One of the main contributions of the philosophers discussed in this chapter consists in the clarification of this passivity.

A. Affective processes are automatic

Emotions are not the product of reflective choice. Even when we work ourselves up to an emotion through deliberation, we cannot simply command the emotion to be aroused. Griffiths uses Fodor's term "mandatory" to describe this feature. He says: "People often respond with fear or anger to a given stimulus whether they choose to or not."[1] That is, emotional episodes are triggered without any intervention of the person qua agent.

The manner in which the passionate or expressive aspect of an emotional episode unfolds also does not require any "conscious direction."[2] The passionate or expressive aspect of an emotion constitutes a condition we suffer as patients rather than do as agents. Following Paul Ekman, Griffiths claims that the physiological and behavioral manifestation of an emotional episode, such as facial expressions, physiological feelings, involuntary bodily movements (e.g. flinching in fear) and also neurological and hormonal changes, unfold in an "automated" way.[3]

The word choice "automated" indicates the presupposition that emotionally expressive behavior is governed by a causal mechanism that operates in a law-like way. This is indeed Griffiths' view, as will be explicated in the next section. But the observation that the various expressive features of any given emotional episode are not deliberate or under one's conscious control need not indicate such a law-like causal mechanism.

Especially when it comes to action tendencies of emotions, such as fight or flight for fear, people vary in their reactions and may react in different ways on different occasions. The very same circumstances, such as a man making a sudden violent gesture toward people in a café, as if about to attack them, may make one person flinch and the other seek an improvised weapon (such as a bottle of water). Furthermore, the same person may react differently on different days. Indeed, to a certain limited extent, we judge and assess people according to their unreflective emotionally expressive behavior. In this example, many of us will celebrate the one willing to fight a threat and some of us will regard the one who flinches as a coward or as a weak person.

1 Griffiths, *What Emotions Really Are*, 93.
2 Ibid., 77.
3 Ibid.

I thus prefer to use the less committing word "automatic" to describe this feature of the passivity of emotions, namely that emotional episodes are triggered and also proceed without our conscious direction. Solomon's "spontaneity" is ascribed to the person qua a rational agent, either an Anscombian agent who knows what she is feeling and why, or a Kantian agent in Moran's sense who can step back from her emotion to examine whether to endorse and sustain it or revoke and dim it down (see discussion in Chapter 1.1). The term "automatic," conversely, stresses the uninvolvement of one's rational agency in triggering or expressing emotional episodes, without assuming that rationality must be replaced with a causal mechanism.

B. *Opacity: affective processes (may) operate below the level of awareness*

Given that emotions happen to us, that they are an episode we undergo, we are not able to track exactly the processes that gave rise to them and sustain them as they occur. These processes are opaque to us.[4] In fact, we are sometimes not even aware of the trigger in the here-and-now situation that initiated the process.

This unawareness of the trigger of an emotional episode is familiar from ordinary experience, when it comes to emotions that take some effort to verbally express. Say I feel irritated by someone over lunch. Later I tell a friend about my feelings, but when asked, "Why were you irritated?", I am unable to answer the question. I find that I cannot easily describe what exactly triggered my irritation. When I try and reconstruct in memory when exactly I began to feel irritated and what happened at that moment, I can come to identify what about that person caused my irritation. Only then can I fully describe my emotion, that is, I can label my physiological and behavioral perturbation and excitement with an emotion-type word, identify the emotionally salient person or thing and further specify what exactly it is about that person or thing that makes them emotionally salient to me. In a way, my irritation can alert me to things I have not noticed during our lunch or rather to things that I have not noticed (via recognition) that I noticed (via affect). Saying that affective processes are in general opaque to us means that even when our emotional episode is more readily describable, affect strikes us before we can describe it. How to understand the kind of unawareness that characterizes the noticing via affect?

A conceptualist about emotions, whether it is a judgmentalist or a seeing-as conceptualist, would say that such unawareness amounts to the lack of self-awareness of an intentional mental state. That is, the emotion comes with implicit "subtitles," namely its conceptual content, that the subject

4 Ibid., 93.

merely has to read out. But the sub-personalists make a stronger claim about how low the level of awareness of an emotion trigger can be.

They all refer to experiments performed by R. B. Zajonc.[5] The experiments were more about preferences and aversions than about what we normally call emotions. But they also included disgust in its most literal sense (of food), and fear in the most reflex-like sense ("emergency response" or the "fight or flight" reaction).[6]

I will not survey all the Zajonc experiments but will shortly describe one, conducted on humans, which I find most telling. In that experiment, subjects were conditioned to have a fear or an emergency response to five out of ten five-letter nonsense words, using electric shocks. Then they were presented with the words at a speed that is too fast for recognition. Although they were unable to identify the words with which they were presented, their skin reacted with a galvanic response prototypical of the emergency response in face of the words that were associated with electric shocks. No object in the environment was here made salient, since those words were presented too fast to recognize, let alone pay attention to. But the measured bodily reaction is prototypical of fear and understandable as such (who wouldn't fear the prospect of extreme circumstances such as electric shocks?).

The triggers of this fear response were in principle unrecognizable as triggers or as anything at all for that matter. Such triggers can never be reported as having been perceived and they cannot be recollected in memory since they were not recognizable at the time of their occurrence. These are not ordinary triggers of emotions. People are not often exposed to extremely fast moving objects. So what can be learned then from those experiments? The gist of these experiments was to show that one can experience affect without any prior inference.[7]

Examine more closely the issue of awareness and inferences. As explained in the previous chapter through the discussion of Moran and Anscombe, inferences may be performed swiftly and on auto-pilot mode (Chapter 1.1). In other words, one need not explicitly deliberate or articulate one's reasoning in order to modify one's beliefs in reference to norms of rational inference or in order to act intentionally in a manner that effectively reflects one's reasons to act. That is, although we may not be aware or self-aware of our operative reasons to believe or to act, they nevertheless guide our beliefs and actions and they can be called to attention through inquiry and the elicitation of reasons.

5 I will not provide details on the experiments here. See Griffiths, *What Emotions Really Are*, 26–27; Robinson, *Deeper than Reason*, 39–41; Prinz, *Gut Reactions*, 33–36.

6 See Robinson, *Deeper than Reason*, 29–30.

7 As can be seen from the name of the paper all sub-personalists refer to, that is, Robert Zajonc, "Feeling and Thinking: Preferences Need No Inferences", *American Psychologist* 35, (1980).

If emotions required rational inferences, no matter how swift and auto-pilot, the inference in question would lead from the trigger to the emotion and its affective expression. Even without deliberation or articulation, to qualify as a premise of an inference, the trigger must, at the very least, be perceived via sensation under a certain description. The subject would be implicitly aware of that description and it is via that description that the trigger is attended to in the first place. And that description would be propositional in form, since inferences connect propositions to one another.

What the Zajonc experiments show is that it is possible that an object in the here-and-now situation will trigger an affective response without the subject's being aware of this object. If an unrecognizable object can trigger an affective response, then surely affective responses do not require the perception of that object under a propositional description. If emotions can be aroused without a trigger that may qualify as a premise for a rational inference, then emotional episodes do not require inferences for their occurrence.

Triggers that do not qualify as a premise for inference would include those that are in principle unrecognizable. But they also include triggers that are not attended to at the time of their occurrence via a certain propositional description, even if they are recognizable at the time of their occurrence and can, in principle, be remembered after-the-fact. To say it differently, if affect can be aroused even in extreme modes of unawareness then it stands to reason that it could also be caused in less extreme modes of unawareness. The unawareness in question here is the lack of a certain kind of attention – the kind that is readily articulable in the form of a proposition. That is, although often one can describe the trigger of one's emotion in the form of a proposition during or after an emotional episode, that description need not be, in the first instance, available to the subject or play any role in the subject's psychology.

The Zajonc experiments examine the limit case where one cannot in principle be aware of what triggered one's affective reaction in order to rule out the necessity of the other limit case where one is able to easily and quickly describe what triggered their emotion in propositional form. In between these two limit cases, there may be intermediary cases of unawareness. In particular, triggers may be mere perceptions that are not conceptually laden. That is, they can be perceived as isolated objects, indeed as mere images or sensations, and they need not be perceived under a propositional description or under a concept at all.

The Zajonc experiments thus challenge not just judgmentalism, which presupposes rationally inferential processes as affective processes, but also any kind of conceptualism about emotion. Any view that says that emotions have intentional content would have to explain where this conceptual content comes from. A seeing-as conceptualist may say this conceptual content is inherited from the conceptually laden perception that caused it. Such a seeing-as conceptualist still owes us an explanation as to the nature of this causal relation if it is not an inferential relation. But in any case, the conceptualist seeing-as view will not be able to account for the kind of emotions that are aroused in those experiments that are clearly caused by perceptions that are not conceptually laden.

The extreme opacity of affective processes in the Zajonc experiments also indicates that these processes may operate or perhaps always operate entirely below the level of awareness. This feature of affective processes that the sub-personalists stress, their opacity or operation below the level of awareness comprises perhaps the most significant novelty of the sub-personalist accounts, and will prove extremely important in this book.

C. *The "separateness" of affective process (the information encapsulation thesis)*

Another aspect of the phenomenology of passivity has to do with the limited control we have on our emotions. Our endorsed beliefs seem to have limited effect on our emotions. A verbally expressed emotional reaction can sometimes "contradict" one's endorsed beliefs insofar as the described emotion appears to include an evaluation of the situation that does not cohere with or that is the inverse of one's explicit evaluative judgment. And these avowed beliefs, in turn, need not fix the contradiction, that is, they do not always or even often succeed in dimming down the emotional reaction or replacing it with another emotional reaction that one would judge to be fitting to the situation. In some sense that is yet to be clarified, affective processes are "separate" from the rational processes that govern our endorsed beliefs and our intentional actions.[8]

As Griffiths insightfully says, affective processes have a "narrow inferential role."[9] The connection beliefs usually have with other states of mind (such as intentions) is an inferential connection. If there were such an inferential connection, then one would expect emotions to be much better synchronized with the subject's endorsed beliefs. The inferential role of affective processes is "narrow" insofar as they do not connect with one's inferential belief system. In fact, in light of the possibility that the triggers of affective processes are not perceived under a propositional description or under a concept, and considering the criticism of rational inferential processes presented in the previous chapter, one wonders why we should say that the inferential role of affective is "narrow" rather than simply say that they are not inferential at all.

A sub-personalist such as Griffiths spells out this "separateness" of affective processes from the rationally inferential processes that give rise to beliefs and intentions in terms of accessibility or rather inaccessibility of "information." First, the affective processes do not access the information

8 Griffiths, *What Emotions Really Are*, 92–93.
9 Griffiths, "Towards a Machiavellian Theory," 95.

embedded in beliefs. Presumably the term "information" here refers to the conceptual content of beliefs, which would have a propositional form. This inaccessibility is meant to account for emotions that contradict beliefs.

However, it is a familiar fact of ordinary experience that thoughts and beliefs do sometimes serve to trigger an emotion, and in that sense their conceptual content seems available to affective processes. My thoughts and speculations about my friend being late for dinner may lead me to worry about and fear for her safety, if I know that she is a punctual and reliable person and remember that she texted me a little while ago to say she is on her way. Or my thoughts about her lateness may lead me to anger if I know from experience that she is always late to our meetings despite continuously promising to change her ways. Anyone who opposes the idea that affective processes are rationally inferential processes, sub-personalists included, would have to provide for an alternative causal relation that would connect beliefs and thoughts with emotions.

Furthermore, some thoughts seem to be involved in certain emotions. How can we understand what regret means without ascribing to the subjects the thought that a certain action or occurrence was the consequence of a bad decision? Griffiths does not include emotions that involve thoughts in the same group with emotions that do not. He calls the first "complex" and the latter "basic" and treats them as quite different phenomena.[10] D'Arms and Jacobson also separate these two groups of emotions, renaming the basic emotions "natural emotions."[11] Robinson and Prinz, on the other hand, although they acknowledge the differences between basic and complex emotions, explain the latter as based on the former, thus proposing a unified account. I will discuss their (very similar) accounts later in this chapter. For the sake of simplicity, I limit myself for the moment only to what Griffiths would call biologically basic emotions.[12]

That the conceptual content of beliefs remains inaccessible to affective processes is also meant to explain the possibility of recalcitrance of emotional episodes to reasons. That is why, for example, according to Griffiths, "knowledge that the cockroach in my drink has been completely sterilized does not eliminate the disgust response."[13] Prinz (whose account encompasses both basic and complex emotions) also mentions in connection to this encapsulation the familiar fact that even when one's emotional episode subsides as a response to one's judgment against it, the affective or

10 This distinction is presented most clearly in Paul Griffiths, "Is Emotion a Natural Kind?" in *Thinking About Feeling*, ed. Robert Solomon (New York, NY: Oxford University Press, 2004).

11 D'Arms and Jacobson, "The Significance of Recalcitrant Emotion," 138.

12 See Paul Griffiths and Andréa Scarantino, "Don't Give Up on Basic Emotions," *Emotion Review* 3, no. 4 (2011).

13 Griffiths, "Towards a Machiavellian theory," 95. See also Griffiths' discussion on fear of earthworms that persists despite the judgment that they are harmless: Griffiths, *What Emotions Really Are*, 28, 93.

expressive aspect of one's emotion lingers and subsides only in a gradual manner. Once the expressive, physiological and behavioral responses have been triggered they cannot be stopped at the same speed as one's thoughts.[14]

The inaccessibility between affective processes and beliefs goes both ways. Beliefs do not access the "information" of affective processes either. Whatever the nature of this "information" may be, it remains "not available for inspection."[15] I shall discuss the notion of information encapsulation and how it bears on the issue of sensitivity to reason later in the chapter. Even if I criticize and reject this notion of inaccessibility of information as a way of clarifying what "separateness" amounts to, I still agree with Griffiths on the basic crucial insight, namely that affective processes are distinct from rational processes.

D. *The affective processes for basic emotions are non-conceptual and non-linguistic*

Given the "narrow inferential role" of affective processes, then whatever the "information" processed by the affective system is, it is not the conceptual content of propositions. This claim is coherent with the fact that at least some triggers that are the input of the affective system are not propositions or conceptually laden perceptions at all. If we understand concepts to be nodes in an inferential network of beliefs,[16] then affective processes, which are not rationally inferential, cannot be conceptual. Griffiths further claims that this means that emotions do not have conceptual content, that they are not intentional attitudes. He says:

> If the concepts that figure in the content ascribed to a representation do not have their usual inferential role, then what is meant by attributing

14 See Prinz on how a negative feeling can linger after one discovers that their bout of jealousy is unjustified: Prinz, *Gut Reactions*, 96. See also: Carman, "First Persons," 403.

15 Griffiths, "Towards a Machiavellian theory," 95. What kind of inspection would that be? Perhaps it could be the kind of inspection Moran describes when saying that our beliefs form and readjust in reference to norms of rationality, without our agential involvement (see discussion in Chapter 1.1.B). And yet this kind of auto-pilot rational inspection operates on states of mind of propositional form with conceptual content. As will be shortly explained, Griffiths (rightly) claims that concepts (the nodes of one's inferential network of beliefs) do not play a role in affective processes. It is thus not clear how Griffiths understands the term "inspection." How can such rational inspection occur in the first place with "information" that is not conceptual content? What is the nature of this information and how can it relate to the conceptual content of mental states that have propositional form? I here just raise the question without pursuing it. For a critique of the sub-personalist notion of information see: D. D. Hutto and E. Myin, *Radicalizing Enactivism: Basic Minds without Content* (Cambridge, MA: MIT Press, 2013), Chapter 4.

16 Robert Brandom, *Articulating Reason: An Introduction to Inferentialism* (Cambridge, MA: Harvard University Press, 2000).

> that content? The very idea that the state has conceptual content is thereby called into question.[17]

Affective processes of basic emotions are thus claimed to be non-conceptual and non-linguistic, and all the philosophers discussed in this chapter share this view.

This non-linguistic and non-conceptual feature that the sub-personalists ascribe to affective processes coheres well with the familiar claim that infants and animals also have emotions and thereby have the same kind of affective system as human adults. If human adults, animals and infants have the same kind of affective system, and given that animals and infants do not have concepts that they use in making inferential connections among propositions in language, then affective processes cannot be linguistic or conceptual.[18]

E. Prototypical outputs for the affective processes that produce basic emotions

The output of affective processes involves the passionate or expressive aspect of an emotional reaction, its involuntary, physiological and behavioral aspect, which together with certain action tendencies is what emotionality amounts to. Those physiological and behavioral phenomena are precisely what we suffer passively during an emotional episode.

Following the work of Paul Ekman, Griffiths, Robinson, and Prinz agree that basic emotions come with typical physiological and behavioral expressions. These usually include, as Griffiths says: "(a) expressive facial changes, (b) musculoskeletal responses such as flinching and orienting, (c) expressive vocal changes, (d) endocrine system changes and consequent changes in the level of hormones, and (e) autonomic nervous system changes."[19]

The philosophers in question vary in their interpretation of the available experimental data. It sometimes seems that Griffiths believes that the above features are all the result of a single underlying neurological mechanism and that these features are accordingly "coordinated."[20] Robinson finds Griffiths' demands on the typicality of physiological expression too strict. She claims

17 Griffiths, "Towards a Machiavellian Theory," 95–96.

18 In fact, Robinson, and D'Arms and Jacobson use this argument as their reason to claim that the affective system is non-conceptual: D'Arms and Jacobson, "The Significance of Recalcitrant Emotion," 133. See also Robinson, *Deeper than Reason*, 18. The only exception here is Prinz, who claims that basic emotions are non-conceptual for different reasons: Prinz, *Gut* Reactions, 41–50; and who thinks human and animal emotions should be distinguished: ibid., 115.

19 Griffiths, *What Emotions Really Are*, 77.

20 Ibid.

that not all the features Griffiths mentions appear in a pre-determined coordinated manner for every instance of a basic emotion; not all basic emotions have a distinct facial expression; and some action tendencies may be activated without an emotion. Robinson also doubts the "coordination" of those elements and claims that each of them may develop independently.[21]

I leave aside the question of a common "essence" or an underlying mechanism to all occasions of this or that basic emotion, as well as the empirical question of how strict are actually the outputs for basic emotions. The characteristics Griffiths lists may be regarded as a prototype. As with any prototype that is representative of many instances of a certain category, particulars are judged to be members of that category if they are similar enough to the relevant prototype.[22] Regarded in this manner, Griffiths, Robinson, and Prinz agree that basic emotions come with prototypical physiological and behavioral expressions. They disagree about the standards for the degree of similarity to the prototype required from each instance of a basic emotional reaction.

2. The sub-personalist account

The above considerations lead all philosophers of this persuasion to make the distinction between basic and complex emotions. They vary in the way they classify and characterize basic emotions. They also vary in the way they treat complex emotions. They share, however, the same foundations: basic emotions come with prototypical physiological and behavioral characteristic that are the result of affective processes characterized as automatic, opaque, "separate," a "separateness" understood in terms of informational encapsulation, and non-linguistic. The characteristics of affective processes described in the previous section are motivated by experiments as well as by ordinary experience of emotional episodes. The full-blown sub-personalist account relies on further considerations.

A. Affective processes are law-like causal mechanisms

I formulate this consideration differently from the philosophers in question, but it nevertheless seems to be the presupposition behind their account. The consideration seems to be the following: the affective processes that give rise to emotional reactions are not inferential in the sense of connecting propositions to one another so as to reach a valid conclusion in reference to norms. So if they are not rational then affective processes are causal processes. Crucially, the kind of causal processes the sub-personalists have

21 Robinson, *Deeper than Reason*, 92–93.

22 Eleanor Rosch, "Principles of Categorization," in *Cognition and Categorization*, ed. Eleanor Rosch and Barbara B. Lloyd (Hillsdale, NJ: Lawrence Erlbaum Associates, 1978).

in mind are causal mechanisms that operate according to predetermined law-like principles.

According to the sub-personalists, given certain typical inputs these causal mechanisms operate "very reliably" to produce a certain typical output, characterized over a "large domain" of properties. They constitute the underlying structure by virtue of which basic emotions have their prototypical physiological and behavioral features and may be considered as a "natural kind."[23]

Being law-like causal mechanisms, the affective processes proposed by the philosophers discussed in this chapter have no normative dimension. As will be later explained, Prinz allows for normativity to sneak back in, since he allows for some emotional reactions not to be as passive as we normally regard them to be. As will be explained in the fourth section of this chapter, Prinz, much like Moran, allows for certain emotional reactions to result from active and agential deliberation. But even for him, most of the time, the affective processes that operate spontaneously and automatically and produce an emotional reaction without the subject's control or involvement, are not normative processes in any way, shape or form. This lack of a normative dimension is precisely what makes the affective processes proposed by the philosophers discussed in this chapter "sub-personal."

The person level is characterized by processes that have a normative dimension or that operate in what we may call a normative space, where people acknowledge what we do or say or otherwise express and hold us responsible for it. Person level processes call for their acknowledgement by other persons. As Cavell says: "I am a being who to exist must say I exist, or must acknowledge my existence – claim it, stake it, enact it."[24] And claiming is to others, staking is for others, and enacting is to others in the inter-personal space where one is held responsible and holds others responsible for their actions, reactions, and verbal or other expressive behaviors in reference to normative demands.

The person level is characterized by the normative and by the demand for a meaningful description, and that is precisely what is missing from merely causal processes governed by law-like principles of operation. Similar to the reflexes that make our knee jump when we hit it on the right spot or to the operations of mitochondria in cells, the affective processes proposed by the philosophers discussed in this chapter are sub-personal. This difference comes hand in hand with another distinction, namely that person level processes are available, at least in principle, to awareness, whereas the issue of awareness does not even come up for sub-personal processes.[25]

23 Griffiths, "Is Emotion A Natural Kind?"

24 Stanley Cavell, *In Quest for the Ordinary: Lines of Skepticism and Romanticism* (Chicago: Chicago University Press, 1988), 109.

25 Sensations may perhaps also count as person level phenomena on this account, since they demand a meaningful description, and we expect that description to have some kind of valence. I cannot explore the issue of sensations here, but I nevertheless want to suggest that they may bear important similarities to affective states.

B. Affective processes are appraisal mechanisms

What is the nature of this law-like relation between the input and the output of affective processes? According to the sub-personalists, the causal mechanism that produces emotional responses accepts as input perceptions of the external situation and produces a physiological and behavioral response, which in turn represents a relation between the environment and the organism that bears on the organism's well-being. In other words, the philosophers discussed in this chapter claim that the sub-personal mechanism in question is an *appraisal* mechanism. It is the way we are "wired" or "programmed" to respond to certain typical situations that bear on our well-being in certain typical ways.

Those typical ways in which the environment bears on the well-being of an organism are by and large what the psychologist Lazarus called "core relational themes."[26] The content of those themes is precisely the rough-and-ready characterizations of the norms of emotion-type fittingness that match types of circumstances with types of affect, such as danger to fear, an insult to anger, benefit for joy, improvement or cessation of a bad situation for relief, and so forth. The content of these themes is also what is known in the philosophical literature as the "formal objects" of emotions.[27] The difference between the names these "matching rules" are given has to do with the various options to understand what "rule" means.

A rule can mean a linguistic rule, which for the typical analytic philosopher would mean a rule that can be specified by a full analysis of the necessary and sufficient conditions for the application of an emotion-type word or concept to circumstances that are specified under a certain description. This is probably what most judgmentalists mean when they use the term "formal object." The kind of judgmentalist that I have presented in the first chapter (not identified with any particular figure) would conceive of these rules in much more flexible ways. This kind of judgmentalist treats these "matching rules" as norms of fittingness and takes into consideration the fact that different people from different social niches may have different norms and that individuals may change their endorsed norms of fit over time.

The key similarity between these two kinds of judgmentalists is that the rules in reference to which the judgments are made are linguistic. Judgments involve verbal descriptions of the situation at hand, they involve the application of concepts to objects in the situation, and those concepts in turn also function as nodes in inferential network of beliefs. The two kinds of judgmentalists would have a different understanding of what concept application entails. The first would have necessary and sufficient conditions of application and the second would have instead more flexible and in-flux criteria.

26 Lazarus, *Emotion and Adaptation.*

27 E.g. Annette Baier, "What Emotions Are About," *Philosophical Perspectives* 4, (1990): 5.

Although Griffiths and Robinson use the term "core relational themes" and Prinz uses the term "formal objects," these philosophers certainly do not imply any linguistic or conceptual understanding of these terms. In fact, the "matching rules" are not rules at all, since rules are for persons who have standards of correctness for rule-application. Sub-personally, we can have only mechanistic law-like principles of operation. For the sub-personalist, a situation matches an emotional response of a certain type because it bears on certain aspects of the organism's well-being, and this "bearing" relation such as danger or a loss does not require the application of concepts. As D'Arms and Jacobson say:

> The fear system, for instance, can plausibly be described as monitoring the environment for threats to the organism ... There may be no better way of articulating that appraisal than by saying that it involves construing oneself to be in imminent danger; but it does not follow that, in order to feel fear, one must deploy this or any other concept ... Jealousy monitors the social environment for potential losses of affection or allegiance, especially (though not solely) from mate. Its characteristic appraisal is perhaps best interpreted in term of *defection.* Again, though, the fact that this concept is part of the best articulation of the emotion's locus of concern does not imply that the capacity for jealousy requires possession of the concept of defection – or even that it can only be articulated in those terms. Similarly for anger and *slights*, shame and *disability of mine*, contempt and *disability of yours*, disgust and *contamination*, amusement and *incongruity*, or envy and the concept of *difference in possession or position between myself and a rival that considered in itself, bad for me.*[28]

What does this "monitoring" consist in? How does the affective system classify a certain perception as a threat or as a loss? Griffiths speaks of "dimensions" of appraisal:

> A model of emotional appraisal takes the form of a set of dimensions against which potentially emotion-eliciting situations are assessed. The dimensions of the emotion hyperspace might include, for example, whether the eliciting situation fulfills or frustrates the subject's goals.[29]

For Griffiths then, as well as for Lazarus, the assessment that a "core relational theme" such as "threat" has been detected is a "summary" of the various appraisals in the relevant dimensions. The crucial difference between

28 D'Arms and Jacobson, "The Significance of Recalcitrant Emotion," 139–140. Emphasis in original.

29 Griffiths, "Towards a Machiavellian theory," 89.

Lazarus and Griffiths is that for Lazarus, the psychologist-judgmentalist, these appraisals are "cognitive" or concept-involving, and are summed up by a judgment.[30] For Griffiths, these appraisals are non-linguistic.

For Prinz and Robinson the appraisal involved in basic emotions consists in an instantiation relation that matches a singular here-and-now perception with a general schematic representation, which is imagistic or otherwise sensory. For example, a here-and-now perception of a snake triggers the schematic representation of a snake, which in turn causes the physiological and behavioral reaction that is prototypical of fear. And it is that reaction that represents the core relational theme "threat." As Prinz would put it, emotions are caused by their "calibration files," which contain schematic representations that "encode eliciting conditions."[31] They qualify as appraisals since the result is a representation of a core relational theme.

No matter how exactly these sub-personal appraisals are spelled-out, the sub-personalist accounts describe affective processes as processes of evaluation, much like the judgmentalist. As discussed in Chapter 1, judgments of emotion fittingness at the person level qualify as inferences, where inference is conceived of as normative and linguistic. Person level inferences have propositions with conceptual content as premises and conclusions and they are made in reference to norms of emotion-fittingness and of language use. Sub-personalists explicitly say that appraisals are also inferences. These are not rational but "computational inferences."[32] Prinz is clear about this point when it comes to his calibration files:

> The calibration file is a mechanism that uses premises to trigger an emotional response. It specifies what kinds of information can serve as an emotion trigger. In that respect, it is like a collection of inference rules (e.g. *If you see a snake, experience fear)*. The transition from a representation of an elicitor to an emotion can be regarded as an inference. It is a move from one group of meaningful mental states (representations of elicitors) to another (the emotion), and one can describe the former as reasons for the latter. Representations of elicitors trigger emotions precisely because emotions are more likely to be accurate when those eliciting conditions obtain. Fear is likely to be accurate (i.e. one is likely to be in danger) when one sees a snake. Therefore, the triggering process is not arbitrary. It is more like an inference.[33]

Griffiths' multi-dimensional appraisals qualify as inferences in this computational sense as well. The computation here is more complicated, since it

30 See also Prinz's discussion on dimensional appraisal theories: Prinz, *Gut Reactions*, 15–17.

31 Ibid., 151.

32 See for example, Griffiths, "Towards a Machiavellian theory," 95.

33 Prinz, *Gut Reactions*, 238. Emphasis in original.

runs through various appraisal dimensions, but it will still involve a series of if → then commands (if input then output). No matter how exactly a sub-personalist conceives of the details of the computations, this computational character of affective appraisals is what is supposed to make the relation between typical circumstances and typical affective responses "very reliable."

To sum up, the notion of salience proposed by the sub-personalists is thus the following: the terms in which the situation is seen as provoking a certain basic emotion are core relational themes (and also appraisal dimensions for Griffiths, and also sensory schemas for Prinz). Those terms should not be understood as concepts, and the manner in which they are brought to bear on the situation is through a process of evaluation that involves law-like computational inference, and not rational inference in reference to norms.

These terms reflect organism-environment relations and are said to bear on the organism's well-being. Griffiths talks about the computational appraisals as "survival enhancing."[34] Robinson talks about affective appraisals as modes of paying selective attention to the environment in terms of wants, interests, and goals (and also values when it comes to human adults), where each basic emotion has its own typical interests and goals.[35] In fact, goals are one of the appraisal dimensions Griffiths talks about in the above quote. Prinz, like Robinson, talks about the core relational themes of basic emotions as important and valued "matters of concern."[36] Emotions, Prinz says, "are like bodily radar detectors that alert us to concerns."[37]

Just like judgmentalists, the sub-personalists also include cares and concerns as part of the terms through which a situation is seen as provoking a basic emotion. In fact, as can be seen from the above quote of Griffiths and from the discussion of Robinson's account in the next section, sub-personalists regard the care-factor(s) as appraisal dimensions. I am puzzled as to how cares and concerns, goals and values regarding one's social world and relationships, that are so infused with language and normativity, could ever be regarded as lacking conceptual content or as participating in sub-personal, non-linguistic and non-normative mechanistic processes. But I will not explore this issue here.

Generally speaking, the sub-personalist account maps the judgmentalist account from the person level, characterized by language and normativity, to the sub-personal level, characterized as non-linguistic and law-like mechanistic. Both accounts regard emotions as resulting from an evaluation in terms of core relational themes as well as cares and concerns. Instead of judgments we have appraisals; instead of rational inferences in a normative

34 Griffiths, "Towards a Machiavellian theory," 95.
35 Robinson, *Deeper than Reason*, 24, 26, 46, 57, 69.
36 Prinz, *Gut Reactions*, 69.
37 Ibid., 240.

space we have computational inferences that follow law-like commands. And what triggers the emotional reaction, at least when it comes to basic emotions, is not a judgment or a perception under a certain conceptual or propositional description, but a non-linguistic perception of aspects of the here-and-now situation that bear on one's well-being in the relevant ways.

3. The return of the care-factor problem

Moving evaluations from the person level to the sub-personal level does not change their basic function as an evaluation. As such, sub-personal evaluations are subject to the same problem as person level evaluations, namely that evaluations need not be affective, no matter how fast they occur or how opaque they are to the person.

Similar to judgmentalists, sub-personalists add a care-factor to their appraisals in the form of interests, wants, goals, values, concerns, likes, and dislikes. In fact, sub-personalists regard care-factors as appraisals. For Griffiths, as mentioned above, they are appraisal dimensions. For Prinz, the appraisals that represent core relational themes already embed their relevance to the subject's concerns. As Prinz says: "The point is that core relational themes are directly relevant to our needs and interests."[38] The relevance to one's cares and concerns, in other words, is already implied in the affective appraisal. But this amounts to a subtle difference. Prinz (and Robinson[39]) basically claim that the appraisal is of the relevance of the situation to one's cares and concerns in certain specified aspects, such as dangers or achievements or other core relational themes.[40]

Judgmentalism takes recourse to a care-factor evaluative judgment and sub-personalists to a care-factor appraisal. But evaluations of the situation as bearing on specific interests, concerns, likes and dislikes, desires, needs or values, as stressed in the previous chapter, need not be "hot" or passionate. At the person level we have the problem of unemotional care-factor judgments and at the sub-personal level have the problem of unemotional or un-affective appraisals.

Perhaps the best illustration of this problem is Robinson's use of the semi-bold letters strategy, used to demonstrate that what she is "talking about is not just some dispassionate evaluation ... but rather a fast, automatic, 'hot' evaluation of what is important to me and my wants and values, and which *because of this* leads to physiological activity and action tendencies."[41] The semi-bold letters strategy is used a number of times throughout Robinson's book, including when it comes to the appraisals that she endorses:

38 Ibid., 66.

39 Robinson, *Deeper than Reason*, 46.

40 See also Prinz on sadness and a *valued* loss as well as his discussion on valence as representing that certain dangers or other core relational themes *matter*: Prinz, *Gut Reactions*, 226, 188 respectively.

41 Robinson, *Deeper than Reason*, 64. Emphasis in original.

> An emotional response of fear, for example, is evoked by an affective appraisal: **This is a *threat*.** Disgust is evoked by an affective appraisal, **This is *nauseating*.** Anger is evoked by an affective appraisal, **This *wrongs* me (or mine)** or **This is an *offence*.**[42]

As explained in the previous chapter, the semi-bold letter strategy will not do. It amounts to saying that these appraisals are affective because they are "hot" and involve "physiological activity and action tendencies." This will not qualify as an explanation of emotions or of emotionality that would account for the difference between an affective appraisal and a un-affective appraisal. It is just a description of this difference, of the passionate aspect of emotions.

After Robinson completes the description of her account of automatic affective appraisals, she appears to recognize that the key question as to what causes emotional reactions is still unanswered. She says:

> Why am I emotional about something on some occasions and on other occasions not? Or why does the very same event make me emotional and not you, although we are both evaluate [sic] the event in an angry or fearful way? There are almost certainly a number of variables involved here.[43]

Robinson here clearly acknowledges a fact about our ordinary experience of emotions. And the fact is that emotions are not "very reliable." People differ in their emotional patterns, even when considering only the ones we would judge to be fitting. Different insults get to different people; different benefits give joy to different people. Those differences function as a way to distinguish people's characters. Those characters that we ascribe to people are based on their distinctive collection of emotional patterns. But even at the level of the individual emotions are not so very reliable. Although individuals are to a certain extent predictable to the ones closest to them, they often surprise those who know them very well and also surprise themselves with their emotional reactions. If people's emotional patterns were law-like, we would manage our close relationships as we manage machines. Our relationships would lack the drama, mystery and suspense that so obviously characterize them.

People's emotional patterns are stable enough for us to ascribe to them an emotional character, the one we like or dislike, the one we may fall in love with or reject. And these emotional patterns are also flexible enough for us to keep wondering about people, even those closest to us, wondering how they feel, what motivates them, to sometimes ascribe to them moods when we cannot make sense of their reactions, and to sometimes watch

42 Ibid., 68.
43 Ibid., 95.

them change – becoming more joyous, more forgiving, more bitter, more fearful, and to sometimes see how they go back to their old ways. This basic mystery of other people as well as of ourselves, the flexibility of the emotional aspect of our characters, is implicitly widely acknowledged, not just by writers of fiction, films, and TV series, but by our interest in those stories, by the way we gossip about other people, by our hopes and fears that people can change.

This basic ordinary fact, that emotional patterns are actually not law-like, is what Robinson acknowledges in the above quote. But a sub-personalist is ontologically committed to the existence of a very reliable causal mechanism. How can Robinson hold her sub-personalist account of an affective appraisal system that is meant to be "programmed" in us and still claim that it sometimes works and sometimes does not?[44]

Her solution is to suggest further "variables."[45] Where are these further variables meant to fit in the causal structure? Presumably we can imagine a switch that turns the affective system on and off according to these variables. To allow for more variability we can imagine a switch with intermediary states between on and off, perhaps even something like the old analogue volume button that comes with the possibility to dim down or tune-up the affect in a continuous manner. The affective system can still be a reliable causal mechanism and the entire process can still be sub-personal if we can find the variables that turn the switch on and off, tunes it up or dims it down.

The first variable Robinson considers is what I have been calling the informative care-factor, which includes specific wants, wishes, goals, core-values, concerns and the like, all of which can be appraised un-affectively. Here, too, Robinson reiterates that the care-factor is unhelpful. She also notes that people sometimes emote over trivial circumstances, which they would not classify as care-worthy.[46] I devote the rest of this section to the examination of the other variables Robinson proposes.

A. *A further notion of salience*

> Sometimes I am distracted … one has to be alert or paying attention in some sense to the offensive event, in order to register it as an offence.[47]

But was it not the job of the affective appraisal system to render a perception emotionally salient in the first place? The Zajonc experiments were meant to show precisely that if we are in a state of unconsciousness (how

44 "Programmed" is the term Robinson often uses in her book. She allows for some biological pre-programming and further programming that depends on one's developmental history. Just a few examples: ibid., 63, 70, 71, 72, 74, 75.

45 Ibid., 95–97.

46 Ibid., 96.

47 Ibid.

can one be more distracted?) we can still register affectively something as disgusting. The seeing-as view, which Robinson explicitly adopts, regards emotions as ways of attending to certain aspects of the environment and making them salient. As Robinson says:

> [A]ffective appraisal ... serves to pick out and focus attention on those things in the internal or external environment that matter to the animal or human being and to appraise or evaluate them in terms of *how* they matter, for example, whether they are a good or a bad thing, a threat or an offence.[48]

A sub-personalist about emotions that claims that in order to emote one cannot be distracted and must focus "in some sense" on the features of the situation that are then to be affectively appraised has sold out.

B. Individual temperament

> Different people have in any case different thresholds for responding emotionally because of temperamental differences, such as optimism and pessimism: I am more prone to respond negatively than you are; you are more inclined to positive responses.[49]

It seems true to ordinary experience that some people are angry more often than others, some people feel joy more often than others, some people feel guilty more often than others and so forth. We could say perhaps that some people's guilt sub-system is tuned-up in comparison to other people's guilt-system as well as in comparison to their other affective systems, so that they feel guilty more often than others and more often than they feel joy.

We could say that temperament consists in the initial conditions of one's affective appraisal system. But this would still not explain why such a person feels guilty at all on any specific occasion. Some people feel guilty very often, but what it is that makes them feel guilty need not follow a consistent or law-like pattern. Some days I feel very guilty about stepping on an ant and other days I don't. What we need is a way to explain *that* variability.

C. Bodily readiness

> One *must* be in a state of bodily readiness. Notoriously, if one is short of sleep, it is easier to *see* the ordinary mishaps of life *as* wrongs or

48 Ibid., 42.
49 Ibid., 96.

> offences deliberately inflicted by an uncaring world; one is more prone to respond negatively. If one is full of energy one is more likely to *think* of the world *as* one's oyster.[50]

Surely some bodily states have an effect on emotions. Taking drugs can have a very immediate and clear effect. I am skeptical as to whether fatigue very reliably makes people more irritable or negative or more anything. But it seems right that a bodily state can have an effect on one's general mood. In fact, the seeing-as patterns that Robinson identifies with fatigue and high-energy can be described as moods. As she says: "A mood is a *bodily state* that lowers the threshold for getting into a bona fide emotional state."[51] I thus think that this variable is basically identical to the next.

D. Mood dependence

"The emotion states I get into are partly a function of my current *mood*."[52] Robinson claims that the same here-and-now perception can provoke different emotions or leave one indifferent depending on one's mood. This seems true. Some days I am generally irritable and various life events such as the rudeness of a waiter are more likely to bother me and make me angry, whereas the same event may amuse me on another day when I am in a playful mood or perhaps just leave me indifferent if I am in an optimistic and confident mood. In other words, the specific affect is already there, coloring my life experiences. I am already under the influence of a dominant affect and my day consists in finding suitable objects that my mood can turn into emotionally salient objects. Again, I think this insight is true to ordinary experience. When in a mood we often "take it out", as we way, on various people and things. Presumably, in such cases, the affective appraisal mechanism serves to boost the affect into a more noticeable episode.

We are left with moods as the only variable that can indeed account for the variability of singular emotional reactions, for the fact that many relatively stable patterns of emotional reaction are not so very reliable. But if mood is the only relevant variable, then moods would be the extra spice that makes an appraisal into an emotion, and a mood would be required each time a subject emotes. We would then need an account of moods to account for the emotionality of emotions. This is not only *ad hoc*, but it means that emotions are just as subjective as moods famously are. It would mean that the appraisal system would only track themes that are relevant to a present mood and would not track anything else. In fact, governed by subjective moods, an appraisal system might settle on objects that do not

50 Ibid. Emphasis added.
51 Ibid. Emphasis added.
52 Ibid.

objectively instantiate the relevant core relational theme. A sub-personalist that believes that emotions reliably track core relational themes, that they reliably alert the subject to where she objectively stands in the world, and who has to take recourse to moods in order to answer the singularity question and to explain emotionality, in order to explain why we emote when we do – has sold out.

This attempts to add variables to the affective system that would explain why some appraisals are affective and some are not fails. Just as we could not explain why some judgments are emotional and some are not within the rational and normative framework of judgmentalism – we cannot explain why some appraisals are affective and some are not within the causal-mechanistic framework of the sub-personalists. In fact, this result is not that surprising. Any account of emotion that treats them as evaluations is going to encounter the emotionality problem and thereby be unable to answer the singularity question: Why is this specific person expressing this specific emotional reaction here and now?

4. The problem of reason-sensitivity and recalcitrant emotions

The sub-personalist account claims to have the very important advantage that it can explain or at least make room for recalcitrant emotions, those emotions that persist despite the person's explicit judgment that they are unfitting to the situation in which they arose. The sub-personalist says the affective appraisal system produces emotions via a causal, non-linguistic mechanism, whereas beliefs are produced via rational and linguistic processes. Governed by two different processes, the two systems may evaluate the situation differently. In other words, the affective appraisal of a situation as fear- or anger-provoking may contradict the normative evaluative judgment that the situation is in fact not fear- or anger-provoking. Since the systems are governed by different kinds of principles – one normative and the other causal-mechanistic – the evaluative judgment will not alter the affective appraisal. As D'Arms and Jacobson say:

> [R]ecalcitrance is the product of two distinct evaluative systems, one emotional and the other linguistic. Because these are discrete modes of evaluation, only one of which involves the deployment of conceptual capacities, it is possible for them diverge systematically.[53]

D'Arms and Jacobson say that this divergence is "systematic" precisely because the affective appraisal system is a law-like causal mechanism and

53 D'Arms and Jacobson, "The Significance of Recalcitrant Emotion," 140–141.

hence very reliable. This works well with the example all sub-personalists keep repeating, namely phobias. And the phobias they speak of are stable ones from which a person suffers throughout most of her life: fear of heights, spiders, or snakes, where the objects of the phobia may be regarded as related to the evolutionary history of the species.

But what if the recalcitrance is not of a basic emotion? What about recalcitrant complex emotions, those emotions whose trigger clearly involves concepts? Unlike Griffiths and D'Arms and Jacobson, Robinson and Prinz regard complex emotions as continuous with basic emotions. What triggers a "calibration file" does not have to be a mere perception, a perceived image, or a smell or a sound; it can also be a conceptually laden perception, indeed even a perception under a propositional description, namely a judgment. For example, the jealousy calibration file may contain the schematic judgment that one's lover is unusually late from work.[54]

The calibration file of a certain emotion-type thus contains not just visual (or otherwise sensual) schemas but also explicit judgments or schemas of a typical scenario for that emotion-type.[55] The affective response is still fast, automatic and mandatory, and the relation between the conceptually structured perception and the calibration file of a complex emotion is still claimed to be a causal and not a normative relation.

As Prinz emphasizes, the emotion may be still informationally encapsulated. The emotion itself, the embodied representation of a core relational theme, need not directly interact with the information in the calibration file, and that includes information that corresponds to the conceptual content of judgments. "The calibration file causes a body response, and the body response causes the emotion. There is no need for direct talk between somatosensory areas of the brain and those areas that harbor evaluative judgments about social practices."[56]

Therefore, Prinz and Robinson may, perhaps, also account for stable recalcitrance of complex emotions such as the fear or disgust of homosexuals and contempt of black people and women. The prejudiced judgment can be included in a calibration file, nevertheless encapsulated from the rest of that person's beliefs, intentions and so forth. A theory of calibration files may even be able to account for recalcitrant phobias whose objects have nothing to do with the evolutionary history of the species such as fear of dolls, clowns, or scarves.

None of the sub-personalists discusses occasional recalcitrance, which is not "systematic" but limited by a period of time or a specific relationship. An occasional recalcitrance can also be of clearly basic emotions. Say I have been living in the same old house for years. I am familiar with the various sounds it makes, so to speak: the pipes squeak sometimes; other times it is

54 Prinz, *Gut Reactions*,101.
55 Ibid., 101, 222–223; Robinson, *Deeper than Reason*, 70, 73.
56 Prinz, *Gut Reactions*, 235.

the wind or the neighbors. Every now and again I suffer from short periods where I am startled by every noise and fear that maybe there is someone in the house. I know when it happens that it was the pipes or the neighbors and yet I still "jump" and feel compelled to take a look and see if anybody is in the house. This anxiety lasts for a few days, a few weeks or a few months and then it goes away, and then it returns. And during those times it is only those sounds that make me anxious or "jumpy." Otherwise my "fear-system" has not been disturbed. No mood can account for this kind of variability, since a mood does not include a preference for certain objects whose perception would boost the general affective state into an emotional episode. Occasional recalcitrance is a neglected issue in emotion studies, but it is familiar to many people and psychotherapists.

I leave aside for now the issue of occasional recalcitrance. Sub-personalists do not have the resources to deal with such cases, and to my knowledge they do not even mention their existence as data to be explained. In the rest of this section I examine the kinds of recalcitrance that the sub-personalists claim they can explain.

On Griffiths' account (and equally on the much less worked-out account of D'Arms and Jacobson), the affective appraisal system is isolated from and works independently of the linguistic evaluative system. As Griffiths emphasizes, the affective system is "informationally encapsulated." It is then unclear how or why these systems should ever connect to allow for an evaluative judgment passed after the formation of an emotional reaction to influence one's affective in the relevant way.

When it comes to fear of snakes or heights, which is meant to relate to the evolution of the species and be to some extent universal in young infants, why or how would some people stop having these reactions as adults? Complete "informational encapsulation" basically rules out reason-sensitivity and this seems to imply that all basic emotions should be recalcitrant in all people. This is surely not the case.

D'Arms and Jacobson use the term "immunize" to suggest that in the normal course of development most people stop feeling these basic fears.[57] But they never explain or elucidate the meaning of this "immunization" and how it should occur. Although the term suggests a causal relation such as receiving a vaccine shot, it is unclear how a rational judgment could cause a change in one's dispositions to emote with a certain affect in certain typical circumstances, especially when these dispositions have perceptions and not concepts as triggers.

Phrases like "top down" are commonly used when speaking of the influence conscious and explicitly articulated judgments have on brain states, and yet they are non-explanatory. One wants to know how the "top"

57 D'Arms and Jacobson, "The Significance of Recalcitrant Emotion," 144; see also D'Arms and Jacobson, "The Moralistic Fallacy," 81.

linguistic person level reaches and influences the "bottom" sub-personal level that is meant to be non-linguistic and non-conceptual.

The data is clear – conceptually structured judgments often serve to dim down emotional states in the relevant way, and most of us somehow stop being afraid of heights or harmless spiders over time, as we grow up. If we cannot account for this phenomenon in any other way then we may have to settle for a vague expression like "top-down" and hope that they may be made explicit in the future. But if we can account for this phenomenon in another way then there is no good reason to wait.

One way of allowing for reason-sensitivity consists in allowing, in some sense, the affective appraisal system to be conceptual, while still retaining the general principle that emotions are not the outcome of rational and normative inferences. Prinz's sub-personalist account brings concepts into the process by allowing the calibration file, which causes an emotion, to contain not just schematic images or other sensory representations but also concepts, judgments, and conceptually structured scenarios. Emotions are nevertheless informationally encapsulated since the relation between the concepts in the calibration file and the emotion is indirect. The here-and-now trigger elicits the relevant calibration file, which in turn causes a bodily change. It is the bodily change (and not the calibration file) that directly causes the emotion.

Reason-sensitivity then amounts to the access one's explicit reflection, which is rational and linguistic, can have to the calibration file itself. Prinz explicitly says that "calibration files can be modified through education and experience," that we can "cultivate" our calibration files.[58] In other words, we can control our emotional patterns through the deliberate alteration of a calibration file.

How does one change a calibration file according to Prinz? The general picture is this: basic emotions may be re-calibrated to include conceptually structured judgments and scenarios. This is, by and large, how we get complex emotions from basic emotions. They may also be calibrated, in a manner described below, to include imagistic or other sensory schematic representations that they did not initially include. The way in which those further schematic representations enter the calibration file also shows the way in which those additional calibrations can be removed from the file.

I begin by examining the issue of reason-sensitivity for complex emotions, those whose file, at some point in an individual's history, was calibrated to include further representations, in particular schematic judgments. Although Prinz is not a declared judgmentalist, he remarks that judgmenatlists have "hit upon one of the ways in which emotions occur."[59] And so, Prinz concedes, explicit deliberative judgments, that a core relational theme has been instantiated in a way that bears on one's interests

58 Prinz, *Gut Reactions*, 236. See also 234, 99, 100.
59 Ibid., 76.

and concerns, can elicit an emotional reaction. Although fear is generally caused by a perception of an object that automatically elicits the relevant imagistic schema in a calibration file, fear may also be caused by an explicit belief that a specific object is dangerous.[60] Does this mean that Prinz thinks such beliefs will always cause fear? If so, then this view is liable to the problem of unemotional judgments. And if not, then we need to know more, in particular why some judgments would cause emotions and others will not? For the sake of argument, I leave that difficulty aside.

If the same kind of judgment – that exams are scary for example – repeatedly elicits an emotion, in this case fear, then gradually, through habit, that judgment becomes a part of the calibration file of that emotion. At some point, it will be enough just to perceive the relevant object, in this case an exam, in order to trigger the schematic judgment and elicit the fear response automatically through the affective appraisal system.[61]

Prinz does not elaborate much on dimming down an emotion via explicit judgment. But one can find evidence in the text that he also concedes that in cases where an emotion was elicited by an explicit judgment, the emotion may subside by making the contrary judgment. For example, "If you do not believe you did anything wrong, you will not feel ashamed. Shame can be caused by beliefs and cured by beliefs."[62] This last phrase could have been written by Robert Solomon. But for Prinz, not all cases of shame are like that, only some cases.

Prinz allows for a revision of a calibration file that would consist in removing certain schematic judgments out of it. He gives the example of a woman who is proud of her genetically determined looks. If she has access to the "information" that the appropriate core relational theme for pride is one's achievements, and if she has the right "skills," then she should be able to "banish looks from her calibration file."[63]

Presumably, the "skill" in question would be to repeatedly control her pride feelings whenever she looks in the mirror or thinks about her figure by reminding herself that she does not believe that genetically determined looks count as an achievement. Eventually she should be able, through cultivating this habit, to eradicate her looks from her pride calibration file.

According to Prinz, the source of stable recalcitrance that will not be cured by repeated reasoning are calibration files that include an unfitting imagistic or some other sensory schema and not an unfitting schematic judgment. He gives the example of fear of flying:

> Calibration files can include perceptual triggers that operate at a fairly low level of processing. A person with fear of flying may have a link

60 Ibid.

61 See Prinz's discussion about *schadenfreude* acquisition: ibid., 148.

62 Ibid., 83.

63 Ibid., 238.

> between visual representation of airplanes and the amygdala. Because this link operates from within the visual system, judgments about the safety of air travel cannot preempt the fear response.[64]

An image of a plane certainly does not qualify as the kind of trigger that would "get a boost from the genes"[65] and so fear of flying cannot be a basic emotion. So how has such an image earned its right of entry to the calibration file? Almost all calibrations Prinz talks about are made through habits of judgment. So, one obvious option is that the image of a plane piggybacked on a schematic judgment that flying is dangerous, which entered the fear file through habit.

Flying is indeed dangerous. It is perhaps a low-probability danger but very high risk. Furthermore, the risk is completely beyond one's control. When driving long distances, the risk may be just as high and yet the driver (or the back seat driver) feels that to some extent she has some control on the level of risk. According to Solomon, and apparently according to Prinz as well, if I reflectively judge that flying is life threatening then I will feel fear. And according to Prinz, if I repeat this sequence enough times, my fear file will become calibrated in such a way, that at some point, no reflection would be necessary to feel this fear.

If this is how the fear file was originally calibrated then it could also be that every time I made the relevant reflective judgment I either saw or imagined a visual image of a plane. It could be that through association or constant conjunction of judgment and perception, a schematic image of a plane also became a part of the calibration file.

Prinz's account suggests that the manner in which a schematic representation has become a part of a calibration file is also the key for removing it. Habits can be undone if their source is addressed enough times. If the image of the plane got into the calibration file through association, then it is consistent with Prinz's account to claim that such an image can also be removed via the association.

When I repeatedly make the contrary judgment, namely that flying is not fitting of fear, so as to remove the schematic judgment about flying from my calibration file, it is more than likely that I am also perceiving an actual plane or imagining one. Each time I repeat my new judgment I would either be at the airport looking at the plane or at home watching a representation of a plane on TV, or online, or imagining one. Over time these perceptions would become linked to the thought that flying is not dangerous. Banishing the "flying is dangerous" schematic judgment from the calibration file would also banish the associated image.

The same procedure would also apply for the case of the woman who is proud of her looks. It is actually plausible that infants naturally experience

64 Ibid., 236.
65 Ibid., 152.

some highly positive affect when they look at themselves in the mirror. But pride requires more than that. Judging that one is pretty and being proud of that would be a conceptually laden calibration on Prinz's account. Given that looks are imagistic in the first place, it is highly likely that this woman was looking in the mirror or at her photos or at the very least imagining her looks as she was cultivating the habit that eventually calibrated the judgment about her looks into her pride file. It is thus highly likely that this woman does not just have a schematic judgment about her looks in her pride calibration file, but also a schematic image of herself, that got there through associative learning.

Prinz maintains that this woman is criticizable for this pride, that she can banish her looks from her calibration file and stop having that emotion. If Prinz's framework is to be consistent then he should allow schematic images that associatively piggyback schematic judgments into a calibration file to also associatively piggyback schematic judgments when those are banished.

If indeed we have this capacity "to banish" schematic representations from a calibration file that got there through repeated judgments, then it begins to be hard to explain why we should have recalcitrant emotions at all, whether basic (like snake phobia) or complex (like fear of scarves). Whereas on Griffiths' account it is hard to see why we do not all suffer from phobias (of snakes, spiders, etc.), on Prinz's account it appears that stable recalcitrance, whether of basic or complex emotions, is curable through repeated reasoning. Prinz claims that we can, through the right kind of self-education, "make sure" that our emotions are "always caused" by a fitting trigger, and "insulate them against normative censure."[66] If it is possible to have a "well-tuned calibration file," as Prinz explicitly claims,[67] then through repeated reasoning we can cure ourselves from unfitting emotional patterns that bother us. This is an extraordinarily optimistic ideal of how reason may rule our emotional lives. There may be people who think of themselves as always emoting appropriately, or as consistently approaching this ideal, but do we actually know anyone like that? The prevalence of recalcitrance, both stable and occasional, the prevalence of over-reactions, of dramatic arguments and emotional turmoil, makes this ideal seem unrealistic.

Complex emotions like resentment and homesickness can also be subject to stable recalcitrance.[68] In fact, for Prinz, jealousy is anger recalibrated by a judgment about infidelity.[69] Some of these schematic judgments can be

66 Ibid., 239.

67 Ibid.

68 D'Arms and Jacobson explicitly say that such emotions, which they call "cognitive sharpenings" are not normally subject to stable recalcitrance: D'Arms and Jacobson, "The Significance of Recalcitrant Emotion," 141. But this claim is not in tune with ordinary experience. In the next chapter, I will discuss at length a case of recalcitrant resentment.

69 Prinz, *Gut Reactions*, 100.

quite unfitting, for example: "masturbation is a form of infidelity," or "having very close friends other than one's partner is a form of infidelity." And yet there are many couples out there that despite their sincere disavowal of such judgments live in a stable nightmare of recalcitrant jealousy. Judgmentalism cannot explain recalcitrance, whether it is at the person level or at the sub-personal level via cultivation of calibration files.

There is nonetheless room for recalcitrance in Prinz's framework. He suggests another option for an image to be *directly* calibrated in a fear file, where the "associative learning" does not pass through habits of judgment: "Suppose I become terrified upon seeing a bowl of spaghetti. It may be that I was eating spaghetti during a traumatic earthquake, and the mere sight of it has instilled terror in me ever since."[70] This example is a caricature of a deep point. It could be that a certain image entered a calibration file due to its association with a traumatic event in the history of the individual that aroused, at the time of its occurrence, the emotion of that file.

For an image to become "wired" into the calibration file and "very reliably" elicit the relevant emotion, a pretty extreme experience is required: an earthquake, rape, torture, the premature or sudden death of a loved one, or some other physical injury or natural disaster. When it comes to food aversion, one would also have to go through an exceptionally bad experience. An extremely bad hangover from vodka may permanently put one off drinking vodka. Or getting bad food poisoning from rancid spaghetti may put one off from ever eating spaghetti again.[71]

Instead of a short-lived trauma, a series of very unpleasant events or an unpleasant period of time can also qualify, provided the affective experiences were strong enough. The traumatic affect may spread over, so to speak, a few events or a period of time. Prinz gives the example of "a person who develops a lifelong aversion to the color yellow after being domiciled in a yellow room during a long childhood illness."[72] Being stuck sick in a room for a long time is very unpleasant for anyone, but certainly for a child, for whom a period of a few months or a year of sickness is like an eternity of suffering. Crucially the overall affect over this period of time needs to be quite extreme in comparison to most emotional episodes to leave such an associative mark on the calibration file.

If all that were needed to directly imprint a schematic image in a calibration file was some experience that triggered an emotion of moderate intensity – we would have so many strange elicitors in our files that they would lose their general feature of tracking a core relational theme. And Prinz, like all sub-personalists, is committed to an affective system whose main function is to track threats, wrongs, infidelities, and other core

70 Ibid., 77.
71 Ibid.
72 Ibid., 75.

relational themes. Indeed, elicitation files would be flooded with schematic representations that got there by association, and would plausibly give rise mostly to unfitting emotions.

Presumably, an intense experience is also needed for images of spiders, snakes and heights to remain in one's fear calibration file. Even if these images can be said to "get a boost from the genes" and perhaps every infant feels fear the first time they see those objects – more is needed for their schematic images to be granted a fixed position in the fear calibration file. Otherwise, we would all have these phobias. One would need either to have been severely bitten by a spider or have endured some other unrelated trauma that somehow included a spider or an image of a spider on the scene.

I think it is probably correct that some stable recalcitrance can be explained in this manner. This is a Freudian cliché, as it were. However, the events recounted by Freud's patients often do not qualify as traumas, as extreme events that clearly stand out in those patients' emotional histories as particularly disturbing; they do not normally involve a catastrophic natural event, rape or physical injury.

On Prinz's account, nothing short of an objective trauma will do. Otherwise, as explained above, too many events will trigger associative learning and our calibration files would be swamped by schematic elicitors that do not fit the emotion in question. But objective traumas are not common events. The problem for Prinz's account is that this is the only family of cases of recalcitrant emotions that are explainable within his sub-personalist framework.

I conclude that Prinz's account does not have the resources to answer the second condition that any account of emotion should comply with, namely to allow for both reason-sensitivity on some occasions and recalcitrance to reason on other occasions. The kind of reason-sensitivity Prinz's account grants is too far-reaching when it comes to complex emotions and assumes that people have the possibility to "tune" their calibration file over time so that their file contains only fitting schematic judgments. The kind of recalcitrance that this account allows for is far too limited. It leaves out occasional recalcitrance as well as stable recalcitrance of most emotions, whether complex or basic, that do not trace back to an objective trauma.

5. The constraints on any causal account for emotional reactions

The sub-personalist accounts regard emotions as the result of an affective appraisal mechanism. Since emotions are appraisals, no matter how non-conceptual or non-linguistic they may be, they encounter the same problem that evaluations at the person level do, namely the problem of unaffective appraisals. Even a sub-personalist like Robinson, who recognizes the insufficiency of adding a care-factor to appraisals, cannot solve this problem.

The sub-personalist accounts (e.g. Griffiths) that insist that concepts do not play a role in the affective system fail to account for reason-sensitivity and do not propose any other notion of reason responsiveness. Accounts that grant some role to concepts and judgments encounter the same problem judgmentalism does: their notion of reason-sensitivity is too demanding and not in tune with ordinary experience. Unlike judgmentalism, Prinz's account allows for stable recalcitrance, but only for a very limited and uncommon sort that requires that the individual in question has experienced an objectively traumatic event.

I conclude that the sub-personalist accounts fail to comply with the two conditions for any account of the causal processes that yield an emotional reaction articulated in the end of the first chapter. However, there are some important insights in the sub-personalist characterization of affective processes that pose further constraints on any account of emotion. I summarize these constraints below and add to them the conclusions that can be drawn from the criticism of the sub-personalist account:

1. Whatever the affective processes are, they may operate below the level of awareness.
2. This means that whatever triggers these processes may be a perception that is not propositionally structured.
3. Whatever the affective processes are, they are not inferential in the rational sense that implies reference to norms of emotion fittingness. If they were inferential in this way, they would always be sensitive to reason and recalcitrance would not occur.
4. Not rationally inferential, and admitting triggers that are not conceptually laden – affective processes are non-conceptual and non-linguistic, if by concepts we mean nodes in an inferential network of beliefs. This means that those who want to be conceptualists about emotions and hold on to the orthodox view that emotions have intentional content, would have to say that emotions that are caused by perceptions that are not conceptually laden are not emotions. They would also have to provide a causal story whereby a conceptually laden perception or a full-blown belief causes intentional states not through an inferential connection.
5. Even if affective processes are not rationally inferential and are non-conceptual, ordinary experience shows that sometimes, maybe even often, explicit beliefs (that P) and judgments (that E fits P) can – sometimes, or even often – cause an emotional episode. Any account of emotion should have the resources to explain this causal (and non-inferential) connection.
6. It seems true that we identify certain affective prototypical physiological and behavioral patterns, and label those with emotion-type words, which we use to refer to affective manifestations on the basis of varying degrees of similarity to the prototype. Perhaps all the prototypical

physiological features are even neurologically coordinated, as Griffiths believes.

However, that there are significant similarities in the physiological and behavioral expressions of an emotions that are thereby labeled as being of a certain type, does not necessitate that these emotional episodes are all caused by the same "very reliable" mechanism that causally connects typical *external* circumstances with those prototypical expressions. To say it differently, although it may be the case that the expressive outputs of affective processes comprise a category whose properties can be characterized via controlled experiments, it is not necessary that the perceptual inputs be a viable scientific category connected to the outputs in a law-like way. But this necessity is assumed by sub-personalists, who further claim that the inputs are core relational themes.

Sub-personalists claim, in other words, that the affective system connects inputs (core relational themes) and outputs (prototypical physiological and behavioral manifestations) in a law-like way. Prinz sums up the sub-personalist claim: "Emotions are certainly set off by core relational themes. That is, they are *reliably caused* by relational properties that pertain to well-being."[73] Sub-personalists are committed to the claim that the affective tracking system is reliably *sensitive* to core relational themes, namely that it is normally set off whenever a core relational theme is instantiated in the nearby environment, and that it is, by and large and most of the time, an *accurate* system that successfully detects core relational themes.

What scientific evidence is there for these claims? The experiments mentioned in the books of Griffiths, Robinson, and Prinz, which explicitly aim to match external circumstances with emotional responses of a specific type, are conducted on human babies.[74] Other experiments, such as those that show that we develop phobias to snakes much more easily than we develop phobias to flowers,[75] or that we very easily learn to fear spiders,[76] demonstrate perhaps that we are all born with a tendency to fear snakes and also spiders. Perhaps we are also all born with a tendency to be disgusted by cockroaches and fear earthworms.[77]

When it comes to human adults, the cited experiments do not aim to show tracking, but they are consistent with it. But those experiments are manipulative so as to induce emotional responses. Sometimes they manipulate a certain physiological feature of the prototypical emotion expression

73 Prinz, *Gut Reactions*, 66. Emphasis added.

74 Robinson, *Deeper than Reason*, 37–38; Griffiths, *What Emotions Really Are*, 88.

75 Griffiths, *What Emotions Really Are*, 88.

76 Robinson, *Deeper than Reason*, 37.

77 Griffiths, "Towards a Machiavellian Theory," 95; and Griffiths, *What Emotions Really Are*, 28, 93.

so that it is forced on the subjects.[78] Other times they present the subjects with extreme external circumstances that would elicit an emotional response in most people, such as memories or perceptions describing most unpleasant scenarios.[79]

Common knowledge suggests that there are many obvious circumstances where most of us would emote similarly: grief when a loved one dies, disappointment in face of a big failure, joy at a grand success, or at one's wedding or graduation ceremony. Football fans or political left-wingers are very likely to experience joy when their team or party wins and many of us like babies. Those reasonably reliable responses are often exploited in advertisements.

However, most of our everyday emotional episodes occur in ordinary circumstances, that are neither manipulated nor clichéd or obvious, but personal – at work, at home, at the café, the grocery store, at social gatherings, usually involving the people and things we know well, even very well – our family members, romantic partners, roommates, colleagues, our pets, our stuff, and also acquaintances such as the barista, the neighbors, the cleaner. There are no experiments that would prove the sensitivity and accuracy of tracking for those cases, which comprise the majority of emotional episodes.

In fact, ordinary experience suggests that those ordinary and personal emotions of human adults are not very reliable. Emotional responses vary from one individual to another facing the same circumstances and even the same individual may respond differently to very similar circumstance on different occasions, as Robinson acknowledges. This is precisely the fact that Robison attempts to reconcile by adding more variables to the otherwise very reliable affective system, an attempt that fails, as shown in the third section of this chapter.

Even if the affective system were largely accurate in tracking core relational themes, it cannot be as sensitive as the sub-personalists presuppose. The fact is that we often do not emotionally react to situations that instantiate core relational themes and that bear on our cares and concerns. That is the experiential aspect of the problem of unemotional judgments or of unaffective appraisals. If we did reliably emote in the way the sub-personalists envision, we would not be able to judge or appraise that a core relational theme has been instantiated and fail to emote.

78 Recall the famous Schachter and Singer experiment where subjects are injected with adrenaline so as to manipulate their level of arousal, discussed for example in Griffiths, *What Emotions Really Are*, 25, 81; Prinz, *Gut Reactions*, 71; Robinson, *Deeper than Reason*, 83–85. Other experiments manipulate facial expressions as in Robinson, *Deeper than Reason*, 36; Prinz, *Gut Reactions*, 36.

79 For example, gory films that arouse disgust: Robinson, *Deeper than Reason*, 34; Prinz, *Gut Reactions*, 137. Or images of genital surgery that arouse stress: Prinz, *Gut Reactions*, 30. Or experiments where people who were injected with adrenaline were asked to recall life-changing events such as the death of a loved one: Prinz, *Gut Reactions*, 70–71.

Ordinary experience further suggests that if the affective system were indeed tracking core relational themes, then it often misfires and cannot be said to be, by and large, reliably accurate. We often judge people as over-reacting and as having various emotional "issues," as we say, that make them respond in ways that are not fitting to the situation at hand. We talk about people as being "touchy" or "over-sensitive" about various issues, we ask them not to "shoot the messenger," advise them to "not take things so personally," or to simply "move on already."

The sensitivity and accuracy claims also suggest that people are highly consistent and predictable in their emotional reactions. Even if we try to personalize a calibration file per person as Prinz does, people are not *that* consistent in their emotionally expressive behavior. Although people exhibit identifiable emotional patterns, and when we know someone very well we can describe those patterns, these patterns are not law-like. If people's emotional reactions were so very predictable, we would have a lot less drama and suspense in our personal lives, in literature, in film, and on TV series. When it comes to human adults, the sub-personalist reliability claim, which includes both sensitivity and accuracy, is dogmatic, an empirical hypothesis without empirical support.

The sub-personalists seem to be motivated by the purposiveness of the action tendencies of what they call basic emotions such as running away in fear of a bear or turning away in disgust from rancid food. The thought seems to be that if fear has the as-if purpose to save us from being killed by bears, then it also has the as-if purpose to save us from dangers in general and a further, even more over-arching, purpose to be conducive to our well-being.

It is crucial, however, to note the difference in kind between categories such as "bears" or "lions" and categories such as "danger." Objects that fall under the category "bear" look and smell and sound similar to one another. They can be identified by their shape (or any other sense modality) or by the way they move, the kind of characteristics that can plausibly be identified by a biological function. Categories like "bears" are those that Eleanor Rosch calls "natural categories," whose members are "basic objects."[80] The members of the category "danger," on the other hand, do not normally look or behave alike. In order to describe the similarity among different kinds of dangers, say bears, lightning storms, or drought, we would have to use abstract concepts. "Danger," much like "wrong" or "achievement", qualifies as what Rosch calls "superordinate categories," used by people with conceptual capacities and instrumental rationality.

Claiming that the fear system monitors for dangers, effectively ascribes to that system instrumental rationality, and is in fact in stark contrast to the lesson of Darwinian evolutionary theory, which aims to remove this kind of

80 Eleanor Rosch et al., "Basic Objects in Natural Categories," *Cognitive Psychology* 8, (1976).

purposiveness or design from nature. Compare this with Fodor's criticism of teleosemantic theories of intentional content: "Darwin doesn't care how you describe the intentional object of frog snaps ... Darwin cares how many flies you eat, but not what description you eat them under."[81] Biological functions, in other words, do not act under description in the manner that people do. They are not rational and they do not track the members of superordinate categories such as "danger."

"Danger" is a synoptic description we may or may not give to the triggers of fear once we take into account the plurality of objects that people are afraid of. The fear reactions of pre-civilized people were perhaps mainly triggered by objects that could be synoptically described as dangerous. Generally speaking, the emotional reactions of the pre-civilized human species, which lived in a naturally hostile environment and in a primitive social structure, could have perhaps been synoptically described as occurring in the face of core relational themes. Or they may have not. It may have been advantageous enough to be afraid of bears and lions even if many other fear triggers were not in fact dangerous (e.g. shadows that look like bears).[82] Whatever the case may be, emotions never actually tracked core relational themes under *that* description. The purposiveness of the physiological and behavioral expressions of our emotions is inherited from the history of our species, but this purposiveness is and was without a purpose.[83]

Admitting that affective processes do not reliably track core relational themes does not stand in contradiction to the obvious fact about our practices of criticism, namely, that we have social norms that match typical external circumstances with emotion-types, and that we use core relational themes to justify or criticize emotions. And finally, this claim does not contradict that people are often afraid when in dangerous circumstances or proud of their genuine achievements and so forth.

The remaining constraints and demands on an account of affective processes are therefore:

7. People often, even if not always or even most of the time, have fitting emotions, and any casual account for emotional reactions should have the resources to account for that fact.
8. If emotions do not reliably track core relational themes, then what may we salvage of the notion of biologically basic emotions? I propose we change our notion of basic emotions from emotions that do not involve

81 Jerry Fodor, *A Theory of Content and Other Essays* (Cambridge, MA: MIT Press, 1990), 73.

82 For a different critique of an evolutionary argument in support of a rationalist account, see: Karen Jones, "Quick and Smart? Modularity and the Pro-Emotion Consensus," *Canadian Journal of Philosophy* 36, s32 (2006).

83 Daniel Dennett, *Darwin's Dangerous Idea* (New York: Simon & Schuster, 1995).

thoughts and that reliably track core relational themes (e.g. dangers) to emotions that, in infancy, are reliably triggered by certain typical basic objects inherited from the history of our species (e.g. bears, heights). What we need is an account that shows how most adults do not experience fear of spiders or heights, and that further shows how the relatively limited pool of objects that reliably trigger emotions in infancy grows later in life to a much larger pool of objects that trigger our emotions in a not so reliable manner.

9. Not-so reliable, the affective processes are not computationally inferential. And since they are not rationally inferential either, these processes are simply non-inferential. Being non-inferential, it becomes very unclear how whatever it is that is being processed can count as "information," so I will stop using this term in the chapters to come.
10. Whatever the affective processes are, they are not processes of evaluation. Any account that treats emotions as evaluations will encounter the same problem, that of unemotional evaluations. Not being able to account for what makes an evaluation emotional inevitably means that evolutionist accounts cannot answer the singularity question either, that is, they cannot explain what causes a specific emotional reaction of a specific person in certain specified circumstances.
11. If emotions are not the product of evaluations or inferences, one would have to insist on a conceptualist account in order to continue to maintain the view that emotions are evaluative states. But, if one wants to include the kind of affective states that are produced in the experiments cited by sub-personalists in the category of emotions, if one wants to include emotional triggers that are not conceptually laden, then one would have to concede that affective processes are not conceptual, that emotions do not have conceptual content, and – if they are not the products of evaluation – then altogether it becomes hard to see why we should consider them evaluative at all. This would mean that philosophers have traditionally understood emotions to be evaluative because people *treat* them that way, submitting them to norms of appropriateness. As said in the previous chapter, people judge themselves and one another in this manner because emotions implicate other people. If we end up holding a non-conceptualist account, then we will have to accept that the force norms of appropriateness have on us is not the force of rational norms on rational agents but needs to be otherwise explained.
12. One of the main challenges for any account of emotion, as said in the previous chapter, is to make sense of how emotions are sometimes responsive to the rational norms of emotion appropriateness they are submitted to and sometimes not. On the one hand, affective processes that produce emotions are distinct from the rational and inferential processes that produce avowed beliefs, just as Griffiths claims. Keeping these processes distinct allows for recalcitrance. On the other hand,

> these *distinct* processes need to somehow *interact*, so as to allow for some kind of reason responsiveness, even if partial. Sub-personalists cannot make sense of this partly successful interaction and the variety of types of recalcitrance within their "information encapsulation" thesis.

Affective processes and rational-inferential processes, although distinct, have something in common by virtue of which they can interact. I will claim in Chapter 5 that this common feature consists in them both operating at the person level. According to the account I propose, although affective processes have all the features sub-personalists say they should have, the features described in the first section of this chapter, although they are automatic, operate below the level of awareness, separate from rational processes (that is, non-inferential) and non-conceptual – they are nevertheless normative, even if in a very thin sense, they are available to awareness, even if in a very qualified sense, and they call for their verbal description and acknowledgment by others. I will show in Chapter 5, that operating at the person level rather than the sub-personal level, allows affective processes to be influenced by verbal description. Reasoning may influence one's emotional episodes precisely since reasoning involves speaking, even if only via inner speech. But before I turn to the formulation of my account, I dedicate the next two chapters to the discussion of other accounts that are available in the literature and examine their insights and oversights.

3 The "primal scene" accounts

Developmental etiologies

The philosophers I engage with in this chapter all speak of emotions as modes of seeing-as that are, by and large, conceptually structured scenarios, general schemas that match an emotion-type to characteristic objects. They all assume that the infant's basic emotions develop through and in relation to language acquisition, into more or less normatively accepted dispositions to express a certain emotion-type in typical circumstances. The terms that are brought to bear on a situation and make certain aspects of that situation emotionally salient are thus normally a scenario under description, when it comes to human adults.

Ronald de Sousa, for example, says that the first emotional responses in childhood, like fear, are "genetically programmed."[1] They become scenarios through teaching the child the name for the emotion-type in the relevant context, thus teaching the child that they are having an emotional reaction of a certain type. The acquisition of linguistic skills allows these basic scenarios to be "reinforced by the stories and fairy tales to which we are exposed, and later still, supplemented and refined by literature and art."[2] The resulting scenarios are schemas of characteristic emotional responses to certain characteristic objects. These mature, normative, and conceptually structured scenarios are the terms that an adult brings to bear on a certain situation that thereby gives rise to an episode of a certain emotion-type.

The philosophers discussed in this chapter thus hold conceptualist seeing-as accounts. But unlike the conceptualist seeing-as accounts discussed in Chapter 1.3.C, the accounts discussed in this chapter do not require a care-factor to explain emotionality. This is because they explicitly regard each emotional reaction as part of a pattern. What needs explaining then is not the emotionality of each emotional episode, but the emotionality of the pattern as a whole. They all offer developmental accounts of emotional dispositions: biologically determined dispositions that change through social influences and to some extent also through one's particular biography.

1 De Sousa, "The Rationality of Emotions," 142–123.
2 Ibid., 142.

The discussions from the previous chapters demonstrate the disadvantages of speaking of the terms that are brought to bear on a situation – and that make certain objects within it emotionally salient – as conceptually structured propositions or scenarios. Such accounts rule out emotions that are caused by perceptions that are not conceptually laden, such as the startle reaction or the reactions studied in the experiments cited by the sub-personalists. Also, saying that a subject emotes since her perception under the description P has activated her disposition to emote E in circumstances P, gives rise to the singularity question: Why does the subject sometimes emote when P instantiates and sometimes does not?

But the strength of the developmental accounts, here represented by Amélie Rorty, Ronald de Sousa, and Jonathan Lear, consists in their offering an explanation and not just a mere description for recalcitrant emotions. They all claim that in order to explain recalcitrance, we must look at the individual's particular biography. Since the framework of these accounts is at the person level, the kind of explanation they suggest for recalcitrance differs from Prinz's account, the only account described thus far to offer any explanation for recalcitrance.

Recall how Prinz explained a very limited class of recalcitrance. He allowed for an image from a traumatic emotional experience to calibrate a schematic image or a memory image into the elicitation file of an emotion-type. By a perceived "image" I mean a perception that is not conceptually laden, whether it is a visual image of an object, or a perception of any other sense modality, like a smell or a sound. For Prinz, the schematic or memory image calibrated into the elicitation file through trauma had a merely extensional relation with the emotional experience that included the respective image. The yellow color of the room in which someone stayed during a long period of illness does not bear any meaningful relation to the illness and the affective experience of that illness. The developmentalists discussed in this chapter, on the other hand, talk about a conceptual relation between the concept or the image (which for them would be conceptually laden) that that is embedded in a paradigm scenario, and the resulting occurrent emotional scenario.

In that manner, the philosophers discussed in this chapter do justice to a very common phenomenon, familiar in everyday experience as well as in psychotherapeutic experience. People often explain their idiosyncratic patterns of emotional reactions by taking recourse to a detail in their biography, which need not be so very traumatic and which appears to make sense of their emotional "pathology." Some typical examples: I am a jealous husband because my first girlfriend cheated on me and I was very hurt; I am often too offended by criticism, since my mother always found something wrong with anything I did; I can't help feeling contempt for black people since a black guy stole my computer when I was a teenager; I am always anxious when I'm alone on the street, even in the daytime, because my mother kept graphically warning me about rape when I was a child; I am always disappointed with my achievements, because nothing I did was ever good enough for my father; I fear to spend money even if I'm rich, because I was brought up in a poor home; I have trust issues with men since my father left home when I was a child; and so on and so forth. We are all familiar with these kinds of stories people tell about themselves and their emotional patterns. This phenomenon needs to be explained in any account of emotion.

Although I will argue that the accounts discussed in this chapter are not fully successful, and that the relation between an emotional symptom and a past event is not conceptual in the way they envisage, critically discussing these accounts and identifying their insights can guide the way to further inquiry. In particular, this chapter demonstrates that the contemporary developmental accounts can all be understood as similar to and inspired by the early Freudian account for psychological symptoms, including recalcitrant emotions. When discussing the contemporary accounts I will thus talk about emotions as having intentional content, since this is how the developmentalist conceptualists speak about the describable aspect of emotional episodes. But Freud did not have a clear theory of emotions. When I discuss Freud's developmentalist account, I will talk about the describable aspect of emotional episodes without committing to them being intentional states.

Since the force of these accounts lies in their explanation of recalcitrant emotions (and also of other emotional pathologies) I focus the discussion on such pathological emotions. This focus is also methodological. If we have a satisfactory account of emotional pathologies, which are far more common than is normally acknowledged in the literature, we can learn from those cases about emotions in general, whatever their relation to after-the-fact rational judgment may be. As Rorty says:

> When people act or react in ways that can be explained by reasonable beliefs and desires, we tend to suppose that these beliefs and desires are the causes of their behavior. We then try to construct our explanations of the more complex cases, using only what was necessary to explain the simple ones. Not surprisingly, we often then find that we are left with bizarre cases at the margins of our theory: self-deception, *akrasia*, and the irrational conservation of emotions [recalcitrance]. By beginning with the fringe cases, we may find the more complex structures that underlie the apparently straightforward cases but which are difficult to discern when everything is going as we expect.[3]

3 Rorty, "Explaining Emotions," 103. See also Freud: "pathology, by making things larger and coarser, can draw our attention to normal conditions which would otherwise have escaped us," in Freud, *New Introductory Lectures*, Lecture 26, S.E, 22, 58.

1. Rorty's "magnetized" dispositions

Rorty articulates her explanation for recalcitrant emotions through an example. She does not say whether her example is based on a real case study or whether it is fictional. What matters is that this case is a possible case, whether or not it is an actual case. And her explanation of this example aims to show what counts as a causal explanation for (stable) emotional recalcitrance. I thus allow myself to add some speculated details to the example I see as plausible. Rorty introduces her case study as follows:

> Jonah, a newswriter, resents Esther, his editor, whom he thinks domineering, even tyrannical. But as bosses go, Esther is exceptionally careful to consult with the staff, often following consensus even when it conflicts with her judgment. His colleagues try to convince Jonah that Esther's assignments are not demeaning, her requests not arbitrary. Jonah comes to believe he was mistaken in thinking her actions dictatorial; he retreats to remarking that she derives secret pleasure from the demands that circumstances require. Where his colleagues see a smile, he sees a smirk. After a time of working with Esther, Jonah realizes that she is not a petty tyrant, but he still receives her assignments with a dull resentful ache; and when Anita, the new editor, arrives, he is seething with hostility even before she has had time to settle in and put her family photographs on her desk. Although many of the women on the secretarial staff are more hard-edged in mind and personality than either Esther or Jonah, he regards them all as charmingly endowed with intuitive insight. He patronizes rather than resents them.[4]

Jonah was partly responsive to rational criticism. He came to judge his resentment of Esther as unfitting, and he succeeded to mitigate it to some extent. But although he ended up having no considerations in favor of resenting Esther, his resentment did not perish completely. Most likely, as Rorty hints, the same kind of recalcitrance would have eventually occurred with his resentment to Anita.

Rorty describes Jonah as having the "magnetizing disposition" to resent women in a position of authority.[5] It is typical, says Rorty, that subjects are unaware that they have such a disposition.[6] One could say he suffered from the prejudice that women in power are domineering and hostile. But Jonah did not believe that female bosses are inherently "bitchy," and he did not acquire any such prejudice from his environment.[7] The significant cause for

4 Rorty, "Explaining Emotions," 106.
5 Jonah does not resent men in position of power, only women: ibid., 114.
6 Ibid., 106–107.
7 Rorty says that "Jonah is a skeptical sort of fellow, who rarely leaps to generalizations, let alone wild ones," ibid.

the magnetizing disposition should be looked for, according to Rorty, in his biography.

Jonah also suffered from nightmares and obsessive thoughts that his mother was trying to kill him. He also detested scarves and refused to wear them no matter how cold it was, and became very anxious whenever he was in the scarves section of department stores. In his childhood, Jonah's mother used to "swathe him in scarves that she knitted herself" from the "the itchiest wool imaginable; and when she bundled him up in winter, she used to tie the scarf with a swift harsh motion, pulling it tightly around his throat."[8]

Young Jonah suffered from those scarf-tying scenarios, and experienced them as something unpleasant that his mother, his female "boss" at the time, forced him to endure. In other words, he saw her as domineering and hostile. He probably did not believe his mother was trying to kill him, but he may have had a passing thought, "Why so harsh? Are you trying to suffocate me?" But Jonah was an obedient child, and suffered quietly and repeatedly. He never expressed his distress, for if he had, his mother may have changed her ways with the scarves. Rorty does not mention Jonah's old emotions, but it is plausible that Jonah became resentful of his mother in this connection.

Rorty does not give much detail, but says that those old scarf-tying scenes are what caused Jonah's magnetizing disposition to see women that have authority over him as domineering and hostile and resent them for that. Although his editor Esther did not tie scarves around his neck, by the time he was her employee, he already had the magnetizing disposition to see his female bosses as badly motivated tyrants and resent them.

Like any mother, Jonah's mother would sometimes get angry or be ambivalent in her affections. But Jonah's mother was not generally hostile. She was an affectionate woman, even if a bit awkward. Rorty notes that Jonah could have experienced those old scarf-tying scenes differently. Instead of experiencing that tying of the scarf as unpleasant, and the pressure of the scarf as painful, he could have felt comforted and reassured. Jonah's way of seeing those scarf-tying scenes as harsh or aggressive indicates that at the time he already had another magnetizing disposition, namely to be "sensitive to the negative overtones of [his mother's] attitudes."[9]

Jonah's brother had gone through the same scarf-tying scenes and did not develop the disposition to resent women in positions of authority. Jonah's brother did not experience those old scenes as expressions of his mother's hostility. And so, "we have not got the significant cause in all its glory: though our explanation is fuller, it is not yet complete."[10] That old magnetizing disposition calls for further explanation. Rorty thus continues to

8 Ibid., 109.
9 Ibid., 109.
10 Ibid., 110.

search in Jonah's biography the significant cause for the older disposition to be on the lookout for his mother's anger and domination.

Just before Jonah's brother was born, Jonah's father went away to serve in the army. When his mother was in hospital with the newborn, Jonah was sent to stay with his grandfather. The grandfather detested Jonah's mother. He saw her as "a domineering and angry woman, the ruination of his son."[11] During Jonah's stay with his grandfather, the grandfather conveyed his opinion, probably unintentionally, to Jonah.

Now, for Jonah to be influenced by his grandfather's attitude toward his mother and make it his own, a further explanation is needed. Jonah was somehow prone to that particular influence. At the time, Jonah may have been upset that his mother sent him away, and was probably jealous of the newborn, who got her affections at the time instead of him. Moreover, he adored his grandfather, who also played the role of a father figure during that time.

Jonah's susceptibility to his grandfather's influence does not qualify as a magnetized disposition. Magnetized dispositions are intentional in the sense that they are under description. They are manifested in situations that can be seen as instantiating that description. Esther and Anita are "women in a position of authority," and Jonah's mother tying scarfs around his neck is "domineering and hostile." Jonah's susceptibility was only "quasi-intentional," since it functioned at the time as "patterns of focusing and salience without determining the description of that pattern."[12]

That is, although Jonah was to some extent upset with his mother and jealous of his newborn brother, he was probably unable to describe those feelings as such. This is not just because he may have not been fully aware of them but also because they were actually too vague to be describable. They were a mere "mood,"[13] roughly describable as antagonistic, a term that would itself be unknown to young Jonah. That mood would have probably passed if not for the grandfather's influence that turned it into an intentional disposition to be alert to any hint of harshness or domination in his mother.

Neither was the identification with his grandfather something young Jonah could have intended. Children often absorb the views and dispositions of their loved parental figures, and they do not do that intentionally or reflectively. It is probably a tendency determined by evolutionary considerations. It is normally "beneficial for children to tend to absorb the intentional dispositions of the crucial figures around them, even at the cost of generating confusion and conflict."[14]

11 Ibid.
12 Ibid., 113.
13 Ibid., 111.
14 Ibid., 122.

To say it differently, magnetized dispositions determine what kind of describable behavior would occur in certain circumstances, whose features can be adequately described. Susceptibility, on the other hand, is not a describable pattern, even if it can evolve into such a pattern. Susceptibility does not come with a "recipe" that would articulate what emotion-type would be manifested on what occasion. It is rather a vague and often temporary proneness or sensitivity.

The causal story ends here. If for any reason we feel that the last or rather first link in the developmental chain needs further explanation, we can look for another link farther in Jonah's biography. If we want to explain recalcitrant emotions we have to identify a magnetizing disposition and look for its significant cause in the subject's biography. And if that significant cause involves another prior magnetized disposition we can continue with the same method until we arrive at a point that requires no further explanation. That point is a certain *scene* in the subject's past. It is the starting point of a developmental etiology that explains how the current magnetized disposition came about, in such way that it conflicts with the subject's judgment of fittingness.

Rorty's developmental etiologies are not merely causal etiologies. They serve to make sense of recalcitrant emotions. Jonah cannot help seeing his female bosses as resentment-provoking, because he has issues with his mother, whom he perceives as unpleasantly bossy. She isn't *that* bossy really. It is just that Jonah was too easily influenced by his grandfather's negative views about his mother. Jonah was very young and impressionable in those days, and he was in any case upset with his mother who sent him away from her.

> [we] now have an account of why a reasonable person might, in a perfectly reasonable way, have developed an intentional set [that is, a magnetized disposition][15] that, as it happens, generates wildly askew interpretations and reactions.[16]

Jonah's susceptibility to adopt his grandfather's attitudes was quasi-intentional, as explained above, and thus caused his magnetized disposition toward his mother without being a reason for it. But that latter disposition had both a causal connection and a "logical"[17] connection to the disposition toward women in position of authority.

The term "logical" may sound strange, given that Jonah's resentment of Esther is not rationally justifiable, nor is the seeing-as disposition that explains it an avowable belief for Jonah. In what sense can the connection

15 Rorty defines a magnetized disposition as intentional set in ibid., 107.
16 Ibid., 111.
17 Ibid., 113.

between the disposition toward the mother and the disposition toward female bosses be characterized as "logical"? Both dispositions are intentional. They match an emotion-type with typical circumstances that are seen under a specific description. These dispositions embed descriptions, and so the connection between them is a conceptual connection.

The first disposition to see his mother as domineering and hostile is directed at his mother; the second disposition to see female authority figures as domineering and hostile is directed at the women who have authority over Jonah. The logical connection between these dispositions is a generalization: from a particular female authority figure, namely his mother, to all female authority figures.

2. Lear's emotional capacities

Before I turn to critically assess Rorty's account, I want to demonstrate the force of a very similar account of a different kind of emotional pathology, brought to discussion by Jonathan Lear. Lear focuses on patterns of emotional reaction, where each emotional reaction survives the subject's reflective judgments.

Some people get angry more often than others or feel guilty more often than others. And each time they get angry or feel guilty they look "out there" to the emotionally salient object and endorse their emotional reaction as fitting. If anyone asked such a person, "Why are you angry?", that person would be able to articulate reasons for their emotions. If asked, "Why are you taking this so personally?", such a person would probably be able to articulate further reasons, to do with their core-values, cares, and concerns.

If emotions are modes of seeing-as, then people whose affective life is dominated by a certain emotion-type can be regarded as having the disposition to construe situations as provoking that emotion-type. In other words, such people feel guilty, for example, whenever they can interpret their actions as wrongs, whether or not other people agree that the emotion is fitting or necessary. The kind of emoting subject Lear talks about is always able to justify and endorse reactions of that pattern. The subject, in other words, experiences no gap between her emotional reactions and her evaluative fittingness judgments.

Should we regard such patterns as pathological? Insofar as the person's well-being is compromised by that emotional pattern, then it is a problem for them. A person who is often angry lives in a world that keeps wronging her. A person who often feels guilty is often tortured by her own actions and thoughts. These are not pleasant emotions. Even if such a person does not see any problem with her emotional pattern, the people close to that person may judge her as having issues that are compromising her relationships.

Lear tells about his patient Mr. A ("A" for "Avowal"), who feels betrayed more often than others. Betrayal or rather anger (combined with thoughts about betrayal or simply caused by betrayal) is the affect-type that dominates his emotional life. Lear describes Mr. A as living "in a world of betrayal."[18] That is, Mr. A has the disposition to construe situations as situations of betrayal situations. Does Mr. A suffer from pathology? Lear seems to think so. Indeed, Mr. A is unhappy in his relationships. Lear describes Mr. A's problematic relationship with his girlfriend:

> Freud teaches us that emotional ambivalence lies at the heart of the human condition. Thus not only is it inevitable for us to feel ambivalently toward our loved ones, but it is inevitable for them to feel ambivalently toward us. So even with our loved ones, who genuinely love us "wholeheartedly," there will be moments when irritation, anger, disappointment slip out and find some form of expression. Now Mr. A would wait for those moments, and then give them astonishing weight. His girlfriend's irritable outburst would reveal her "true feelings" towards him, and the rest of her care and concern for him would be dismissed as a cover-up. Not only that, but her outburst would be experienced as a "betrayal" because he had made himself so vulnerable. Now he could see that he had been lulled into a false sense of trust by her deceptively caring exterior; in fact, she was ready to betray him at the first opportunity.[19]

Lear seems to suggest here that Mr. A can be judged on rational grounds. Lear criticizes Mr. A for exaggerated and unrealistic demands of "wholeheartedness" from his girlfriend and for judging her too harshly and therefore wrongly. However, Lear's criticism in this paragraph relies on Lear's norm of fittingness according to which more than "moments of irritation" are needed to qualify as betrayal. I share Lear's norm of fit, and I also believe that emotional ambivalence is "at the heart of the human condition." But people are allowed to have different norms of fittingness. And this is precisely why reason is not the route to convince Mr. A that he should not feel betrayed.

Lear could explain to Mr. A why he believes Freud was right and that although it is understandable why one wishes for "wholeheartedness" in relationships, the mature adult should accept ambivalence as a fact of life. Mr. A may reply that unlike most people perhaps, he is not emotionally ambivalent about his girlfriend. He loves her and is loyal to her without the slightest reserve. If people are not as loyal as him, this only shows their own moral weaknesses, or that they are incapable of "true love." They should be more like him. His norm of fittingness may not be popular, but he stands

18 Jonathan Lear, "Avowal and Unfreedom," *Philosophy and Phenomenological Research* LXIX, no. 2 (2004): 450.

19 Ibid., 450.

behind it and endorses it as one of his core-values. He can justify his loyal and devoted way of being in the world. Norms are not laws; they can change. And Mr. A feels a moral obligation to serve an example for others. He hopes there is someone else out there for him, someone just as loyal and wholehearted like himself.

Lear may insist that such "true love" is a myth, an unattainable ideal that is causing Mr. A trouble. They may argue for hours, and each of them may be able to provide good reasons for the norm of fittingness they advocate. It is hard to imagine what would count as proof that would decide if love is inevitably ambivalent or alternatively that love is either wholehearted or severely compromised. Mr. A may end the argument by saying "let's agree to disagree," and feel more justified in his belief than ever.

Lear also tells us about Mr. A's problems at work:

> Mr. B was trying to get assigned to a project that Mr. A wanted – typical rivalry at work – and yet this was a betrayal because Mr. A had earlier taken him into his confidence, had helped guide Mr. B up the ladder of success, etc. As far as I could tell, Mr. A had genuinely helped Mr. B in the ways he described. What Mr. A did not understand about himself was that part of his motivation for helping Mr. B was so that he could later feel betrayed by him. In countless ways such as this, Mr. [A][20] unconsciously sustained his own world of betrayal.[21]

Lear notices that the circumstances that gave rise to the betrayal were the result of Mr. A's actions. Lear would probably not ascribe to Mr. A such "unconscious motivations" to feel betrayed if it were not for the fact that Mr. A repeatedly found himself in such situations. Mr. A, in general, was a master "in fostering occurrences in which he actually would be betrayed (or, at least, severely let down)."[22]

On every such occasion Mr. A could endorse his feelings of betrayal and articulate reasons for his emotion that he would judge to be good reasons. Lear could point out to Mr. A that instead of focusing on each such occasion, the very fact that he feels betrayed so often needs explaining. Mr. A could then reasonably claim that he has been unlucky in life to have been betrayed so many times. Lear could say that the very fact that Mr. A's actions led to these situations makes him responsible for them. But Mr. A could reasonably reply that being betrayed is not something a person can do, since it is done by others. He is not telling those who betray him what to do. They are free agents who make their own choices independently of him.

20 The original text says "Mr. B," but that is obviously a typing mistake.
21 Ibid., 450.
22 Ibid., 451.

Lear can still insist and tell Mr. A that he is naïve and childish to think that one can have "wholehearted" friends at work: "[T]he workplace is often an arena of jealousies, competitive strivings and pronounced ambivalent feelings."[23] Mr. A may accuse Lear in turn of cynicism and lack of hope and faith in human nature. Mr. A may admit that he is too kind for this cruel world, and yet he will never give up his belief in people and he is committed to charitably assuming people are as good and as loyal as himself, and continues to hope that the world can change thanks to people like him.

Reason need not change Mr. A's emotional pattern. In fact, it may serve to entrench this pattern. Lear goes as far as saying that Mr. A's pathology consists in this rationalization of his seeing-as disposition: "Reason – at least, *his* reason – conspires, as it were, to keep him in a betrayed world. He is more than willing to take responsibility for feeling betrayed – indeed, one wants to say, *that* is his problem."[24] This is why Lear calls this pathology "pathology of avowal."[25]

It is true that reason need not be able to help Mr. A, and that reason can play in the service of his pathology. But this is not Mr. A's problem. His problem is that he does not enjoy healthy relationships. Neither is reason the primary cause of Mr. A's emotional pattern of betrayal. Mr. A is under the grip of a betrayal construal, and whatever causes that construal is at the heart of Mr. A's problems. In the above quotes Lear says that what causes this construal is Mr. A's unconscious motivations to feel betrayed.

I am skeptical about "unconscious motivations" in the manner Lear speaks of them, as if they were desires or purposes. Presumably these are the person's motivations, and the unconscious is here posited to contrive strategies on behalf of the person, to devise the means to achieve the person's ends. But the unconscious cannot be analogized to an adult who may instrumentally reason on behalf of a child or rather, as a child that finds infantile solutions for the adult, as the analogy is usually put.[26] The access the mind of one person has to the mind of another is limited and fallible, whereas the unconscious is posited to have unlimited and immediate access to the desires and goals of the person. Therefore, in order to do the job it was posited to do, the unconscious part of the mind does not just attempt to reason on behalf of another – it is as a matter of fact rationally connected to that other. Yet, as Donald Davidson has shown, if two parts of the mind that are posited to be separate connect rationally with one another, then

23 Ibid., 450.
24 Ibid., 453.
25 Ibid., 451.
26 See Jonathan Lear, "Wisdom Won From Illness: The Psychoanalytic Grasp of Human Being," *International Journal of Psychoanalysis* (2014) 95: 677–693. See also Lear on "strategic value": Jonathan Lear, *Freud* (London: Routledge, 2006), 37.

they are not separate at all.[27] An unconscious that was posited as a separate part of the mind in order to explain strange behaviors such as Mr. A's persistent pattern of feelings of betrayal and at the same time is claimed to be reasoning on behalf of the conscious part of the mind is thus an incoherent notion.

Could those motivations be the motivations of the unconscious itself? If so, the inevitable question will be why does this little person within have these wants or why does that unconscious function produce these wants? The explanatory question at the person level: Why does Mr. A keep creating situations that are likely to fit a betrayal construal? – is now replaced by an explanatory question at the unconscious level: Why does Mr. A's unconscious want to create situations that are likely to fit a betrayal construal? Positing such unconscious motivations is thus unhelpful and non-explanatory.[28]

In any case, Lear's ultimate explanation need not take recourse to such motivations. Lear indicates that in the case of Mr. A, an unconscious emotion is at play. Lear's guess is that this specific old emotional reaction was "some primordial parental disappointment [that] served as an occasion for the infant A to cast a mold that would shape his later experience."[29] In order for Mr. A to resolve his dominant affect of betrayal, he needs to express that specific emotional attitude (from and about his past) and only when that specific emotion is identified and expressed will rational reflection about its justification would be relevant. As Lear says:

> Roughly speaking, the avowal has to "grab onto" the very emotion that has hitherto remained unconscious. It cannot merely be an expression of the very same *type* of emotion (betrayal), it has to be an expression of that very emotion.[30]

Similar to Rorty, Lear also claims that this original scene where Mr. A felt betrayed, had a causal role to play in a developmental story that ended in his disposition to feel betrayed. Whereas Rorty speaks of quasi-intentional dispositions that turn into magnetizing dispositions, Lear speaks of emotional capacities.

> [A]n emotion such as fear has a developmental history. Babies can feel and express fear; so can adults. But in healthy circumstances the emotion develops in complexity and becomes even more integrated into

27 Donald Davidson, "Paradoxes of Irrationality," in *Philosophical Essays on Freud*, ed. Richard Wollheim and James Hopkins (Cambridge: Cambridge University Press, 1982).

28 Much more can be said about homuncularism and its problems in Freudian thought that I will not explore here.

29 Lear, "Avowal and Unfreedom," 451.

30 Ibid., 452.

> a person's rational assessment of the world. In the mature adult, fear not only reaches down into bodily reactions, it reaches out to the world and *makes a claim* that it is an *appropriate* response. However, in unhealthy circumstances, this developmental trajectory can be inhibited or disrupted. The outcome will be a biologically mature adult who is expressing an infantile form of fear.[31]

According to Lear's approach, Mr. A's emotional capacity to feel betrayed did not go through the normative course of development. His "developmental trajectory" was inhibited due to a certain scene of "parental disappointment" in his childhood, where he felt betrayed. Presumably an adult going through the same scene would not have felt so severely betrayed. But children often see the world in an all-or-nothing extreme manner.

The healthy course of development would entail refining this emotional capacity, say by accepting norms of fittingness that allow for emotional ambivalence with loved ones and colleagues, and which confine betrayal to more clear-cut circumstances. Instead, that old reaction, which was probably characterized by an all-or-nothing infantile way of seeing the world, has become his only way to feel betrayed. If, in the past, say, he felt betrayed by his father, then consequently he has developed the disposition to see other people as somehow cast in the role of his betraying father. Moreover, unconsciously, he still feels betrayed by his father.

When it comes to cases like Jonah, Lear would presumably say that the scenes with the mother inhibited the normal development of resentment. A child may resent being told to do something he does not want to do. Adults, on the other hand, accept that they may not always be able to do what they want and that sometimes they have to do something simply because an authority figure said so, whether that figure is male or female. But in Jonah's case, the scenes with his mother fixed his capacity for resentment into an emotion that from then on has been typically directed at female authority figures.

No extra "unconscious motivation" is needed in Lear's account. He can say instead that the primordial scene caused an emotional reaction that was somehow never expressed and dealt with properly. That specific emotion has become unconscious but left a mark on the subject's capacity to experience that emotion-type. Whenever the typical circumstances arise, circumstances that fit the "mold" cast by that primordial emotional scene, the subject would experience that emotion type and regard the here-and-now circumstances as the reason for the emotional reaction. Nothing short of re-living that old event and expressing the old unconscious emotion can put the subject on the right track to develop the capacity to experience that emotion-type in a mature manner.

31 Lear, *Freud*, 53.

3. De Sousa's "paradigm scenarios," the singularity question and the problem of non-traumatic traumas

The developmental etiologies Rorty and Lear suggest share problems encountered in other accounts of emotions. First, both Rorty's magnetizing dispositions and Lear's emotional capacities assume stability. Rorty's dispositions to experience an emotion-type in circumstances that fit the description embedded in the disposition assume that every time such circumstances arise the disposition would be manifested. The only kind of recalcitrance Rorty can account for would thus be stable recalcitrance. Occasional recalcitrance, limited by a period of time or by a certain relationship, cannot be accommodated in this framework.

In fact, even stable recalcitrance is here assumed to be ultra-stable. Rorty indicates that Jonah is automatically resentful of Anita, his new female boss, before she even has the chance to interact with him. It is true that people may be quite predictable. It is likely that Jonah's colleagues are not even that surprised when Jonah begins to complain about Anita. But must Jonah be resentful in response to each and every assignment Anita gives him? It seems possible or even likely that Jonah will have better and worse days when it comes to his interactions with Anita.

Furthermore, is it not possible that when Rachel replaces Anita, Jonah will not be resentful at all? Is it impossible to imagine that there is something about Rachel that disarms Jonah and releases him, insofar as Rachel is concerned, from his usual patterns of interaction with female bosses? People's emotional patterns, even the stable ones, are not that reliable. People surprise themselves and others with their emotional reactions. Even without therapy that exposes emotional patterns, people can change their habits of emotional reaction.

Some women, for example, spend years fearful and resentful of the men who show interest in them, and then another suitor comes along with whom they instantly feel safe and unguarded. Will they go back to their old emotional pattern once the relationship with this particular person is over? Maybe they will and maybe they won't. The interaction with Rachel may put an end to Jonah's previous behavioral pattern; or this pattern may return when he needs to confront a new female authority figure. It seems dogmatic and *ad hoc* to retroactively reconstruct increasingly detailed dispositions that would account for such differences and changes in a person's emotional patterns.

But perhaps this reading of Rorty and Lear is uncharitable. Perhaps we can say that the disposition to emote E in situations perceived under the description P may or may not manifest whenever the subject perceives a situation under the description P. Conceptualist seeing-as experiences are like that. I may or may not see the drawing as a duck or as a rabbit. But then these accounts face the singularity question: Why do people sometimes emote according to their pathological pattern and sometimes not?

Ronald de Sousa's developmental account clearly allows for occasional recalcitrance. He offers an account to the development of the paradigm scenarios for each emotion-type, but nothing in his account suggests that a paradigm scenario must be brought to bear on any situation that instantiates the scenario. In this sense, de Sousa's account leaves room for the singularity of emotional reactions, for the familiar fact that one may be angry about certain circumstances today and not be angry when very similar circumstances arise tomorrow or next year. But this also means that de Sousa's account is incomplete. One of the main challenges of any account of emotion, as I have been stressing in the previous chapters, is to answer the singularity question: What makes one emote in this particular way here-and-now?

De Sousa regards a recalcitrant emotion as a case of "muddled scenarios,"[32] where the subject fails to apply a normative paradigm scenario. Instead, the subject unconsciously invokes a paradigm scenario that does not "*objectively* resemble"[33] the actual contemporary situation. Somehow the typical scarf-tying scene has become Jonah's paradigm scenario for his relations with Esther and Anita. But Jonah is not aware that he is unconsciously muddling scenarios, and that is why his here-and-now reactions are recalcitrant. If we want to understand how Jonah came to have this resentment scenario, we need to investigate into its development until we find the "original scenario."[34] In Jonah's case, the original scenario would be Jonah's more or less vague frustration and anger toward his mother who sent him away while in hospital with his newborn brother.

Here too, nothing in de Sousa's account suggests that one must always muddle the same scenario in the face of the same typical circumstances. Jonah may apply the scarf-tying scenario today and not tomorrow. In this sense, de Sousa's account allows for occasional recalcitrance as well as for stable but not necessarily permanent recalcitrance. However, de Sousa's account still does not answer the singularity question: Why is the scenario muddled today and not tomorrow? What is the nature of the connection between the here-and-now situation and a paradigm scenario? How does one trigger the other?

The developmental accounts, that is, magnetized dispositions (Rorty), emotional capacities (Lear) and paradigm scenarios (de Sousa), share another problem. The muddled scenario or the original scenario, the actual emotionally laden event that took place in the subject's life, is not necessarily that traumatic. No war, torture, rape, natural disaster or a long illness or physical injury are required for an event to magnetize Rorty's dispositions, to inhibit the development of Lear's emotional capacities or to be a candidate for a muddled scenario.

32 De Sousa, "The Rationality of Emotions," 146.

33 Ibid. Emphasis in original.

34 Ibid.

It seems arbitrary, or at the very least unexplained, that certain events would cause such problematic emotional patterns whereas others do not. Jonah was sent away from his mother, probably like many children at the time. Can such an event qualify as traumatic? Even if we say that somehow that event was very unpleasant for *him* in particular, due to some subjective factor (another disposition perhaps?) Why was this event or the scarf-tying scenes more important than say the first time Jonah had a fight with friends at kindergarten and got beaten up, or the first time Jonah got scolded by a beloved teacher, or the few years young Jonah was in love with a girl at school who didn't give him the time of day that were equally unpleasant for Jonah?

If all such not-so-traumatic unpleasant events modified one's dispositions then pathological emotions would be the rule. And yet all these accounts assume that many (if not most) of our emotions arise in more or less normatively acceptable circumstances. Although it seems right that many of our emotions are over-reactions or part of a more or less problematic patterns, many of our emotions do fit the circumstances in which they arise. Surely etiological developmental accounts need to provide an explanation as to why certain past scenes give rise to problematic emotional patterns whereas others do not.

4. The "Primal Scene" accounts and the early Freudian version

The etiological accounts presented in this chapter structurally resemble Freud's early account of neurosis. Neuroses for Freud included hysteria, namely physiological symptoms that cannot be physiologically explained, obsessional neurosis, that is compulsive actions that cannot be rationally explained, and recalcitrant emotions such as phobias. Recalcitrant emotions (fear, jealousy, guilt) both stable and occasional count as neuroses in the Freudian framework, since they are emotional reactions that are not rationally explainable or modifiable by the subject when the subject expects them to be amenable or sensitive to reason. Freud explained these psychological symptoms by tracing a developmental history through a series of events in the patient's life story. In various texts, Freud claims that the first scene in the relevant series of events is of a sexual nature and occurs very early in one's childhood.[35]

Freud sometimes referred to that first event as the "primal scene." Freud introduced this term in his case study known as the "Wolf Man," where the scene in question was of sexual intercourse between the parents.[36] Jean

35 E.g. S. Freud, "My Views on the Part Played by Sexuality in the Aetiology of the Neuroses," (1906 [1905]) S.E., 7, 278. See also Freud's first informal use of the term in a letter to Fleiss: Letter 61, S.E., 1, 247. He there obviously refers to scenes of seduction in early childhood.

36 S. Freud, *From the History of an Infantile Neurosis* (1918 [1914]), S.E., 17, 7–122.

Laplanche and Jean-Bertrand Pontalis, for example, reserve the use of this term only to scenes such as the one that the Wolf Man experienced.[37] And it is probably what most people associate with this term.

It is true that the majority of Freud's patients describe scenes that have some sexual tone to them, even if in some case studies the connection to sexuality is relatively weak.[38] But crucially, those scenes, including the scenes of witnessing parental intercourse, are said to have developmental significance due to their emotional import. It is by virtue of the emotional experience of those scenes that they can inhibit one's emotional development.[39] In that sense, many of the first scenes described in Freud's developmental etiologies can be called primal scenes.[40]

The model for Freud's primal scene etiologies is that of physical trauma.[41] Just as physical trauma is caused by an *external event* and leaves the body damaged *from that moment on*, so can an *external event* be emotionally disturbing in such a way that the emotional reaction to the event may cause, *from that moment on*, a damaging change in one's patterns of reactions of that emotion-type. This emotional disturbance is called "traumatic" precisely because of this analogy with physical trauma. The etiological importance of the primal scene thus comes from its emotional import, and so there is no reason to suppose that the actual content of the scene must be sexual, although it can be.

I will use the term "primal scene" to denote any scene that is the first in such developmental etiologies whose goal is to explain psychological pathology. Here I only discuss the pathology that is relevant to the inquiry of this chapter, namely emotional patterns such as recalcitrance or any other avowed pattern that nevertheless compromises one's relationships (such as Mr. A's repeated emotional experiences of betrayal). I emphasize again that my use of the term carries no distinctively sexual connotation. Although the primal scene may carry sexual significance it need not carry such significance. The scene is "primal" in the following sense: it is chronologically *the first* scene of the series of scenes that comprises a certain etiology; it carries *great causal weight* as it launches the developmental etiology, which ends with psychological pathology; and it is considered to be emotionally traumatic, since it is both disturbing and since it leaves an emotional scar,

37 Jean Laplanche and Jean-Bertrand Pontalis, *The Language of Psychoanalysis*, trans. Donald Nicholson-Smith (London: Karnac, 2006[1973]), 335.

38 See for example, Lucy's case, where the scene that begins the etiology is a scene where Lucy realizes (indirectly) that her employer does not reciprocate her love. Freud, "The Case of Lucy R," in *Studies on Hysteria* [1893–1895], S.E., 2, 106–124.

39 See how Lear reads the case known as the Rat Man in Lear, *Freud*, Chapter 1.

40 In Chapter 4, I will discuss cases where Freud claims that the emotional reaction to the primal scene often occurs years after the event.

41 Josef Breuer and Sigmund Freud, "On the Psychical Mechanism of Hysterical Phenomena: Preliminary Communication," [1893] in *Studies on Hysteria*, S.E., 2, 3–17, 6.

as it were, on the person's psychology (on her emotional dispositions or capacities).

In this generalized use of the term, the contemporary developmental accounts discussed in this chapter all take recourse to such a primal scene. It is the first link in the causal chain of development of a magnetizing disposition, the one Rorty calls "the significant cause in all its glory." It is the "primordial" scene that Lear refers to as the childhood event that inhibited the normal development of a certain emotional capacity and fixated its typical objects in the mold of the object from that old scene, toward which the infantile emotional reaction was directed at the time. And finally, the primal scene is the "original scenario" de Sousa invokes when discussing the "muddled scenario." The "original" or "primal" scene develops into a schematic scenario that is brought to bear on, yet does not "objectively resemble", a here-and-now situation, thereby giving rise to an unfitting emotional reaction.

In fact, even in Freud's very first publication on the causal etiologies of hysteria written with Josef Breuer, he already speaks of the trauma as not necessarily the emotional effect of one single scene. The trauma may also be the cumulative effect of a number of scenes or of repeated scenes over a period of time. Or it may be the effect of two events, where the second (such as Jonah's stay with his grandfather) somehow "seals," to use Rorty's expression, the first event (Jonah's being sent away from his mother) as traumatic.[42] Another way for a trauma to be spread over two events would be that the first event causes a susceptibility or a magnetizing disposition, such as Jonah's disposition to see his mother as domineering and hostile, due to which the second event seems much worse than it actually is, as with the first scarf-scene in Jonah's case. As Freud says:

> it not infrequently happens that, instead of a single, major trauma, we find a number of partial traumas forming a *group* of provoking causes. These have only been able to exercise a traumatic effect by summation and they belong together in so far as they are in part components of a single story of suffering. There are other cases in which an apparently trivial circumstance combines with the actually operative event or occurs at a time of peculiar susceptibility to stimulation and in this way attains the dignity of a trauma which it would not otherwise have possessed but which thenceforward persists.[43]

Instead of talking of a "primal scene" we may often talk of what I will call from now on the "primal series." These are the chronologically ordered events (or periods) taken from a subject's biography so as to construct a

42 Rorty, "Explaining Emotions", 111.
43 Breuer and Freud, "Preliminary Communication," 6. Emphasis in original.

causal etiology whose aim is to explain the current pathological emotional pattern. Together, the events of the primal series form a "single story of suffering." Crucially, the suffering here is caused by external events, and so is still modeled on the kind of damage one suffers from physical trauma. The primal series account is thus a complication of the primal scene account.

I now turn to examine more closely the early (indeed the earliest) Freudian account, which is clearly the inspiration for all the accounts in this chapter. The main text I rely on and from which the above quote is taken is Freud's earliest publication from 1893, written together with Joseph Breuer: *Studies on Hysteria*, and in particular the very beginning of this book, that is, On the Psychical Mechanism of Hysterical Phenomena: Preliminary Communication.

Freud's early account is probably closest to de Sousa's; in a sense, it can be seen as enriching the account of paradigm scenarios. De Sousa claims that recalcitrant emotions result from unconsciously bringing to bear on the here-and-now situation a certain "muddled" scenario that does not "objectively resemble" it. The early Freudian account explains more about how certain scenarios may become "unconscious" in the first place, and sheds some light about what "not objectively resembling" means.

According to the early Freud, not every emotionally distressing event can potentially be a primal scene that has long-term effects on one's psychological health. An emotionally unpleasant event qualifies as mentally traumatic and may potentially cause a psychological symptom, if the subject's emotional reaction to the event itself is submitted to two conditions: suppression; and repression of the emotion. Although I shall eventually reject the early Freudian account as well as the other developmental accounts discussed in this chapter, the account proposed in the second part of the book relies on the following discussions of suppression and repression. I will thus stop talking about emotions as having intentional content, as required by conceptualist seeing-as accounts. Instead, I will use the minimalist definition for emotions given in the Introduction and in Chapter 1 and will talk about emotions as having a describable aspect, namely the emotionally salient features of the situation. This minimalist conception is consistent with both a conceptualist and an imagistic seeing-as account.

When I talk about emotional episodes as emotional reactions to a situation – a conceptualist may read this as meaning "emotional reactions towards an intentional object," a tracking sub-personalist may read this as meaning "emotional reactions towards a target that is not conceptually laden," and it may also be read as an emotional episode triggered by something or someone in the situation, where the trigger need not be a target nor an intentional object. On this last conception, the trigger is often (but not always) also the emotionally salient feature of the situation at hand. And so when I speak of the "object of an emotion," then for the moment, "object" may be read as "intentional object" or as "target" or as "the emotionally salient features of the here-and-now situation" where no intentionality or targeting needs to be presupposed. On this last conception, the salient object of the emotion may be perceived under description or it may be perceived without the involvement of concepts. The issue of intentionality and targeting need not be settled for the purposes of this first part of the book.

A. Suppression of the emotional reaction to the "primal scene"

The first condition for an event to count as a "primal scene" is that the emotional reaction to that event is not properly experienced. That is, the affective or passionate aspect of the emotion is somehow suppressed. It is not fully or not at all expressed, "whether in deeds or words."[44] A subject stops herself from expressing an emotion when that emotion itself is somehow conflictual for her.[45]

Certain emotional reactions, even if perfectly fitting to the situation in which they arise, even if they are justified and in that sense normative, can nevertheless be considered socially inappropriate, often on moral, or rather moralistic grounds. Envy, for example, is a natural and understandable emotion, and it fits a competitive situation where someone has something one wants. And yet envy is hardly what one would call a socially graceful emotion. Indeed, Christianity declared envy (and pride) to be a moral sin.

We encountered four notions of emotion appropriateness in Chapter 1. The first two notions are of emotion fittingness – of type and intensity. Judging an emotional reaction in reference to norms of fittingness decides whether an emotional reaction is reasonable or justified. The third notion is fittingness to character, used by others about the emotions of a subject whom they know well. And the fourth notion introduced in Chapter 1.2.A has gone hitherto unnoticed in the literature. That is the notion of fittingness to one's self-image as having and cultivating certain cares and concerns, including desires, interests, values, virtues, attachments and aversions. It is a notion of appropriateness that is used first-personally. We may judge our own emotional reaction in reference to this notion of appropriateness and decide whether or not this emotional reaction suits us, who we think we are and what we care about. As explained in Chapter 1.2, we may use this notion of appropriateness to our self-image in order to formulate care-factor reasons for or against the emotional reaction, whether or not the emotion is fitting in type or intensity.

Social, moral or moralistic appropriateness thus comprises a fifth notion of emotion appropriateness, recently brought to discussion by D'Arms and Jacobson.[46] In fact, even here we could make a further distinction between

44 Ibid., 8.
45 Ibid., 10.
46 D'Arms and Jacboson, "The Moralistic Fallacy."

norms about the social propriety of *publicly expressing* emotions, and norms about the social propriety of *having* certain types of emotional attitudes *at all*. Whereas the norms about expressing socially ungraceful emotions can be regarded as norms of politeness or of social prudence, norms that demand we simply not have certain emotions, such as envy or pride can be regarded as moralistic norms for the following reasons: (1) They demand that a moral consideration should trump fittingness considerations; (2) the general moral call for the prevention and avoidance of harm can be easily met by the weaker norm to be polite and prudent and not express such emotions publicly; and (3) moralistic norms of social propriety deny emotions that are natural and arguably make a cruel and virtually impossible demand to comply with, namely to not have what is natural and normal to have.[47]

Moralistic norms of appropriateness, given they address the very having of an emotion, may be confused, as D'Arms and Jacobson show, with norms of fittingness, which are also used to judge against the very having of an emotional reaction. Some will say, for example, that anger is never a fitting response or that envying a friend (who is not a rival) is never a fitting response, no matter if that friend just achieved something we wanted for ourselves.[48]

Someone who is not moralistic about envy, say, may experience perfectly fitting envy and feel that she should not express her envy so as not to be judged by other people as immoral. Such a person may allow herself to express her emotion in private, via inner speech or by writing about it later in a journal, but in public will try her best to keep a "poker face," as we say, or otherwise hide or fake her emotional response. This kind of emotion suppression consists in suppressing the *public expression* of the emotional reaction in order to avoid conflict with another person. Such suppression takes into account the moralisms of other people and the manner in which they would judge one's emotional reaction as inappropriate in reference to norms of social propriety (or even as unfitting, even if that judgment is a "moralistic fallacy," as D'Arms and Jacobson say).

The kind of suppression Freud talks about is not only of public expression of the emotion but also of its *private* expression. That is, the emotion is denied private acknowledgement altogether. Freudian suppression, which

47 These are not meant to be necessary and sufficient conditions for moralism. Indeed, according to these criteria moral taboos could be considered moralistic. I will not discuss the issue of taboos here. For an illuminating discussion of moralism see Cora Diamond, "Henry James, Moral Philosophers, Moralism," *The Henry James Review* 18, no. 3 (1997).

48 D'Arms and Jacobson give a few such examples for philosophical accounts that promote moralistic norms of fit: Gabrielle Taylor on anger, Patricia Greenspan on grief, Elizabeth Anderson about amusement of sexist jokes: D'Arms and Jacobson, "The Moralistic Fallacy," 78–80. The envy example is discussed extensively in their paper and is reminiscent of Greenspan's example of mixed feeling discussed in the previous chapter.

is the only kind of suppression I shall discuss from now on, is a self-deceptive moment where one pushes the emotion or the emotionally laden thought out of one's awareness. By "awareness" I merely mean what is explicitly on one's mind, what one is attending to. One is aware of whatever one is explicitly thinking or imagining to oneself, or of various feelings, perceptions and other experiences that one focuses on.[49] And the conflict that motivates such suppression is not merely the potential conflict a person would have with other people on the scene if she allowed herself to publicly express a socially inappropriate emotion. The conflict is rather within the subject herself.

What is the nature of this conflict? Freud calls such emotions "incompatible."[50] That is, the emotional reaction to the primal scene is incompatible with that person's own moralistic and social standards, to that person's self-conception as a moral person with various cares and concerns. Emotions that are incompatible in this manner could themselves give rise to most unpleasant emotions. A person, who holds the view that envy is indeed immoral and yet finds herself in a situation where she feels envy, would feel guilt and shame or perhaps even self-directed disgust or contempt. Such an internal conflict need not be moral or moralistic. Emotions can be unfitting to one's self-conception as having certain virtues or character traits, such as being cool (and therefore not easily irritated or embarrassed) or being confident (and therefore never jealous, envious or embarrassed) and so forth.

In fact, if one reflects on one's emotion in reference to various norms of appropriateness, one is likely to end up reflecting on one's self-image as well: (1) an emotion that is fitting in type and intensity but that the subject finds immoral and thereby unfitting to one's self-image as a moral person; (2) an emotion that is fitting in type and intensity but that the subject finds too risky, such as feelings of anger, betrayal or disappointment toward a loved one – such emotions may not fit one's self-image as having a loving close relationship with that specific person; (3) an emotion that is unfitting to the situation in type or intensity may cause conflict when one is attached to one's self-image as being a reasonable person who can rationally control her emotions to be in alignment with her avowed beliefs.

This notion of "incompatibility" sounds like a rational notion. It sounds as if Freud thinks that one judges one's passing thought or emotion to be

49 This is how I interpret what Freud called the descriptive quality of "being conscious" which he defines as follows: "'Being conscious' is in the first place a purely descriptive term, resting on perception of the most immediate and certain character," Freud, "The Ego and the Id," [1923] S.E., 19, 13–14. This is also how Hume conceives of awareness, he writes: "We may observe, that it is universally allowed by philosophers, and is besides pretty obvious of itself, that nothing is ever really present with the mind but its perceptions or impressions and ideas, and that external objects become known to us only by those perceptions they occasion. To hate, to love, to think, to feel, to see; all this is nothing but to perceive" [to perceive in Hume's sense is to be aware of impressions and ideas] Hume, *Treatise*, Book 1, Part 2, Sect vi.

50 See for example, Freud, "The Case of Lucy R," 123.

incompatible with one's self-conception as having certain moral standards and other cares and concerns and thereby suppresses both its public and private expressions. Indeed, Freud sometimes speaks of "intentional repression,"[51] by which he means intentional suppression that results in rendering the mental state in question unconscious.

This intentional quality inevitably raises the well-known difficulty or paradox of self-deception. How can one intentionally decide to ignore an emotion and be successful in this endeavor? If one would be told, for example, not to think of an elephant one will probably think about elephants more than ever.[52] Similarly, if one attempts to suppress or ignore or deny an emotion under *that* description, if one can say to oneself that one is pushing a certain thought or emotion out of one's mind, one will more likely be unable to think of anything but that emotion.

A person can still suppress an emotion, just not under *that* description. A person can just divert her attention elsewhere or distract herself and think about something else. A person who shifts her attention away from a certain emotion is suppressing her emotion; this is a good description of what that person is doing. And yet that person is unaware of that description.

Compare this diversion of attention to what Kent Bach says about self-deception: "although the self-deceiver does what he does intentionally, he does not do it under the description of 'deceiving myself' or anything of the sort."[53] Bach proceeds then to talk about what the self-deceptive person is actually doing. She may be just thinking of something else, which Bach calls "evasion."[54] The person who feels betrayed or insulted when their best friend more or less gently mocks her in public, may just deflect the conversation in a new direction and thereby manage to ignore the friend's comment.

Or one can shift one's attention from an emotion by thinking thoughts that contradict the state of mind one is self-deceptive about (in our case, an emotion) and cohere well with one's self-image, which is what Bach names "jamming."[55] So a person who feels relief when a relative who has been sick for a long time dies and is conflicted about such relief given her close relationship and the apparent contradiction with the loss and grief she feels, can shift her attention from the momentary relief by thinking about how sad she is. And finally, Bach speaks of "rationalization,"[56] that is, engaging in giving

51 E.g. Breuer and Freud, "Preliminary Communication," 10; Freud, "Lucy," 116.

52 George Lakoff, *Don't Think of an Elephant: Know Your Values and Frame the Debate* (White River Junction, VT: Chelsea Green Publishing, 2004). "The exercise is: Don't think of an elephant! Whatever you do, do *not* think of an elephant. I've never found a student who's able to do this." Ibid., 3.

53 Kent Bach, "An Analysis of Self-Deception," *Philosophy and Phenomenological Research* 41, no. 3 (1981): 368.

54 Ibid., 360.

55 Ibid., 361–362.

56 Ibid., 368–359.

reasons against the troubling emotion or for an alternative, contrary emotion, in reference to various notions of emotion appropriateness. If one engages in explicit disavowal of a certain emotion, if one says to oneself that one should not feel or have a certain emotion since it is incompatible with who one is or who one wants to be, then one is likely to think that one has genuinely eliminated the emotion rather than just using this deliberation to distract oneself from it.

Kent Bach says in the above quote that the "self-deceiver does what he does intentionally." But can we still say that this action of suppression, this diversion of attention, is done intentionally? Anscombe insists that intentional action is action done under description. That is, if the agent is asked, "What are you doing?", she can provide a description of what she is doing. And if the agent is asked, "Why are doing it?", she can easily elicit reasons for her action, in terms of her goals and ends, which effectively comprise another description of what she is doing (see discussion in Chapter 1.1.B). According to Anscombe, the subject that acts intentionally is aware of what she is doing and why she is doing it and attention can easily be called to those descriptions – while the action is taking place.[57]

Freudian suppression is not an intentional action in Anscombe's sense since the subject can only very partly answer Anscombe's questions in the manner she demands. The subject is aware that she is now attending to something she did not attend to before, to some new thought or activity, and in that limited sense she can answer the question, "What are you doing?" and say, "I am looking at/thinking about/doing this or that." But she is not telling herself or able to say, "I am now diverting my attention away from this emotional state of mind." She will not describe herself or be aware of herself as "evading", "jamming" or "rationalizing."

Neither is the self-deceiving subject able to answer the question: "Why are you diverting your attention?" She cannot provide a description such as: "I am forcefully ignoring my emotion since it is incompatible with my self-image as a rational and moral person with certain cares and concerns, and this incompatibility is too disagreeable to contemplate." As Sartre says, "Bad faith dare not speak its name."[58]

Indeed, in most cases, the subject diverts her attention after a fleeting awareness of the incompatible emotion, before she would bother to describe it or explicitly acknowledge it, let alone be able to say that it is incompatible with her self-image or that she is deflecting her attention away from it. The subject has a fleeting awareness of the emotion and, sometimes

57 For a detailed discussion on the self-awareness involved in Anscombian intentional action, see Moran's discussion: Richard Moran, "Anscombe on Practical Knowledge," in *Agency and Action*, ed. J. Hyman & H. Steward, Royal Institute of Philosophy Supplementary 55 (Cambridge: Cambridge University Press, 2004), 43–68.

58 Jean-Paul Sartre, *Being and Nothingness: An Essay on Phenomenological Ontology*, trans. Hazel E. Barnes (New York: Philosophical Library, 1956[1943]), 68.

(but by no means always or usually), the subject may even have a fleeting thought such as "that's disgusting!" or an incredulous "no...," but the emotion is not seen as a consideration in favour of ignoring it in reference to one's endorsed cares and concerns.

But this does not mean that Freudian suppression is a mere behaviour like a reflex or a merely causal operation like the operations of mitochondria in cells. It is quite possible, that many years later and after years of therapy, the subject may come to see this suppression as rationalizable. That is, the subject may be able to specify the respects in which the emotion in question was incompatible with her moral standards or too risky for her relationships and her other social commitments and see how these respects can be regarded as considerations in favour of that old suppression, even if they were not considerations at all at the time the action was performed.

Although these considerations were not psychologically operative at the time the action was performed, and did not guide or cause the action at the time, they nevertheless make sense of that action in a larger context of one's personality as having various normative and social commitments. And giving those "reasons" after-the-fact, even much longer after-the-fact, nevertheless contributes to one's self-understanding. If the subject further comes to realize that such normative considerations (moral, prudential, even considerations of fit) ultimately also implicate her self-image as a moral and rational person with various cares and concerns, then she may further redescribe past suppressions as having spared her self-image from incompatible emotions. Although the subject may learn in this way about her self-image, this self-image was not in itself causally operative at the time the suppression took place, and it would be a mistaken rationalizing move to say that the suppression originally occurred in order to spare oneself from incompatibility.

Nevertheless, even if these suppressions were not rationally motivated by the subject's normative commitments or self-image, even if they were done without self-awareness, they implicate the subject's own well-being and her relationships with others. In that sense, we are still responsible for those retroactively describable suppressions, even if we did not know what we were doing at the time we were doing it. This kind of responsibility is to be distinguished from blame or from the kind of accountability people have for their intentional actions (see Chapter 6.4 and 6.5).

Although the Anscombian why-question that asks for operative reasons does not have application here, another why-question that asks for retroactive rationalizations does. If we allow reason-giving to be retroactive, if we allow for responsibility to be divorced from blame, then Freudian suppression is still an action, even if it is not an intentional action. Actions may be under description, in the way Anscombe conceives them, or they may be not under description and yet describable. I will call this kind of action "non-Anscombian action."

The role of elicitable reasons for Anscombe is to guide the very performance of the intentional action. This is precisely why one can answer Anscombe's why-questions while performing the action. Non-Anscombian action is not guided by reason. What would then be the source of motivation for non-Anscombian actions that are not done under description? I suggest that at least when it comes to Freudian suppression, the source of motivation consists in that action being emotionally expressive.

Although we do not yet have an account for affective processes, we already know that emotions are not judgments and that affective processes are automatic, non-inferential and not guided by us qua Anscombian or Kantian agents. Action tendencies of emotions need not be done under description, especially those that are so clearly automatic and involuntary emotional behaviors, such as flinching in fear. I suggest that Freudian self-deceptive suppression, the non-Anscombian action of shifting one's attention, is an action tendency of an emotion-type that I call "alienating aversion."

Alienating aversion resembles other aversive emotion-types such as shame, guilt, and disgust, that are often expressed through an explicit averting of one's gaze, as if gesturing a separation from the object of the emotional response and oneself. In a sense, feeling alienating aversion effectively preempts or prevents shame, guilt, and self-disgust. This aversive emotional reaction effectively alienates a certain thought or emotion by looking away or turning a blind eye to a certain passing thought or feeling and thinking of or focusing on something else.

As with any emotional reaction, alienating aversion may be accompanied by an evaluative thought such as "that's disgusting!" or "Na…" And yet, just as with any other emotional reaction, the emotional reaction itself, including its expressive activity, need not have been caused by this thought, and even if it were so caused it would not be by virtue of an inferential or rational connection. Indeed, in many cases, without the affective aversive reaction such thoughts would not come to the subject's mind in the first place.

If we continued saying like Freud that a subject suppresses an emotion due to its incompatibility with that subject's self-image, then we would be judgmentalist, basically claiming that alienating aversion is the judgment that a certain emotion is incompatible or that it does not cohere with one's endorsed cares and concerns. If we reject judgmentalism, then we had better reject that rational notion of incompatibility as well. Suppressed emotions are simply those emotions that we cannot tolerate having on an emotional level. When describing later in life such aversive suppressions, we can understand them as emotionally (and not rationally) conflictual with certain aspects of the subject's self-image.

B. Repression of the emotional reaction to the "primal scene"

We still do not have an account for the affective processes that yield such a rejected emotion in the first place. But whatever these processes may be, the resulting emotion has a passionate or expressive aspect, that is the affect of that emotion-type, as well as a describable aspect. Suppression prevents the affect from being expressed, and furthermore, denies the describable aspect from being acknowledged. That is, suppression renders the emotion unavailable to speech, whether inner or out loud, since it is unavailable to one's attention, at least temporarily.

The second condition that renders a scene traumatic and turns it into a "primal scene" consists in making the emotion not just temporarily unavailable to consciousness or to awareness or to one's attention, but unavailable for the long term. The emotion is not just suppressed, but is also repressed. Once the emotional attitude is repressed, the subject is unable to acknowledge verbally that she is angry that P or that she is jealous that P. In other words, the emotion becomes unavailable to self-aware verbal expression in the form of a propositional attitude: "I E that P," where P would be the description of the emotionally salient features of the primal scene.

This repression may mean that the memory of the primal scene becomes unavailable to consciousness or recollection. When a memory is "unconscious" the subject cannot recall it,[59] or rather, the subject is just not thinking about the primal scene. We can often be reminded through some association of various memories, and may often react emotionally similarly to how we reacted at the time. But when an emotional reaction or a memory is repressed, no thoughts or associations will cause that memory or emotion to cross one's mind. No thought, whether explicit reasoning, storytelling or just a thought that spontaneously crosses one's mind, leads to the recollection of this emotionally laden memory. It is in that sense that a memory is unavailable to consciousness or that the describable aspect of an emotion can be called "unconscious." As Freud says later in his career:

> Forgetting impressions, scenes or experiences nearly always reduces itself to shutting them off. When the patient talks about these 'forgotten' things he seldom fails to add: 'As a matter of fact I've always known it; only I've never thought of it.'[60]

Repression of the emotional reaction to the primal scene need not result in the full repression of the memory of the primal scene. The subject may remember the scene and even be able to articulate its description P, but P or rather the described objects of the there-and-then situation will not be acknowledged as having been emotionally salient. People who remember their primal scene often remember it only in "highly summary form."[61] Not thinking about the scene in detail serves to prevent the acknowledgment of

59 Breuer and Freud, "Preliminary Communication," S.E., 2, 9.
60 Freud, "Remembering, Repeating and Working-Through" [1914] S.E. 12, 148.
61 Breuer and Freud, "Preliminary Communication," S.E., 2, 9.

its emotional significance and the expression of the affective aspect that is intertwined with the describable aspect of the emotion.

Early Freud emphasizes the repression of memory rather than the repression of emotion, which I describe here, as I rationally reconstruct his account. Freud and Breuer famously said that "[h]ysterics suffer mainly from reminiscences."[62] Freud and Breuer there assumes that since the repression of the memory of the primal scene caused the psychological symptom, recovering that memory would cure the patient. And yet, he also emphasizes the emotionality of that memory or the emotional reaction to the primal scene when he says that "[r]ecollection without affect almost invariably produces no result."[63] It is thus consistent with the original text to say that it is an emotion, rather than the memory, that has undergone repression.

The emotion has not been eradicated, but it somehow becomes isolated from conscious thought processes. It is now an unconscious emotion in the sense that it is unacknowledgable, not thought about, and thereby not experienced affectively nor available for verbal report. This inaccessibility or isolation involved in repression needs further explication. Without such explication, the unconscious, as a quality of certain emotions, is difficult to understand. How could some mental states be excluded from one's awareness? How can one succeed not to think about and thereby virtually forget about a disturbing event? It could sound as if a repressed mental state exists in some metaphorical "place," which is how Freud sometimes conceives of the unconscious, but this would be a mysterious conception of unavailability (and also incoherent, as shown by Sartre, but I will not defend this claim here).[64] I will turn to this issue in Chapter 5.4. For now, I will just accept, as other philosophers do, that there are such mental states as unconscious emotions.[65]

C. *Unconscious emotions and neurotic (in particular emotional) symptoms*

Unconscious emotions were not properly expressed at the time of their formation, and under most circumstances their affective aspect remains numb and unexpressed. But that affective aspect has not thereby been destroyed. The emotion has sunk into a mere dispositional state, and

62 Ibid., 7.

63 Ibid., 6. Freud also emphasizes that affect can be expressed verbally and need not be expressed in a grand cathartic moment of intense feeling or an action tendency. He says: "language serves as a substitute for action; by its help, an affect can be 'abreacted' almost as effectively." Ibid., 8. See also Lear's discussion on Freud's actual practice, reflected even from the earliest case studies, as not necessitating a cathartic moment of intense feeling: Jonathan Lear, *Love and its Place in Nature* (New York: Farrar, Straus & Giroux, 1990), 64–65.

64 Sartre, *Being and Nothingness*, Part 1, Chapter 2: "Bad Faith."

65 See Introduction, fn 12.

normally that disposition is "latent," not manifested. Under certain circumstances, however, which may arise many years after the original repression, the unconscious emotion may be enlivened.

Latency and enlivenment of emotions are familiar from our everyday experience of emotions. Although emotions are episodes that often run their course in such a way that we forget about them and move on, we may sometimes remember emotional reactions and re-feel them. Say that I was angry years ago when I found out that my ex-girlfriend shared details about our sex life with a mutual friend. I was angry for about an hour or so at the time but never confronted her. A few months later, that friend reminded me of that detail and I was angry about it again. In a sense, I never stopped being angry about it. I was not "over it", as we say, when I stopped thinking about it after the original anger episode. My anger was enlivened when I remembered it. Ten years later when I think about it I find that I am not angry at all. I remember that I was angry about it, but now I am over it. Emotional episodes that were not properly exhausted at the original time of their arousal may calm down and their affect will not be felt, but if one is not over them, they may be enlivened later in life. In fact, I can be over it and then years later suddenly get angry yet again.

Latent unconscious emotions can also be enlivened. Somehow, in a manner yet to be explained, the here-and-now situation triggers the unconscious emotion into partial manifestation. Although Freud and Breuer talk primarily about hysterical symptoms, the primal series account, as I call it here, is applied to other neurotic symptoms in Freud's writings. Here I am only concerned to articulate this partial manifestation of the unconscious emotion in a way that produces a distinctively emotional symptom.

This manifestation is only partial since the describable aspect of the unconscious emotion remains unacknowledged and is not available for reporting or for verbal expression. The affective aspect, on the other hand, is now expressed. The here-and-now situation is then experienced as having triggered the aroused affect, and certain features of the situation become emotionally salient. If the subject attends to and describes those here-and-now salient features of the situation, those current salient features become the recognized object of the occurrent emotion, which is the one judged to be inappropriate or pathological. To say it in de Sousa's terms, the original scenario (the unconscious emotion) is brought to bear on the current situation, which it does not objectively resemble, thereby producing the current emotional pathology.

We now have two emotions, if by "emotions" we designate affect and emotionally salient features of a certain situation. One emotion is the enlivened unconscious emotion, whose emotionally salient features belong to a specific past situation or experience and are currently unacknowledged and not available for description or report, and the second is the occurrent emotion, whose emotionally salient features belong to the here-and-now situation. And the enlivenment of the unconscious emotion serves to explain the occurrent emotion. Or we could say that we have an affective experience with two objects – one in the here-and-now situation, which is emotionally salient and available for description, and the second that belongs to a past situation and that remains unconscious.

Freud and Breuer say that there is a "symbolic relation" between the occurrent psychological symptom and the emotional reaction to the primal scene (or rather between the describable aspect of the occurrent emotion, namely the here-and-now object, and the describable aspect of the unconscious emotion, that is the there-and-then object).[66] This symbolic relation is also claimed to be a causal relation between the enlivened unconscious emotion and the occurrrent pathological reaction. In other words, it is by virtue of this symbolic relation between the here-and-now and the unconscious emotion that one is now emotionally reacting in pathological ways.

The word symbolic appears in scare quotes. Is it because the connection need not be exactly a symbol? The term symbolic indicates that although the subject would not judge the object of the enlivened emotion (an object that remains unconscious and unavailable for description) to be straightforwardly similar to the object of the current emotion – there is nevertheless some kind of non-arbitrary connection between them, some kind of non-straightforward similarity. The subject suffering from the psychological symptom, in our case an emotional pathology, does not see or understand or is simply not aware of this "symbolic" and causal connection.[67] This incapacity to see the connection results from the isolation of the unconscious emotion from one's regular thought processes.

It may be the case that the new emotionally salient people or things fit the emotion-type of the enlivened affect, as is the case with Mr. A's repeated experiences of betrayal. Mr. A can then avow his current emotional reactions as justified. Or it may be the case that the manifest emotion does not stand rational scrutiny and the new emotionally salient object may be judged to be unfitting to the manifested emotion-type, as is the case with Jonah's resentment of his female bosses. Given that the affective aspect of Jonah's current reaction comes from unconscious resentment of his mother (that has been somehow enlivened), rational judgments against the emotion, which consider reasons to do with the here-and-now relation to his boss, will not help to subside the affect.

The early Freudian version of the etiological explanation for emotional patterns thus also consists in an extended form of rationality. As Freud says elsewhere, "*the emotional state, as such, is always justified*,"[68] only that it is not necessarily justifiable by reasons that come from the reality of the

66 Breuer and Freud, "Preliminary Communication," S.E., 2, 5.

67 Ibid., 4–5.

68 S. Freud, "Obsessions and Phobias: Their Psychical Mechanism and Their Aetiology" (1895 [1894]), S.E., 3, 75.

here-and-now situation. The reasons that may serve to justify the affective state come from the describable but unacknowledged aspect of the enlivened unconscious emotion. In other words, the current affective state is justifiable when considering the original event in which it arose in the first place, namely the primal scene or the "original scenario," as de Sousa would call it.

This early Freudian account regards therapy as bringing an unconscious emotion to consciousness. In order to remove the principal cause and change the patient's pathological patterns of emotional salience, the isolation of the emotion from conscious thought processes somehow has to be broken down, and through that process, the subject can come to see and understand the symbolic and causal connections between the symptom and the hitherto unconscious emotion. As said above, the unconscious emotion is made available for verbal report and expression and the subject can express the emotion's affective aspect and let the emotion run its course.

5. Insights and oversights of the "primal scene" account

The early Freudian account does not provide a general theory of emotion in the manner the accounts of Rorty, Lear, and de Sousa do. This is largely because Freud never saw his goal as providing such an account. But if we run with Rorty's methodological principle and look first for an explanatory account of pathological emotions, then the early Freudian version of the primal scene account seems promising.

The early Freudian version leaves room for the singularity of emotional reactions. Although Freud does not explain why the unconscious emotion is enlivened in certain specific circumstances and not others, he does not commit to any law-like rule that characterizes the types of circumstances in which those unconscious emotions would be enlivened. This feature allows Jonah, for example, to have better and worse days when it comes to his relations with Esther. It also allows for Jonah to abandon his emotional pattern with a different female boss. But in order to answer the singularity question we need to know more about the triggering process, through which an unconscious emotion can be enlivened. In this sense, the early Freudian account, much like de Sousa's, is incomplete.

The Freudian version importantly adds the symbolic connection between the "original scenario" or the relevant unconscious emotions and the pathological here-and-now emotional reaction. In other words, de Sousa's "not objective resemblance" is here characterized positively, namely that there is some resemblance between the current salient object and the old one (from the original scenario), but not a strong or straightforward resemblance. That is, there would be some respects in which the scenarios do resemble – but not that many. This is not to repeat the philosophical cliché that anything is similar to anything in some respect or other. Rather, the resemblance in question, although not straightforward, is nonetheless salient. In other words, there is a notable thematic affinity between the here-and-now emotionally salient features and the object of the unconscious emotion, the object that is brought to bear on the here-and-now situation and that gives rise to the current emotional salience in the first place.

Indeed, it is this thematic affinity that allows Rorty to declare that there is a conceptual connection between the emotional reaction to the there-and-then and the emotional reaction to the here-and-now (through the postulation of a disposition). It is such thematic affinity that people use when they tell stories about themselves in order to explain their emotional issues. Whatever causal account we end up with should explain the source of this thematic affinity.

However, Freud goes astray when he basically declares this thematic affinity to be a causal connection. Indeed, by calling the connection between the enlivened unconscious emotion and the here-and-now psychological symptom "symbolic," Freud has caused great confusion in the psychoanalytic literature ever since. The term "symbolic" suggests a semantic relation between the unconscious emotion (or few emotions) and the here-and-now pathological emotional reaction. It is as if Freud was saying that the here-and-now reaction is an expression of the unconscious emotion, which is the "real" emotion in this emotional experience. It is as if the here-and-now reaction is merely a representation of the enlivened unconscious emotion. Are we to think that the unconscious is a little person within us speaking its emotion through symbolic representations? I will not pursue this line of criticism here.

In Chapter 5.2 I will explain why it is a mistake to call this connection "symbolic," and that it is not a semantic connection at all. In fact, this should not surprise those who think that emotions (be they pathological or not) are imagistic modes of seeing-as. Imagistic seeing-as is not a representational relation. When I see one face in terms of another, when suddenly certain features of the face become salient by virtue of the similarity I see – the one face does not represent the other and does not stand for it in any way. Imagistic seeing-as relations can turn into representational relations if one intends to use them this way, but they are not inherently representational when they occur passively and strike our attention. As will be explained in Chapter 5.2, the term "symbolic" is misleading and should be discarded.

Another major problem with the early Freudian account for emotional pathologies consists in the haunting skepticism about the importance of the primal scene. Its alleged emotional importance makes more sense in light of the hypothesis of the incompatibility of the old emotional reaction with the subject's self-conception. Yet it still remains unclear why the reactions to the scene designated as "primal" carry so much more causal weight in comparison to other scenes that also give rise to unpleasant emotions that in turn provoke alienating aversion.

That is, we would expect many emotions to have been suppressed and repressed. Why is one repressed emotion or a series of few unconscious emotions somehow more important than other emotions that have been repressed? Why are they the ones that get enlivened later in life and cause an emotional symptom? We need to know more about what repression actually consists in (except "rendering unconscious") if we want to answer this question and be convinced of the plausibility of a Freudian account for pathological emotions.

The explanation that considers unconscious emotions to be the terms that are brought to bear on the situation at hand and make certain aspects of it emotionally salient seems promising. But a Freudian approach still needs to provide an explication for repression, for the triggering process that enlivens unconscious emotions, and for the thematic affinity between the describable aspect of the unconscious emotion and the object of the here-and-now pathological reaction. But before these challenges can be addressed, we need to consider another important problem with primal-scene accounts. This objection is described in the next chapter, which gives rise to another Freudian account.

4 The primal memory accounts

The narrative approach

This chapter considers another explanatory approach to the formation of psychological symptom that is also based on Freudian insights, but from writings published after the *Studies on Hysteria*. Although this approach is meant to apply to all psychological symptoms, the chapter addresses only the application of this approach to distinctively emotional symptoms, namely to pathological patterns of emotional reaction such as recalcitrance.

The approach discussed in this chapter distances itself from the primal scene account in the following sense: the significant cause is here conceived not as the primal scene and the emotional reaction to it at the time of the event, but rather as the memory of that primal scene, which becomes traumatic and is thereby repressed later in life. The muddled scenario that is brought to bear on the here-and-now situation and makes certain aspects of that situation emotionally salient is thus not a faithful emotionally laden memory of the primal scene, which bears a straightforward causal connection to the event. It is rather a memory that has undergone some kind of modification that renders it traumatic and thereby significant enough to later be enlivened and cause a problematic emotional reaction.

The resulting account shares an advantage with the primal scene account, namely that the relation between the memory and the emotional symptom lends itself to the kind of storytelling familiar from everyday life and the therapeutic setting. However, it also shares a similar problem with the primal scene account, namely that the manner in which the memory is modified does not render it as significant as it should be in comparison to other memories in order to cause the pathological emotional reaction. The critical presentation of this approach will show its merits and its problems, which in turn will pave the way for the account I propose in the next chapter for both pathological and non-pathological emotions.

1. When Freud left kindergarten

In *Rewriting the Soul*, Ian Hacking criticizes developmental etiologies of the early Freudian style:

> How come we are stuck with the very earliest, kindergarten Freud, the stock-in-trade of those prewar black-and-white psychodramas shown on late television? How come we have not even gone so far as Freud has gone by 1899 – how come we have not thought seriously about what Freud called screen memories? Why have we been so literalist, so mechanical, and imagined that an illness produced by trauma is produced at the time of the trauma, in early childhood? Why can't we at least discuss the idea that the experience of the original event, apparently kept in memory, is not what causes distress and dysfunction; why can't we ask whether the problem comes from the possibly repressed memory itself, much later in life, and the way in which the mind has worked on and recomposed that memory?[1]

For the sake of simplicity, I focus, as Hacking does, on imagistic memories, which can be regarded as analogous to a video recording, in a very qualified sense that will soon be explicated. The kind of memory modification that interests Hacking does not consist in a distortion of the images of that "video recording." No extra images have been inserted into the "video" of the primal scene and no images have been taken out of it. Such imagistic distortion may occur, but I shall leave that possibility aside, for the sake of simplicity. Hacking's point about memory modification is philosophical, and relies on conceptual clarity about ordinary everyday experiences. It is precisely the logical nature of his argument that makes it so convincing.

Hacking does not talk of memory as a latent disposition that may manifest when a subject is reminded of it. He is concerned with actual remembering, that is the experience one goes through when the memory is consciously manifested. Since the scene in question involves people and their intentional actions, remembering the scene cannot merely involve visualizing a sequence of moving images. "[A]ctions are not simply activities, movements that show up on video."[2]

Hacking refers to Anscombe's claim that an intentional action is under description. Actions can be minimally described in terms of bodily movements, such as "I am moving my arm up and down."[3] But what makes an action intentional in Anscombe's sense is that the subject's reasons for it, her goals and interests, guide the subject's bodily movement. This is why when the subject elicits reasons for her action, she also further describes what she is doing. Intentional actions, in other words, come with "subtitles," with conceptual content. It is this feature of intentional action that allows for a distortion in memory without changing its respective "video recording."

1 Ian Hacking, *Rewriting the Soul: Multiple Personality and the Sciences of Memory* (Princeton: Princeton University Press, 1995), 137.

2 Ibid., 234.

3 See the discussion of Anscombe's example in Chapter 1.1.

By the time a past event is remembered later in life, the subject has developed conceptual resources that were not available to her at the time of the event. The old event was experienced then as an action under a description that employed there-and-then conceptual capacities. The manner in which the subject describes here-and-now what happened or what was done back then, the concepts and categories that the subject applies to the old situation, may thus be different to the description under which the past action was originally done. Remembering the event can thereby differ from the way the event was originally experienced. So, the redescription of the old actions distorts, in a certain logical sense, the content of the past event. As Hacking explains:

> Old actions under new descriptions may be re-experienced in memory. And if these are genuinely new descriptions, descriptions not available or perhaps nonexistent at the time of the episodes remembered, then something is experienced now, in memory, that in a certain sense did not exist before. The action took place, but not the action under the new description.[4]

Hacking emphasizes the phenomenological aspect of memory as an experience, or rather as a re-experience of the past event: "When we remember what we did, or what other people did, we may also rethink, redescribe, and refeel the past."[5] It is this re-experiencing that may make the subject believe that what happened in the past was actually done under this new description.

As indicated in Hacking's words, the difference between the re-experience and the past experience can sometimes be due to the redescription of past actions that includes concepts acquired only later in life. The difference can also be due to the employment of a concept that was not available to anyone at all at the time of the event. It is the latter case that is of great interest to Hacking, since the main concept he deals with in this book is "child abuse," a concept whose criteria of application have an intricate history.

We need not turn to extreme examples where the moral concept in question did not exist at all at the time of the original event. Many of us experience a "generation gap" with our parents as we grow up. We may begin our lives endorsing the norms they teach us and in the course of time reject them and endorse different norms. The issue of applying contemporary moral concepts to past events is a complex issue that may involve an emotional reaction.

Take for example a woman whose father discouraged her from going to university in the late 1960s. He then said it would make it difficult for her

4 Hacking, *Rewriting the Soul*, 249.
5 Ibid.

to find a man. He said that men do not want a woman who is "too smart." At the time she thought her father was right and that there was nothing wrong with his views and advice.

Twenty-five years later, as she encourages her own daughter to go to university, she may remember that past event and realize that her father has wronged her. His advice held her back and did not allow her to fulfill herself professionally. In fact, she now thinks, he was sexist toward his own daughter. He did not respect her enough to support her wishes to get a university education.

But was this father indeed disrespectful at the time? Has this father wronged his daughter? Could he have seen himself as what we call "sexist"? The term itself was not widely used or accepted at the time, and this particular father was not a very up-to-date kind of man. He was just the average man of his generation. The now middle-aged woman may think that there is something morally questionable with that generation, and indeed with her father.

We do not yet have an account for the formation of an emotional reaction. But there is no need to be a judgmentalist or a conceptualist about emotions to think that sometimes thoughts and judgments cause an emotional episode – in some indirect and non-inferential way that is yet to be clarified. It is thus possible that as this woman reflects on the role her father played in her life, she may find herself retroactively angry. The "video-recording" of the past event may not change, but the opportunity arises for the distortion of its "subtitles." This distortion may give rise to an emotional episode in the present. The woman may look back and mistakenly "realize" she was in fact angry at the time, insulted and disappointed, only that she was not able to fully comprehend her emotions back then. This refeeling of the past that Hacking talks about is consistent with both a conceptualist and a non-conceptualist seeing-as account of emotion.

Hacking seems to be concerned with the question, "What did he do?" which is a question about the past event. But I am more concerned with the question about the past experience of the event. Namely, what did this woman *feel* back then? What kind of emotional impact did that event have on her – then? She may have been disappointed and frustrated that the world poses such difficulties on her, but was she angry with her father at the time?

Consider next how redescription of remembered scenes from childhood makes a difference mainly due to concepts that are available to the remembering adult but were not available to the child. It is in this connection that Hacking makes an explicit reference to Freud:

> The old, and valuable, Freudian insight is that scenes that are recovered, whether it is in flashbacks, or through memory therapy, or through more ordinary reflective but unassisted recollection, become

> invested with meanings that they did not have at the time they were experienced.[6]

Hacking also makes explicit reference to primal scenes: "The idea, that the primal scene has a different meaning when experienced by the child from what it means when remembered or repressed by the adolescent, is of fundamental importance."[7]

Given the sexual character of the primal scenes Hacking is interested in, namely those of sexual abuse, he refers to Freud's claim that childhood memories become sexualized in adolescence.[8] Hacking claims that this theory depends on the presupposition of the asexuality of children (a presupposition Freud held and then abandoned in favor of his theory of infantile sexuality).

The sexuality of the adolescent colors the past childhood event in a sexual meaning it could not have had at the time of its occurrence. It is only later, in adolescence, that the event is redescribed and receives the meaning of something not innocent and perhaps even morally wrong. If the adolescent reacts emotionally to the memory with shame or anger and further feels an alienating aversion towards those emotions (which can later be seen as conflictual with her self-image as sexually innocent or with her loving idealization of the adults that were involved in the past scene) – then the emotion may be suppressed and repressed.[9] That later repression grants the redescribed memory its new emotional significance as traumatic. Hacking says that although the premise (namely infantile asexuality) was false, the insight about the effects of redescription should nevertheless be preserved.

To be accurate, Freud talked about the sexualization of childhood memories in puberty and their subsequent repression after the publication of *Three Essays on Sexuality* (1905), where he presented his theory of infantile sexuality.[10] Infantile sexuality is nevertheless different to adult sexuality; in particular, what is acceptable for a child becomes unacceptable or perverse for the adult.

Freud claimed that the childhood memory is re-modeled and consolidated in puberty, where it is colored with a mature sexual overtone, whereas the past experience itself was of an infantile-sexual nature. The adolescent may then emotionally react to the redescribed scene with alienating aversion, and the emotion with the redescribed memory as its salient

6 Ibid., 254.
7 Ibid., 249.
8 Ibid., 248–249.
9 Richard Wollheim, *The Tread of Life* (New Haven, CT: Yale University Press, 1999[1984]), 137.
10 See for example the elaborate footnote in Freud, *Notes Upon a Case of Obsessional Neurosis* [1909], S.E., 10, 206–208, fn. 1; and also in Freud, "My Views on Sexuality," S.E., 7, 274.

object will be suppressed and repressed and might further cause a psychological symptom in the future.

Hacking's logic goes astray when he claims that the "retroactive redescription changes the past".[11] He explains:

> If a description did not exist, or was not available, at an earlier time, then at that time one could not act intentionally under that description. Only later did it become true that, at that time, one performed an action under that description.[12]

This assertion is not only provocative; it is also logically inconsistent. If intentional action is under description, then the relevant description that correctly determines the action is the one the agent is aware of at the time of the action. The description under which an action is performed is the one the agent can provide as an answer to a why-question while the action is taking place. If the agent cannot in principle be aware of certain descriptions of one's actions, then that action was not performed under that description.[13] We may retroactively judge what someone did in the past as morally questionable, and we may even say that the action was indeed morally questionable *at the time*, whether or not the agent could have been aware of the relevant moral concept. But we cannot say that someone *intended* to do something that falls under a newly available moral concept.[14]

The logic of redescription thus justifies a more modest claim: subtitle-distortion changes the meaning of the event in memory. The remodeled memory may then arouse in the remembering subject an unpleasant emotional reaction that is itself aversion-provoking. Now, we can reiterate the early Freudian account of mental trauma from the previous chapter, this time not addressed to the primal scene itself, but to its redescribed memory. That is, the new emotional reaction to the redescribed scene is both suppressed and repressed and may cause a psychological symptom later in life.

The symptom, therefore, is less dependent on primal scene than in the account described in the previous chapter. It is not the emotional reaction to the primal scene that is repressed, but the emotional reaction to the re-described and re-modeled memory. What is "primal" in this account is the memory. People may tell explanatory stories that begin in a primal scene, but they are often confused. Their symptom is actually caused by the

11 Hacking, *Rewriting the Soul*, 243.

12 Ibid.

13 See Anscombe on how we may ascribe to actions descriptions, even if the agent does not elicit them as reasons for her actions, when the agent possesses the knowledge necessary to infer this further description from the ones she explicitly provides: G. E. M. Anscombe, *Intention* 2nd edn (Oxford: Basil Blackwell, 1985[1963]), §28.

14 See Barry Allen's criticism of Hacking's *Rewriting the Soul* in "Review: The Soul of Knowledge," *History and Theory* 36, no. 1 (1997).

traumatic reaction to the remembering of the scene, yet they claim that they have experienced the trauma at the time of the scene itself.

One may think that this is not such a significant difference. The redescribed memory is nonetheless causally connected to the primal scene whose "video" is given new "subtitles." Perhaps the difference is merely temporal – the scene and the emotional reaction to it are separated by the time it takes for the subject to acquire the conceptual resources required to redescribe the scene in a way that would cause a traumatic reaction to it.

However, whether or not one acquires the relevant concepts and whether or not one applies them to the memory in such a way that it arouses an unpleasant and aversion-provoking emotional reaction is a contingent matter. This is particularly evident when the concepts in question did not exist at the time of the past event. As Hacking says: "it was not determinate that these events would be experienced in these new ways, for it was not determinate, at the time that the events occurred, that in the future new descriptions would come into being."[15]

At the time of the event, there was no fact of the matter that these specific new concepts would become a part of one's language in the future. Whether or not these new concepts would be created was, back then, a completely contingent matter. And so, the scene, when it actually happened, was not necessarily destined to be "primal" at all. If those concepts had not come into being years later that scene could not have been remembered through a redescription that would in turn cause a traumatic emotional response. That is, the scene could not have been re-modeled in memory as traumatic (thereby becoming a potential cause for a psychological symptom later in life).

The contingency here at stake is that of social and thereby linguistic development, which affects the possibilities that may or may not arise to redescribe certain remembered scenes, possibilities that depend on the subject's conceptual resources and available categories. Given that redescription may serve to traumatize a memory so that it may causally contribute to the formation of a psychological symptom, the contingency in question also characterizes the potential of a memory to cause a symptom. What is indeterminate is not the past itself, as Hacking claims, but rather the causal efficacy its memory may acquire through the acquisition of further conceptual resources.

Hacking speaks of this contingency as dependent on new descriptions coming into being. New descriptions need not be entirely new concepts or words. Language is in any case in flux. In particular, the application of emotion-type words depends on norms of fittingness, which change to some extent from generation to generation, from childhood to adulthood. The indeterminacy described above is thus far-reaching.

15 Ibid., 249.

Even a sexual event in childhood, likely to be re-described in puberty as not-so-innocent is not pre-determined to be re-modeled as traumatic. Freud gives the example of two girls who were brought up in the same household and engaged in "naughty" sexual games when they were very young. One is the daughter of the landlord and the other of the caretaker. Freud says that the first may end up with neurosis as she is brought up on ideals of "feminine purity and abstinence" and the second, growing up in a much more sexually liberated environment, can end up as an actress leading a pathology-free life.[16] Importantly, even the daughter of the landlord need not feel so guilty and ashamed when she comes to understand her past games as sexual. She may just dismiss the event as infantile foolishness.

2. The story of reiterated redescriptions of the primal memory

Hacking's primal memory account involves redescription that happens via conscious reflection and explicit remembering and a re-living of the past event later in life. That redescription occurs just before the repression of the memory with its new emotionally traumatic significance. Another such re-descriptive remembering or re-experiencing of that scene or already re-described memory can occur after the formation of the symptom, whether alone or in the form of "flashbacks" or in therapy.[17]

Paul Ricoeur complicates this approach by stressing that such re-modeling of the memory occurs more than once prior to the outbreak of a psychological symptom.

> Freud discovers that the subject's history does not conform to a linear determinism which would place the present in the firm grasp of the past in a univocal fashion. On the contrary, recovering traumatic events through the work of analysis reveals that "at the time they were experiences they could not be fully integrated in a meaningful context." It is only the arrival of new events and new situations that precipitates the subsequent reworking of these earlier events ... generally speaking, numerous repressed memories become traumas after the event. It is a question of more than just a delay or a deferred action. Here we see that we are far removed from the notion of a memory which would simply reproduce real events in a sort of perception of the past; this is, instead, a work which goes over and over extremely complex structurations. It is this work of memory that is implied, among other things, by the notion of the story or narrative structure of existence.[18]

16 Freud, *Introductory Lectures on Psychoanalysis*, S.E. 16, Lecture 22, 352–354.

17 See Hacking's discussion on flashbacks in Hacking, *Rewriting the Soul*, 252–254.

18 Paul Ricoeur, "The Question of Proof in Freud's Psychoanalytic Writings," in *The Philosophy of Paul Ricoeur: An Anthology of His Work*, ed. Charles E. Reagan and David Steward (Boston: Beacon Press, 1978), 191.

Ricoeur does not explicate exactly what he means by "reworking" of an event or rather of a memory of an event. But given he says that this "reworking" ultimately provides a "meaningful context," then it can be assumed that he is talking about re-describing the old event or memory, giving it new meaning by matching it with a new description, by applying certain concepts. That is, Ricoeur complicates Hacking's account by allowing for a few occasions for the redescription of the memory.

The occasion for re-describing a memory arises with "the arrival of new events and new situations." Ricoeur does not explain how or why these new events "precipitate" the activity of redescription. I assume that Ricoeur means that the new event somehow sheds light on and is used to re-interpret the old memory. In Jonah's case, for example, it was his stay at his grandfather's place that may have induced in Jonah the belief that his mother is (at least sometimes or in some respects) domineering and hostile, a belief he somehow acquired from his grandfather. Jonah may then redescribe his memory of being sent from the hospital as an instance of his mother's domineering and hostile comportment. The new event that "precipitates the subsequent reworking" of the old memory is thus thematically relevant to that old memory. The stay at the grandfather's place, for example, is a relevant occasion to redescribe the hospital scene since it includes the communication of views about Jonah's mother that are applicable to the old memory.

The scarf scenes may have also been an occasion for Jonah to redescribe the old hospital scenes. During those scenes, Jonah may come to resent his mother and form the view that his mother is submitting him to these itchy scarves, not as a genuine way to show her love, but rather as a demonstration of her power to make him suffer. That is, Jonah may form the view that his mother expresses her hostile authority through a pretense of love and care. This new belief is applicable to that old hospital scene. Jonah may now redescribe that scene: his mother sent him away with a smile, saying it was for his own good, but in fact, she used her loving attitude to sweeten her hostile rejection of him.

According to this account, by the time the repressed memory may cause a psychological symptom, that memory has been redescribed on a number of occasions, each further granting that memory with further meaning that renders it even more unpleasant or traumatic, and Ricoeur does not specify if this occurs through judgment or through some other causal and non-inferential process. Ricoeur describes the symptom as the result of two opposing mental "forces." The first is the force of repression, which struggles to keep the traumatic reworked memory unconscious. The second is the force of regression, which works to bring the primal memory into consciousness in its original form.

The symptom is the result of a "compromise" between those two forces. On the one hand, repression succeeds to keep the memory unconscious and on the other hand regression succeeds to express the affect invested in or associated with that memory. This compromise is achieved through the work of "censorship," which allows the primal memory to reach consciousness in "disguise," namely in the form of a symptom.[19] The intentional term "disguise" suggests that Ricoeur thinks that the here-and-now psychological symptom, which in our case is an emotional reaction, consists in the (distorted) expression of the emotionally laden memory. This is the "real" emotion that is being expressed. The here-and-now reaction stands for the expression of the repressed memory. That is, for Ricoeur, as for early Freud, the relation between the repressed emotionally laden memory and the symptom is symbolic, that is, semantic.

The "subject's history," which, according to Ricoeur, will ultimately comprise the explanation for the current symptom, resembles to some extent the stories of the developmental etiologies discussed in the previous chapter. The story will include not just the primal scene or period that often dates in childhood, but also further experiences in the subject's life, "new events and new situations." All these events together comprise a version of the primal series, the significant events in the subject's life that somehow combine to produce a psychological symptom.

I assume that the primal series that Ricoeur considers as the chronicle for a history of the reworkings of the primal memory contains the same list of events that would appear in a developmental etiology of the sort Rorty describes. This assumption relies partly on the fact that both kinds of narrative accounts are ultimately inspired by Freud's case studies. Each narrative account thus proposes a way to understand the chronicles described in those cases, namely the chronologically ordered series of emotionally laden events, the patient's "story of suffering." I will also partly justify this assumption from conceptual considerations shortly.

Although both kinds of narratives use the same chronicle of events, each narrative connects those events to one another differently. Each narrative, in other words, involves its own "causal hypothesis," as Graeme Marshall calls it, which "structures the narrative beyond its chronological ordering."[20]

Examine first developmental etiologies. The primal scene accounts propose a clear *forward* temporal direction of development. A primal scene occurs, the reaction to it changes something in the subject *at the time* of its occurrence, whether it is a magnetizing disposition for Rorty (Chapter 3.1), the inhibition of normal emotional development for Lear (Chapter 2.3), or the creation of a memory disposition for early Freud (Chapter 3.4) and for de Sousa (according to the interpretation presented in Chapter 3.3).

Then another scene in the series occurs, the response to which is determined by the disposition created after the primal scene. That new event may

19 These metaphorical terms appear for example in ibid., 194.

20 Graeme Marshall, "Overdetermination and the Emotions," in *Explaining Emotions*, ed. Amélie Rorty (Berkeley: University of California Press, 1980), 217.

further create another magnetizing disposition or another memory disposition that conceptually relates to the first disposition. Recall the "logical" connection between such two dispositions that Rorty talks about. According to Rorty, before the scarf scenes Jonah had the disposition to regard his mother as domineering and hostile, which affected the way those scenes were experienced. After or during the scarf scenes, Jonah develops the new disposition to see female authority figures in general as domineering and hostile. The later disposition is a generalization of the first, through the concept "female authority figures," which is effectively the theme through which we can regard Jonah's boss Esther and Jonah's mother as part of the same "story of suffering."

Rorty's developmental account can be represented diagrammatically as a linear line (see Figure 4.1).

Primal Scene→ disp. A → Scene 2 → disp. B → ...... → here-and-now symptom

Figure 4.1 Developmental etiologies

Each two consecutive scenes in such a linear etiology connect thematically, according to this model, in a manner that would enable the conceptual connections between the dispositions they cause, as described above. The emerging themes such as "mother," "domineering and hostile" or "female authority figures" stress the aspects of each scene that play a significant role in forming the emotional dispositions. This thematic affinity among the scenes comprises the "dominance hypothesis" of the developmental narrative, which "supplies the terms in which the events emerging as significant are to be redescribed, and thus makes explicit the aspects to be dealt with."[21]

Compare this with Ricoeur's primal memory narrative. Ricoeur's narrative account can be represent diagrammatically (see Figure 4.2). The causal structure Riceour assumes no longer presupposes clear linear development. Each scene in the series serves as a relevant occasion to redescribe the primal memory. Those redescriptions turn the memory into an emotionally disturbing one in various aspects and lead to the memory's repression. That repression, in turn, struggles with regression, and the primal memory may reach consciousness in the symbolic form of a symptom. The causal hypothesis of the primal memory account is the primal memory, which glues together, so to speak, the chronologically ordered events. It is the primal memory that is redescribed during the scenes of the series, that gets

21 Marshall, "Overdetermination," 216.

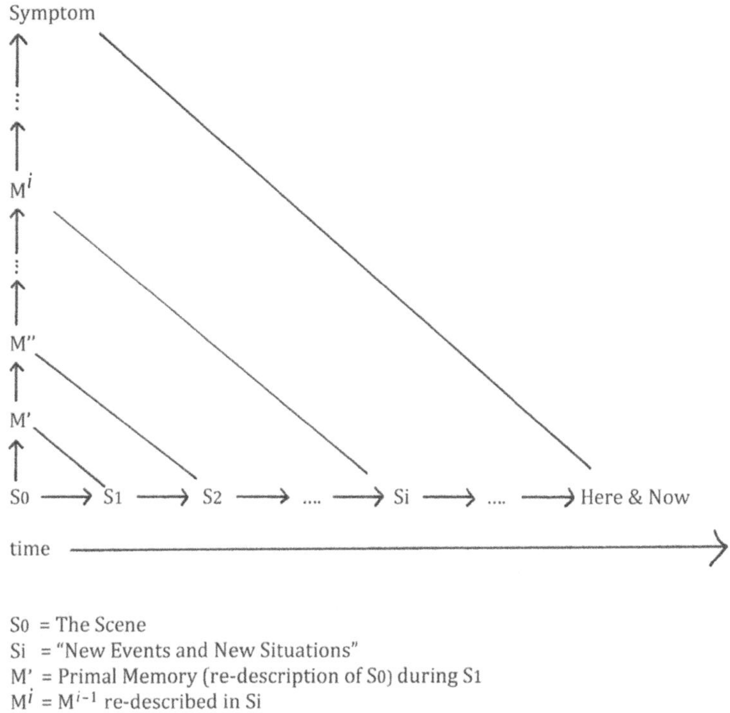

Figure 4.2 Primal memory account (Ricoeur)

repressed, and that finally gets distorted into an occurrent (emotional) symptom.

Although Ricoeur does not say this, it is consistent with his account that each scene would bear a certain thematic affinity with the primal memory. This affinity allows the subject to apply certain aspects of the new event or situation to the primal memory and thereby redescribe it. The dominance hypothesis in Ricoeur's narrative and the theme that runs through it is also the primal memory, redescribed and further redescribed during the events of the chronicle. The events selected to take part in the chronicle would therefore be those that can be regarded as bearing thematic affinity to the primal memory. The primal memory is both the thematic and the causal thread that runs through the chronicle and makes it into a causal story.

Since the causal thread that runs through the narrative is a conceptually laden thematic thread, Ricoeur seems to be committed to a conceptualist view of emotions that regards them as intentional states with conceptual content. When it comes to explaining emotional pathologies, then, the reworked primal memory comprises the terms in which one sees the situation as E-provoking. The affective aspect of the current pathological emotional episode more or less matches that of the reworked and traumatized primal memory, and the describable aspect of the emotionally salient features of the here-and-now situation (here understood as the occurrent emotion's intentional content), bears thematic affinity with the primal memory.

Therapy, on Ricoeur's account, consists in an "epistemological inquiry"[22] that reveals the primal memory, and that inquiry includes bringing to light the series of events that contributed to that redescription. The purpose of therapy is to "reopen the path of memory,"[23] and as such it is conceived as the struggle against the force of repression, which in the therapeutic context is named "resistance." [24]

Ricoeur does not elaborate on the concept of repression, why we should consider it a "force" or what it means for a memory to be repressed. In the previous chapter I proposed that an emotionally laden repressed memory is not entirely unavailable to consciousness. This unavailability to awareness amounts to not being thought about. A repressed mental state is isolated from the normal thought processes (in a way yet to be explained). If the subject's thought somehow manages to wander in such a way that it reaches or arouses the repressed memory, the content of the memory is remembered "in highly summary form" and its affective significance is denied expression.

On the narrative account (which assumes a conceptualist view of emotions as intentional states), what is repressed then is more simply understandable as an emotion whose intentional content is the content of the primal memory. As said in the previous chapter, due to the isolation of this emotion from the rest of one's thought processes, the subject cannot see the thematic affinity between that isolated emotion and the here-and-now pathological emotion. Bringing such an emotion to consciousness breaks down its isolation and thereby involves the articulation of its intentional content, the expression of its affective aspect, and the understanding of thematic affinity between that hitherto unacknowledged emotion and the here-and-now symptom – where thematic affinity is here conceived to be a symbolic and causal connection.

But the philosophers discussed in this chapter prefer to talk in terms of a repressed memory, which is emotionally laden. Using the primal memory terminology, remembering involves describing or rather re-describing the content of the memory and also expressing or acknowledging its affective importance. This removal of repression or extraction from isolation also involves the recognition of the symbolic and causal connection between the primal memory and the symptom. Removing repression also involves the

22 Ricoeur, "The Question of Proof," 195.
23 Ibid.,190.
24 Ibid., 195.

contextualization of that memory as the thematic thread that runs through the series of events that affected that memory and thereby its later symbolic manifestation in the form of a psychological symptom. Removing the repression from the primal memory and the process of narrating thus go hand in hand. As Ricoeur says:

> But what is it to remember? It is not just to recall certain isolated events, but to become capable of forming meaningful sequences and ordered connections. In short, it is to be able to constitute one's own existence in the form of a story where a memory as such is only a fragment of the story. It is the narrative structure of such life-stories that makes a case a case history.[25]

Effectively, therapy itself and the process of narration it involves is the final event of the chronicle. That is, therapy is another new situation in which the subject remembers the old event and redescribes it. In one sense, the resulting primal memory is "only a fragment of the story," since it is the final redescription of the primal scene, an event that is circumscribed in certain past circumstances. But in another sense, exposing this memory also entails the identification of the primal series – the series of events, each of which played a part in the reworking of the memory of that old event.

Therapy begins with the description of the symptom and is equipped with the general causal-thematic schema described above. As Habermas explains, the schematic narrative gets "filled out and become[s] a complete history,"[26] through the investigation of the individual chronicle. Each case history will thus be a particularized instantiation of this general schema.

Habermas emphasizes that the resulting narrative is not comprised of a person's rationalized intentional actions. The story is not the kind of biography that would track a subject's goals and purposes and how they were decided upon, achieved, or failed. The evolution of a symptom is something a subject suffers rather than does intentionally. Habermas then calls each case history the "drama" of the patient.[27]

Yet the drama is not so much the story of the person as it is the tale of the adventures of a memory, the true hero of the case history. The memory is born at the time of the old childhood scene. That memory is then later redescribed, receives the meaning of an emotional trauma and is submitted to repression. Then, during a period of relative mental health the memory may get further redescribed "over and over."[28]

25 Ibid., 190.

26 Jürgen Habermas, "The Interpretation of a Case," in *Philosophy and Psychoanalysis*, ed. Brian A. Farrell (New York: Macmillan College, 1994 [1972]), 44.

27 Ibid. 44.

28 Paul Ricoeur, "Psychoanalysis and the Movement of Contemporary Culture," in *The Conflict of Interpretations: Essays in Hermeneutics*, trans. Willis Domingo, ed. Don Ihde (Evanston, IL: Northwestern University Press: 1974 [1969]), 136.

The main event the memory then goes through is described in what Ricoeur admits to be "semimetaphorical" terminology.[29] That is, at some point the memory is pushed and pulled by two opposing forces, those of repression and regression. Having gone through censorship and imaginative distortion, the memory then returns to consciousness in the form of a symptom.[30] The symptom can be removed through a therapeutic struggle against the forces of repression or resistance that finally reveal the primal memory and the various adventures it went through over the course of the events that redescribed it. It is only then that the primal memory can go back to its original temporal home, in the past, and be free of both repression and regression.

This semimetaphorical language leaves the whole process quite mysterious. The term "regression" indicates some kind of going backwards in time, of experiencing again an old emotional reaction, but it remains unclear what initiates regression or why we should consider it to be a force. And Ricoeur does not elucidate the concept of repression on which the entire story rests. I delay the discussion on repression and regression and what sense can be made of those concepts to the next chapter.

3. The (subtle) rationalism of the narrative account and the return of the problem of non-traumatic traumas

A difficulty arises when it comes to the scenes of the series that are meant to contribute to its redescription. Redescription, as Hacking so clearly explains, occurs via actual remembering, a re-living or a re-experiencing of the old event through the filter of new concepts or meanings. Such redescription involves explicit reflection. It is a rational activity that involves judgment, namely the application of concepts and even the articulation of the new description.

This means that every time the primal memory is redescribed the subject actually remembers it, even if via "subtitle distortion." Are we to assume that after each such iteration the memory is repressed again? Since redescription occurs through reflection and even explicit verbal expression it becomes hard to imagine how repression would succeed or why later in life the subject would remember this event only in "highly summary form." Perhaps this is why Hacking talks about "the *possibly* repressed memory" rather than the repressed memory.[31]

In fact, if the primal series consists in such explicit reflections, then it seems possible or even likely that the subject would readily know that her

29 Ricoeur, "The Question of Proof," 194.

30 Note that "returns" is an intentional term, as is "disguise" and "compromise." Is the memory a little person within us? Is the unconscious a little person within us? Homucularism is to be found virtually everywhere in psychoanalytic literature as well in the philosophy of psychoanalysis.

31 Hacking, *Rewriting the Soul*, 137. Emphasis added.

symptom is connected with this trauma and indeed refer to that trauma as the cause of her symptoms from the very start. Some people may begin therapy with statements like "my father left home when I was a child and that ruined my chances for a normal love relationship." In such cases there appears to be no need to conduct an epistemological inquiry that would reveal the memory and the subject's story of suffering. And then it is not clear, on this account, what else could be done to help the patient get relief.

Does Ricoeur mean that the subject redescribes the memory unconsciously? A picture like this would entail a conception of the unconscious mind as having rational capacities to redescribe memories via propositions. But Ricoeur remarks that Freud, who is the avowed source of inspiration for his account, explicitly rejects a rational conception of the unconscious. He quotes Freud who says in the *Interpretation of Dreams* that the unconscious "does not think, calculate or judge in any way at all."[32]

Whatever is Ricoeur's claim on the matter, his account commits him to a rational picture of the unconscious, namely to a homuncular view of the unconscious as a little interpreter in the mind. Such a little interpreter would, for example, access Jonah's new belief – the one he absorbed from his grandfather – that his mother is domineering and hostile, and use that belief to redescribe the memory of the hospital scene as a scene where his mother forced him to leave, demonstrating her hostility. This picture, however, is incoherent on similar grounds to those presented in Chapter 3.2.

On the one hand, this little interpreter is posited to be a separate part of the mind, separate from consciousness. On the other hand, for this unconscious part of the mind to engage in such redescriptions, it needs immediate and complete access to the newly acquired conceptual resources of the conscious mind and to its newly formed beliefs. It is not in the fallible and charitable position a separate interpreter would be. And those concepts and beliefs are then the ones that are supposed to be applied to an unconscious memory, thereby creating a rational connection between those two supposedly separate parts. To repeat the Davidsonian point, the notion of a divided mind requires that the two (or more) parts in question cannot have a rational connection between them. If the two (or more) parts of the mind rationally connect then they are not separate.[33]

Finally, the very idea that a redescription of a memory renders it traumatic enough to potentially cause a symptom poses the same difficulty that arises for the primal scene accounts. The scene is admitted to be not intrinsically traumatic at the time of the event, and its original memory is not destined to become traumatic but rather its status as traumatic is contingent on the occurrence of further events as well as the acquisition of new

32 Freud, *Interpretation of Dreams* [1900], S.E., 5, 506–507; quoted in Ricoeur, "The Question of Proof," 194.

33 Davidson, "Paradoxes of Irrationality."

concepts and beliefs. But the redescribed memory is still considered a trauma, a memory that is more predisposed than others to cause pathology by virtue of its exceptionally strong emotional import. The subject may only have the "meaningful context" later on in life, but it is the rational activity of redescription of the memory that grants it trauma-worthy.

The primal memory account requires the memory to be indeed traumatic, to clearly stand out from other moderately disturbing memories. Otherwise, we would have too many such primal memories for each subject. People would be obsessively re-describing many memories and would potentially have respectively many troubling emotional symptoms. Ordinary experience as well as Freud's case-studies show, however, that people do not tell so many such stories of suffering about themselves. Rather, they usually tell one such story that focuses on one or few such primal memories.

Moreover, the redescribed primal memory, especially in stories like Jonah's, need not be that much more unpleasant or aversion-provoking than other memories that have gained their emotional import through later redescription. Being sent away from one's mother for a vacation with a beloved grandfather, or playing "naughty" infantile-sexual games with the caretaker's daughter, hardly qualify as objectively traumatic, no matter at what point in time they are described or in reference to what beliefs. There is no reasonable difference between those memories and many other memories that would make these primal memories so much more significant than say a physical fight with a friend or a sibling, or a temporary rejection by one's social group at kindergarten, or the loss of one's pet.

Rational judgment, whether at the time of the event or many years later, will not turn a memory of a scene into an objectively traumatic memory that clearly stands out in one's biography. And the rare occurrences of intrinsically traumatic scenes, such as rape, torture or natural disaster, do not require retroactive redescriptions to receive their traumatic affective weight. Is there some other way to salvage this trauma model? Or should we simply give up on the attempt to explain a pathological emotional pattern via a thematically connected emotionally laden memory? Grünbaum does not find the thematic feature of etiologies indicative of the truth of their causal hypothesis:

> no matter how strong the *thematic affinity* between a conjectured repressed thought and a maladaptive, neurotic action, this "meaning kinship" does not itself suffice to attest the hypothesized repression is "the hidden intentionality" behind a given behavior. For thematic affinity alone does not vouch for etiologic lineage in the absence of further evidence that a thematically kindred repression actually *engendered* the behavior.[34]

34 Grünbaum, *The Foundations of Psychoanalysis*, 55.

Grünbaum speaks of "conjectured" repression, but the memories I am concerned with here are not strictly unavailable to consciousness. What makes these emotionally laden memories unconscious, as I have been stressing, is that the subject does not normally think about them. And if they are thought about, the subject remembers their content only in "highly summary form" and does not express their affective aspect nor acknowledges that they have such affective significance. Unconscious emotionally laden memories – or more simply put, unconscious emotions – are (somehow) isolated from one's normal thought processes. This is the concept of a repressed or an unconscious mental state that is used in this book and so skepticism about guessing the content of primal memories or scenes is not relevant. No guessing or making-up memories must occur in therapy. This book relates only to memories that are brought to discussion in therapy by the patient (and not by guesses of the analyst).

Grünbaum's skepticism can be rephrased in the context of this chapter as follows: Although we can find a thematic affinity or a symbolic connection between certain memories or past emotional reactions and the current psychological symptom, does this thematic affinity mean that these memories cause symptoms? Can we say that repression has caused the symptom just because we can find such thematic affinities? In other words, what justifies the identification of a thematic or the symbolic connection with a causal connection?

Denying any causal significance whatsoever from the thematic affinity between symptom and memory does not do justice to the proliferation of such causal-thematic stories that are told by people who never even went to therapy and of stories that we read about in countless novels, including those written before *Studies on Hysteria*. Are all these causal stories simply wrong? Are these thematic affinities simply a coincidence?

On the one hand, one cannot help but notice that these stories often sound like excuses. People often tell such stories in such a way that relieves them from responsibility of their "maladaptive" behavior. These people present themselves to be in the grip of a primal memory that compels them to behave or to emotionally react in certain ways. That memory is the consequence of what happened to them during the primal scene as well as later in life. They claim to be suffering from trauma, which is at the end of the day not of their doing. They suffer from their pathological patterns, but what can they do about it?

These stories sound only half-convincing, since many of them do not refer to intrinsically traumatic events such as rape, torture, physical injury, or a natural disaster, and do not actually stand out in one's biography as objectively so much more disturbing than other memories or past events. How come only certain unpleasant events or memories leave such a distinct mark and define these people? In that sense, it is reasonable to suspect that there is something not quite right about such stories.

On the other hand, the thematic thread that runs through such narratives (whether primal scene or primal memory narratives) does not seem arbitrary or completely *ad hoc*. People are often puzzled about the meaning or the genesis of their pathological patterns and when they find a symbolic connection between those patterns and certain memories they often feel that the riddle has been solved. Even distinguished philosophers such as Rorty and de Sousa, who hardly mention Freud's name explicitly in their accounts of emotions, take recourse to thematic affinities.

Furthermore, although we can find many unpleasant events for each such person and wonder why *those* particular events or their redescribed memories would plausibly cause so much trouble, it is possible that the person in question will be particularly "touchy", as we say, about those particular memories. That is, although rational judgment may equalize the harm involved in many events or the emotional import of many memories, somehow people can be more selective as to which memories they feel very strongly about.

We need not rule out that there is some causal connection, yet to be explicated, between emotional (and other psychological) symptoms and certain unconscious emotions or emotionally laden memories, and that somehow thematic affinity is indicative of this causal connection (even if thematic affinity need not be *the* causal connection *per se*). The doubt is about characterizing those primal memories as traumatic, a characterization that is meant to account for their potential to cause a symptom. In other words, the doubt is about the source of the affective importance of those memories, here claimed to be the result of redescription.

Whether Ricoeur or Hacking would identify themselves as judgmentalists or sub-personalists about emotions, it certainly seems that according to both of them, the memory is rendered traumatic through its evaluation as traumatic, or at the very least that the reflective re-describing subject would be able to provide reasons for the reaction and claim that it is justified by the redescribed circumstances of the memory. There is no rational justification, however, for the great importance of memories such as Jonah's. And yet these are the memories that get imaginatively expressed in the symptom. The pertinent question is why or what about such memories makes them so "primal" if it is not their rational assessment as distressful? Why is their significance over-emphasized?

4. Is there another way to understand regression?

It is again in Freud's texts that we can find yet another approach to the thematic affinity between memory and symptom, which does not require the memory to be traumatic or *the* significant cause of the symptom. This option, however, also ultimately fails to explain the over-emphasis of those repressed emotionally laden memories.

Freud suggests the possibility that it is a "current conflict" that primarily causes the symptom.[35] To say it very generally, the subject is going through an emotionally difficult period, and partly expresses her distress through a psychological symptom. The psychological symptom, in turn, bears a symbolic connection with a certain memory. That is, the memory is mobilized to give symbolic shape, as it were, to the psychological symptom. The symptom stands for the current conflict, and in the case of distinctively emotional symptoms, the here-and-now emotionally salient features comprise the imaginative distortion of some there-and-then emotionally salient people or things. The expression "symbolic" presupposes that the here-and-now is not only seen as the there-and-then but also imaginatively represents the there-and then emotion.

If the subject remembers the memory that is imaginatively represented in the symptom, and recognizes the thematic affinity between that memory and her symptom, she may mislead herself to think that the affective aspect of the symptom originates from this memory. As the subject redescribes this memory in therapy, in the manner Hacking suggests, she re-lives that old memory as an emotional experience. But the experienced intertwinement of the redescribed memory and the affect conceals the fact that the affect experienced actually expresses the patient's emotional attitude toward the here-and-now conflict. As such, a subject recognizes the thematic affinity between the memory and her symptom, she can then falsely declare that memory to be the source of her troubles and perhaps further accuse the actual past scene as the principal cause of her illness.

In such cases, Freud talks about causality in the "regressive direction,"[36] where the current emotional distress mobilizes a past event to function as its cause. Regression here is not pictured as a force that pulls a memory to consciousness against the forces of repression, where the repression of the (reworked) memory is conceived as the principal cause of the symptom. Regression here is rather pictured as a way to mobilize the past for the disguised expression of one's current emotional distress about one's current situation in life, which is the principal cause of the symptom.

For Freud, the main opposition is between such regressive cases and the cases explicable in terms of a primal scene account or a developmental etiology, which presuppose a causality of a "forward direction," where an external event causes a change in the subject.[37] Most cases, Freud claimed in later writings, combine both kinds of causal factors:

> There are cases in which the whole weight of causation falls on the sexual experiences of childhood, cases in which those impressions exert

35 Freud, *From The History Of An Infantile Neurosis*, S.E., 17, 54. This line of thought has been associated with Jung, as a critic of Freud, even in Freud's time. See Freud's angry footnote on this matter of originality in this case study, known as the Wolf Man in Freud, *Infantile Neurosis*, 103.

36 Ibid., 54.

37 Ibid.

> a definitely traumatic effect and call for no other support than can be afforded them by an average sexual constitution and the fact of its incomplete development. Alongside of these cases there are others in which the whole accent lies on the later conflicts and the emphasis we find the analysis laid on the impressions of childhood appears entirely as the work of regression. Thus we have extremes of "developmental inhibition" and "regression" and between them every degree of co-operation between two factors.[38]

This quote describes a combination of an emotionally disturbing event and a regression to its memory via a current conflict. But in light of the critique of the primal scene account presented in this chapter, we can reformulate this suggestion in terms of a combination between a primal memory and its regressive mobilization. In any case, a primal memory can include both the memory of an event that was traumatic at the time of its occurrence as well as a redescribed memory that received its traumatic significance through that later redescription.

The primal memory account traces the origin of the here-and-now expressed affect in an emotionally laden memory alone. The "regressive causation" option ascribes the source of the affect only to a current conflict. These two options need not exclude one another. They can be considered as vectors of affect, so to speak, each works independently of the other and together they recombine into the resulting pathological emotion.

That is, the current situation may be the cause of some of the affect and so can the arousal of the old memory. The old memory need not be traumatic on this conception. It suffices that it be moderately unpleasant and thereby contribute to the total affect of the resulting occurrent emotion. The enlivened emotionally laden memory also makes certain features of the here-and-now emotionally salient, that is, selects the object of the occurrent emotion via symbolism. The symptom can thus be said to result from both.

This suggestion is appealing since it seems right that people would be more likely to suffer from emotional pathologies or other psychological symptoms when they are in any case not so happy with their lives. Furthermore, the combination option does not necessitate that the aroused memory be traumatic. In fact, it may be that when one remembers, the memory would seem more emotionally significant than it actually is, since the remembering subject would be re-living that old memory with additional affect, borrowed, so to speak, from the current conflict.

And yet one wonders why certain emotional conflicts mobilize past memories so as to express themselves during that time through a symptom, whereas other emotional conflicts do not (but instead, say, get repressed themselves and stay latent for a long time). Some people can remain

38 Freud, *Introductory Lectures*, Lecture 23, S.E., 16, 366.

completely functional and relatively symptom-free even through hard times to which they turn a blind eye. Imagine a woman who discovers the man she just married is a criminal. She moves out to a new place and files for a divorce, and during all that time does not miss a day of work, almost pretending that this never happened, or that it means nothing since she was deceived and can accept that and move on. And although such a person is clearly cutting too short emotions such as disappointment, heartache and self-doubt, she need not experience any emotional pathologies that would bother her. Some of us would describe this person as strong and resilient, using her capacity to turn a blind eye for her own mental benefit.

The singularity question for emotional pathologies remains unanswered: Why is this person experiencing this emotional pathology here and now? Why does one conflict give rise to a symptom by mobilizing an old memory and another doesn't? Is there something special about those current conflicts that do causally contribute to the formation of a symptom? Is there something special about the memories they mobilize? Any account that explains a pathological emotional reaction in term of a primal series of emotions about the present and the past would need to account for the affective significance of the emotions of the series. This understanding of regression does not provide the resources to explain this affective significance.

In the second part of the book, I propose an account for emotional pathologies that makes use of a notion of salience similar to the notion implied by the primal series accounts, namely that the manifest emotional pathology results from seeing a certain situation in terms of few other unconscious emotions. The account I propose is an imagistic and non-conceptual seeing-as account. The account proposed, although Freudian in spirit, resists the idea that here-and-now pathological emotions symbolize or represent those causally relevant old emotions. The affective processes proposed are used to explicate what exactly may be meant by "regression" and "repression" and what gives rise to thematic affinity. In particular, the proposed processes explain the source of the affective importance of the emotions in the relevant series. That is, they explain why these are the emotions that are brought to bear on a certain here-and-now situation and make certain aspects of it emotionally salient, thereby giving rise to a pathological emotion.

Part II

5 An associative account of emotions

The first part of this book presented a critical assessment of various philosophical approaches to the explanation of emotions. The critique of judgmentalism (Chapter 1.2) gave rise to various "seeing-as" accounts: the seeing-as conceptualists (Chapter 1.3.C), sub-personalism (Chapter 2), developmental accounts (Chapter 3), and narrative accounts (Chapter 4). The two latter accounts focus on emotional pathologies. Although these accounts differ in the causal processes they propose or in their identification of the terms in which one *sees* a situation *as* provoking this or that emotion-type, similar problems emerge in them.

None of the accounts can answer the singularity question: Why does this individual emote in this specific way here and now? Judgmentalism contradicts the familiar and ordinary fact that very similar external circumstances that can all be judged as fitting a certain emotion-type and as bearing on one's wants, needs and values, sometimes give rise to emotional reaction and sometimes not. The sub-personalists who assume a law-like connection between certain external circumstances and certain emotion-types either ignore the singularity question or attempt to add variables that would explain it – but with no success. And the seeing-as conceptualists, although they leave room for the possibility of singularity, do not have the resources to answer the singularity question.

All accounts also fail to provide a framework that would explicate the complex issue of reason-sensitivity, namely allow that some emotions be responsive to reason in reference to various notions of emotion appropriateness and some not. None of the accounts presented so far, in other words, does justice with our ordinary experience, which on the one hand shows that we often can dim down our emotions as a response to our deliberation against it, and that on the other hand demonstrates the relative prevalence of recalcitrance, stable or occasional. Although the developmental and narrative accounts (primal series accounts) specifically address the problem of emotional pathologies, both accounts rely on a peculiar overemphasis of certain emotional episodes or memories, an overemphasis that these accounts lack the resources to explain.

In fact, all the accounts presented thus far share a general common feature that gives rise to these problems: a subtle form of rationalism. The rationalism of judgmentalism, namely that emotions are evaluative judgments that embed operative reasons, has been recognized and widely criticized in the literature. The affective processes of the sub-personalists (mostly) escape judgment at the person level, and yet something very similar to judgment, an appraisal that results from "computational" inferences and equally "computational" reasons, emerges at the sub-personal level, giving rise to the very same problems that judgmentalism faces at the person level. Although sub-personalists conceive themselves as very different to judgmentalists and in particular as "causalists" rather than "rationalists," their sub-personal causal mechanism works in a way that maps onto rational processes. Indeed, for Prinz, the sub-personal processes explicitly depend on rational judgments which serve to re-calibrate elicitation files.

The conceptualist seeing-as accounts all hold that emotions have an intentional object, that they are characterized by "aboutness." And they also hold that the perceptions of those objects are conceptually and even propositionally structured, ending up as being seen-as dangerous or as a wrong etc. Just like the judgementalists, these philosophers hold that emotions are intentional states with conceptual content – evaluative states of mind. They insist that these emotions are not judgments and are only belief-like rather than embedding a full-blown belief, but any intentional state of mind with conceptual content is by definition rationally assessable and indeed reason-sensitive, since concepts exist in the space of reasons. Although this view allows for recalcitrance (and hence for irrationality), it is nonetheless a rationalist view insofar as emotions are presupposed to be inherently rationally assessable.

The developmental and narrative approaches, that is the primal scene and the primal memory accounts, not only talk about conceptually (and even propositionally) structured emotional scenarios, but further rely on identifying emotionally salient past scenarios or memories that are reasonably assessable as traumas, (redescribed) memories that clearly stand out in a person's biography as having an extremely intense emotional import that is incompatible with that person's self-image. Rationality sneaks in to all these primal series accounts, since at some stage or other in the affective processes they suggest an evaluation takes place. And yet, as is clear from Jonah's case, from Freud's case studies and also from the stories people tell about themselves in everyday life, the relevant memories need not be assessable in that way, no matter how redescribed.

Indeed, even the typical sexual childhood scenes that appear in some of Freud's case studies, such as witnessing one's parents having sex,[1] being beaten up by one's father as a punishment for some sexual behavior,[2] seeing

1 The Wolf Man in Freud, *Infantile Neurosis*, p. 39.
2 The Rat Man in Freud, *Notes Upon a Case of Obsessional Neurosis* [1909], S.E. vol. 10, pp. 155–249.

one's uncle in bed with one's cousin (not actually having sex, but somehow in an inappropriate situation),[3] need not be that traumatic nor have a long-lasting effect on one's psychology. Surely not all people that have undergone such experiences and redescribed them later in life as utterly immoral and disgusting must suffer from neurosis.[4]

Although Freud's social niche could be said to generally have issues with sexuality and color any such event as intensely disturbing, emotional attitude to sex (provoking guilt, shame and disgust) would have plausibly colored as objectionable many moments in the lives Freud's patients. It seems arbitrary to choose just one childhood occasion and ascribe to it or to its memory the status of *the* cause for a patient's symptoms or for her inhibitions and emotional issues with sexuality. People can be excessively touchy about certain details in their biography – but that touchiness is hard to explain when taking into consideration only one scene or memory under a certain description, circumscribed in certain spatio-temporal circumstances, and certain newly acquired norms of fit.

This reliance of the primal scene and memory accounts for pathological emotions on just one or few traumatic scenes or memories comes from their reliance on some kind of an evaluation or judgment. The unit for rational inference is a proposition, a description that serves to circumscribe external circumstances or a memory as well as a norm of fit, a belief about which emotion-type fits which type of circumstances. The computational inferences of sub-personalism connect here-and-now individualized perceived images or judgments with specific images (that is, visual or otherwise sensory schemas or memories) or judgments of a specific calibration file. The subtle rationalism of the accounts presented thus far, which in most accounts appears as an inferential feature, therefore yields another feature that all these accounts share: a form of atomism, whereby each emotional reaction is considered on its own, or at most it is considered together with those that are very similar to it and a few other memories of emotional episodes. Indeed, each emotion-type instantiation is also considered to result from a "discrete" mechanism[5] or from the similarity of the situation to a type-specific emotional scenario.

In this chapter, I propose an account that incorporates the insights of the previous accounts and makes two intertwined moves. The first is a move away from rationality and inference altogether. Unlike all the other approaches considered so far that involve at some stage an evaluation, whether at the person or the sub-personal level, the account I suggest does not include an activity of evaluation at all. This radical move away from inferentialism also results in a move away from atomism and toward a holistic picture of one's emotional life. Each emotional reaction depends on

3 Katarina in Freud and Breuer, *Studies on Hysteria*, S.E., 2, 125–134.

4 Grünbaum: "Is the occurrence of childhood seduction not equally frequent among those who are well enough never to see a psychotherapist?" Grünbaum, *The Foundations of Psychoanalysis*, 256.

5 E.g. D'Arms and Jacobson, "The Significance of Recalcitrant Emotion," 138, 139, 141.

many other emotions for its formation, and some of these need not be of the same emotion-type.

I here follow the methodology Rorty describes (see Chapter 3.1). That is, I first propose an account for pathological emotions and then generalize it for the rest of our emotional reactions. This chapter is respectively divided into two parts. The first part presents an account for emotional pathologies, which, much like the primal series accounts, takes recourse to unconscious emotions. My account further draws on Freudian insights about distinctively non-rational imaginative capacities.

The distinctive non-rational imaginative capacities I invoke in this chapter are associative capacities more or less familiar from early Modern philosophy, in particular from the philosophy of David Hume. Associations have since fallen out of fashion, precisely because of Hume's claim that they can account for the operations of the mind as a whole. Hume's associations are law-like "dumb" operations of the mind, whose role is to create the sense that there is a world of mind-independent objects at all; that is, to make the perceived world of objects comprehensible and reliably stick together. Hume's associations have this role, since he is constructing from a fragmentary experiential atomist starting point, a starting point this book does not share. Hume's associations were of course also meant to account for the sense that nature is stable, that induction is reasonable, and for general ideas (universals), personal identity (although here Hume admitted defeat) and much else.[6]

The associations proposed in this chapter operate blindly, but they are not law-like nor arbitrary and are therefore not entirely "dumb." They are simple imaginative relations: *similarity*, *inversion*, *part–whole and part–part* (of the same whole). Although the imagination does not follow reliable rules or laws, it is nevertheless a habitual capacity in such a way that we can ascribe to it patterns of association. Furthermore, imaginative connections are not arbitrary. Whether clichéd or idiosyncratic, connections such as similarities and inversions can be pointed out and described and others, at least those who know us well, may come to share them, that is, see the similarities or inversions that we can see and describe to them.

In the first part of this chapter, I introduce these imaginative associations and draw on Freudian insights to describe their manner of operation. I do not engage explicitly with Freud's texts, but I rely mostly on his work on dreams, jokes, the psychopathology of everyday life, and his papers on the unconscious and repression.[7] I then use those associative processes and

6 Hume, *A Treatise*, Book 1

7 Freud, *The Interpretation of Dreams* [1900], S.E., 4 and 5; Freud, *The Psychopathology of Everyday Life* [1901], S.E., 6; Freud, *Jokes and their Relation to the Unconscious* [1905], S.E., 8; Freud, "Repression" [1915], S.E., 14, 143–158. Freud, "The Unconscious" [1915], S.E., 14, 161–215; Freud, *Inhibitions, Symptoms and Anxiety* [1926], S.E., 20, 77–174. I also rely on *Studies on Hysteria*, and on Freud, "Screen Memories," [1899] S.E. vol. 3, pp. 303–322."

propose another explanation for emotional pathologies such as Jonah's recalcitrant resentment. The associative processes that cause emotional pathologies also serve to make sense of the manner in which aversive suppression turns into repression, and thereby de-mystify the concept of the Freudian unconscious.

In the second part of this chapter, I generalize the account for pathological emotions for all emotions. I propose that the associative processes of the imagination are the affective processes that yield emotional reactions in general. I then show that these affective–associative processes comply with the conditions and constraints that have been articulated in the previous chapters. Imaginative associations, I argue, are just enough to "stitch together" our emotional life in a way that allows for their singularity as well as their occasional stability in identifiable patterns, their sensitivity or insensitivity to reason, and their intelligibility (as fitting, or as cases of mixed feelings, or as understandable in light of past reactions).

i. THE ASSOCIATIVE EXPLANATION FOR PATHOLOGICAL EMOTIONS

1. Imaginative associations

A. Association, condensation, displacement; and similar faces

The associative processes of the imagination that this chapter relies on presuppose a few imaginative operations: the basic capacity of association, and the synthetic capacities of condensation (which works on associations) and displacement (which often accompanies condensation). Begin with the basic capacity of association. To say it most simply, the associative imagination separates or extracts objects or parts of objects from a wider context or situation and connects them to one another. The types of connections that concern me in this book are: *similarity*, *contrariety or inversion*, *part–whole*, *and part–part* (of the same whole).[8] The basic capacity of association is the capacity to produce imaginatively coupled fragments. When I say "fragments" I do not mean actual fragments, but imaginative fragments, objects and parts of objects that the imagination considers in isolation from their surroundings, as if "cutting" them out of the picture they are in. As will become clear in this chapter, I find this basic associative capacity in Freud's texts.

I claim that we imaginatively associate in that manner all the time. We do not get constantly distracted by noting such connections between objects or parts of objects, since this basic capacity of association operates *below the level of awareness*. By "below the level of awareness" I simply mean that associations occur automatically, without our conscious direction, and without our noticing them. In other words, basic associations are unattended to; we are blind to their ongoing operation.

This is inevitably an empirical claim and requires some kind of empirical support. As will become clear in this section, only indirect empirical support can be found for this speculative claim. But the hypothesis is nonetheless compelling, since it can make sense of a variety of mental phenomena such as getting and explaining jokes, experiencing and interpreting art, sudden and uninvited thoughts or memories that cross one's mind, and some of our communicative gestures. These are the kinds of experiences I appeal to in this section, so as to make plausible this claim about this associative activity of the imagination. Only in the next section, I show how associative processes relate specifically to emotions.

The first phenomenon I examine is the one described by Wittgenstein and discussed in Chapter 1.3.A in reference to Roberts, that is:

8 There may be other types of connections made by the associative imagination. In this book, however, I am only concerned with these four.

> I contemplate a face, and then suddenly notice its likeness to another. I *see* that it has not changed; and yet I see it differently. I call this experience "noticing an aspect."[9]

This kind of "suddenly" noticing a similarity is different to the basic association via similarity that occurs below the level of awareness. My imagination may associate one face to another via similarity blindly, without my noticing it. The experience Wittgenstein describes is different. In this case I am struck by the similarity of the two faces; it suddenly comes over me, as a passive affliction of a sensual experience. Such a similarity is not implicit or in the background of my ongoing comportment. Rather, my attention is focused on it, captivated by it, drawn to it.

I claim that *this* kind of explicit experience of similarity is the synthetic result of an *accumulation* of a few basic associations, which connect a few fragments of one face to a few fragments of the second face. That is, for such a similarity to strike us, *enough* similarities between different parts (nose, eyes) or aspects (expression, color) of two faces have accumulated, and the imagination further synthesized those accumulated associations.

What one suddenly becomes aware of and finds oneself focused on is the synthetic result of those accumulated associations, which in this case is the general similarity of the two faces considered as wholes. This synthesis of associations is precisely the "act of the imagination," that Roberts suggests (see Chapter 1.3), which makes one see one face in terms of another. As Wittgenstein says, although the face has not changed, one sees it differently, one notices an aspect that one has not noticed before. The synthesis of accumulated associations causally effects what the subject sees as salient and determines the terms that characterize this salience. That is, certain features of each face have become salient through their being seen in terms of certain features of the other face.

This synthetic associative capacity is what Freud called "*condensation*." As claimed above, we do not notice each basic or individual association on its own – if we did, then our attention would be flooded by the noticing of similarities all the time. It is when an accumulation of such associations, which connect a few fragments of an individuated whole with a few fragments of another well-circumscribed whole or a few wholes, pass a certain threshold – that they are synthesized and strike our awareness. In other words, the basic capacity of association blindly fragments and connects all the time and every now and again condensations of those associations surface to our attention.

There is another way in which a face seen in terms of another face may look different. If one face belongs to a person that I generally characterize as nice or bossy or feminine, I may see the other similar face as having that

9 Wittgenstein, *Philosophical Investigations*, §113.

general characteristic. For example, after watching Tina Fey imitate Sarah Palin on *Saturday Night Live*, I could not help laughing each time I saw Sarah Palin speak on TV.[10] Although I know that Palin takes herself seriously, I could not help but see her as if she were imitating herself. Or, when I meet a person that looks like someone I like, I cannot help but have an a priori good view about him.

Sometimes, then, condensation may be accompanied by what Freud called "*displacement*." That is, once the fragments of (at least) two separate wholes heavily connect and once the fragments of one whole are seen in terms of the fragments of (at least one) other whole, a general feature or aspect of the other whole may infect, so to speak, the first. The comic aspect of Fey may be "transferred" or "displaced" onto Palin, and the characteristic I like about my friend may be displaced onto the person I just met. Crucially, this does not mean that Fey has stopped being funny or that I don't like my friend any more. It is not as if the aspect of one whole has abandoned it and moved on to the other whole. Displacement is more like catching a cold – when I catch a cold from you we now both have a cold. Through the condensed connections, one whole infects another with some general aspect.

I would like to note in passing, that although Freud kept changing or even abandoning his theories and inventing new ones, he kept making use of condensation and displacement, what he called "primary processes," throughout his entire career. In the rest of this section I will focus only on condensation and I shall return to displacement in the third section of this chapter.

Condensations of this sort, such as the similarity between two faces, strike us. The awareness of the synthetic result of condensation is characterized by a phenomenology of passivity. When we suddenly notice a similarity between two objects or images, we feel that we suddenly become aware of something that is there anyway to see and now came to mind. In a certain respect, noticing a similarity via imagination resembles seeing an object through the senses. And yet the relation of perception to a physical object differs from the relation of the imagination to similarity.

If I see a cat in the bushes and you don't, we can go and check if the cat is there. If the cat is indeed in the bushes then we will both see it and can point at it. Perception is directly caused by the object and operates through the senses and if both of us face the same circumstances and have ordinary healthy eyesight, we will both see the same objects. Perception occurs in a third-personal space, where anyone would be sensually affected in the same way by the same objects under the same circumstances. Perception happens to us qua members of a species with certain shared capacities.

Pointing may suffice to communicate and share a perception, that is, to get someone else, anyone or everyone, to see what we see. Communicating

10 The award-winning sketch: "A Nonpartisan Message from Governor Sarah Palin & Senator Hilary Clinton." In Saturday Night Live, 34th season (SNL: September 13, 2008).

or sharing a similarity, on the other hand, invites and often depends on unpacking the condensation of a general similarity into individual associations. If I notice a similarity and you don't, I can try and show you this similarity but not by getting closer to the objects in question or by pointing at them. I will break down or analyze the general similarity between two faces, say, and show or describe various associations of coupled fragments, of the parts or aspects of the faces that are similar to one another. These are the explanatory "specifications" I briefly spoke about in the connection to Roberts' discussion of Wittgenstein in Chapter 1.2.

We cannot presuppose that everyone will immediately notice the similarity we see, whether it is the general similarity between two faces that initially struck our awareness in the kind of passive affliction described in this section, or whether it is a specific association of coupled fragments that we see as similar when we unpack the condensation that initially struck us into individual associations to which we now pay attention. And this is the case even if we all have equally good eyesight and are standing in exactly the same spot. The relation between the similarity I see and my imagination (through which I see it) is not a merely causal relation and does not occur in a third-personal space. Even if some people can see or come to see the similarity I see, it could be that some people will never see the similarity I see.

Neither is the relation between the imagination and the similarity that strikes us a rational relation. Condensations are not candidates for reassessment through deliberation in Moran's sense. If I see a similarity I cannot argue myself out of it. It is only if I find out that I misperceived one of the faces (e.g. it was dark or the face was behind a slightly distorting glass) and now I see it as basically a changed face that I will stop seeing the two faces as similar.

Furthermore, condensations of imaginative associations are an activity where the Anscombian why-question, which calls for purposive reasons, does not have application. Suddenly noticing similarities, being afflicted by their recognition, is not something we intentionally do or that serves any goal or purpose. Even if we play a game of seeing similarities and deliberately look for them for the purpose of playing a game, the similarities that we find also strike us. When we play such a game, we are effectively paying attention to the otherwise unnoticed blind associations that we make all the time anyway. Basic or individual associations that connect objects or parts of objects via similarity occur in the first instance below the level of awareness, but they can be called to attention.

Whether it is the condensation of associations that surfaced our attention or whether it is an individual association that we deliberately try to attend to, the Anscombian dialogue does not fit the occasion:

- Oh! Look at that!
- What? What are you seeing?
- I see that these faces are similar to one another!
- Why are they similar?

If that last question is answered in terms of means-end reasoning, it would require a special purposive context, such as:

- They are similar because these two are wearing masks so that we don't know who is who.

But this kind of special context did not guide my seeing that the two faces are similar in the way that my goal to poison the inhabitants of a certain house guides my pumping the water (see Anscombe's example in Chapter 1.1).

Otherwise we may answer this "why" by stating a cause rather than a reason, such as:

- They are twins.

That they are twins is the cause for them being actually similar, but it is not an answer to the "why" that asks about my being struck by their similarity.

Nevertheless, condensations are an activity about which one can ask a how-question or rather a show-me-how-question, a question that calls for specifications, specifications that explain how the faces are seen as similar.

- These faces are similar to one another!
- Show me how?
- Look – they have similar noses, similar facial expressions, similar hair.

These specific associations are between noses, facial expressions and hair, and not between a shape of a star or some other arbitrary shape that can in principle be painted on the cheek of one face as well as on the cheek of the second face. That is, the imagination connects objects or parts of objects that are perceptually salient.

If my interlocutor fails to recognize the similarity I try to show her, even after having specified the component or the more basic similarities, I will find it hard to let go of the demand for the recognition of another and say in frustration "can't you see?" If I am the only person in the world that sees that similarity I will begin to suspect my sanity. Associations and their condensations come with a built-in demand that others could, in principle, recognize the same connection. Each association presupposes that there is something there to be seen, which effectively means that there is at least one person out there in the world that can see the connections I see. Although people's visual imagination may be highly creative and idiosyncratic, and they may see original connections that nobody else has seen before, associations nevertheless come with the *demand for their sharability* with other persons.

In that sense, associations are *expressive* of *the way we see the world*. Indeed, when condensations strike us, even in this simple case of noting a similarity between two faces, we often explicitly share with others that we have just identified a similarity and seek their acknowledgement. Recall Kant's discussion of aesthetic judgment according to which one speaks with a universal voice, demanding others to agree with one's judgment, even if that judgment expresses a subjective experience.[11] This demand for sharability of imaginative associations also reminds us of Stanley Cavell's first-personal use of "we" in describing ordinary language grammatical connections.[12]

Imaginative associations thus operate in a *problematic second-personal space*. Ordinary utterances in language address another person in a linguistic communicative act that presupposes being understood.[13] Imaginative associations do not address anyone specific or anyone at all. They do not aim at conveying meaning or at being understood. They belong to the realm of what we may call expressive sensibility. They express an identification of a seeable connection, be it similarity, inversion, part–whole or part–part, and come with a built-in demand for their sharability, *without* assurance that they will indeed be shared with anyone specific. In that very thin and qualified sense – imaginative associations are normative.

Imaginative associations operate automatically and below the level of awareness, and unless they condense into a sensible or embodied mental state that forces its way, as it were, into our attention, they proceed unnoticed. Nevertheless, and even if imaginative associations are not something we do, associative activity does not qualify as sub-personal in the way the operations of the mitochondria in the cells do. Each individual association operates in this problematic second-personal space and it can, at least in principle, be brought to awareness or be called to attention, unlike the operations that cause reflex movement or the operations of mitochondria in cells. Imaginative associations, in other words, operate *at the person level*.

Condensations are sensible or embodied experiences that come over us together with the sense that they are expressive of our personal, even if sharable, imagistic take on the world. It is the kind of expressivity that calls for sharing, for showing to another, often through verbal expression, even if that other is oneself via some kind of inner speech, which in the case of suddenly noticing a similarity would be something like "hmm…!" perhaps with a little eye-brow lift.

Furthermore, condensations come with the feeling that they are explainable, and that what explains them is something we can become aware of.

11 This is what Kant calls "a claim to subjective universality" in the "Second Moment of a Judgment of Taste" in *Critique of Judgment*, trans. Werner S. Pluhar (Indianapolis: Hackett Publishing Company, 1987 [1790]), § 6–9.

12 Stanley Cavell, "Aesthetic Problems of Modern Philosophy," in *Must We Mean What We Say* (Cambridge: Cambridge University Press, 1998 [1969]).

13 Rebecca Kukkla and Mark Lance, *Yo and Lo* (Cambridge, MA: Harvard University Press, 2009).

This is why we try to unpack them into individual associations. And this is why some of us, verbal people with a critical capacity, tend to "rationalize" them. That is, if my interlocutor fails to see the similarity between two faces even after I unpacked the condensation and pointed to the various more specific similarities of two faces, I may continue to specify in what respects this nose is similar to that nose (e.g. they are both small and reddish) or in what respects this facial expression is similar to that facial expression (e.g. they both have a cheeky smile) and so forth. Importantly, however, those concepts (e.g. "small", "cheeky") were not originally written into the associations. Associations do not come with "subtitles" and do not have conceptual content, not even implicitly. Associations nevertheless lend themselves to this meaning-giving, since they are not arbitrary. In the faces example, as mentioned above, the specific associations are between noses, facial expressions and hair, and not between a shape of a star or some other arbitrary shape that can in principle be painted on one cheek as well as another. That is, the imagination connects objects or parts of objects that are perceptually salient, and perceptual salience can in turn be further described with concept-words.

I have implicitly assumed above that the associations one specifies after-the-fact in order to explain how or in what way one sees the similarity between the two faces, played a causal role in the process that led one to be struck by that similarity in the first place. But how can I know if the associations I specify after-the-fact were indeed the ones that causally brought about the similarity that struck me? Is it not possible that they are all new associations? Freud acknowledges the difficulty of retroactively ascribing a causal role to associations made after-the-fact.[14] Freud insisted that although some associations identified after-the-fact may be new, most of them did in fact play a causal role in the formation of the condensation. Freud did not explain this insistence, but the framework of imaginative associations can point to an answer.

Imaginative associations are not arbitrary or random. They connect perceptually salient objects or parts of objects, and the connection itself is there to be seen inasmuch as others can recognize it as well. I connect via similarity one nose to another because they are indeed similar in the sense that others should be able recognize the same connection. It is possible that there will be many similarities between two generally similar faces, and yet there will not be *that* many similarities, if those are constrained to connect perceptually salient objects or parts of objects, such as nose, eyes, ears, beauty mark etc. When I explicitly attempt to specify them, there may be similarities that I notice now and that did not play a causal role in the initial condensation, and yet it is likely that if I list many similarities now, at least some of them did play that causal role.

14 Freud, The interpretation of Dreams, S.E., 4, 280.

Furthermore, the associative imagination is a creature of habit.[15] Once an association is made once, it tends to repeat itself on later occasions. Once I see Sarah Palin as Tina Fey on one occasion, I find I cannot help but see Tina Fey in Palin's face almost every time I see Palin on TV. Habits are not laws or rules and they may come and go. But if a similarity between two faces has just struck me, then it is likely that I will repeat the associations I have just made beforehand, and that at least some of them will "come to me" again. That is, it is likely that when I deliberately try to identify specified associations, those I will find now will overlap with or echo some of the associations that indeed sustain the condensation. This after-the-fact unpacking of condensations is familiar from other contexts that I will soon explore, where it is clear to the subject that they are repeating previously made associations.

B. Broadening the scope of imaginative associations

The imagination may associate the fragments of the faces in the above example even if one face is not present. That is, the imagination may fragment, connect and synthesize not just presently perceived images, but also schematic images and memories of images. When the imagination works on memories, then, when it fragments or extracts an object or a part of an object from a memory – it is from an imagistic or otherwise sensual memory. Memories, as far as the associative imagination is concerned, do not come with "subtitles," and are not under description, as they are when one explicitly remembers and describes what one remembers as Hacking explains (see Chapter 4.1). Whenever I use the term "memory," I will thus always mean something like a photograph or a video-recording, or any other sense modality, and never a semantic memory. This means that there is indeed an ambiguity as to what the video recording or the photograph is of. But this is how the associative imagination – rather than the understanding – works.

As implied above for the case of memory, associations may operate not just on imagistic perceptions, schemas or memories but also on other sensual objects such as smells and sounds, whether experienced now, imagined schematically, or remembered. Inasmuch as those schematic or remembered images, smells, sounds etc. participate in associative processes without agential involvement or control, and since such images may strike one's awareness uninvited, they are like perceptions. Since the imagination may connect a perception to these other schematic and remembered images, I will call the fragmented perceived images (or smells or sounds), the sensual

15 Cp. Hume: "Men will scarce ever be persuaded, that effects of such consequence can flow from principles [of the imagination] which are seemingly so inconsiderable, and that the far greatest part of our reasonings, with all our actions and passions, can be derived from nothing but custom and habit". Hume, *A Treatise*, Book 1, Part 3, Sect. 10.

schemas and the imagistic or otherwise sensible memory-fragments by the inclusive term "images." And although the term "image" suggests a visual image, I include under this term all the other sense modalities as well.

Neither is the imagination confined to similarities. Other imaginative relations may strike us, such as inversions. For example, I notice the inversion that characterizes two cats, one black and one white, which brings out their color as a salient feature. Imaginative relations may serve to lead one from one image to another. For example, I see someone wearing the same glasses my husband wears and my imagination leads me, through a part–whole relation, to see (with my eyes closed) a schematic image of my husband or an image of him from a memory. As said in the beginning of the chapter, the kinds of associations that are relevant to the imaginative activity described in this book are fourfold: similarity, inversion, part–whole, and part–part.

I now want to make the further claim that the imagination may associate not only images with images but it may also associate *words* to one another as well as images with words. Indeed, I claim that *the associative imagination is blind to the difference between words and images.* Crucially, however, *as far as the imagination is concerned – words are not semantic items.* The imagination regards words as objects or parts of objects. There are two ways for words to be objects: (1) words qua marks and noises; and (2) words qua the imagistic or sensory schemas or memories that are *in wake of* the semantic item. The word "father" for example qua semantic item is surrounded with a halo of private associations such as schematic images or images from memory of *my* father, an (admittedly stereotypical) image of a man with a suit and tie sitting at the head of the dinner table, a memory-image of a strong man holding me tight when a big wave approaches in the ocean, and so forth. As will be emphasized in the next sub-section, these are precisely the private associations that are excluded from consideration when one treats words as semantic items that are used in propositions that can be true or false.

Verbal expressions or words or images also come to mind spontaneously, without deliberately directing our thoughts to them. Those words or images too are the result of condensation. Certain fragments of the here-and-now situation may connect heavily enough to a certain word or image, which would then come to mind or strike our awareness. For example, my daughter asked me what the word "to brood" meant. I immediately had the passing image of Angel (from the TV series *Angel*) on my mind.[16]

Usually we ignore such associations. Although we may recognize that we had this passing thought or that a certain image has suddenly come to our minds and then another one consecutively, we usually do not bother to

16 An American television series, a spin-off from the television series *Buffy the Vampire Slayer*. *Angel*, created by Joss Whedon and David Greenwalt, 5 seasons (The WB: October 5, 1999 – May 19, 2004); *Buffy the Vampire Slayer*, created by Joss Whedon, 7 seasons (UPN: March 10, 1997 – May 20, 2003)

specify how these two impressions or thoughts connect imaginatively. In fact, we are rarely motivated to verbally express such a connection. We simply disregard it as meaningless, since the two consecutive images or words do not rationally follow from one another.

It is less easy to do so out loud. If instead of just explaining to my daughter what the word "brood" means I start talking about Angel, and if Angel has nothing to do with our earlier conversation and the conversation seems to have now lost its original thread, my daughter or perhaps my husband may ask, "What made you think of Angel?" This question presupposes that the thought of Angel did not come out of nowhere to my mind. Although reason did not lead me to it, something did.

I trust that the "what made you think of that?" question is familiar to most readers from ordinary experience. When we ask this question we assume that although the expressed thought does not reasonably relate to the here-and-now conversation or situation, something – an image or a word from the here-and-now or the just-a-moment-ago – nevertheless causally triggered the expressed thought, and that this triggering relation is not arbitrary. Somehow, we assume, what was said did not come out of nowhere but is (imaginatively) connected with something else and that this connection caused the expressed thought to appear in that person's mind in the first place.

Sometimes, if one bothers to answer the "what made you think of that?" question, one can trace the associations that led to it. If I wonder why indeed am I thinking of Angel, or rather why his image came into my mind, I remember that Angel is often said to be "brooding" on the show. Indeed, the image that came to my mind was of Angel in a typical brooding position at his desk. I then further remember that this image is from a scene where Angel's colleagues and friends are staring at him from the window and Cordelia saying "He's brooding" (this may not have been her exact words but that is how I remember it). The word "brood," *qua sound or noise*, and the image of Angel connect through a part–part relation. The word, here considered as a sound, and the image of Angel at his desk are both parts of the same whole, the scene I saw on TV years ago.

In fact, I further remember, I heard the word "brood" for the first time on that TV show. That memory of myself watching that show in the late 1990s feeling puzzled (by the word "brood") also connects with my daughter now via similarity in the respect that we both did not know the meaning of the word "brood." In a way, I then explicitly think to myself via inner speech, since English is not my native tongue, I still feel like a child in respect to some English words. Providing these themes of childhood and language-learning does not trace any causal process but may perhaps give me some satisfaction, as a person who appreciates meaning, and who may be otherwise frustrated with a collection of associations.

The fragments of the here-and-now situation: my daughter, the word "brood," and the puzzlement or questioning, connected with fragments of the there-and-then experience of watching Angel: myself, Angel, and the word "brood." These connections condensed into an image of Angel, which then struck my awareness. One can (although not always) unpack condensations after-the-fact and become aware of these connections and nature of the connections (similarity, inversion, part–whole, and part–part) and further provide the respects in which these connections hold – even if those respects were not originally causally operative but result from after-the-fact thematizing. The "what made you think of that?" question is thus a how-question or show-me-how question, which calls for explanatory specifications that in turn lend themselves to thematic meaning-giving.

Thoughts or words or images that strike us suddenly or that come to our minds without our conscious control are such condensations. We usually call such thoughts that come to mind without conscious direction "associations," although they are in fact the condensation of what I have been calling basic or individual associations. But I will call all of them "associations," since individual associations may too come to mind when we unpack condensations after-the-fact.

This practice of unpacking condensations is especially familiar when it comes to what we may call creative condensations that synthesize associations into a new whole. Some game shows display an image of a face that is composed of a few faces of famous people and ask the viewers to recognize who those people are. The strange looking face is a condensation of a few faces, that is "pictorially arranged" into a new synthesized face.[17] When we look at such an image we explicitly try to break it down to parts and find what (whole) face they are a part of. In this case, we are unpacking the condensation of part–whole associations another person has deliberately synthesized.

Perhaps the most obvious example for unpacking condensations occurs when we explain jokes. As Freud says, jokes are condensations of imaginative associations that strike us with laughter.[18] We laugh precisely because we notice how the words of the joke (or the images in case of visual comedy) connect with certain images or other words. This is what is meant by getting a joke.

Take for example a joke my daughter used to tell. Whenever she heard the German word "Vater," she would say "Farter!" Here the two words *qua marks and noises* associate via similarity of sound. They are associated through phonetic (and also visual) resemblance. In the previous example of Angel and "brood," "brood" was also considered as a sound in a part–part relation.

Another association between "Vater" and "Farter" is an inversion. In the wake of the semantic item "Vater" is an image of my daughter's father speaking in an authoritative tone, telling her to do her homework, and also

17 "Pictorial arrangement" is another primary process that sometimes, not always occurs in dreams according to Freud: Freud, "On Dreams" [1901] S.E., 5, 631–685, section 7.

18 E.g. Freud, *Jokes*, 19–23.

an image of him sitting on *his* chair reading his book with a serious face, and also an image of all the fathers of the kids at her school standing around the classroom on father's day with their suits and ties, and so forth. In the wake of the semantic item "Farter" is an image of a bad smell,[19] of the funny sound, a visual memory of one of my daughter's friends farting loudly by accident and everybody laughing while he blushes in embarrassment, and so forth. The association here connects one or more such images of "Vater" with one or more such images of "Farter." The association is of inversion.

And if I want to ruin the joke even more than I already have, I can continue to analyze it and say that it is an inversion because the images in wake of "Vater" inspire respect and dignity whereas the images of "Farter" inspire the contrary. When explaining how these images relate to another through inversion, I can provide the respects in which they hold, which in this case is the concept or the conceptual theme "dignity." But the association itself in its causal operation is not semantically linguistic and did not come with the subtitle "dignity." But imaginative associations, although imagistic and non-conceptual, nonetheless lend themselves to such thematizing.

Someone who didn't get the joke may ask us, "Why are you laughing?" or "What's funny?" or "How is this funny?" That is, we can ask the show-me-how question for jokes that calls for the unpacking of its condensation. If we try to explain what was funny many of us will be able to spell out the relevant imaginative connections easily. When we explain a joke, we are tracing the associations whose condensation has just made us laugh, and repeat them, as it were, much more slowly as we verbally express them. If we specify the associations that in the first instance were automatically made and further provide respects in which these connections hold, we will most likely kill the joke. It is the condensed nature of the connections as they penetrated our attention, the fact that they all struck us at once, that made them funny.

Although we normally disregard our spontaneous associations, there are specific contexts where some of us have the habit of explicitly attending to them as they occur, as they strike our awareness. This special attention is familiar to anyone who views a work of art, reads fiction or a poem, or watches a film, with the prospect of criticizing or giving some interpretation of it.

When I watch a movie or a TV show I "listen" carefully to my inner speech (the words and phrases that come to my mind) and to my imagistic associations. I trust my associations not to be random or meaningless. I take the trouble to specify them and further provide respects in which they hold. This is the way I begin to think about the movie, make sense of it. In other words,

19 A reminder that I use the term "image" in a generalized sense to include not just visual images but other sense modalities as well.

I treat the film (or any work of art) as the synthetic result of such associations. Effectively, by "listening" to my associations as I face a work of art I am attempting to unpack the condensation that supports that work of art.

This trust of or attention to one's associative imagination when facing a work of art has to do with the way that work itself was made. The synthetic result of an artist's imaginative associations enjoys a special kind of unity. Poems and paintings, films or installations are very well arranged synthetic wholes. This is because the associations the artist used to construct their work of art are not entirely "dumb." An artist or a poet selects in a self-aware manner a significant portion of the associations that are condensed into the work.

That is, the poet identifies many (if not most) of those associations and thinks about the respects in which they hold *before* their place in the poem is secured. Such associations *do* come with "subtitles." Pre-articulated they become communicative; they address the viewer or reader; they convey meaning.[20] It is in this manner that similarities can become metaphors or similes or symbols and it is in this manner that part–whole relations can become metonyms. In the next section, I shall demonstrate through a specific example why imaginative associations such as part–whole should not be confused with semantic and communicative literary means such as metonyms.

These intentionally planted associations and the way they interrelate may thus exhibit aesthetic depth. For example, Captain Beefheart's song title "Ice Cream for Crow" includes the planted inversion in respect of color, which brings out the color white as a salient feature of "ice cream," and the color black as a salient feature of "crow." Note that in this example, words are considered as designators of images, as they often are in poems.

My condensation of associations need not be exactly as yours or as the artist's, and yet they are likely to overlap to some extent. This is because associations trace what is there to be associated and the perceptually salient objects or parts of objects (including words qua objects) that are being connected are perceptually salient for other people from the same social niche who share certain cultural references.

It could be that some imaginative associations are widely shared among many subjects across many cultures, languages, and historical eras. It could be the case, for example, that most or even all of us associate an image of eating with the associations in the wake of the words "destruction" and "desire."[21] Many other associations are shared or are sharable among

20 For a view of art as a form of communicative action in a similar sense see David Macarthur, "Remarks on 'Architecture is a *Gesture*' (Wittgenstein),"*Paragrana* 23, no. 1 (2014), 88–100.

21 This is perhaps the plausible source for and the salvageable insight of the otherwise strange and inflated theory of Melanie Klein about implausibly elaborate fantasies and beliefs of infants who do not even have beliefs at that young age: Melanie Klein, *Love, Guilt and Reparation and Other Works 1921–1945* (London: Hogarth Press, 1975), Chapter 17.

subjects who speak the same language and come from the same social niche. This sharability causes many of us to laugh at the same jokes, enjoy the same art works, and have our favorite literary critics.

We trust our associations when we face a work of art precisely because we assume that the associations we have will overlap to some extent with the associations of the artist who made the work, whether these were deliberately "planted" associations of the artist or the artist's automatic and unaware associations. And we trust the work inasmuch we expect that spelling out these associations will be aesthetically rewarding. Alternatively, and this is especially the case for works of art from a different time and place, we assume that our associations are, or at least can be or should be, sharable with other viewers that are in some way like us, a linguistic and cultural likeness or a likeness of sensibility. Indeed, as many have noticed, we often seek to express the meaning we find in an artwork and expect people to see what we see. This is the source of what Kant called "subjective universality" of aesthetic judgment mentioned above. This sharability is also the source of Cavell's qualification of Kant when he speaks of an inherently subjective judgment that is at the same time a search for community.[22]

The more we know of a person, the more sharable and overlapping our associations would be. Many of us can make private jokes with our partners and closest friends or say to them very short phrases or even just one word or a facial expression to convey a message, as if by way of a code, invented and used for the first time with no prior agreement. The code here consists in the trust we have that those closest to us will make a similar imaginative association between what we just said and some idea, the idea that we want to secretly convey.

We are accustomed to "listen" to our associations when we attend to what another person is expressing through their art, their jokes or their "codes." We trust our own associations in such cases because we are thereby effectively trying to repeat or reconstruct someone else's association, that was originally invested with meaning, that was deliberately selected by the artist or joker or close friend because the respects in which the connection holds are somehow deep or funny or useful.

Our own private, spontaneous, and purely imagistic imagination does not normally yield such well-arranged unities nor make especially profound connections that merit the attention of others, even if there are some exceptions, such as slips of the tongue, those mistakes in speech that people note as meaningful and as revealing of one's secret thoughts or emotions. It is a

22 Stanley Cavell, *The Claim of Reason* (Oxford: Oxford University Press, 1979), 20. For elaboration of Cavell's position here see David Macarthur, "Cavell on Skepticism & the Importance of Not-Knowing". *Conversations: The Journal of Cavellian Studies* 2, (2014). On-line: https://uottawa.scholarsportal.info/ojs/ index.php/conversations/issue/view/222. There is much more to say about imaginative associations and art-works, but I will not pursue this here.

"slip" precisely because it was not intentional or semantic to begin with. But sometimes, slips can be accidently quite well arranged, and in such cases they can be mistaken for a deliberate joke.[23] Usually, however, the condensations that strike our awareness do not enjoy the unity of creative condensations. Private associations need not make an impression on anyone; they are not selected for their merits, and indeed are not selected at all – they are done blindly. This is why, even if it is possible to identify associations as similarities, inversions, part–whole, and part–part relations, and to conceptually describe some respects in which these imaginative connections hold, this verbal exercise will not normally qualify as aesthetically deep or funny. That is why it is often (although not always) easy to ignore passing thoughts and images that suddenly come to our minds as meaningless background noise.

C. *The non-rationality of imaginative associations*[24]

The connective capacity of the imagination is strictly non-rational or, more precisely, non-inferential. The unit of inferential reasoning is a proposition. It takes in proposition(s) and produces a conclusion in the form of a proposition. What are propositions? They are linguistic sentences comprised of words, and they are considered only insofar as they may have a truth-value and can play a part in inferential relations with other such sentences.

Two different sentences that have the same truth-value and occupy the same place in an inferential belief system would be two verbal forms of the same proposition. Words, as far as reason is concerned, have meaning only insofar as they appear in a sentence that can count as the verbal form of a proposition. As Frege says: "never to ask for the meaning of a word in isolation, but only in the context of a proposition."[25]

When reason works well, its inferences are truth preserving, indeed, that is their purpose. Even when we misuse or abuse reason, we do it to fool ourselves (or others) and convince ourselves (or others) that we are right, that truth is on our side. That is why it is important to distinguish between operative reasons and objectively valid reasons (see Chapter 1.1). Reason has its psychological aspect, since we all engage in reasoning and take certain considerations to be in favor of this or that belief or action. But importantly, reasons also have their objective aspect, according to which

23 See Lacan's discussion about jokes and slips of the tongue: Jacques Lacan, *Le séminaire de Jacques Lacan, Livre V, Les formations de l'inconscient*, ed. Jacques-Alain Miller (Paris: Seuil, 1998 [1957–1958]).

24 This section has enormously profited from conversations with David Macarthur, who noted the inversion between the operations of imaginative associations as articulated in this book and Frege's principles of enquiry: Gottlob Frege, *The Foundations of Arithmetic: The Logico-Mathematical Enquiry into the Concept of Number*, trans. J. L. Austin (Oxford: Basil Blackwell, 1980 [1884]).

25 Frege, *The Foundations of Arithmetic*, p. x.

they may be either good or bad reasons. Operative reasons are always up for scrutiny and can always be held to standards of truth and justification so that we can determine whether or not they are objectively valid reasons.

Once we obey Frege's principle, "always to separate sharply the psychological from the logical, the subjective from the objective,"[26] we can start talking about concepts rather than words. Concepts are the abstract counterpart of words. They partake in propositions that in turn inferentially connect with other propositions in a system of beliefs, which is, at least ideally, objectively valid. The meaning of concepts is twofold. On the one hand they derive their meaning from the place they occupy in an inferential belief system (*de dicto*). On the other hand, their sense also includes the actual objects they serve to designate in any particular use of the relevant words (*de re*). Proper names are thus concepts *de re*. There is thus a clear distinction between concepts and images of objects, where the latter may be considered as the sense of the former, but the two should never be confused. Only concepts take part in reasoning. As Frege says: "never to lose sight of the distinction between concept and object."[27]

The associative imagination disobeys the three Fregean principles. The imagination considers words *in isolation* from their place in a proposition. In fact, this kind of fragmentation is precisely the condition of the connective imaginative activity I have described above. The imagination may associate such de-contextualized words *subjectively* with other such words that are also extracted from their place in a proposition.

The associative imagination does not operate according to rules, certainly not logical rules. Even when an imaginative association appears to be logical it is in fact psychological. For example, an association between the word "mother" (qua marks and noises) and an image which takes part in the halo around the semantic item "mother" – say a schematic image of one's own mother – is not a matter of logical identity "mother" = "mother." It is a psychological connection.

In fact, as will become clear in this chapter, the imagination always sees the subjective in the objective. When I see a similarity between two faces, when I see one face in terms of another, I see the same (objective) face, and yet, as Wittgenstein says, I see it differently. That is, imaginative salience is on the one hand of something that is objectively out there and on the other hand a result of subjective associations. Imaginative associations, in other words, provide the terms in which certain features of the (objective) situation become (subjectively) salient. There is no distinction between subjective and objective as far as the imagination is concerned.

Finally, as has been claimed and exemplified in this section, the imagination is blind to the difference between words and images, between the abstraction of words (concepts) and objects or images, between thing and

26 Ibid.
27 Ibid.

property. The imaginative connection between the word "mother" and the schematic image of my mother is not a semantic connection of intentional designation. This connection does not convey any de re meaning. It is a causal connection. But once this connection is verbally expressed or described, it might seem as if the connection is semantic. But in the first instance, the imaginative connection does not designate anything.

As emphasized in the previous sub-section, insofar as the imagination is concerned words are not concepts. They can be considered as mere marks and noises. And the only affinity they bear to their semantic counterpart is their connection to the imagistic or otherwise sensory schemas or memories that are in the wake of the semantic item.

It is almost as if Frege formulated his principles of enquiry in order to exclude from it any recourse to private imaginative associations. Elsewhere Frege says:

> An indicative sentence often contains, as well as a thought and the assertion, a third component over which the assertion does not extend. This is often said to act on the feelings, the mood of the hearer or to arouse his imagination. Words like "alas" and "thank God" belong here. Such constituents of sentences are more noticeably prominent in poetry, but are seldom wholly absent from prose. They occur more rarely in mathematical, physical, or chemical than in historical expositions. What are called the humanities are more closely connected with poetry and are therefore less scientific than the exact sciences which are drier the more exact they are, for exact science is directed toward truth and only the truth. Therefore all constituents of sentences to which the assertive force does not reach do not belong to scientific exposition.[28]

Fragmentary, psychological, and blind to the distinctions between subjective and objective, words and images – the associative imagination is a distinctively non-rational, non-inferential, and non-conceptual capacity. The synthetic capacity of the associative imagination that condenses such associations into one whole is therefore also distinctively non-rational.

When characterized through the comparison to reason, imaginative associations appear to have a merely negative characterization as not rational. This might seem as if the connections I am calling imaginative are merely the leftovers, so to speak, of our rational thought. As if there are inferential connections, and then there is all the rest of which we can say nothing. It is true that we cannot use rationality to describe imaginative connections, and yet it is false that this means imaginative associations are merely negatively characterized. Similarities, inversions, part–whole, and part–part relations can be *shown* to others, and others can agree that these are indeed the

28 Gottlob Frege, "The Thought: A Logical Inquiry," *Mind* 65, no. 259 (1956): 295.

connections instantiated. Imaginative associations are a positively different species of a sharable and thinly normative activity of the mind, that lend themselves to what I have been calling "thematizing," an activity through which one can add-on a conceptual meaning to originally non-conceptual associations. I claimed in the beginning of this section that we imaginatively make such associations all the time and that when enough associations to fragments or aspects of the same whole accumulate, their condensation (which may be pictorially arranged) reaches one's awareness. The condensed associations, thoughts, and images that come to mind, do not happen at every moment, but if one is attentive to one's wandering mind one discovers that they happen quite often.

I cannot think of a scientific experiment that would verify this claim, as I cannot think of how one would measure the private thoughts and associations that come to another person's mind. There may be such a way, some kind of mind reading, but I cannot think of one. I can only refer to common knowledge as well as to my own experience of my own passing thoughts and impressions that spontaneously come to my mind without any conscious direction and ask the reader to do the same.

Has anyone tried to stare or to close their eyes and think of absolutely nothing, to have no words or images cross their mind? Can anyone honestly say that they are able to empty their minds from passing thoughts, memories, images and the like? People go all the way to Peru or India to try and achieve such emptiness. Meditation aims precisely at getting one's mind to stop associating. Indeed, the meditation tapes I heard explicitly ask the listener to gently push aside thoughts that come to mind. The tapes, however, do not include mere silence.

Some of those methods include humming a particular musical note, others repeating a word (via inner speech) and yet others ask people to focus on certain bodily sensations. In other words, those methods force attention on a specific image (usually a specific perceived bodily sensation) or word so as to block the associative imagination. The block could perhaps prevent or at least put an obstacle on the associative formation of coupled fragments. If I focus on only one perception or word, I am less likely to notice other particulars in my environment. That is, I am less likely to fragment the rest of my environment and connect it with other images or words.

And yet, since imaginative associations work below the level of awareness, it is quite possible that I continue to associate nonetheless. But, if enough associations accumulate and condense into the same thought or image, then, perhaps, if I am already focused on some particular word or image (in the generalized sense introduced above that also includes perceived sensations) I am less likely to attend to my condensed association. Although it may fleetingly strike my awareness, I may not even notice it. If I focus on only one image or word, there will be little to no room for another to come to my attention, or rather no moment available for another image or word to pop-up in the temporal sequence of my inner experience.

Blocking associations requires continuous effort of selective attention. One's attention needs to somehow steer away from elements of the environment that would otherwise trigger associations as well as maintain a focus that would block one's capacity to notice an association that would otherwise strike one's awareness.

Even when we direct our thought deliberately via reasoning or reach high focus and concentration when solving a problem or making an argument, imaginative associations may sneak in. Sometimes these associations may even help with our rational tasks, since they fragment an image or a word from the problem we are thinking about and therefore relate to it, and since similarities, inversions, part–whole, and part–part relations are not random. Their accumulation or condensation may turn out to be insightful.

To sum up this section I claim that each of us may be ascribed with a rich imaginative or associative network of fragmented images and words, that is in constant flux. Every time we make a new association either through our own originality or by repeating or assimilating someone else's association, the network changes a bit.

Some of the associations in an imaginative network may be cross-culturally shared or sharable. Many of those associations are culturally shared or sharable. The more we circumscribe the group of people in space and time or in age or social class, the more comparable the people in the group – the more associations they will share. Although no two people share an entire associative network and many associations are idiosyncratic to a specific person, even those, once identified and described *should* be sharable with another person, even if that sharability is not assured nor presupposed.

This chapter's main claim is that affective processes are associative processes of the imagination. Associative processes can be affective when they connect elements from the here-and-now situation to latent emotions. Latent emotions, I remind, are dispositional states that have a describable aspect and an affective aspect that remains dormant, unfelt, or non-episodic, unless they are somehow enlivened, an enlivenment which, I will claim, occurs through associative processes.

These affective processes comply with all the conditions articulated at the end of Chapter 2. They are automatic (occur without conscious or explicit direction), non-propositional and non-inferential, and operate below the level of awareness. They are indeed non-linguistic and non-conceptual as demanded by Griffiths, but they do make use of words, only that those words do not function qua semantic items. Associative processes are nonetheless expressive and describable and occur in the problematic second-personal space described above. Their sharability, which comes with a thin or a weak normativity and the possibility to call them to attention renders them *person level* processes.

This means that on the proposed account, emotions are not intentional states with conceptual content. When I talk about the describable aspect of the emotion, then, I talk about the emotionally salient object of the emotion, the emotionally salient people or things in the here-and-now situation, and not about the intentional object of the emotion or its intentional content. And so I use the terms "describable aspect," "object," and "emotionally salient people and things" interchangeably. By "object" I do not mean to designate anything intentional nor do I presuppose targeting, an issue I shall return to in the second part of this chapter, which presents the full account that covers all emotions, whether pathological or not. Even if this is an imagistic seeing-as account, I nevertheless claim that it can also explain emotions that involve thoughts. There is thus a question about how to understand "complex emotions" that involve thoughts (see Chapter 2.1.C) on this non-conceptual associative account. I assume for now that this explanation is possible, and will allay certain concerns about "complex" or "cognitive" emotions in the next part of this chapter (5.2.B).

2. Enlivening and synthesizing emotions: the associative explanation for emotional pathologies

In Chapters 3 and 4 I have spoken about latent emotions, whether conscious or unconscious and the possibility of their being enlivened. I now propose that it is the associative imagination that enlivens latent emotions. The associative imagination, which fragments and connects, may also fragment and connect elements from the describable aspect of a latent emotion. If the latent emotion becomes heavily connected with fragments of the here-and-now situation, if enough such associations accumulate, then the emotion is enlivened. Its affective aspect is triggered and experienced and its describable aspect (the emotionally salient object of the emotion) reaches awareness and, if it is not an unconscious latent emotion it may be described and expressed in words.

Say that a few years ago, I was envious of my colleague when she got a position I was also applying for. I have since then been promoted to a similar position and I enjoy a healthy and productive work relationship with my colleague. I basically forgot about that old envy. In fact, that envy is no longer fitting. The situation in which it arose is over.

Then one morning, I see from a distance my colleague and my boss, who rarely comes to the office, saying hello to one another and exchanging a handshake. I am suddenly overcome by the feeling of envy that my colleague got the promotion more than a year before I did. I now remember seeing through the glass walls of my boss's office the warm handshake he gave her at the time, which was enough for me to realize back then that she got the promotion I wanted for myself. I now remember, re-experience, and refeel the envy I felt back then.

How come I was suddenly "reminded" of that old emotion and felt it again? This is not the first time since my colleague's promotion that I see my boss say hello to my colleague or give her a handshake. Why was my envy enlivened here and now and not the previous time I saw them exchange a handshake? My connective imagination may have previously fragmented similar handshakes and connected them with that old scene I saw from the glass wall through a part–whole relation, and yet my envy was not enlivened and I did not become aware of it and re-feel it. Why now? According to the associative explanation, what makes this moment different to others is that now more associations have accumulated that together cause the old envy to be enlivened.

My imagination fragments the smiles they exchange in their "hello," associating them by way of *similarity* with the smiles they exchanged when my colleague got her promotion at the time. These warmhearted smiles also connect, by way of *inversion*, to the fake smile I received from my boss just a few minutes ago when he said hello to me.

I further associate through *similarity* the boss's current visit with his previous visit that took place last month (the boss does not come often to our office since he works at a different building in another part of town). A new client came for a meeting and my boss introduced my colleague to that client before me and so she shook his hand first. That imagistic sequence of introductory handshakes from a month ago – first my colleague and then me – connects through *part–part* relation to the handshake I saw a few years ago through the glass wall. That is, the old promotion handshake is a part of a situation stretched over time in which first my colleague gets this promotion handshake and then months later I get a promotion handshake. And the current handshake (that is the trigger for the current enlivenment of the envy about the distant past) connects with both these handshake memories (from a year ago and from a month ago) through *similarity* in a straightforward imagistic sense as well as in the respect that all these handshakes made me feel that the boss favors my colleague over me. It is the synthesized or condensed accumulation of these connections from the here-and-now to the past emotion that enliven it and bring it to awareness as can be seen in Figure 5.1.

Now one may be tempted, after identifying all these connections and providing the respects in which they hold, to say that there is a symbolic connection in some broad sense between the here-and-now situation and the memory of the scene where I realized my colleague has won the promotion I wanted. Indeed, after the specification of the relevant associations we find that there is a thematic affinity between those scenes as well as with the scene from a month ago with the new client: they all seem indicative of my boss's favoring my colleague over me, they imply that my colleague is more successful than me and that I am always a step behind my colleague.

Crucially, however, this connection is not symbolic or representational. The here-and-now does not stand for the there-and then. The here-and-now was not selected to convey any meaning. This thematic affinity, although it can be provided after-the-fact, did not cause my envy to be enlivened at that specific moment. It is the accumulation of such connective associations to

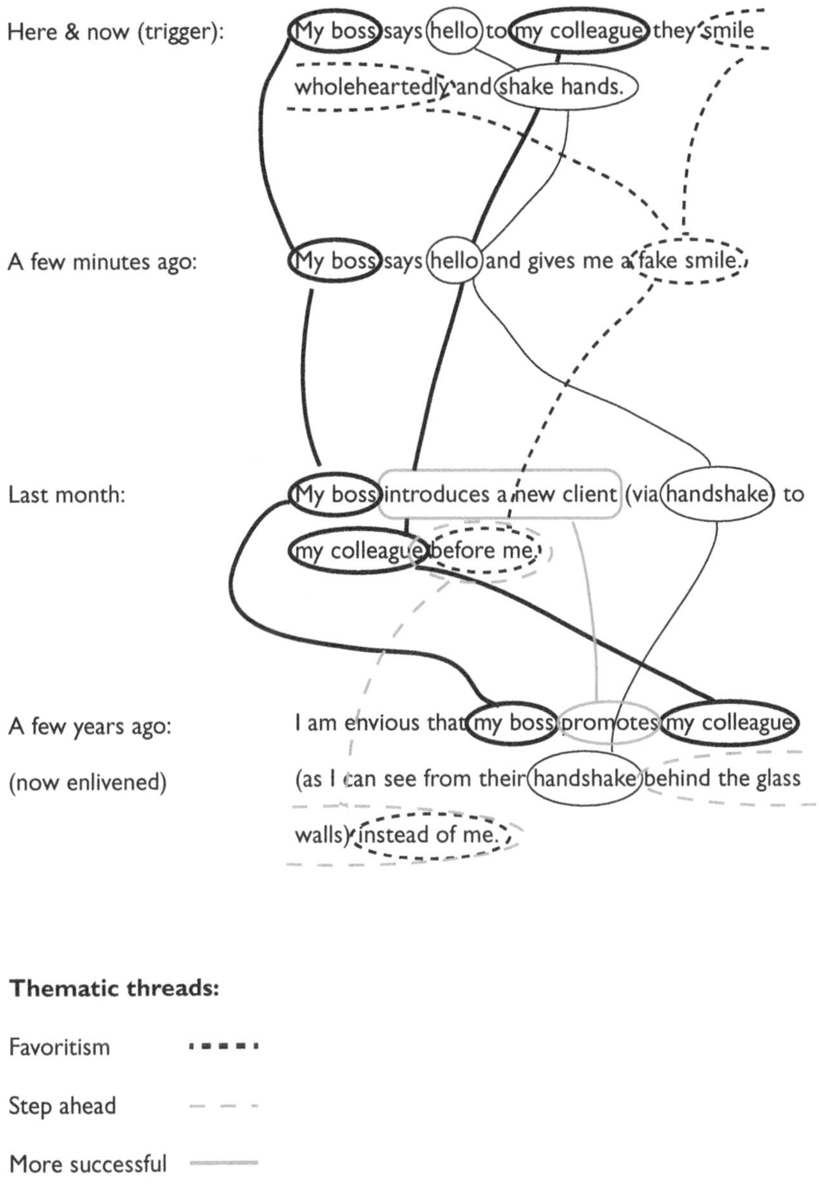

Figure 5.1 Enlivenment of a latent emotion

fragments or elements of the describable aspect of the emotion that enlivens it. It is only because such connections rely on perceptual saliences and comprise imaginative connections that are not random or arbitrary that they lend themselves to the identification of thematic threads. These thematic threads are more like inventions than they are discoveries. They were not written into the associations in their causal operation. The imaginative-causal connections themselves are not semantic connections and do not have the purpose to convey any meaning. They are blind operations of the mind.

If I am a person that values self-awareness I may wonder about this sudden re-experiencing of an old envy. I may then undo the condensation and remember the event from my boss's previous visit with the new client. Although I did not care so much about it at the time, I now consciously re-describe that event as another instance of favoritism. I may now be retroactively angry and envious about this unfair bias.

Unconscious emotions may be enlivened through associative triggering as well. In such cases, however, one cannot become self-aware of one's emotion. I will explain what exactly this "cannot" amounts to in the next section when I discuss repression. For now I will just say that unlike other thoughts or images that cross one's mind in association, fragmented elements of unconscious emotions will not be "listened" or attended to. And, once the unconscious emotion is enlivened, its affective aspect will be manifest, but one will not recognize or be able to describe the emotionally salient object of that emotion.

Re-visit Jonah's case. As far as we know from Rorty's description of the case, Jonah has unconscious emotions about the scarf-tying scenes and about being sent away from his mother. Jonah resents that his mother harshly tied those itchy scarves around his neck and is probably also frustrated that his brother never complained about them. The describable aspect of these emotions is remembered "in highly summary form" or Rorty would not be able to tell us about them. It is the affective significance of these scarf-scenes that Jonah has probably been sparing himself from.

Although we still need a full account of how suppression leads to repression, we know that by and large, unconscious emotions are those that can be said on reflection to be incompatible with one's self-conception. As a child, Jonah would have found it risky to acknowledge such resentment of his mother. Jonah surely loved his mother very much and was dependent on her love and could not risk that relationship. Indeed, although Jonah was aware that he did not like those itchy scarves, he never complained about them. If he did, then surely his mother would have stopped knitting them from that material.

Jonah further resents that his mother sent him away from the hospital after his brother was born and while his father was away. Presumably Jonah was at the time also jealous of his newborn brother who replaced his position with his mother. Up until the brother was born, Jonah was the sole receiver of his parents' affection. Indeed, when his father went away he became the only little man in his mother's emotional life, and enjoyed an exclusive place with her.

We know very little about the time Jonah spent with his grandfather. But Rorty indicates that Jonah was somehow aware of the grandfather's anger and contempt toward his mother. One would imagine that it would not be such a simple matter to assimilate, even partly, the grandfather's views, as Rorty seems to suggest. A young child is much more likely to protect his love to his mother, indeed even if everyone agrees that the mother is truly harsh and hostile. We know that Jonah adored his grandfather. Loving two caregivers that dislike each other is an obvious source of conflict for a child. And so, it is much more likely that Jonah felt that his own negative feelings toward his mother would make this conflict explicit and should thus be kept at bay. I am thus going to assume that these resentful emotions toward his mother are unconscious.

Below is a (possible) list of the associations Jonah's imagination makes at moments where he feels a bout of resentment toward Esther. I take as an example a moment where Esther gives Jonah an assignment and he resents her for that and yet does not complain about it to anyone, since he knows his colleagues disagree with him and that he is probably wrong about Esther. I emphasize that this is not meant to be an empirical hypothesis. The associations below need not correspond exactly with the associations that Jonah has actually made, although there would plausibly be some overlap, if only since Jonah and I speak the same language. My discussion of Jonah's resentment aims to demonstrate what would count as an associative explanation for Jonah's pathological emotional reaction.

Jonah imaginatively fragments the situation at hand and connects those fragments to fragmented elements of the unconscious emotions regarding his mother listed above. I first list the associations, which are also demonstrated in Figure 5.2.

I put in quotes fragments of the here-and-now that are most likely words or fragments of the "subtitles" Jonah explicitly gives to his feelings via inner speech. Also in quotes are fragments from sentences that may have been said during the scarf-scenes or the hospital scene. For example, Jonah may have said to himself during the scarf-scenes "I shouldn't complain about those scarves, mother will be offended," or "Look at him, he just loves those scarves, he'll never complain." During the hospital scene, Jonah's mother would have verbally explained that she has to send him away to his grandfather. When Jonah protested his mother probably said something like: "I'm sorry darling, it's not up to you, you don't have a say in this, it's adult business."

The unquoted words in Figure 5.2 are meant to represent images (perceived or remembered images or schemas, that need not be just visual but could also be a feeling, a smell etc.). The words in quotes are fragments of inner speech or things actually said. After listing the imaginative connections, I will then proceed to provide respects in which these connections hold. Such aspects can only be given after-the-fact, perhaps in therapy, and are not assumed to have played any causal role.

Symptoms:

SCARF PHOBIA

Obsessional thought: My *mother* is going to kill me

I resent that *Esther* gives me this demeaning assignment

Colleagues smile to *Esther* and I cannot complain anymore.

I am suffocating at work!

Unconscious Emotions (and related associations):

I resent that my *mother* is harshly tying an itchy scarf around my neck (my ***brother*** smiles and I keep quiet)

STRANGULATION

I resent that *mother* sent me away to my grandfather when in hospital with my ***brother*** while my father was away.

I said "No!"

Mother said: "You don't have a say"

Emerging Thematic Threads

Women in position of authority

Strangulation

Peers (brotherhood vs. rivalry)

Domination (submission vs. rebellion)

Unpleasant physical feeling

Current resentment		**scarf-scenes resentment**		**hospital resentment**
Esther	←→	Mother	←→	Mother
Colleagues	←→	Brother	←→	Brother
gives me this assignment "demeaning"	←→	harshly ties a scarf around my neck ←→	←→	"send away"
"suffocated at work"	←→	strangulation		
smile, "not complain"	←→	keep quiet strangulation	←→	"not have a say" "no!"

Figure 5.2 Associative explanation for Jonah's symptoms

Esther ←→ Mother: Many of us are familiar with the simile that bosses are like parents. The boss telling me what to do is, in some respects, like a parent telling me what to do; I expect my boss not only to take an interest in my work, but also to care about me, to wish me well, to guide me, like a parent. My boss has other employees, other "children" (my colleagues), of which I may be jealous, with whom I may compete for the boss's favor, similar to a sibling dynamic around the parents, and so forth. But Jonah does not merely liken Esther to *a* mother under specified respects as some general metaphor for their relationship. Esther is *similar* to *his* mother. Unlike the verbal simile "bosses are like parents," which brings out certain aspects of our bosses, the imaginative association of similarity is bi-directional. As will be explained below, it is not just that Esther is seen in terms of Mother but also that Mother is seen in terms of Esther. Esther and Mother are similar in a number of respects: they both tell me what to do; they are both expected to care and be responsible for me.

Colleagues ←→ Brother: It is not simply that there is a general simile that colleagues are like siblings. Rather, Jonah's colleagues are *similar* to *his* brother. Another idiosyncratic aspect in which the similarity can later be said to hold is acceptance and appreciation of kindness. That is, the colleagues accept Esther's assignments as relatively kind instructions at work, and Jonah's brother accepts Mother's scarves as loving gestures during the scarf-scenes. Also, the colleagues are happy with Esther and smile when she gives them assignments, *similar* to the smiles of Jonah's brother to their mother as she was tying scarves around his neck. And both these visual smiles, perhaps accompanied by "thanks", via *inversion* to Jonah's protest when he was sent away from the hospital.

Gives me a "demeaning" assignment ←→ harshly ties an itchy scarf around my neck ←→ "send away": All these fragments are *similar* to one another. All of them are activities or happenings to which Jonah is submitted by a woman present on the scene. It could be that Jonah actually does not like his assignments or his job in general, and that the itchiness and the unpleasantness of being sent away connect through similarity to the "demeaning" assignment. Or it could be that the assignment was not so bad, but felt "demeaning" due to the displacement that accompanied the connections with those other unpleasant orders. The theme of female authority figures was the one stressed by Rorty. But crucially, on the present account, this theme played no causal role, but can be added-on from above, as it were, to Jonah's imaginative network.

The image of harshly tying a scarf around someone's neck is *similar* to the image of strangulation or of hanging. Jonah may have already associated the scarf scenes with strangulation at the time of those scenes, as he may have seen such images on TV or visually imagined them when he heard of them in stories. We can all see how there is a sense in which the harsh tying of a scarf tightly around one's neck resembles the image of strangulation and/or hanging. But this is not the normal association we make when our loved one puts a scarf on us or tightens our tie. It is Jonah's idiosyncratic association.

The image of strangulation is also imaginatively *similar* to "send away," in certain respects. Strangulation literally gets rid of someone, and telling someone to go away is more abstractly or figuratively getting rid of someone. Strangulation also involves an inability to speak (as its part), and thus stands in a part–whole relation to the old hospital scene, where Jonah was told to go away and he does "not have a say." This in turn associates through similarity with Jonah's incapacity to complain about the scarves (a complaint that would have been justified) and about Esther (exactly because everyone else thinks it is not justified). Silencing oneself comes with a feeling of closing one's mouth while the resentful words are said via inner speech.

Jonah's associative imagination fragments the current situation into elements: Esther, colleagues, assignment, "demeaning," "not complain," and couples each of them with elements from the salient objects of two unconscious emotions, whose fragments also interconnect imaginatively. It is not just one imaginative association, but the accumulation of these associations that together enlivens Jonah's two resentful unconscious emotions as demonstrated in Figure 5.2. The imaginative process of triggering "wakes up" those latent emotions into an episodic state.

"Regression," on this associative account, consists in this imaginative process of enlivening latent emotions or emotionally laden memories. There is no "push" from the memory to "return," as Ricoeur would have it, only the accumulation of imaginative associations from a here-and-now situation to an unconscious emotion. If a current conflict plays a role in such a regression, then it is by joining the series of emotions that get enlivened through the same triggering process.

Once an emotion is enlivened, then at least in principle it is available to awareness. But since the emotion is unconscious, a quality yet to be explained, Jonah does not attend to or recognize the describable aspects of those emotions. Indeed, in any case, given our practices of emotion expression both in words and through behavior, practices that expect us to find the cause and indeed the justification for our emotions in the here-and-now situation, Jonah focuses on the here-and-now situation in order to verbally express and describe, at least to himself, what he is feeling and why.

Although Jonah is not aware of this, he sees the subjective, namely the elements of the describable aspects of his unconscious emotions, in the objective, namely in the elements of the here-and-now situation. He sees his colleagues in terms of his brother, he sees Esther in terms of his mother, he sees the assignment in terms of the itchy scarf tied around the neck and in terms of being sent away. Seen in terms of strangulation, Jonah can see these assignments as "suffocating" him, indeed an expression that is usable in such contexts.

In other words, the bi-directional associations that triggered the latent emotions, those that connect elements from the here-and-now with fragments of the describable aspects of the latent emotions, are *condensed* into the now salient aspects of the here-and-now situation. In Jonah's case, the triggering elements are also the ones that become imaginatively salient through this process, and this is probably often the case.

But we can imagine a situation where the trigger would be different to the elements that thereby become salient. Say I see a sports car passing by that associatively reminds me through a part–part relation of my ex-boyfriend who left me due to his unfitting jealousy (the sports car and the boyfriend were both parts of the breakup scene as well as many other scenes with that boyfriend, who was obsessed about his car). This association (together with a few others) triggers certain latent emotions of disappointment, anger and heartache. I then see my husband in his car coming to pick me up and see him as having a suspicious expression (which then makes me angry). In this latter case, new associations (husband ↔ ex-boyfriend; husband's car ↔ boyfriend's sports car), and not the ones that triggered the latent emotions, condense so as to make salient certain aspects of the situation, in this case my husband, or see them in terms of the elements of the enlivened emotions.

But as in the case of the two similar faces, where *both* faces seem different once the similarity is noticed, here too it is not just that the current situation is seen in terms of the objects of the enlivened emotions – these hitherto latent emotions are also affected by this process. Just as Esther seems more like Jonah's mother, Jonah's mother seems more like Esther. Just as the colleagues begin to look more like Jonah's brother, Jonah's brother begins to look more like a colleague. *Imaginative associations are bi-directional.*

This bi-directionality is another feature that excludes imaginative associations from being semantic literary connections of the sort used in poems. Consider the metaphor "All the world's a stage." The metaphor tells us something about the world – not about stages. Neither is Esther a symbol for Mother in the literary sense. A statue of a leader symbolizes the leader or stands for the leader, but the leader does not stand for the statue. The imaginative association Esther–Mother, on the other hand, brings out aspects in both Esther and Mother.

This is not redescription in Hacking's sense. Jonah is not even aware that emotions that have past scenes or imagistic memories as their salient objects have been enlivened. Although Jonah is not attending to his enlivened emotions in real-time, their describable aspect has acquired a new dimension. In fact, when Jonah visits his mother that evening and she keeps nagging him to put another sweater on since the house is cold, he may suddenly have an image of Esther cross his mind and think to himself that his mother is quite "bossy," rather than, say, a "nagging nuisance," or a "sweet" concerned mother.

Since the terms in which certain aspects of the situation have become salient originate from now enlivened emotions, this condensation is also accompanied by the *displacement* of affect. That is, the aspects of the here-and-now situation that have become salient through condensation are affectively salient. In other words, the describable salient aspect of the here-and-now situation is now intertwined with the aroused affect. A new occurrent describable emotional attitude has been formed.

The describable aspect of this new synthesized emotional reaction (the here-and-now emotionally salient people or things) is what I called the "look-alike reason" of an emotional reaction in Chapter 1.3.B. The description of the emotionally salient features of Esther is what Jonah will say if someone asks him why he is emoting in this way, that is, it will be the answer to a why-question that calls for justification. However, it was not, in the first instance, an operative reason, but rather the condensation achieved by the distinctively non-inferential connective and synthetic imagination. These look-alike reasons are retroactive rationalizations. We treat them like reasons, we treat them as though they should be rationally assessable, but they are actually not reasons at all.

In order to eliminate this occurrent emotion, Jonah has to undo the displacement of affect. If Jonah was able to even partly undo the condensation that supports this occurrent emotion, if he became aware of the describable aspects of his enlivened emotions rather than be aware merely of their condensed manifestation, then his affective attention would be redistributed over these few there-and-then objects and the here-and-now situation may lose its affective salience either partly or completely. In that manner, Jonah would be able to dim down his occurrent emotion, at least on this particular occasion. This occurrent emotional salience of Esther is recalcitrant to Jonah's reasoning against it, precisely because Jonah does not recognize that the emotional salience of the relevant aspects of the here-and-now situation stems from their coupling with elements of describable aspects of other emotions.

Recalcitrant emotions in general, as here exemplified through Jonah's case, can be explained associatively as the result of the condensation and displacement of enlivened unconscious emotions. As can be seen in Figure 5.2, the associative explanation includes three stratifications, each represented differently in the diagram.[29]

The first is *temporal*. The describable aspect of each emotion in the diagram refers to some moment or period in time. Each emotional reaction, as a whole, also originated at some moment in time, whether at the time of the event (as the primal scene developmental account would have it) or retroactively later in life through redescription in Hacking's sense, and as demonstrated in the example of the colleague-promotion-envy in the beginning of this section. And, the suppression of the affect of those emotions which (somehow) leads to the repression of their describable aspect also happens at some moment in time.

These temporal phases can be represented *linearly*. That is, each latent emotion with its describable aspect is located either above or below another. The temporal stratification thus presents a temporally ordered series of few

29 Early Freud identifies these stratifications, and I here use Freud's terms to name these stratifications. Freud's text indicates similar if not identical diagrammatic representation. His understanding of these stratifications is, however, different to the one presented here. In particular, Freud calls the associations "logical" rather than "imaginative." Breuer and Freud, "The Psychotherapy of Hysteria," in *Studies on Hysteria*, S.E., 2, 288–290.

emotions, which is the primal series, used by the accounts presented in the two previous chapters. In Figure 5.2 I put the earliest repression at the bottom of the page, and the axis of time goes upwards. The symptomatic emotional reaction is thus the most recent and appears at the top of the diagram.

In any case, as elaborated in Chapters 3 and 4, no primal series of emotional reactions, whether synchronized with the time of the events or with an episode of later remembering, can causally account on its own for pathological emotional reactions. It is thus less important for the sake of this discussion whether the emotions in Jonah's primal series were experienced at the time of the events or later. In fact, in the next section, I will claim that this series is not "primal" at all, in the sense that the affective significance of each emotion of the series does not stem from any well-circumscribed spatio-temporal situation.

The second stratification is of *imaginative associations*, which serve to enliven the latent emotions, and also to condense and displace them into the emotional symptom. This is the stratification that comprises the causal affective processes that bring about emotional pathologies. Without it, latent emotions would remain latent and no symptom would be formed.

These imaginative associations are represented by zigzag lines, such as those that appear in Figure 5.1 for the colleague–promotion–envy example. Figure 5.2 for Jonah's case does not include the zigzag lines. Instead, I styled the connected fragments of the describable aspects of the emotions. The fragments that are styled in the same way (e.g. bold) are the ones that are imaginatively associated with one another. Imaginative associations ignore the temporal order of the emotions in question. This is how I interpret Freud's insistence that unconscious processes are characterized by "*timelessness*."[30] This feature will also be discussed in the next section.

Finally, the third stratification is *thematic*. Since imaginative associations rely on perceptual saliences and are not random or arbitrary, their identification further lends itself to the formulation of themes that run through the (temporally stratified) series. The themes of an associative diagram are the aspects in which the various imaginative connections can be said to hold. In Jonah's case, the connection mother ←→ Esther holds, amongst other things, in the respect that both are female authority figures. The thematic stratification can be represented by the lines that are composed of zigzag lines, namely the threads that run through the temporal stratification, or alternatively, it can be represented by the different font styles, as it is in Figure 5.2. The styles or the threads, that can be traced in the network due to the various associations or the zigzag lines, are potential place-holders, as it were, onto which we can add themes, once we formulate or provide the respects in which the associations hold. That is how, for example, we can ascribe the theme of female authority figures to the italic font style in Figure 5.2.

30 Freud, "The Unconscious," S.E.,14, 187. Emphasis in original.

Thematic affinity *per se*, however, does not cause emotional symptoms. It is the synthesis of an *accumulation* of simple and bi-directional imaginative associations that triggers unconscious emotions and condenses and displaces the elements of those emotions into a new occurrent reaction. And those connections do not come with "subtitles" that spell out the respects in which they hold. Thematic affinity is the storytelling we can tell after-the-fact. Conceptual themes are adds-on, a way to give meaning to the imagistic causal network. The thematic stratification is thus not part of the causal stratification, but any associative network allows for its later addition.

And so, it is best to abandon the term "symbolic" which Freud used to characterize the connection between the symptom and the repressed memory or the latent emotion (see Chapter 3.4). The synthesis of associations is not a semantic relation, as explained above, and it is not a communicative activity that creates a symptom as means of representation for the unconscious emotions, as it is taken to be in psychoanalytic literature.[31] A symptom – in our case an emotional symptom – is not a representation or a symbol for an unconscious emotion, just as in the Wittgenstein example one face does not represent or stand for another face when the faces suddenly strike us as similar. Seeing-as, in other words, is not a representational relation. It can be made into a representational relation if one intends to use it that way, but it is not inherently representational.

The describable aspect of a pathological emotion is an imaginative synthesis of unconscious emotions. Pathological emotional reactions are synthesized emotions. Pathological emotional episodes, just like any other condensation that strikes our awareness, are *expressive* (of the way we see the situation as emotionally salient), but they are not communicative. They seek acknowledgement from another person, but they do not address another person in the manner ordinary language does. They feel explainable, they come with the *feeling* that there is something to become aware of – but they do not come with "subtitles." In the next part of this chapter, I will claim that all emotional reactions, pathological or not, can be characterized in this manner.

3. Why *those* unconscious emotions?

Once we have this kind of diagram for an emotional symptom, we have deciphered the symptom. The occurrent pathological emotion is a kind of riddle, solved by detangling the condensation and displacement that caused it, and revealing the relevant unconscious emotions. The thematic stratification of

31 See, for example, the entry on "Symbolism" in Laplanche and Pontalis, *The Language of Psychoanalysis*, 442–446. Indeed, this confusion around the term "symbolic" is largely responsible for the homuncularism that infects psychoanalytic literature and the philosophy of psychoanalysis. For if something is being communicated, then it appears that the unconscious or *It* speaks! But I will not pursue further this line of criticism here.

such diagrams allows for the construction of narratives of the sort described in the two previous chapters. What is the difference then if all accounts end up with the same series? In this section, I show that whereas the primal series is the endpoint for the developmental and narrative accounts, it is where the challenge begins for the associative explanation.

Narratives appear to be complete and to make sense through the themes that run through them. Narrative accounts thus focus on the emotions of the primal series only insofar as they imaginatively connect to and thematically interrelate with one another. The narrator leaves out of the story elements of these emotions that do not participate in any theme. In Jonah's case, as can be seen in Figure 5.2, the grandfather and the father appear as elements of the first emotion in the series but they are not connected to any other element in the diagram. Indeed, the grandfather and especially the father play a very marginal role in Rorty's narrative.

R. G. Collingwood likens such selective thematic emphasis of certain aspects of events in the chronicle to the work of a landscape painter: "he is always selecting, simplifying, schematizing, leaving out what he thinks unimportant and putting in what he regards as essential."[32] A narrative account for an emotional pathology, which effectively adds-on the thematic structuration to the associative diagram, basically ignores those under-connected elements or marginal figures as part of its methodology of explanation.

The aim of a narrative explanation is to turn the chronicle (the primal series of emotions) into a *coherent* and *consistent* whole. As Marshall says: "The explanatory power of any narrative lies in its consistently tying together a wealth of material, including biographical material, into a coherent whole."[33] It is only if Jonah had other symptoms that could not be deciphered through those particular unconscious emotions that a narrative explanation would look for other unconscious emotions. In such cases, a narrator may be a pluralist and accept a few narratives per person.

But each such narrative nonetheless marginalizes issues in the subject's life that do not directly connect through imaginative associations with the symptom. Why do we hear almost nothing about Jonah's father? Is it because their relationship was so great? Is it because this relationship has nothing to do with the symptom? Is it plausible that Jonah's relationship with his mother can be isolated from and uninfluenced by his emotional relationship with his father?

This is what makes primal series accounts questionable in the first place. Why are those scenes with those particular emotional interactions said to be represented in the symptom and not others? What makes these scenes or

32 R. G. Collingwood, "The Historical Imagination" [1935], in *The Idea of History* (Oxford: Oxford University Press, 1994 [1946]), 236.

33 Marshall, "Overdetermination," 208.

emotions so important? With the conceptual resources of the associative explanation we can formulate the question differently: Why does the imagination go there and not elsewhere in its associations? Why are these particular unconscious emotions overemphasized at the expense of others?

In all Freudian accounts, including the one presented in this chapter, the overemphasis of these unconscious emotions is the source of the symptom. It requires explanation. When approaching these emotions of the primal series with the associative methodology, they too are regarded as fragmented wholes connected to other emotions, some of which are in the series, but others are not. The elements that seem under-connected when one only wants to decipher the symptom actually connect with *other* latent emotions that do not directly connect with the symptom. These other emotions, which do not appear in the primal series, are latent, inasmuch that the subject is not over them. Many of these emotions are also unconscious, in the sense that the subject has never properly dealt with them, verbally expressed or acknowledged them.

According to the associative account then, Jonah's unconscious emotions that partake in the primal series connect to other latent emotions. They may connect, for example, to Jonah's embarrassment and anger that he felt when he first realized that his father did not pursue a creative profession because he wanted to please his mother and provide well for the family. They may further connect with Jonah's shame whenever he sees his father say "yes" with a smile to his mother against his own wishes, and so appear weak and spineless; and with Jonah's recent disappointment regarding a love interest who ended up with his neighbor; and with Jonah's feelings of loneliness within his own group of friends where he often feels he does not quite fit in; and with Jonah's anger that two of his beloved friends hate each other; and so on and so forth. Each such further emotion contains fragments that imaginatively associate with fragments of the unconscious emotions that directly connect to the symptom, that are its terms of salience.

The unconscious emotions of Jonah's primal series further connect with other emotions that have past scenes or memories as their objects, such as, say, Jonah's anger at his grandfather who has such a low view of his mother, Jonah's jealousy of his best high-school friend that all the girls like, his anger and disappointment that his father seems to be interested only in his mother and not at all in him and his brother and so on and so forth. When we press on the associative methodology, the imaginative diagram "branches out" to include many more emotions than those that directly connect with the describable aspect of the symptom.

The associative explanation for emotional pathologies treats the emotional issues of the subject holistically, as an interconnected network. This is an *imaginative* holism (unlike, say, a rational and inferential holism of beliefs). There is not just one or few occasions or memories or emotions whose objects merit their affective importance when considered individually (through rational justification or through a developmental story). The symptom is not caused only by those few emotions to which it is directly and heavily connected. There are rather many moderately unpleasant emotions that do not sit well with one's self-conception, and these emotions interconnect imaginatively. Certain emotions within those many problematic ones condense and displace more emotions than the others do. They are nodes in an imaginative-emotional network, nodal emotions that "radiate"[34] many other emotions. These nodal emotions get enlivened frequently and function as the terms in which situations are seen as emotionally salient exactly because many associative routes lead there.

These densely synthesized unconscious emotions function effectively as the subject's pictures or imaginative models for everything that is going wrong in her emotional life. The unconscious nodal emotions, in other words, imaginatively capture the subject's diverse and complex plurality of emotional difficulties, a variety of issues the subject has not acknowledged properly and has not dealt with. This is the source of their curious affective importance; this is why they stand out from the rest of one's latent emotions.

Condensation or associative synthesis, we may say, *is the imagination's way to generalize*, to create the terms in which we see the world as emotionally salient in various disturbing ways. In that sense, when a here-and-now situation triggers such synthesized unconscious emotions, the resulting occurrent pathological emotion expresses not just those few unconscious emotions of the primal series, but the subject's multi-faceted emotional discontent. I will thus stop calling those emotions "primal," since their affective importance does not come from their objects regarded on their own. I will call them "synthesized" or "nodal" emotions.

If we do not branch out diagrams such as the one drawn here for Jonah's case, we might be tempted to say that the occurrent emotional pathology is a mere illusion whereas the unconscious emotions of the series are the ones actually being expressed. We might say that Jonah is misled to think that he resents Esther, whereas in fact, it is his mother that he *really* resents. Associative diagrams that do not zigzag their way out of the series of nodal emotions appear to separate "illusory" from "real" emotions.

I will claim in the next part of this chapter that this distinction between "real" and "illusory" is highly misleading for the case of emotions in general. I now just want to note that for the case of pathological emotions, the emotions of the primal series do not have any privileged status as "more real" than the occurrent pathological emotion. The emotions of the series of nodal emotions, just like the occurrent here-and-now reaction, condense and displace other emotions in the subject's imaginative-emotional network. That is, each of those emotions gets its affective weight from and

34 This is the term Freud uses to describe such nodes that condense many associations, e.g. Freud, *The Interpretation of Dreams*, S.E., 4, 306–7; and also Freud, *An Infantile Neurosis*, 52.

carries the baggage of other latent emotions, as it were. The describable aspect of such an emotion as circumscribed in specified spatio-temporal circumstances is not the source of the affective aspect of a synthesized nodal emotion.

Jonah's "real" problem in life is not that he resents his mother for the itchy scarves or for sending him away from her when his brother was born. Jonah, rather, has many emotional issues of which he is not self-aware and an imaginative habit of seeing situations in terms of a few emotions that imaginatively capture and synthesize those issues. In fact, Jonah's emotional landscape may change and other unconscious emotions may become more heavily associated than the emotions Rorty tells us about. The series of nodal emotions is not fixed and neither is the symptom that imaginatively connects with them.

Enlivening nodal synthesized emotions depends on an accumulation of associations from the here-and-now situation to those latent emotions, as well as the accumulation of associations from many other emotions to those specific unconscious emotions. Imaginative associations may operate idiosyncratically and capriciously. Nothing ensures that I will imaginatively associate and synthesize today in the same way that I did yesterday. Although the imagination has its habits of association and synthesis, these habits may change and the dominant synthesized emotions may change. It is basically a cliché that neurotics such as Jonah have periods of remission. This dependence of the symptom on the accumulation of associations thus allows for occasional recalcitrance, stable recalcitrance and on-and-off recalcitrance (and the same range of stability also applies to pathologies of avowal).

The associative explanation makes use of the same series of unconscious emotions invoked by the other accounts for emotional pathologies available in the philosophical literature. But only this account has the methodological resources to branch out the emotional-imaginative network. It is thus the only explanation for emotional pathologies that can answer the question of the overemphasis of certain emotions (or emotional scenes or memories) over others. And that emphasis is not due to being "primal" or traumatic, but to being heavily condensed and to synthesizing one's emotional issues that spread over, as it were, many other emotionally laden spatio-temporal circumstances, disregarding their temporal order. The associative explanation is therefore far removed from the developmental etiologies.

4. Repression

Every account for emotional pathologies, including the associative explanation proposed, takes recourse to unconscious emotions, and so any such account should include the resources to spell out the process of repression, on which the existence of unconscious emotions depends. Chapter 3.4

presented the early Freudian claim that an emotion becomes unconscious through being submitted to two conditions: suppression and repression. In this section I use the associative approach to make sense of the concept of repression as a consequence of suppression. This approach will serve to demystify the notion of the unconscious, as a quality of certain mental states, in particular of certain emotions, and explain how such states can on the one hand be unavailable to consciousness and on the other hand cause psychological symptoms.

As said in Chapter 3.4, the suppression we are all explicitly familiar with is the suppression of the public expression of certain thoughts and emotions. That is the capacity to keep a poker face or deflect the topic of conversation to something else so as to conceal one's affective episodes from other people. The one who suppresses the public expression of her emotion may allow herself to express her emotion privately. She may do so by talking to herself at the moment of the reaction (through inner speech), or hold on until she gets home and express herself privately by crying or screaming into a pillow, banging on the wall, or writing in her journal.

The kind of suppression that ends in repression involves not just the suppression of affect from being expressed publicly, but also the prevention of private expression. That is, the one who prevents any expression at all effectively prevents the very acknowledgement of having the emotion. A fleeting moment of awareness of the emotion, perhaps demonstrated in some involuntary behavior (such as very brief facial expressions known as "microexpressions"[35]), is all it usually takes for that person to divert attention away from both the describable and affective aspects of the emotion.

As explained in Chapter 3.4, early Freud says that these rejected thoughts and emotions are incompatible with one's moral standards or with one's self-image. But, it is not normally the case that we suppress both public and private expressions of an emotion through deliberation in reference to an explicit ideal of our moral standards and our regulating conception of ourselves with which we guide our intentional actions and reflective judgments as much as we can.

As claimed in Chapter 3.4, this public and private suppression, the diversion of attention away from both the describable and affective aspects of the emotion, qualifies as an action, a non-Anscombian action. This action is not done under description or in a self-aware manner, and one cannot easily recognize what one is doing, let alone provide reasons for what one is doing during the action's performance. But a non-Anscombian action is nonetheless describable and one can, in principle, ask and answer a retroactive why-question about it, even if such self-understanding is not causally operative during the performance of the action but only retroactively achievable.

35 Paul Ekman, *Emotions Revealed: Recognizing Faces and Feelings to Improve Communication and Emotional Life* (New-York: Henry Hold and Co., 2003).

As suggested in Chapter 3.4, suppressive action of the sort that leads to repression is an aversive *affective* reaction that I call "alienating aversion" and the diversion of one's attention is its action tendency, namely its behavioral expression.

How is this aversive suppression caused? I will claim in the second part of this chapter that the formation of all emotional reactions follows the same associative processes that I have used to explain pathological emotions. For now I just assume that aversive suppression forms in an analogous manner to emotions like Jonah's resentment of Esther. That is, the passing thought or emotion that triggers an aversive response associatively connects (via more than one connection) to a series of a few other past aversive responses.

These may be past occasions of aversive suppression or past guilts, disgusts, shames, and fears whose objects relate imaginatively through an accumulation of associations to a now rejected passing thought or emotion. These past aversive reactions, whose enlivenment causes the current aversive response, are nodal synthesized emotions that condense and displace many *other* past aversive emotions. They somehow imaginatively capture, encapsulate and synthesize what the subject will not tolerate about herself or others.

Although the associations that interconnect one's aversive subset of one's emotional–imaginative network are non-conceptual, they nevertheless lend themselves to add-on thematic stratification (as explained earlier for pathological emotions such as Jonah's). If somehow one becomes aware of one's imaginative network of aversive responses, one would be able to thematize them, to provide and formulate the respects in which these interconnected responses are similar to, or otherwise imaginatively associate with, one another. These are effectively the respects in which the rejected emotions, which comprise the objects of the aversive responses, are emotionally conflictual with one's self-image. This aversive affective reaction to one's passing thought or emotion is expressed through its typical action tendency, namely the diversion of attention.

But how does aversive suppression end in repression? If the rejected emotion in question relates to a situation that is more or less constant or repetitive, there would be available reminders of this emotion at every corner. If I try to suppress that I am in love with someone while living with them in the same house,[36] or if I try to suppress having had sexual naughty games with the caretaker's daughter, who is around often or most of the time (see Chapter 4.1), if I deny resenting my mother for tying itchy scarves around my neck while having to go through these scarf scenes every day – then the very fact that I am often in the environment of the object of my emotion might repeatedly confront me with the emotion I am trying to avoid.

36 This was Lucy's situation, the governess that suffered from unrequited love to a widower, the father of the children she took care of. Freud, "The Case of Lucy R."

If each time we see these familiar objects that so straightforwardly relate to the suppressed emotion we would be reminded of that suppressed emotion and have to suppress it all over again – we would be likely to be reminded of this emotion so frequently that it would become increasingly difficult to distract ourselves from it. In what follows I use the resources of the associative explanation to show that although the initial suppression of an emotion requires further iterations, each such iteration brings suppression closer to repression. That is, after each iteration, it becomes more difficult and less likely to enliven the denied emotion.

Say I hear a lecture in high school about alcoholism and the criteria to determine whether one is an alcoholic, and then I suddenly realize that my father's drinking habits answer those criteria. I quickly deny this passing angry and shameful thought and suppress it, perhaps by no longer listening to the lecture and drawing in my notebook instead. A few days later, I am fleetingly reminded of my anger and shame when I see an empty glass of scotch in the kitchen before noon, since that image bears a part–whole relation to the lecture I heard. My new aversive response does not just shift my attention away from my emotion but also from the empty scotch glass. Perhaps one or few such iterations are all that is needed to develop a habit of aversive responses to scotch glasses around the house, expressed in averting my gaze away from those glasses, through distraction and deflection, by thinking about or focusing on something else. I may even collect the glasses and wash them while I talk on the phone or listen to the radio without enlivening my anger and shame about my father's alcoholism.

The aversive response of suppression is imaginatively contagious, so to speak. I reach a stage where I ignore or distract myself regularly from some typical objects that would remind me of my father's alcoholism, such as glasses, bottles, alcohol breath, the noise of stumbling into the house at night etc. In other words, I develop *habits of selective attention* that ignore or deflect from typical images and words that bear a strong imaginative relation to my denied emotion. Whereas in the past these images spontaneously enlivened the suppressed emotion, now as soon as I see them I turn my attention elsewhere or think about something unrelated and thereby block them from potentially enlivening my emotion. The describable aspect of a denied emotion, my father's alcoholism, my love for my boss, my infantile sexual history, can become the elephant in the room.

This is how an emotion can get isolated, latent, not thought about, even in the midst of a situation that is likely to enliven it. Suppression turns into repression when the relatively straightforward associations that are likely to enliven an emotion have been blocked by patterns of selective attention or rather of inattention. Repression, as Freud says, is maintained by a continuous effort.[37] It is not a mysterious force but our sustaining of habits of deflection that prevent the imagination from enlivening the emotion.

37 Freud, "Repression," 151; and also in Freud, *Inhibition, Symptoms and Anxiety*, 157.

I stress that when I characterize associations as "straightforward," I refer to the kind of assessment the subject would make were she to identify and describe these associations. A "straightforward" identified similarity would be similarity for which one could find or formulate many respects in which it holds. A not-straightforward similarity, such as the one between Esther and Jonah's mother, would be similarity for which one could provide one or very few respects, and with some effort or with the kind of skill literary critics have. A straightforward part-whole relation such as the relation between empty scotch glasses I see before noon and the lecture I heard, could be regarded after-the-fact as a meaningful connection (even if the connection was not meaningful in its causal operation), given that scotch glasses are used for drinking alcohol, they are part of the concept of alcohol drinking. A not-straightforward part–whole relation would be a connection such as the one between the color yellow and a childhood illness (spent in a yellow room), which can be judged to be a merely extensional relation once considered after-the-fact (this is Prinz's example from Chapter 2.4). But the imagination in its non-conceptual and automatic activity connects without judging these connections to be straightforward or not, since associations do not come with "subtitles" that specify the respects in which they hold.

Repression can successfully keep an emotion latent for a long time. The emotion is buffered, so to speak, from many straightforward associations that would lead to it. It is not available to conscious thought since enough associative routes to it are repeatedly blocked through the diversion of attention. But these straightforward associations are not the only associations that lead to an unconscious emotion.

Rejected emotions associate with one another, and are rejected in the first place through such accumulation of imaginative connections. That is, unconscious emotions interconnect in an imaginative network as described in the previous section. And some of them may become more heavily condensed than others. Since one's emotional–imaginative network is in flux, an unconscious emotion can become nodal after-the-fact.

An unconscious emotion that has become nodal has many associations leading to it. Although an unconscious emotion may be safe from more or less straightforward associations, it may be enlivened through the accumulation of less straightforward associations. One's habits of diversion of attention may be caught off guard, so to speak, when new here-and-now elements of a situation imaginatively connect with it. An enlivened nodal emotion makes certain aspects of the here-and-now situation emotionally salient, and a new occurrent emotion is formed, as described in the previous section.

But even if one's imagination can bypass one's habits of selective attention through new and not straightforward associations, even if the emotion is enlivened, its describable aspect, forcefully ignored by suppression in the past, need not reach consciousness or rather self-awareness (although it may). In fact, it is unlikely that one would attend to or recognize the object of this hitherto repressed emotion. There are two main reasons for this.

First, in any case, we are trained to regard our emotions as caused by something in the here-and-now situation. As soon as an emotional episode begins, we normally look to the situation at hand, in order to describe the emotionally salient features and give reasons for or rather rationalize our emotional reaction.

Second, the now enlivened emotion is already heavily imaginatively associated with many other emotions that have undergone aversive suppression. The describable aspect of the emotion is likely to trigger a new aversive response of suppression or diversion of attention. That is, even if one may be fleetingly aware of a word or an image that crosses one's mind, which partakes in the describable aspect of the hitherto repressed emotion, one will immediately ignore it and focus instead on the here-and-now aspects of the situation that have become emotionally salient. In other words, the now enlivened emotion is suppressed again and will be from now on buffered, as it were, from associations to straightforwardly similar circumstances to those that have just enlivened it. In other words, one attends to and is self-aware of the occurrent emotion, which is describable or actually verbally expressed and reported on, and the unconscious emotion or few such nodal emotions may remain inattended to, un-reportable.

To sum up: the kind of suppression that leads to repression consists in an aversive affective response. That response is caused by an accumulation of associations to previous aversive responses, including not just alienating aversions but also shames, guilts, embarrassments, and disgusts. The aversive response is expressed through the action tendency of attention diversion or deflection. The aversive response to the same mental state goes through some further iterations whereby one diverts one's attention from further images and words that straightforwardly associate with the same mental state. Suppression turns into repression when one's patterns of inattention have stabilized and the straightforward associative routes to the emotion in question are blocked by the continuous activity of attention deflection.

Repression, on this picture, consists in an ongoing activity that expresses one's aversion from an imaginatively connected bundle of many emotions. Should we worry about the temporal stratification of these aversive responses of suppression? If we did, we might find ourselves wondering: If every aversive suppression depends on previous ones, how did the first aversive suppression occur? I propose that aversive suppression begins as a basic emotion. If ostriches indeed put their heads in the sand when a predator approaches then I would have evidence that aversive suppression has an animal analogue. But this is apparently a myth. I trust the Freudian story of the Oedipus complex that presupposes that all children cannot stand being too angry with or hateful to their parents, given their dependence on the caregiver's love and protection, and suppress and repress such strongly negative emotions.[38] At least at some point in time then, we all experience

38 See Lear's discussion on the resolution of the Oedipus Complex: Lear, *Freud*, Chapter 6.

this aversive reaction to the basic object – caregivers. It is a natural reaction, a capacity for psychological survival. As will be explained in the second part of this chapter, the imaginative account requires basic emotions, understood as biologically or evolutionarily determined reactions to basic objects. The associative account does not provide an explanation for basic emotions. It presupposes those basic emotions and serves to provide an account of imaginative associative processes by means of which the objects of emotions become so varied later in life.

Unconscious emotions may become nodal and the imagination may then enliven them through the accumulation of *new* associative routes, less straightforward connections with newly encountered images and words, fragmented out of some new situation. If by "regression" we mean the enlivenment of unconscious emotions, then regression is simply the normal activity of the associative imagination that may enliven emotions. "Regression" is indeed the inverse of "repression" inasmuch as the associative imagination sometimes makes associations that are in turn blocked by patterns of selective attention. Regression "wins" so to speak when new associative routes, not previously blocked by habits of selective attention, enliven the unconscious emotion. But there is nothing mysterious, intentional or purposive about regression. The imagination associates all the time anyway. It is simply a way to describe a situation where an accumulation of imaginative associations enlivens a hitherto unconscious emotion.

And there is nothing mysterious about repression and there is no need to call it a "force." Repression consists in our capacity to develop patterns or habits of selective attention that sustain our affective aversion from certain mental states. Repression, in other words, is precisely the capacity for pervasive bad faith, whereby we notice, acknowledge and identify with the mental states we like and approve of and deny or ignore those mental states that we do not like.

The unconscious is not a storage room for certain mental states nor are those hidden states the result of some foreign force or a little person within us that emotionally reacts and desires in forbidden ways. In fact, there is no single unconscious but two interrelated notions of the unconscious. The first is that of automatic associative processes, whose "media" of operation includes emotions, sexual desires and memories. That is, they operate blindly on embodied mental states, characterized by prototypical physiological and behavioral manifestations, states that come over us with no conscious control and yet feel explainable in the sense that there is something we could become aware of and that would shed light on the current affliction. The second notion is of habits of inattention, which intertwine with associative processes as described in this section, and whose level of unawareness is not as low as that of associative processes. Habits of inattention entail a more agential activity or rather an emotionally expressive action. They are non-Anscombian actions, something that we do, even if they consist in an action tendency of an emotional reaction, which is in turn caused by condensation of imaginative associations. Crucially, the fact that embodied condensations such as emotional pathologies (including habits of inattention) have a describable aspect does not mean that some "other" within us is their source, as if "speaking" to us.

This picture of the Freudian unconscious as imaginatively contagious habits of inattention is, perhaps surprisingly, very similar to Sartre's conception of bad faith.[39] According to this associative account, unconscious emotions originate as consciously formed emotions or thoughts.[40] In the first instance these emotions are describable and at times even verbally expressed through inner speech, and the suppression of both their affective and describable aspects consists in the self-deceptive activity of turning a blind eye and covering up by thinking of or looking at something else.[41] An emotion is "unconscious" when it is under stable repression, which is effectively a consistent denial of parts of one's emotional reality. These emotions are of the person and it is the person that keeps them away from self-awareness, even if not intentionally in Anscombe's sense. There are some moments in Freud's texts that can be read in this manner, as in "*the essence of repression lies simply in turning something away, and keeping it at a distance, from the conscious.*"[42]

There is nevertheless an air of mystery to the pathological emotional reactions that are caused by the Freudian unconscious. When an accumulation of imaginative associations that include similarities that one would not judge to be straightforward (if one were aware of them) enlivens unconscious emotions, the resulting condensation, namely the resulting occurrent reaction, can sometimes seem strange. Indeed, Jonah, for example, probably felt that he did not understand and could not explain his resentment of Esther and the limitations of his lack of rational control over it, and furthermore felt that there was something to understand or know about his emotion that could explain it. In other words, Jonah probably felt that his emotional pattern is enigmatic. As Russell Grigg says, it is this sense of a riddle that leads (or should lead) one to therapy.[43]

39 Sartre, *Being and Nothingness*, Part 1, Chapter 2: "Bad Faith."

40 For a different account see: Sebastian Gardner, "The Unconscious," in *The Cambridge Companion to Freud*, ed. Jerome Neu (Cambridge: Cambridge University Press, 1991).

41 John Steiner does not criticize the notion of the unconscious as complete and total unknowledge nor does he set it aside as I do here. But his interpretation of Sophocles' *Oedipus the King*, which takes recourse to self-deception as an alternative interpretative concept to the orthodox notion of the unconscious, resonates well with the present account of repression. John Steiner, "Turning a Blind Eye: The Cover Up For Oedipus," in *Psychoanalysis and Culture: A Kleinian Perspective*, ed. David Bell (London: Duckworth, 1999).

42 Freud, "Repression," 147.

43 Russell Grigg, private communication.

ii. AFFECTIVE–ASSOCIATIVE PROCESSES

In the second part of this chapter, I follow the methodology described by Rorty (in Chapter 3) and generalize the associative explanation for emotional pathologies, proposing an account for affective processes in general. I present the proposed account and then show that it fulfills the conditions and constraints specified in the first part of the book.

The affective processes I propose are the same for all emotions, whether or not we later regard them as pathological. These are associative processes that constantly fragment and connect one's perceptually salient features of the here-and-now situation to other images, words or fragments of thoughts or memories and to past emotional experiences. When enough such associations to past emotions accumulate, condensation and displacement cause occurrent emotional reactions. That is, the describable aspect of all emotional episodes is caused by the condensation of the describable aspects of certain past emotions, which in turn condense other emotions from one's emotional history. Some of those emotions that take part in the condensation may be unconscious. And the affective aspect of the current episode is the result of triggering of those past emotions. Their enlivened affect then makes here-and-now features of the situation emotionally salient through displacement.

The affective processes I propose comply with the conditions outlined in Chapter 2. Associations, as explained in the first part of this chapter, are strictly non-rational and non-inferential, imagistic and non-conceptual, automatic and operate below the level awareness. And yet the possibility to call attention to them and bring them to awareness as well as their built-in demand for sharability that grants them their expressivity, means they operate at the person level. On the proposed account, then, emotions are not intentional states. As noted in the previous part of this chapter, when I use the term "object" of the emotion, I simply mean the emotionally salient features of the emotion, circumscribed in certain spatio-temporal circumstances, namely the describable aspect of the emotion (a too brief but hopefully suggestive discussion about emotion-type words and the extent to which they describe the affect of the emotion will be presented later in this chapter).

If every reaction depends on one's past experiences, how does one begin one's emotional life? The associative account presupposes the existence of basic emotions. As explained in Chapter 2, these emotions should not be understood as tracking core relational themes. What is basic about them is their objects, such as bears, snakes, falling, and whatever else science will tell us that we all reliably emotionally respond to in infancy. The associative account does not explain why we have those basic emotions in the first place, but provides the processes through which one's emotional experiences admit increasingly more kinds of objects that do not reliably cause us to emote. The variety in question also comes from language acquisition, since words also participate in associative processes, not words qua concepts but as marks and noises or as the associations that are in the wake of concept-words.

The account presented here explains the emotions of human adults – those who already possess language, who are sensitive to moral, social, and prudential norms, and who at some point in childhood have already enacted their capacity to turn a blind eye to certain thoughts, desires and emotions that are too emotionally conflictual for them. They can make judgments about what is morally right or wrong, what is good or bad for them and their relationships, and they can formulate desires about who they want to be or what they want to become. Persons have also been trained by their parents and their social niche to conceal and control the expression of their emotions on certain typical occasions. Furthermore, they have been told that on some typical occasions they should not have certain emotions at all. This kind of training comes hand in hand with the refinement of a capacity to control also the private expression of an emotion, namely the capacity to self-deceptively turn a blind eye to what one is feeling.

By the time an individual is a full-fledged member of a linguistic community, that individual has experienced many emotional episodes. Various bundles of past emotional experiences, even those formed as basic emotions at the time of their occurrence, associate imaginatively in the manner described in the first part of this chapter to other emotions. The person whose emotional reactions this account explains thus has an imaginative-emotional network in place. Some of the emotions of this imaginative network are unconscious, many are not.

Placed in such a network, emotions have an affective weight that does not come from their describable aspect considered on its own, and their objects, which are themselves condensations, capture imagistically other objects and parts of objects of other emotions. As explained in the first part of this chapter, the elements of different emotions within an imaginative network are seen in terms of one another, thereby adding layers of what we may call imagistic significance to one another through these interconnections, the kind of interconnections that would then lend themselves to conceptually-laden add-on descriptions, to thematization. The themes that can be threaded into one's imaginative network serve to identify or describe patterns of emotional reaction, where the theme often describes a more or less typical object of many emotional experiences. Themes can also be more general and be considered as the kind of cares that were discussed in the first part of the book, such as interests, desires, needs, and values. Such cares do not pre-exist in the network and do not play a causal role in the formation of emotional reactions but can be attributed to people in light of their emotional behavior, as an add-on thematic stratification of their imaginative network. And other themes, those that can be ascribed to unacknowledged or unconscious emotional patterns as well as to patterns that we regard as pathological, are what we call emotional "issues" or "sensitivities" that comprise what we call a person's "emotional baggage," such as Jonah's issues with female authority figures.

The associative account is thus an imagistic and non-conceptual seeing-as account for emotions. Although we suffer emotional episodes as patients they nevertheless reflect on us inasmuch as they are *expressive* of *our* way of seeing certain aspects of the situation as emotionally salient. Indeed, we see the situation in terms of other emotional situations or issues of *ours*. Our emotional episodes, in other words, are caused by and are indicative of who we are, of what pushes our buttons and of the emotional baggage we carry with us in our social interactions.

1. All occurrent emotions are mini-symptoms

According to the associative account, every emotional reaction, and not just the emotional reactions we call "pathological," is the manifest synthetic result of the affective–associative processes that connect elements of the here-and-now situation with elements of nodal synthesized emotions. An accumulation of enough associations enlivens nodal emotions whose elements are now the terms in which the here-and-now elements of the situation are seen as emotionally salient. Every occurrent emotional reaction is associated to a certain series of few nodal emotions, each of which condenses and displaces other emotions, which are not the terms in which the here-and-now situation is seen as emotionally salient.

Every occurrent emotional reaction, even the most mundane and rationally endorsable one, bears imaginative connections with some latent emotions that do not straightforwardly resemble the here-and-now situation. The associative explanation regards all emotional reactions as mini-symptoms. This may sound strange if one likes to think of emotions as connected to external circumstances by way of evaluation and thereby ensure their role as alerting us to dangers, achievement, loss of affection, and other core relational themes. But the emotions of human adults do not accurately track core relational themes, or rather, our emotions are often enough unfitting to their objects. To repeat points made in this book, we can convince ourselves that this is the case when we call attention to our ordinary experience of emotions: examine the reactions of your intimates, how often do they overreact or emote in unfitting ways? Recall how often people ascribe moods to one another in order to explain unfitting emotions; recall how often we read about crimes of passion in the newspapers; reflect on your identification with fictional characters and the unjustified emotional spirals they go through; think about all the people the seek psychotherapy to overcome their emotional issues; recall the frequent use of phrases such as "don't take it out on me," or "don't shoot the messenger," and the familiar warnings about the "emotional baggage" of love interests. We can remind ourselves, in other words, of what we all implicitly know, namely that our emotions are too often out of kilter with reality to see them as generally useful means to perceive one's place in the world.

In any case, we have seen in Chapters 1 and 2 that identifying affective processes with an activity of evaluation hopelessly fails to explain emotionality or to answer the singularity question. In order for external circumstances to trigger affect they have to "touch" us somewhere deeper. According to the proposed account, what pushes one over their emotional edge, so to speak, and express affective behavior rather than make a cold judgment or simply ignore the possible emotional significance of the situation, is precisely the accumulation of imaginative associations to synthesized nodal emotions that implicate large areas of one's imaginative-emotional network.

Take the example of irritation with a rude waiter. The waiter is indeed rude. In fact, that waiter has irritated me on many occasions prior to this one. I even have a paradigm scenario for this waiter irritation, some specific past such occasion that imaginatively condenses the others and is enlivened each time the waiter irritates me. In fact, to speak (more or less) like de Sousa, each emotional reaction to a certain situation involves the enlivenment of an emotion whose object can be verbally described as a scenario that indeed "objectively resembles" the current situation. That is, each emotion of this irritation pattern also involves the enlivenment of a nodal emotion that straightforwardly resembles the occurrent emotion. One almost wants to say that I am imaginatively projecting past irritation experiences onto the new similar enough occasion. As if waiter-irritation or simply irritation is a word whose past uses were projected to the present new case. I say "more or less like de Sousa," since for de Sousa those scenarios are conceptually structured and so is the current situation, which comprises the intentional content of the emotion. On the present account, these scenarios, even if they may be perceived in a conceptually laden way, are purely imagistic as far as the associative imagination is concerned. When I use the term "scenario" in this chapter then, I refer to an imagistic (or any other sense modality) scenario, even if the subject can be said to have applied the relevant concepts at the time.

But why does this waiter irritate me and not my friend who also frequents the same café and thinks this waiter is rude and yet gets irritated a lot less often? Somehow this waiter "gets to me," as we say. The rudeness of the waiter or perhaps the waiter himself are seen in terms of highly condensed emotions, some of which have nothing to do with waiters. These nodal emotions imaginatively synthesize other emotional issues that are going on in my life, some of which may be what Freud called a "current conflict" (see discussion in Chapter 4.4). And so, in that sense, the occurrent emotional reaction is also a synthesized emotion. That is, the current scene with the waiter imaginatively captures other emotional difficulties as well. On the associative account, all emotions muddle scenarios, to speak like de Sousa, even the innocent looking ones, those that are easily avowed and are not labeled "pathological."

Even a rationally fitting experience of fear, say of a stranger in an alley, imaginatively connects with other fear memories or experiences that have contained no strangers in allies. Imaginative connections, albeit blind and simple, may be useful and endorsable when they accumulate and condense. Something specific about this stranger "gives me the creeps" via imaginative associations to, say, some character I was warned about years ago, which in turn associates with some highly condensed past fear experience. That nodal fear, in turn, imaginatively captures, condenses, and displaces other emotions that branch out of it. The alley may be similarly associated with, say, a fragmented image from a scary movie or with a word from a recent conversation about the dangers of the neighborhood.

Even the most basic emotions that may be said to occur reliably, like grief when a loved one dies, imaginatively associate with and synthesize various latent emotions, about that person, about others who died, and so forth. Imaginative connections give depth or rather breadth to such basic emotions as they connect with nodal emotions that in turn branch out and interconnect with many other emotions. They make my grief different to your grief.

2. Accounting for the prevalence of emotion-fittingness and pathology

That emotional reactions are all mini-symptoms that "muddle" scenarios may give rise to some concerns: First, muddling scenarios is a source of pathology. Are all occurrent emotions therefore pathological? That is, why would emotions ever fit their describable objects, and if they do, why would they ever not be pathologies of avowal? Second, would not such an account turn all emotions to some kind of an illusion? Are we always mistaken about what our emotional reactions are actually about given that other emotions sustain the emotional episode without our awareness?

I turn to the first concern. If all emotions muddle scenarios, then how can it be that many of them are nonetheless fitting to the external circumstances in which they occur? Emotions are not so reliably predictable and are often pathological and yet they still enjoy stability. Each person can be ascribed with more or less stable patterns of emotional reaction, and the objects of emotions are often describable as core relational themes, the rough-and-ready characterizations such as danger, wrong, achievement, benefit, etc. We often feel gratitude when we are helped, fear when we face danger, guilt when we wronged someone and so forth. Verbally expressed emotional reactions often fit their objects and survive normative judgments of fittingness.

This stability has two main sources. The first has to do with the origin of adult emotions in infantile basic emotions. Our occurrent emotions associatively relate to our emotional history that goes as far as the infantile basic emotional days. That is, the objects of the emotions of an adult imaginatively relate to the objects of basic emotions, objects that typically fit their emotion are suitable occasions for action tendencies such as running away or being aggressive, behaviors that are named with emotion-type words.

Those ancient objects in one's emotional history set the tone for the objects that follow, since the new objects relate to the old objects through not just one but many associations. And these associations, as explained in the first part of this chapter (5.i.1), are not random, but sharable and positively characterizable as similarity, inversion, part–whole, and part–part relations. Their non-arbitrary nature is what makes them amenable to after-the-fact further conceptual description. The fact that an accumulation of associations is needed to produce a new occurrent emotion ensures that many objects of newly formed reactions will relate to previous objects of that emotion-type in ways that can be made sense of. That is, any new occurrent emotion will be "stitched together" well, in a way that can be made intelligible after-the-fact through the more or less creative identification of thematic affinities.

Emotions that imaginatively connect with one another through quite a few associations may well be similar to one another also in the respect that their objects are both dangerous, or qualify as wrongs, or achievements and so forth. The familiar rough-and-ready characterizations of the typical objects of emotion-types, articulable by the adult as norms of fit, are such thematic affinities. They are effectively one of the respects in which many objects of different emotions of the same or similar enough type can be said to be similar to one another. Such themes, as repeatedly said in this chapter, are not causally operative but comprise after-the-fact descriptions of various connective threads that one can trace in an imaginative network. It is precisely this after-the-fact feature of this kind of add-on conceptual description that makes the typical descriptions of "formal objects" or of norms of fit rough-and-ready and not amenable to conceptual analysis Chapter 1). There is no one right way to ascribe themes to an imaginative network.

Imaginative associations are not cohesive enough to reliably produce occurrent emotions that generally fit the external circumstances in which they arise (they are not sameness relations or law-like rules), but neither are they too weak or arbitrary to reliably produce occurrent emotions that generally do not fit the external circumstances. Imaginative associations are just enough to keep our emotional life as stable as ordinary experience shows us that it is. It appears there is nothing intrinsic about the formation of an emotional reaction that would make it fitting or not fitting.

What of the possibility that all fitting emotions are pathologies of avowal? Many of our occurrent fitting emotions lend themselves to the identification of emotional patterns, such as my occasional irritation with the waiter, an occasional typical offence taken with a certain insensitive friend, repeated guilt for being late, compassion for and sadness about certain people in news stories. Probably many, or even most, occurrent fitting emotions also associate with an unconscious nodal emotion, which in turn captures other issues that the subject has not properly acknowledged. If there is no intrinsic feature that separates the production of pathological and non-pathological emotions, are they all pathological? It is strange to call my occasional and relatively minor irritation with the waiter or with rude drivers pathologies.

Some philosophers, such as Plato and Kant, embrace the thought that emotions are largely "bad" or pathological.[44] It is true that often emotions reveal our weaknesses. We often wish that we could be above what nevertheless gets to us. On the other hand, we would regard someone that never experiences emotions as inhuman and even as dangerous or evil.

Emotional reactions, in the first instance, are neither pathological nor healthy. Strictly non-inferential and non-rational, the emotions of human adults have no intrinsic purpose to track core relational themes, to enhance survival or promote one's well-being, and have no intrinsic way of failing to do so (see discussion in Chapter 2.5). In our contemporary civilized environment, whether an emotion is labeled "pathological" is a *pragmatic* matter decided after-the-fact in a manner that is culturally and normatively dependent.

Although the formation of all emotional reactions results from associative processes and not from appraisals of core relational themes, many emotions do not cause much trouble. They may be avowable, not criticized by others, and they do not make us feel that the world is against us in some global way. Other emotions may be criticized by one's social niche but the subject need not mind the criticism and may continue to avow her emotion and feel no need to make it go away.

Even non-avowable emotions need not be pathological. Some recalcitrant emotions, such as fear of spiders, need not be criticized by others nor cause that much inconvenience. They may be considered a forgivable and largely ignorable emotional idiosyncrasy.[45] Finally, some non-avowable emotions may be changeable and controllable in response to criticism and self-criticism in a way that makes them forgivable and manageable (this interaction with reason will be described at the end of this chapter).

Emotional patterns are labeled "pathological" when one can see that they cause great inconvenience or harm to one's relationships at home, at work, with friends, or at the café, in a way that causes self-aware distress either to the emoting subject or to the people with whom she emotionally relates. Whether or not an emotion is pathological is a socially interactive and a cultural matter, depending on what you and your social niche lets you get away with and expects from you.

The second concern regarding this account would be that if all occurrent emotional reactions "muddle" scenarios, then this might mean that we

44 Plato, *The Republic*, *The Complete Works of Plato*, ed. John M. Cooper (Indianapolis: Hackett, 1997). Immanuel Kant, "Anthropology from a Pragmatic Point of View" [1798], ed. and trans. Robert B. Louden (Cambridge: Cambridge University Press, 2006).

45 Carman, "First Persons," 401–402.

never actually or genuinely direct affect of a certain type to someone or something here-and-now. The term "muddle" suggests that we regard the imaginative-causal connections between the here-and-now and nodal emotions that do not straightforwardly resemble the here-and-now as a way of making a mistake. As if I only *appear* to be irritated by the waiter, whereas *really* I am irritated by someone else, the object of the enlivened nodal anger. One may worry that this means I am always under illusion as to which is the true target of my affective behavior.

And yet it is not the case that my affective behavior has one true target, circumscribed by a spatio-temporal context. The occurrent emotion and the nodal emotions are aroused together as an interconnected associative network through the accumulation of imaginative associations. Imaginative associations are bi-directional and disregard the temporal stratification of the network. Every affective episode is "smeared" over a few describable objects from various spatio-temporal circumstances, even if normally we attend only to the here-and-now target.

When it comes to the causal processes that produce affect, there is actually no target at all. On the associative account, there is no targeting, whether conceptual or non-conceptual. When it comes to basic emotions, there is a causal co-variance that matches certain action tendencies as well as physiological manifestations with certain here-and-now objects such as bears and heights. But the imaginative character of all emotions means that emotions have a few objects, most of which are not even present and belong to different spatio-temporal circumstances.

Only when we consider emotions in isolation from other emotions, that is, when we verbally list the series of emotions structured by the temporal stratification of the network, is there sense in talking about an object for each emotional attitude. Insofar as the affective processes are concerned, those describable, emotionally salient objects, the objects of all the emotions in the series, partake in an associative bundle that is intertwined with affect. There is no sense in selecting one of those objects, whether it is the here-and-now object or the objects of the nodal emotions that relate to different spatio-temporal circumstances, and declaring it as the true object or the target of the emotional episode.

And yet, the temporal stratification, namely the series of describable emotions including the occurrent emotion, is there to be exposed through verbal expression and report. All the emotions of the series have the same status insofar as their psychological reality is concerned. One's occurrent emotion is as real as can be. Its affective aspect is felt, and its describable aspect is easily acknowledgeable, at least in the cases dealt with in this book, namely of easily reportable emotional reactions to the here-and-now situation. When I say that I am irritated by the rude waiter or feel admiration for the volunteers at the soup kitchen, I am not confused. This is a good description of what I am feeling, of my experience of emotional salience. Often, I am not even wrong when, through verbal description and report, I identify the object of my emotion as the causal trigger of my emotion. Often, in other words, the object of my occurrent emotion was indeed the trigger for the affective–associative processes that produced that occurrent reaction.

My self-awareness is nevertheless limited or partial, since I am usually not aware that this triggering process has passed through the enlivenment of latent emotions, some of which do not bear a straightforward resemblance to the current reaction. The mistake one makes does not consist in muddling scenarios but in focusing on and attending *only* the here-and-now situation, describing the occurrent emotion and thereby declaring it the *only* emotion that one is experiencing, whereas in fact other describable emotions are also operative during the emotional episode. Although the object of the occurrent emotional reaction to the here-and-now situation may often be the trigger for the emotional episode, it is certainly not *the* cause of the emotional episode, but only one causal factor out of many.

Branching out the network of the series is inevitable on the associative account and demonstrates that no describable emotional reaction is more real than another. They are all real if by "real" we mean that the subject feels them, and they are all illusory if by "illusory" we mean that they are not caused individually and only by their describable object.

Although "muddling" is a misleading term, we can still call the enlivened nodal emotions paradigm scenarios if we wish, even if they are not exactly scenarios nor paradigms. The nodal emotions' significance as models or pictures that are brought to bear on the here-and-now situation making certain aspects of it emotionally salient does not come from their conceptually laden description or the propositional content of their perception (if it were indeed a conceptually laden perception), regarded as matching an emotion-type. These latent "scenarios," that are purely imagistic or otherwise sensual for the imagination, have been broken apart and stitched together again. Their affective intensity and the frequency with which their describable aspects are brought to bear on here-and-now situations comes from the accumulation of associations that their *fragments* participate in within the large emotional-imaginative network.

Neither is the here-and-now trigger of the affective–associative process a scenario, but rather *fragments* (certain perceived images or words) extracted from the here-and-now situation. It is only through attending to the here-and-now situation and through the description of its emotionally salient features that an occurrent emotion can be experienced as related to a scenario under description. Whether it is the occurrent emotion or the latent nodal emotions, it is only through their verbal expression and description that they are properly individuated. Prior to this activity of description, all we have are imagistic objects from various spatio-temporal circumstances and affect that is spread-out, so to speak, over those various inarticulate and not conceptually laden objects that are nonetheless describable. Our occurrent emotional experience includes attending to the here-and-now object, which in turn condenses the other objects (the terms in which the here-and-now object is seen) and whose emotional salience comes from the displacement of enlivened affect.

This new understanding of scenarios, as describable condensations of other emotional scenarios, means that scenarios may imaginatively and causally connect with one another, even if their affective aspect is of different types. In de Sousa's account, all anger episodes connect with other anger scenarios. De Sousa's paradigm scenarios participate in discrete processes; their function is type-preserving. On the associative account, conversely, the synthesized scenarios may imaginatively connect with and thereby be partly caused by scenarios of various emotion-types. This feature of the associative account may sound radical, but it is actually familiar from fiction as well as from the therapeutic experience.

For example, an anger scenario that imagistically presents the subject yelling at someone, may imaginatively connect with a guilt scenario that imaginatively presents someone yelling at the subject. These images imaginatively connect with another both through similarity (one person yelling at another) and through inversion (in the respect of roles, namely who is yelling at whom). Furthermore, the object of these specific anger and guilt scenarios may be quite similar. And so certain anger and guilt scenarios may be heavily associated with one another. In that manner, certain angry reactions may be partly caused by past guilt experiences.

Although certain guilt and anger scenarios are describable as instances of one person wronging another, it is not the case that all anger scenarios relate to all guilt scenarios through the notion of "wrong." "Wrong" is a theme that we can identify after-the-fact and is not causally operative. Rather, specific anger scenarios may be causally related to certain guilt scenarios through the accumulation of imaginative associations between other fragments of their describable aspects, between parts of their salient objects. In other words, specific anger and guilt attitudes may be causally related if their respective objects relate to one another imaginatively. It is almost a cliché to say that people are especially sensitive to wrongs similar to those they feel guilty about.

Consider the quite familiar experience of having a fleeting moment of disgust or contempt followed immediately by pity toward the same person. Both these consecutive occurrent emotions associatively connect with the same series of nodal emotions, or share a subset of such emotions. Indeed, plausibly, the self-aware disgust, most likely quickly ignored or dismissed, further contributes to the formation of pity. Pity comes with inverse action tendencies to disgust: the first comes with approaching the otherwise disgusting; the second with turning away from it. In that manner, experiencing an aversive reaction to one's feelings of disgust or contempt may associatively connect via similarity with previous experiences of pity, those whose salient object was someone miserable and weak that many would find disgusting.

Although such cases may seem contradictory and people may judge them as a demonstration of hypocrisy or as a reproachable incapacity for wholeheartedness, it is not the case that one emotion is more real or genuine than another. It is a case of mixed feelings, not just in the sense of having two ambivalent emotions more or less at the same time (consecutively), but also in the sense that they imaginatively interconnect with one another and with other emotions. Freud famously said that the unconscious knows no contradiction.[46] On the account I propose, the associative imagination knows no contradiction. Inversions positively connect ambivalent emotions to one another; not only are they both real and may both be fitting as implied in Greenspan's treatment of mixed feeling (see Chapter 1.2.A), but they are causally connected.

In fact, cases of mixed feelings are obvious candidates for suppression of both the affective and the describable aspects of one of the two inverse emotional attitudes. Many alienating–aversive reactions have as their objects emotions that are themselves affectively conflictual that can later be said to be incompatible with certain aspects of one's self-image as having a wholehearted positive affective relation with the object of that emotion. In other words, wholeheartedness or rather the lack of it, is a theme that can often be ascribed to aversive reactions after-the-fact. Self-deceptive deflection of one's attention can easily be achieved by focusing on the contrary occurrent emotion. I can thus feel happy for my friend without being aware that I am also envious of her, feel sorry for the homeless person without being aware that he also disgusts me and so forth.

I would like to note in passing, that we can also suffer emotional ambivalences where the two emotions are not in the first instance causally related. One of Freud's more famous patients, the Rat Man, does not acknowledge and keeps unconscious his rage against his father who beat him and especially his siblings when they were children and who has been interfering with his love life since early childhood.[47] He feels an aversion toward these emotions and does not acknowledge he has them.

If such latent anger were to be enlivened, the obvious route to deflect his attention away from it would be to focus on contrary dispositional emotions and enliven their affect, such as how he misses his dead father, his love for and admiration of his father, and so forth. Such positive emotions are real, and yet their affect in such cases would not be enlivened if it were not for the enlivenment of the inverse negative emotion that the Rat Man pushes away from his thoughts. Although the Rat Man indeed loves his father and misses him, he occasionally attends to and feels these emotions as a "cover up" when he turns a blind eye to his rage.

Even if basic emotions consist in specific behavioral and physiological manifestations that are reliably triggered by certain types of objects (e.g.

46 Freud, "The Unconscious," 187.

47 Freud, *Notes upon a Case of Obsessional Neurosis*.

bears, heights, caregivers) in infancy, later in life, emotional experiences with different affective aspects may imaginatively connect and thereby causally influence one another. In fact, I shall conclude this section with the claim that on the associative account, it is misleading to talk about emotion types as entities or mechanisms that correspond to emotion-type words.

On the associative account, emotions are various physiological and behavioral manifestations, whose causal formation is not merely physiological but a process that can be brought to awareness. Emotionally expressive behaviors or action tendencies typically involve certain salient people and things. These objects can be basic and inherited from the history of the species (e.g. bears, snakes). But most salient objects of adult emotions are much more varied due to the imaginative processes that give rise to those saliences. The fact that we classify and type emotional experiences with emotion-type words, does not mean that that those words capture discrete emotion production mechanisms.

Emotion-type words that designate basic emotions are applied to various combinations of prototypical affect and typical objects. It is precisely since they are not applied simply to prototypical physiological and behavioral manifestations that sub-personalists argue about the precision of classifications of basic emotions according to their prototypical output (see Chapter 2.1.E).

But what about emotion-type words that appear to designate what Griffiths calls "complex emotions" or what traditionally has been called "cognitive emotions," such as regret or pride, that involve typical thoughts? Aren't there clearly distinct and discrete complex emotions? Indeed, a conceptualist may worry about the associative account that claims that emotions are non-conceptual and insist: How can one feel regret without believing that one has done something wrong or made a bad mistake? How can one feel pride without believing that one is somehow great or lovely?

Ordinary experience shows that emotional experiences often involve thoughts and beliefs, and some of these beliefs may even be causal factors in the formation of emotions (in a way yet to be explained). But such beliefs, whether they precede or follow the formation of the emotion, are not, according to the associative account, part of the emotion itself. The emotional experience itself is simply its affective aspect, namely the prototypical physiological and behavioral manifestations, and its describable aspect (which emotions typically have), namely the experienced emotional salience of certain people and things. That the emotional experience we call "regret" involves the belief that one has made a mistake is a fact about language rather than about emotions. That is, complex or "cognitive" emotion-type words pick out not just typical affect and typical objects but also typical thoughts and beliefs that one entertains during the emotional episode.[48]

48 I thank David Macarthur for his help in clarifying this point.

When we talk about different cultures having different complex emotion-types, we are thus talking about differences in vocabulary and not about different emotion kinds. People's emotional-imaginative networks lend themselves to the identification of many themes that may be added-on to them, following various paths in the network, and emotion-type words are such themes that we ascribe to such networks. Since thematizing is an after-the-fact conceptual activity, it is no wonder that different cultures and different languages will thematize differently.

3. Person level affective processes, the relation to reason and the singularity question

In this section, I turn to the two main challenges for any causal account of emotion and show that the associative account can provide answers where other accounts fail. These are the challenges inherited from judgementalism that were articulated in Chapter 1.3.D. The first outstanding challenge, it may be recalled, is the question of reason-sensitivity, namely the strange unreliability of our capacity to dim down our emotional reactions through rational criticism in reference to various notions of appropriateness. The second is the singularity question, namely, why is this particular person having this particular describable emotional reaction here and now?

A. Emotions, judgments and reason-sensitivity

The proposed associative account for the formation of emotional reactions is the only account that involves no activity of evaluation. It is never the case, according to this account, that a judgment *per se* causes an emotion, by virtue of the evaluation it embeds. Making explicit judgments of emotion-fittingness may cause an emotional reaction indirectly. That is, what triggers the emotional response is not the judgment qua proposition, but its fragmentation to elements, namely to words with imagistic and associative "halo," and their association with elements of other emotions that are thereby enlivened. Judgments can become emotional once they have been broken apart and stitched back together again through the condensation of the describable aspects of other emotions and the displacement of their affect.

This means that a judgment such as "This remark is not offensive" may trigger an emotional reaction despite the "not" that appears in this judgment. The imagination is indifferent to logical relations. This is actually not such a strange situation. Imagine you are at a dinner party and someone tells a joke of which you are the subject, and you find it funny and laugh with everyone without the slightest bad feeling. The thought or the judgment "This joke is not offensive" did not even cross your mind. Then someone says to you: "oh, don't be offended, this was not an offensive joke." Now suddenly the thought that the joke may have been offensive has been planted in your mind. Now you can start comparing it imagistically with other occasions of offense. Indeed, you might suddenly stop feeling at ease without exactly understanding why. "Not" will not have an effect on our emotional state. There is no image for "not."

Once occurrent emotional episodes are verbally expressed in the form of emotional attitudes they become amenable to why-questions that call for their justification. In other words, once verbally described, emotions embed a look-alike reason that can then be subject to rational criticism in reference to the notions of appropriateness discussed in this book: type and intensity emotion fittingness, social or moral propriety, and fittingness to one's character or to one's self-conception in terms of one's endorsed cares and concerns. But according to the associative account, emotions do not have conceptual content. Although we can verbally express and describe our emotional episode by the sentence "I E that P," P is not the intentional content of the emotion, but just the verbal description of the emotionally salient features of the here-and-now situation. On the associative account, therefore, emotions are not sensitive to reasoning through the power that rational norms have on our rationality. If these norms have any force on emotions, it is peer group pressure to suppress and repress emotions. Nonetheless, the associative account allows for some responsiveness to reason, namely for certain emotions to genuinely dim down in response to reasoning, but that dimming down does not occur by virtue of a conceptual and rational connection between the deliberation and our emotion.

So what happens when we criticize our emotion and aim to dim it down? How can rational reflection have an effect on the non-inferential associations that make certain aspects of the here-and-now situation emotionally salient? Examine first the situation where the verbally expressed emotion, describable as "I E that P" is criticized as unfitting on the grounds that P is false. Reconsider Solomon's example discussed in Chapter 1.1: I am angry that John stole my car, and then I discover that John did not steal my car.

As explained in Chapter 5.ii.1, each series whose condensation sustains an emotional episode contains one nodal emotion that straightforwardly resembles the occurrent emotion. I will call it the "straightforward" nodal emotion, which effectively maps onto de Sousa's paradigm scenario that "objectively resembles" the here-and-now situation. So when I am angry that John stole my car, one of the nodal enlivened emotions would be an emotion that arose in response to some past stealth event in my life, for example, the time when my precious bag with all my personal things got stolen at the swimming pool.

When I realize that John did not steal my car, but that he bought a car just like mine, the association of straightforward similarity to that nodal emotion about my bag gets "unplugged." This is not because of the "not" in "John did not steal my car," but because of the alternative image that is now on my mind, namely that John bought a new car. Effectively, by saying that John did not steal my car but bought a car just like mine, I stop associating the current situation via straightforward similarity to the bag-stealth emotion. Unplugged, that straightforward nodal emotion no longer participates in the condensation that sustains my current emotional episode and no longer contributes any affect to the emotional salience of the here-and-now situation through displacement. That nodal emotion may still "vibrate" and contribute to the affective episode, but will no longer contribute to the salience of the here-and-now situation via displacement.

Now, according to the associative account, an emotional episode is caused by the condensed accumulation of *enough* associations. It could be the case that without the associations to the straightforward nodal emotion there would not be enough associations to sustain the condensation. In that case, the here-and-now situation will cease to be emotionally salient. The affective episode will not instantly subside, since affect has already been triggered, but it will be cut short, since the subject has no salient features to attend to. The hitherto salient object will not function as an ongoing trigger that could continue to sustain the episode. In such cases, subjects will think that their reasoning against the emotion has caused it to subside. And they will be right – but that causal relation is not due to a rationally constitutive relation between the belief that P and the emotional attitude.

If, however, there are enough associations to sustain a condensation even without the associations to the straightforward nodal emotion, that is, if the other synthesized nodal emotions of the series of emotions are themselves highly condensed and strong enough on their own, then the here-and-now situation will continue to be emotionally salient. The salience will not be as intense, since one nodal emotion (the straightforward one) no longer participates in the condensation and no longer contributes any affect via displacement – but the occurrent emotion will not subside. I may thus continue to be angry that John stole my car even when I know that he did not steal my car. Indeed, Freud gives the example of a woman who is jealous that her husband is having an affair with his employee even when she knows and genuinely believes that her husband is not having an affair with his employee.[49] In such cases, the subject may be frustrated that her reasoning against her emotional reaction fails to have the desired effect, the effect that is normatively required of her. In other words, she will describe her emotion as recalcitrant to reason.

Consider now cases where P is true but the emotion is criticized on the grounds that P does not fit E. The associative explanation has the resources to understand the difference between a phobic person that is consistently afraid of harmless spiders and an ignorant person who may be afraid of a harmless spider precisely because she does not know that the spider is harmless. The ignorant person sees a relatively harmless (yet large) Australian huntsman spider and reacts with fear also because one of the nodal

49 Freud, *Introductory Lectures*, Lecture 16, S.E., 16, 248–256.

emotions of the series whose condensation sustains her fear is a straightforward nodal emotion, for example, the fear she felt when she saw the big spider in the Harry Potter movie *Chamber of Secrets* or in the James Bond film *Dr. No*. When her local Aussie friend laughs and says it is not a poisonous spider, the friend's words may trigger an old memory where she picked up a small harmless spider to release in the garden, or perhaps she would need to see her friend calmly do the same with the huntsman in order to trigger that alternative image. The straightforward nodal fear of big and dangerous spiders gets unplugged and stops to contribute affect via displacement. The here-and-now huntsman now stops being emotionally salient. The subject may still feel her heart beat for a couple of minutes or so, she may even explicitly think about the spider from *Dr. No*, but the huntsman will no longer be emotionally salient. The phobic person, on the other hand, whose fear is sustained largely by nodal emotions that non-straightforwardly resemble or are otherwise associated to the here-and-now situation, will not stop being afraid of the huntsman, even if the straightforward nodal emotion has been unplugged.

Examine next the effect care-factor criticisms may have on one's emotional episode. Reconsider the example from Chapter 1, where I am insulted by a drunk on the street (Chapter 1.2.B). Say that the drunk was singing to himself an old children's song that I am familiar with, and as I hum along with him he suddenly yells at me to shut up and that my nose is ugly. Say that one of the nodal emotions that gets enlivened and contributes to the condensation that sustains my episode of offence is the disappointment and sadness which relates to a past occasion, when after breaking my nose, I looked in the mirror and realized that it will no longer be as straight as it was. The connections between the here-and-now and the there-and-then are relatively straightforward.

Other nodal emotions of the series that are less straightforwardly connected may be, for example, the disappointment I felt when I was told I am too old to audition for a certain movie that I was initially offered to act in, and also the envy I felt when my best friend became the girlfriend of the boy I loved when I was 8 years old. I always thought that this friend was more attractive than me, even if at the time my envy was not at all focused on her looks but on her musical talent, which that boy loved, given his own musical interest. Her looks may become implicitly relevant to that old emotion now, many years later, through the associations with the here-and-now situation with the singing drunk.

As I walk away from the drunk on the street feeling offended (an emotion whose affect may be quite similar to sadness), I ask myself, "Why am I taking this so personally? Who cares about this drunk?" I remind myself that although I sometimes look in the mirror, criticize how I look and wonder how I would look if my nose had not been broken, I don't really care so much about my broken nose. If I did care so much I would have gone to plastic surgery.

Effectively, this reasoning against my current offence describes the association between the here-and-now emotionally salient features and the relatively straightforward nodal emotion (regarding the broken nose). That is, the answer to the question, "Why do I care?" is effectively the same as the answer to what I called a how-question in the previous part of this chapter (5.i.1), the question that asks to specify the associations that partake in a condensation. In other words, this reasoning via inner speech amounts to giving an explanatory specification for the condensed occurrent emotion.

But the capacity of imaginative associations to displace affect depends on those associations being unidentified, undescribed. This is their feature as partaking in a condensation. *Verbally describing or identifying imaginative associations unplugs them from condensations.* This does not mean that the relatively straightforward emotion has stopped "vibrating," so to speak. But the condensation that supports the occurrent emotional attitude has been partly undone. My attention has shifted from the drunk and his comment and is now focused on myself and my own issues with my nose. Although I obviously care about my nose enough for this emotion to be latent rather than "dead," talking about it to myself, effectively serves to undo the displacement of affect from this nodal emotion to the current situation.

This partial un-doing of the condensation may cause the occurrent offence to subside, in case the other nodal emotions of the series are not, by themselves, intense enough to continue to sustain the emotional episode. In other words, if those other synthesized emotions are not that heavily condensed, if they do not imaginatively capture or synthesize large enough parts or aspects of my emotional life, then they will not on their own sustain the arousal of affect. In that case, I will take myself to have cut my emotional episode short through my reasoning against it, in reference to my endorsed cares and concerns. And I would be right, even if the subsidence of the here-and-now emotional salience did not occur by virtue of a rational constitutive relation.

But if the other nodal emotions of the series that do not straightforwardly connect with the current situation are heavily associated with fragments of the here-and-now, and if they are themselves highly condensed emotions, then they may continue to sustain on their own the current offence. If that is the case, the offence will be recalcitrant, since listing the respects in which the current situation does not merit my taking offence has no bearing on those synthesized nodal emotions. The more nodal those synthesized emotions of a series are, the more associations they condense to other emotions and to the here-and-now situation – the more recalcitrant the occurrent emotion will be. Perhaps removing the one straightforward nodal emotion may weaken the intensity of the occurrent emotion. Or that removal may alter how the object of the occurrent emotion is seen as emotionally salient, since the terms in which it is seen have altered. For example, my offence that the drunk thinks my nose is ugly may turn into disappointment and feelings of rejection that he did not want me to sing along with him.[50]

Although affective processes are non-inferential and are separate from rational processes, emotions may be responsive to reasoning and dim down due to the possibility to describe imaginative associations, that is, to give explanatory specifications for the condensed emotion and thereby unplug certain associations from the condensation in which they participated. If giving reasons against an emotion effectively addresses certain imagination associations, those can be disconnected as a consequence. Whether or not reasoning or rather the speaking it involves (either out loud or via inner speech) can dim down an emotion thus depends on weight of the nodal emotion that the criticism effectively addresses in comparison to the weight of the other synthesized nodal emotions of the relevant interconnected series. But this responsiveness of an emotion to reasoning effectively comprises a sensitivity to the articulation of explanatory specifications.

Alternatively, some care-factor criticisms may simply serve to motivate the subject to divert her attention elsewhere and think about something else. If I get upset that someone cut in front of me while driving, I may say to myself, "Why waste brain cells on this rude nobody?" And I will be right – yes, it is irritating, but it is not worth the irritation. My emotion need not subside in some genuine way. All I need to do is turn on the radio and think of something else. Turning a blind eye is not always a potentially harmful activity that might cause pathology in the future; it is a basic capacity that helps us cope with our ongoing challenges.

Importantly, rational criticism of any sort, whether care-factor criticism, fittingness criticism and certainly criticism in reference to various moralisms or considerations to do with social propriety, may also trigger an aversive response of suppression, through associative processes that connect the here-and-now criticism with certain nodal aversive reactions. On such occasions, when suppression occurs after verbal expression of the emotion and as a consequence of explicit criticism with reference to one's self-image and moral and social ideals, one turns a blind eye to the emotion precisely by giving reasons that justify the contrary state of mind.[51] In other words, sometimes, rational criticism can merely be a cover-up that facilitates the ignoring of an emotion, and the subject only misleads herself to think that she has caused her emotion to subside through a constitutive rational connection between that rational criticism and her emotional state.

Suppression and repression, our capacity for sustained habits of inattention, are the ones thanks to which, according to associative account, most

50 This section is inspired by Freud's discussion on the role of associations in the formation of dreams, indeed I see it as a transposition of Freud's discussion on the causation of associations from dreams to emotions. See especially Freud, *The Interpretation of Dreams*, S.E., 4, 176, 284, 330.

51 This is the self-deceptive technique that Bach calls "rationalization," mentioned in Chapter 3.4.A.

adults do not experience fear of harmless spiders or fear of heights when safe behind a fence. According to the associative account, we never genuinely get rid of or become "immunized" against basic emotions, namely of emotional reactions to basic objects such as bears, snakes, or caregivers (see Chapter 2.4). We may get "de-sensitized" to them only in the sense that we have strong and entrenched habits of ignoring the relevant nodal emotions. And those habits may be broken when encountering new situations that have not been blocked from triggering those old nodal basic emotions, such as a broken barrier on the roof of a sky-scraper, a big spider of an unfamiliar type, etc.

B. The singularity question

The associative account has the resources not only to make room for singularity (as the conceptualist seeing-as accounts do) but to provide an answer to the singularity question: Why is this specific individual experiencing this particular occurrent emotion with its describable and affective aspects here and now? Affect is triggered when an accumulation of imaginative associations passes a certain threshold. That threshold may be an individual matter or maybe it is more or less universal. I do not take a stand on this question. It could be that some people are more emotional than others. Or it could be that some people are especially skilled at ignoring their emotions or that they express them through their activities or their profession, for which they may have another rationale. Imaginative associations are cumulative causal factors. Once the threshold has been reached, the more associations we add, the more intense and the more recalcitrant an emotion will be.

The imagination has its habits, and certain associations may repeat themselves often enough, and Jonah, for example, associates Esther with his mother quite often. Yet even habitual associations need not always occur due to their "capriciousness," to use Hegel's term (see Introduction). Habits can be broken or abandoned and picked up again. The imagination is creative and may associate in new ways when facing either familiar or new circumstances. At times idiosyncratic, creative and capricious, imaginative associations do not obey laws or law-like generalizations and do not exhibit the kind of regularity that lends itself to very reliable prediction.

I want to note at this point that empirical psychologists have proposed various accounts of emotion that are similar, to some extent, to the one I propose in this book, classified under the heading "network theories."[52] This associative approach has not enjoyed much success precisely because the relevant experiments did not demonstrate the kind of regularity across many people that scientists looks for.

52 Mick Power and Tim Dalgleish, *Cognition and Emotion: From Order to Disorder*, 2nd edn. (Hove: Psychology Press, 2008), 73–81.

In particular, Gordon Bower has suggested a network theory that bears certain similarities to the one I present here.[53] The associations Bower speaks of are not imaginative but "semantic," that is, they connect entire propositions or concepts whose meaning is derived from their everyday linguistic usage within propositions.[54] Bower assumes that these linguistic associations among various concepts and propositionally described memories are stable. Indeed, Bower claims that these associations are permanent fixtures, awaiting activation, which would then link certain occurrent emotions with certain concepts and emotionally laden memories.

Bower thus tried to show that there is a general causal connection between happy/sad moods and the recollection of happy/sad memories while in that mood. One such experiment appeared to confirm the theory.[55] However, Bower admitted that he failed to replicate these results. He thus concluded in frustration: "The effect seems a will-of-the-wisp that appears or not in different experiments in capricious ways that I do not understand."[56]

But if the network is understood to be an imaginative network in flux, then one should not expect experimental consistency. The imagination is "capricious;" it is idiosyncratic and singular, that is, it can make different connections from time to time. More specifically, there is no reason to expect a happy mood to always connect with happy memories let alone the very same happy memories. For example, I may be in a happy mood and remember by way of inversion a day where I failed to achieve something, which in turn somehow imaginatively relate to certain people and things in the here-and-now situation.

The account proposed here does not explain every emotional reaction with reference to law-like regularities that would match external circumstances to emotional episodes of a specific type. Although some of us would prefer a scientific account that would reliably predict singular emotional reactions, the reality of our ordinary experience shows that emotions are not a source of reliable regularity in our lives. That the associative account is not a scientific account with reference to law-like causal processes is a strength rather than a weakness of this account. It is what enables this account to allow that similar circumstances would make one person emote and leave another indifferent or make a person emote today but not tomorrow.

This does not mean that emotions cannot be studied scientifically. Many questions about emotions lend themselves to scientific inquiry. One could

53 As Power and Dalgleish note, Bower's account is the one that is the closest to Freud and Breuer's account, whether or not Bower admits that influence.

54 See for example, Gordon H. Bower, "Mood and Memory," *American Psychologist* 36, no, 2 (1981): 135.

55 Power and Dalgleish, *Cognition and Emotion*, 76.

56 Bower, quoted in ibid., 77.

ask why we have emotions at all; why we have the basic emotions that we have; what are the basic objects that all infants respond to emotionally; what are the prototypical physiological and behavioral changes that characterize various types of affect. The associative account does not answer these questions but simply assumes that there are basic emotions, namely basic physiological and behavioral responses that make salient certain typical objects, inherited from the evolution of our species.

One can also ask about the different emotion-type words in different languages, and about the respective variety of social norms of emotion fittingness. One can also ask about norms of expression and inhibition of emotions, about norms of social propriety and about moralism norms that relate to certain emotions. A social science can study the differences among cultures and other social niches. Such a science cannot explain, however, why one person is moralistic about envy and another about pride. Freud can generalize and claim that, by and large, a young woman who grew up with bourgeois parents in turn-of-the-century Vienna is more likely to be moralistic about sex and sexually inhibited than a young woman who comes from the working class. One can even superimpose further classifications and their characteristic social norms and say that a young bourgeois woman is more likely to be moralistic about sex if she also went to a Catholic school. But each class of people, no matter how specified, would admit a certain variety among its members in relation to the norms of social prudence and the moralistic norms they hold particularly dear.

According to the associative account, one's emotional and imaginative network reflects the norms of one's social niche, at least some of them. Inhibitory norms can be ascribed to an individual inasmuch as they are themes that can be ascribed or added-on to that individual's network, that is, to the unacknowledged and ignored or unconscious part of that network. Indeed, many of the themes that we can add on after-the-fact to one's network can be regarded as the norms this individual is particularly sensitive to, including norms of fit. But the associative account does not explain the social source of those norms or why we have norms at all. The associative account can only serve to identify an individual's issues with certain specific moralisms or other social normative pressures.

One can also ask about trends of emotional response in a certain social niche. A statistical social science can conduct a study on a group of people from a certain social niche and note how they divide in their emotional responses. Statistical studies reveal aspects of our social imagination, that is, of the possibilities to emote and the distribution of responses typical of a social niche. Such studies may enable us to predict more or less how a group of people would emote and how they may express their emotions or what would be the distribution of responses among those people in certain circumstances. But if we want to ask why a specific individual spontaneously emotes in specific circumstances, generalizations about certain social niches will not help.

The associative account is in the realm of singular causation. That is to say, each emotional reaction is singularly caused not just by external circumstances, which in themselves may be reproducible, but by other causal factors: one's style and stable or occasional habits of association and one's habits of selective attention or inattention. Both these factors depend on one's singular biography. In particular, habits of selective attention reflect one's evolving singular self-image as a socially interacting person with certain moral and prudential standards and endorsed styles of social behavior. And importantly, how exactly the imagination associates in every given set of circumstances is a contingent matter. The imagination can associate in new and unpredictable ways, and which emotions are the nodes of one's associative network may change as well. The associative explanation is an explanation per person and that person is itself a moving target, an evolving and relatively inchoate object, given the non-conceptual and in-flux character of imaginative associations. The associative explanation is thus not just per person, but per person in a specific period in that person's life.

The associative account is not explanatory in reference to law-like very reliable processes that match a typical input with a typical output. But this does not mean that the output, the occurrent describable emotion, is left causally unexplained. Consider again what James Woodward says about singular causation:

> Singular causal explanations wear the source of their explanatory efficacy on their face – they explain not because they tacitly invoke a "hidden" law or statement of sufficient conditions, but because they identify conditions such that changes in these conditions would make a difference for whether the explanandum-phenomenon or some specified alternatives to it would ensue.[57]

In other words, imaginative associations are causes in the sense of "difference makers."[58] We can ask after-the-fact the "what-if-things-had-been-different?"[59] question about the associations whose accumulation is claimed to have caused the emotional reaction. That is, we can ask how would the emotional reaction have been different or how it would now change if we removed one or some of the associations that contributed to its formation.

The associative account provides a schematic answer to this question. If we remove associations through speaking, the occurrent emotion will change. The remaining associations may still accumulate beyond the threshold but the emotion will diminish in intensity respectively to the weight of

57 Woodward, "Singular Causal Explanation," 237.

58 Peter Menzies, "Causal Efficacy of Mental States," in *Physicalism and Mental Causation*, ed. Sven Walter and Heinz-Dieter Heckmann (Charlottesville, VA: Imprint Academic, 2003).

59 See for example Woodward, "Singular Causal Explanation," 236–237.

the associations removed. Or the salient object of the occurrent reaction may alter due to the change in the collection of there-and-then objects that partake in the condensation. If not enough associations remain then the emotion may be "turned off" altogether and the affect will subside. The associative account has the resources to answer the "what-if-things-had-been-different?" question in this general way. But these "specified alternatives" are not that specified, only schematic.

Indeed, due to the imaginative holism of the associative explanation, it is hard to imagine that the consequences of removing one or few associations that connect the here-and-now with certain nodal emotions would make a radical difference. Say that I left my last boyfriend following yet another jealousy attack of his. He has been to therapy, he realizes he should not be jealous and promised to stop his suspicions. During those attacks he said very hurtful things. So, after that specific attack, I was overcome with anger and fear that our future children would witness the verbal abuse of their mother and thought there is no way I can let them grow up like this. I said to myself that I had enough and left the relationship.

But what if that attack had not happened? Would I have not left him? I imagine that any reader who has left a relationship would have difficulties pointing to just one reason for leaving that relationship. Normally, there would be many such reasons. Many other occurrences could have triggered this breakup: as I make him a cup of tea I suddenly realize he never made me a cup of tea and that I cannot let my future children witness such an un-equilibrated relationship; or as he makes me dinner I am overcome with resentment that he has never made me dinner before; or after yet another unsatisfying sexual experience I am overcome with frustration and fear that I will never have sexual satisfaction. All of these occasions might have caused that breakup.

My anger and fear that this is not the life I want have become, over the years, nodal emotions with a growing degree of condensation. Although that high degree of condensation was not predetermined and its enlivenment is not a matter of fate, retroactively I can say that many events could have triggered these nodal emotions whose action tendency was to leave my boyfriend (a form of running away in fear and attacking in anger). When nodal emotions condense very many emotions with varied objects, then at some point in time something is likely to enliven them.

This suggests a radical difference between causation in the psychological realm and causation in the physical realm. In the latter we typically identify what we call "*the* cause," without which an event would not have occurred, even in the presence of the same background causal factors or "causal field."[60] In the psychological realm, the distinction between "*the* cause" and the background causal factors breaks down.

60 J. L. Mackie, "Causes and Conditions," *American Philosophical Quarterly* 2, no. 2 (1965).

In any case, practically speaking, we cannot conduct controlled experiments with imaginative associations. In practice, the "what-if-things-had-been-different?" question cannot be asked for all the associations that are said to have accumulated and produced an emotional reaction, since not all associations can be specified in the first place. In practice, we do not have at our disposal a full list of the associations of a specific subject that yielded the emotional reaction, given that these associations are made below the level of awareness. And so we cannot test and see what happens when we remove them one by one or when we remove nodal emotions from the interconnected series one by one in a controlled manner. In other words, although the associative account qualifies as a causal explanation and is therefore empirical, it is a non-scientific account.

Imaginative associations are "unobservable" and the enlivenment of nodal emotions is normally ignored prior to attempts of self-aware description and so, enlivened nodal emotions are not normally reportable.[61] And there is no mind-reading technology, at least for the moment, that would allow us to eavesdrop on someone else's fleetingly passing words and images. That associations are "unobservable" would not pose a problem for a scientific account, since their speculative postulation would be verified through their use in prediction across many people. This is presumably the hope for the (just as unobservable) automatic appraisals hypothesized by the sub-personalists. But since this account produces only singular explanations for specific emotions of an individual, this account appears to be speculative.

Even as a merely speculative account the associative account is methodologically advantageous in comparison to the conceptualist seeing-as account which offers no explanation for singularity, and also to the sub-personalist account, which is just as speculative. The associative account is consistent with our daily experience of emotions, namely that they are not-so-reliable and not-so-predictable, and that they are sometimes responsive to reason and sometimes not. But this account is not merely speculative and in the next chapter I discuss a non-scientific empirical method to inquire into the emotional-imaginative reality of a person.

In the next chapter I will claim that although one is not aware of the individual associations that accumulate into an emotional reaction as they occur, and although another person cannot "eavesdrop" on the fleeting awareness one has of one's nodal emotions, one can nevertheless "listen" to one's own (condensed) associations and identify in "real time" at least one nodal emotion of the relevant interconnected series through introspective awareness. I will claim that although we cannot control exactly the way we undo condensations or know whether or not we have untied all the relevant associations, it is possible nevertheless to partly undo the condensation and thereby manage and sometimes change our emotional patterns.

61 Reports by subject are the main source of empirical data in empirical psychology. See Introduction, fn. 15.

6 The associative method of inquiry into one's emotional patterns

The associative explanation for the formation of emotional reactions belongs to the realm of singular causation. As explained in the previous chapter, this renders the account I propose a non-scientific empirical account. The main concern about explanations such as the one I gave in Jonah's case is that the associations hypothesized might be *ad hoc* interpretations. There may be no way to show that Jonah's imagination actually makes these connections and that those are the ones that cause his emotional episodes of resentment.[1]

For this account to be not merely speculative, we need a method of empirical inquiry in "real-time,"during an emotional episode, that would allow the identification of an enlivened emotion and that would show the relevance of the associations between that emotion and the occurrent emotion. Since we cannot "eavesdrop" on another's fleetingly passing words and images, all we can rely on is the subjects' reports about the words and images that come to them.

Introspection is an empirical and non-scientific method of inquiry to one's own mental states. We may not be self-aware of everything that goes on in our minds and may not be able to describe well our emotions or desires. But we are able to attend to and recognize our passing thoughts, words and images that come to mind and explicitly strike our awareness and call our attention. This introspective capacity is taken for granted in many experiments in empirical psychology that often rely on subjects' reports.[2]

However, one can report only what one recognizes and pays attention to. According to the associative account I propose, one is very unlikely to be able to recognize the enlivenment of unconscious emotions since one normally ignores their describable aspect and attends only to the here-and-now emotionally salient features of the situation. One would need to change one's patterns of inattention and deliberately attempt to "listen" to

1 Power and Dalgleish mention this objection in connection to Bower's network theory of rational rather than imaginative associations (briefly described in the previous chapter): Power and Dalgleish, *Cognition and Emotion*, 78.

2 See Introduction, fn. 15.

one's passing words or images in real-time. The purpose of this chapter is to show that there is an empirical and non-scientific method of inquiry that can enable the modification of patterns of inattention, namely psychoanalytic therapy.

When it comes to our endorsable or tolerable emotional reactions, we usually do not feel the need to find an explanation beyond the one that the here-and-now situation provides us with.[3] Describing the salient object of our emotion often satisfies us and allows us to express our emotional reaction verbally and let our emotion run its course. It is only when one feels puzzled by one's emotional patterns or experiences them as problematic that one would seek further understanding.

In this chapter I aim to spell out how one may change one's patterns of inattention in therapy and become more self-aware of the formation of one's own emotions, in particular those that cause one trouble in social interactions. I emphasize at this point, that although the method I describe may be generalized for the treatment of other psychological symptoms (in particular obsessional neurosis and physiologically unexplainable aches and pains), I only discuss distinctively emotional symptoms such as occasional or stable recalcitrance or pathology of avowal.

The experience of psychoanalysis, I claim in this chapter, may make one more attentive to one's associative processes and use that self-awareness to control or even change one's emotional patterns. Although my claims in this chapter are consistent with the conceptual framework laid out in the previous chapter, these are admittedly empirical (yet non-scientific) claims. The skill to "listen" to one's fleeting associations ultimately refers to an experience that cannot be shown to others or done for others. My presentation of this process of becoming more self-aware relies on my own experience and should appeal to the experience of anyone who has undergone psychoanalytic therapy.

It should be remembered, that when I use the expression "the object of the emotion" I am not talking about an intentional object or about a target, since the associative account, as explained in the previous chapter, does not regard emotions as intentional states with conceptual content, nor as targeting anything. The object of the emotion here simply means the emotionally salient people and things in the here-and-now situation, and indeed, according to the associative account, each emotional experience involves other such objects from other spatio-temporal circumstances.

1. Free association

In the previous chapter I propose that the imagination associates all the time below the level of awareness, and that sometimes, when an accumulation of

3 See also Rorty, "Explaining Emotions," 103.

associations to a particular latent thought or memory surpasses a certain threshold, that thought or memory comes to one's mind. Such condensed associations that strike us may be words or images, laughter or emotions.[4] Such condensations that reach the surface of our awareness are (normally) triggered by words and/or perceived images in the here-and-now situation and they imaginatively relate to those here-and-now aspects.

We notice such condensations when something or someone makes us laugh, and some of us attend to such associations when facing a work of art. Often we simply ignore such associations as insignificant background "noise." At times we react aversively to passing thoughts or memories and deflect our attention away from them. And sometimes we experience them as interruptions in an otherwise rationally directed conversation or debate.

On occasion, associations come to mind when we do not engage in any particular intentional activity or conversation, when we stare at the here-and-now situation without directing our thought to make an argument or answer a question, to solve a problem or to describe our environment. When waiting for the bus, having an afternoon rest, or when sitting alone at a café, our mind "wanders" more or less freely. By "freely" I mean that many of the condensed associations that come to mind while we "stare" are not triggered by external circumstances, which further impose normative demands on what we should say or feel or do, but by previous associations that struck us during our quiet moment at the café or at the bus stop.

As described in the previous chapter (5.i.1.C), when attempting to meditate, we become aware of the difficulty not to free associate. But normally, in situations where we allow our minds to wander from one association to the next, we hardly remember what we were thinking about. Retroactively, we will normally describe ourselves as resting, relaxing, staring, being absent-minded or just bored. It is easy to ignore thoughts as meaningless or to deflect one's attention from an unpleasant association, when we are in the privacy of our own minds.

Although we all experience situations where we let our minds wander, we do not normally associate out loud when someone else is listening. Psychoanalysis is a peculiar situation where one person speaks, not in order to convey views or socially interact in a way that makes rational sense but to vocalize associations, and another person listens, an unusual kind of listening, which I describe in the next section.

Whereas we normally ignore our associations as unwelcome interruptions of our otherwise rationally directed thought, here one is asked to attend to and articulate them. Analysis thus provides a strange environment, where the one and only rule the patient is meant to obey is:

4 And also sexual desires, dreams, and even the experience of suddenly seeing similarity, inversion, part–whole and part–part relation.

> to put himself into a state of quiet, unreflecting self-observation, and to report to [the analyst] feelings, thoughts, memories – in the order in which they occur to him. At the same time [the analyst] warn[s] him expressly against giving way to any motive which would lead him to make a selection among these associations or to exclude any of them, whether on the ground that is too *disagreeable* or too *indiscreet* to say, or that it is too *unimportant* or *irrelevant*, or that it is *nonsensical* and need not be said. [The analyst] urge[s] him always to follow only the surface of his consciousness and to leave aside any criticism of what he finds, whatever shape that criticism may take.[5]

Free association – vocalizing whatever comes to one's mind – consists in the difficult task of breaking one's habits of inattention. The deliberate attempt to "listen" to one's passing thoughts, memories and feelings that one would otherwise ignore or deflect one's attention from, effectively suspends one's aversive reaction to that association. That is, while normally one is not self-aware when one suppresses a passing thought or emotion, the strange attempt to "listen" to oneself confronts a person with her aversion to some associations and her indifferent disregard of others.

The demand to vocalize such associations to an audience may give rise to silence, to a pause in one's speech, and may also give rise to explicit verbal expression, whether vocally or via inner speech, as to why that association should not be vocalized, that it is disgusting or immoral, that it is silly or strange. When a patient pauses before vocalizing a thought or feeling or memory, she is facing an explicit decision – to say or not to say, to be heard or not to be heard.

Suppression normally proceeds without interruptions precisely because it is not done under description. The psychoanalytic situation introduces an articulated version of suppression, where one is aware that one is reluctant to express one's association publicly because it is embarrassing, or shameful, or silly. Unlike merely deflecting one's attention, keeping silent is intentional and the reasons for it are easily articulable. In other words, the therapeutic setting forces reason to intervene in what would otherwise be an affective, non-rational, and non-conceptual process.

Freud says the patient should "leave aside" such reasons to keep silent. The relationship with the analyst differs from the relationships outside of analysis, where one obeys the normative pressure to maintain a certain image and be careful not to express immoral or otherwise ungraceful thoughts and emotions. The norms that govern everyday relationships do not apply to the psychoanalytic situation. That the analyst is a non-judgmental listener, disconnected from the patient's social world, is a reason to "leave aside any criticism" and give voice to an association. Each such

5 Freud, *Introductory Lectures*, Lecture 19, 287.

voicing of associations that one initially hesitates to vocalize cumulatively contributes to the patient's gradual change of her habits of inattention. I elaborate on this process later in this chapter.

2. Listening to oneself, to one's voice (and hypothesizing the series of nodal emotions)

Once associations are voiced, the analyst can listen and attend to them. We usually attend to what another says from the ordinary rational interpretative stance aimed at following an argument or an inference. The analyst listens to those voiced associations as well as to the patient's retreats to pauses, articulation of rehearsed views and apologetic qualifications, regarding them as associations that are imaginatively connected.

Much like a critic's approach to art, the analyst also is especially attentive to her own associations while listening to the patient, as those serve to identify imaginative connections among the patient's voiced associations. As the analyst listens to the patient's speech, fleeting memories to fragments of what the patient said half an hour ago, a day ago, a year ago will cross the analyst's mind, which inform the analyst about the connections between those fragments of speech. Associations to cultural references that cross the analyst's mind may also be helpful and indicative as to what goes on in the patient's imagination, given that they are (or should be, according to the view presented here), from similar social niches.

The analyst identifies similarities, inversions, part–whole and part–part relations among the patient's voiced associations, and these imaginative connections are indeed there to notice. The question remains as to whether or not the imaginative connections that the analyst identifies effectively trace the imaginative associations the patient actually makes and which lead the patient from one voiced association to the next. In his case studies, Freud seems convinced that the connections he, as an analyst, identifies are those that have causal effects on the patient.[6]

In what follows, I imagine an analytic situation in which the patient mentions often enough elements of the describable aspect of the nodal emotions that comprise the terms in which the here-and-now situation is seen as emotionally salient, those synthesized emotions that directly connect to the emotional symptom that the patient originally complained about. This need not be the case. It could be that the (imagistic aspect of the) memories that partake in the nodal emotions are hardly or not at all spoken of and that other emotional scenes receive more focus. I will discuss this possibility at the end of this chapter. For now, I assume that the voiced associations indicate, through various similarities, inversions, part–whole and

6 As mentioned in Chapter 5.i.1.A, Freud acknowledged the difficulty of his assumptions in the context of dream interpretation: see Freud, *The interpretation of Dreams*, S.E., 4, 280.

part–part relations, the presence of the unconscious emotions that "give shape" to the symptom. I treat this scenario first, a scenario that emphasizes the role of the series of the nodal emotions that directly connect with the symptom, mainly because it is the one portrayed in Freud's case studies as well as in contemporary philosophical understandings of Freudian psychoanalysis, such as Ricoeur's (see Chapter 4.2).

The listener of the voiced associations can thus hypothesize that the patient has certain nodal emotions, even if the patient does not affectively express them in a self-aware manner. It is easier for the analyst to identify imaginative connections and hypothesize unconscious emotions since they are not the analyst's emotions and the analyst does not need to counteract habits of inattention or "un-block" imaginative associations in order to identify them. The patient who "listens" to and voices her associations may also listen to her own voice and share the analyst's hypothesis. Richard Moran in his *Authority and Estrangement* describes the situation as follows:

> The person who feels anger at the dead parent for having abandoned her, or who feels betrayed or deprived of something by another child, may only know of this attitude through the eliciting and interpreting of evidence of various kinds. She might become thoroughly convinced, both from the constructions of the analyst, as well as from her own appreciation of the evidence, that this attitude must indeed be attributed to her … She can only learn of it in a fully theoretical manner, taking an empirical stance toward herself as a particular psychological subject.[7]

Moran, in other words, sees the process of identifying nodal emotions as a third-personal inquiry, whereby known concepts with agreed upon criteria of application may be employed to describe and explain evidence, a description available to anyone equipped with those concepts and the theoretical framework in which they partake, as well as with access to the same evidence.[8] The evidence Moran refers to here consists, presumably, of the voiced associations and other spontaneous gestures or pauses and so forth. And the theoretical framework to which this evidence is submitted is psychoanalysis.

The minimal theoretical framework suggested in this book amounts to the supposition that voiced associations imaginatively relate to one another and that those imaginative connections are partly what brought about these voiced associations in the first place. Partly – since on the associative account, there are more imaginative connections to various other fragments of memories, thoughts and emotions that causally contributed to the

7 Moran, *Authority and Estrangement*, 85.
8 Robert B. Pippin, "Natural and Normative," *Daedelus* 138, no. 3 (2009): 39.

formation of a voiced association in addition to the connection to the association that was voiced just beforehand. The empirical assumption then, is that voiced associations, even when they seem rationally disconnected from one another and do not follow any line of reasoning or inference, are not just randomly appearing in the patient's mind one after the other. Rather, they follow an imaginative thread of similarities, inversions, part–whole, and part–part relations, which are not arbitrary. To speak metaphorically, the analyst assumes that there is an imaginative connective tissue among the voiced associations. Identifying imaginative threads, however, is not a matter of applying concepts with clear conditions of application nor is it necessarily accessible to anyone.

Similarities, inversions, part–whole and part–part connections that a listener can identify among another's voiced associations, do not have clear criteria of application. People may or may not be able to see such connections spontaneously and may or may not see connections that others try to show them. The only way to "prove" that a listener is indeed identifying imaginative threads among another's voiced associations consists in getting another listener to see the same imaginative connections.

But listening in analysis does not seek merely to identify imaginative threads as some kind of a creative construction; it aims at "getting" another person, as we say, and how that person's imagination works.[9] That is, the imaginative threads found in analysis should trace, by and large, associations that the patient makes below the level of awareness. To even have a chance of tracing such associations, a listener should speak the same language as the patient and preferably be from a similar social niche and so share many cultural and social references. A listener that has been listening to another's voiced associations for a very long time would gradually begin to share more associations with the person speaking, if only because such a listener would know more about the life experiences of the patient, experiences that partake in the patient's imaginative network. The more the imaginative networks of two people overlap, the more likely they are to get one another.

In fact, on the face of it, if one did not have to face the challenge of changing one's habits of inattention, one would be one's own best listener given that in such a limit case, the speaker's network and the listener's network are identical. And yet the interplay of listening and "listening" to oneself requires the presence of another listener other than oneself. It is that other listener that induces the non-judgmental peculiar atmosphere of analysis, it is the very presence of a listener that requires the use of the voice, which in turn confronts the patient with her habits of inattention, and it is the awareness that someone is listening that encourages one to listen to one's own voice and attend to it from the imaginative perspective of connecting voiced associations.

9 See also Lear, *Freud*, 45.

The special kind of listening involved in analysis occurs in a second-personal space. The existence of imaginative threads cannot be proven to anyone by turning to facts (or poetry and literature would be considered objects for scientific study). Voiced associations are not exactly evidence since the relation between those associations and a hypothesized unconscious emotion is not an inferential relation. The listener is as if painting with the voiced associations, connecting them with zigzag lines to one another. The imaginative character of the zigzag lines lends them to thematizing, and the listener can apply concepts and identify patterns, coloring the zigzag lines with thematic threads, and tracing how the zigzag lines appear to converge into a hypothesized unconscious emotion.

This hypothesis is more like balancing a painting then it is like connecting dots on a graph that is predetermined by some theoretical framework to be linear or sinusoidal, thereby hypothesizing the existence of many more dots. Ultimately, getting how another person's imagination works and identifying its patterns requires a listener qua person, with a specific language, social norms, inhibitions and cultural references, who can be sensitive to the nuances and connotations of what is said or otherwise expressed in analysis.

In Freud's case studies, as well as is implied in the above quote of Moran, it is the analyst that suggests the hypothesis of unconscious mental states to the patient.[10] But even if the imaginative connections Freud identifies indeed play a causal role in the patient's psychology and even if Freud hypothesizes the correct nodal emotions, how could he know that these are in fact causal factors rather than mere interpretations? The early Freud supposed that voicing the hypothesized nodal emotion should enliven that emotion in the patient, who would then verbally express that emotion. Repression would thus be removed and the patient cured.

Often, however, early Freud's patients would listen to Freud's hypothetical explanations of their symptoms with no effect:

> It is as though the patient were saying: "Yes, that's all very nice and interesting, and I'll be very glad to go on with it further. It would change my illness a lot if it were true. But I don't in the least believe that it *is* true; and, so long as I don't believe it, it makes no difference to my illness."[11]

The patient can adopt the stance of the analyst toward her own voiced associations. With the help of the analyst, the patient can also see the

10 For discussions about how the analyst should convey interpretations to the patient see Lear, *Freud*, Chapter 1; Neville Symington, *A Healing Conversation: How Healing Happens* (London: H. Karnac Books, 2006), Chapter 5. See also Marcia Cavell's description of such a particular occasion: Marcia Cavell, *Becoming a Subject* (Oxford: Clarendon Press, 2006), 31–33.

11 Freud, *Introductory Lectures*, Lecture 19, 290.

imaginative connections that the analyst identifies. These connections are described within a second-personal space, and the similarities, inversions, part–whole and part–part relations identified by the analyst are indeed there to be identified and the patient may, at least in principle, identify the same connections the analyst does. The analyst can add on the thematic stratification and construct a "story of suffering." The patient may listen to the narrative that the analyst constructs from her voiced associations and see for herself that the story indeed makes sense of her symptom in terms of her past experiences. But nothing forces the patient to accept the story as a true description of how she came to suffer from the psychological symptom she complains about. The story may be analogous to finding meaning in the night's sky rather than actually tracing causal connections.

Even if the patient believes every word the analyst says and trusts that the series of nodal emotions Freud identifies indeed causes her symptom through condensation and displacement, and even if Freud got the zigzag lines right and identified the correct nodal emotions, and the patient's belief constitutes knowledge. What difference would that newly acquired knowledge make? Later Freud criticizes his early hopes that deciphering the riddle of the symptom in this manner would remove repression:

> If only that was how things happened! ... there are different sorts of knowledge, which are far from equivalent psychologically ... If the doctor transfers his knowledge to the patient as a piece of information, it has no result ... The patient knows after this what he did not know before – the sense of his symptoms; yet he knows it just as little as he did. Thus we learn that there is more than one kind of ignorance ... But our thesis that the symptoms vanish when their sense is known remains true in spite of this. All we have to add is that the knowledge must rest on an internal change in the patient.[12]

In a sense, both patient and analyst share a similar ignorance in the beginning of analysis, namely, neither of them knows the facts about the patient's psychology. This kind of ignorance can be remedied by a correct hypothesis of the operative unconscious emotions in the manner described above. But this is not the kind of ignorance that causes the symptom. The patient suffers from an unawareness of the explanation of her symptom that cannot be shared by the analyst. This psychological (rather than factual or theoretical) unawareness is two-fold.

First, she is unaware of certain emotions in the sense that they are buffered from her immediate awareness by patterns of inattention. And second, she is unaware of the associative processes that causally connect those ignored emotions with her symptom. Once we understand the

12 Freud, *Introductory Lectures*, Lecture 18, 281.

Freudian unconscious as two different kinds of unawareness, making the unconscious conscious can be understood as two different kinds of "internal changes."

The first "internal change" would consist in rendering conscious the nodal unconscious emotions, unconscious in the sense of inattention. Somehow the patterns of inattention break during anaylsis in a way that allows the verbal expression of hitherto ignored emotions. The second "internal change" would be to somehow become aware of certain associative connections between certain unacknowledged emotions and the symptom in a way that would make the patient see that these associative connections are also causal connections and not mere interpretations.

Freud is concerned with the patient's becoming aware of the "sense of [her] symptoms," and by that he refers to the exposure of the synthesized nodal emotions and the manner in which they are condensed into the symptom. According to the associative account I propose, since the nodal emotions cause the symptom due to their high degree of condensation of *other* emotions, the "internal change" that needs to occur in therapy is the un-doing of *that* condensation.

In the next two sections I follow the proposed route of analysis that is largely concerned with deciphering the symptom in the right way, the way that would make a difference in the patient. In the next section I examine how a patient who has been "listening" and listening to herself during analysis and has come to hypothesize certain nodal emotions can go through a kind of internal change that can convince her that indeed those emotions cause her symptom. I then examine what kind of internal change may be involved in verbally expressing hitherto unconscious or unacknowledged emotions, before going on to explain that on the associative account, verbally expressing an emotion involves not only describing its object, but also the gradual undoing of the condensation that sustains it. The associative account thus provides new ways to understand the "internal changes" involved in psychoanalytic therapy.

3. "Listening" to oneself, to one's associations (and self-management)

The very activity of voicing associations, as described above, involves "listening" to one's passing thoughts, images of memory or fantasy, and affective feelings. Introspective awareness, the deliberate attention to words, phrases, and images that pop into our minds and to feelings that come over us, is available to all of us, even if we do not often make use of it. In analysis, the patient effectively cultivates the capacity to "listen" to her passing thoughts and emotions, a skill that manifests itself also outside of the therapeutic situation.

Individual imaginative associations as such, however, cannot, in the first instance, be "listened" to in a straightforward manner, since they are made below the level of awareness. One cannot be aware that one has made various connections and *thereby* caused an emotion or a thought to strike one's awareness. All one can be aware of or "listen" to in the first instance is the condensed result, that is, that various words or images are crossing one's mind in a certain order, or that a specific emotional reaction has come over one.

Although individual imaginative associations are not available to awareness in the first instance, these individual associations remain operative during an emotional episode. An emotional episode is sustained by the condensation and displacement of the series of nodal emotions that gave rise to it. In fact, according to the associative account, the nodal emotions that get enlivened together thereby rendering the present situation emotionally salient, are available to verbal description and expression in the first instance, in the same manner that any enlivened emotion would be describable.

Normally, one immediately and non-reflectively turns away from enlivened nodal emotions in accordance with one's habits of inattention, and focuses on the here-and-now situation to comply with the normal expectation to describe one's occurrent emotion, thereby circumscribing the object of the affect to the here-and-now situation. But the subject who is undergoing therapy is in the process of changing habits of inattention. The verbal expression of the occurrent emotion during therapy is thus less likely to focus the subject's attention entirely on the external circumstances.

In fact, without the subject's habitual turning away from the describable aspect of an enlivened nodal emotion, the verbal description of the here-and-now emotionally salient features is likely to further and more explicitly enliven certain words and images of the describable aspect of at least one nodal emotion. The words the subject uses to express her occurrent emotion, whether out loud or via inner speech, re-trigger specific associations that connect verbalized fragments of the here-and-now situation with fragments of the describable aspect of a nodal emotion. Certain words and images from the describable aspect of the nodal emotion, fleetingly come to one's awareness.

As Jonah resents that Esther just gave him an assignment, he thinks to himself, "Why does she give me these irritating assignments all the time? I feel suffocated in this office!" As Jonah describes to himself what he feels for Esther, he may have a fleeting memory of his childhood scarf scenes. Verbally expressing the occurrent emotion triggers a re-run, so to speak, of the associations that are currently condensed into the occurrent emotion. Trained in analysis, it becomes more difficult to ignore words and images to that come to one's mind. Jonah describes to himself the various inversions and similarities he now sees between the current situation with Esther and the scarf scenes.

How can we know whether Jonah's fleeting image of the scarf scenes was indeed an echo, so to speak, of a causally operative association, or whether

Jonah simply cannot help remembering the scarf scenes since they have been discussed in therapy in connection to the symptom? If the nodal emotion in question is indeed taking part in the condensation of the emotional episode Jonah is now in the midst of, then we should expect that identifying the associations that lead to it would make a difference to Jonah's feelings of resentment.

If those imaginative connections are indeed contributing causal factors of the resentment Jonah is now experiencing, then when Jonah describes the various connections and perhaps also further provides the respects in which they hold he is effectively unpacking, at least partly, the condensation that causally support his resentment. As Jonah attends to the connections between the here-and-now and the scarf scenes, he is effectively separating the here-and-now emotional salience and the old emotion. That is, the displacement of affect from the nodal emotion about the scarf scenes to the here-and-now situation is undone. Instead of experiencing the affect of resentment as addressed to one here-and-now object (namely Esther), Jonah's attention is divided across two different and imaginatively connected objects.

In other words, describing in words the various connections to a certain nodal emotion, namely providing what I called in the previous chapter an "explanatory specification," (5.i.1.A) unplugs this nodal emotion from the condensed series that sustains the current affective episode. As a result, the salient object of the occurrent emotion may alter, or the intensity of the occurrent emotion will dim down or perhaps even subside altogether, depending on the other nodal emotions in the relevant series whose condensation supports the occurrent emotion. Occurrent emotions can be, to some limited extent, as described in the previous chapter (5.ii.3.A), sensitive to explanatory specifications, that is, to the verbally described version of an imaginative association. An explanatory specification traces a causal factor for the blended or condensed co-presence of two describable emotions, a tracing that effectively takes away this blending and thereby cancels the displacement of affect which the association initially caused in its unidentified (or unconscious, inattended) form.

Even if the occurrent emotion does not subside spontaneously as a result of the unplugging of one of the nodal emotions that gave rise to it, the subject may use the explanatory specifications of associations to control or dim down the occurrent emotion. Explanatory specifications are not reasons in the standard normative sense, and there is no sense in saying whether an imaginative association is good or bad. Whether something can be seen as similar or as inverse to something else or as part to a whole is a subjective matter, with no objective counterpart. Although we expect others to see what we see, they may not see what we see and that will not mean that they have poor eyesight or that they are irrational. But we can nevertheless judge whether a similarity is straightforward or not or whether the enlivened nodal emotion in question is relevant to the situation at hand.

Jonah's efforts of verbal description in real-time demonstrate that Esther does not straightforwardly resemble Jonah's mother and that the assignments do not bear a strong or straightforward similarity to the scarves. Jonah can then see that what causes his resentment is not a consideration that bears on whether Esther is resentment-provoking.[13] And he can use that understanding to control and dim down his emotion. Specifically, describing explanatory specifications provides a way out or a distraction from the here-and-now situation. Jonah can turn his attention away from Esther and focus instead on the now unplugged nodal emotion.

Even if Jonah has not fully acknowledged in analysis the presence of that nodal emotion, he is now busy verbally expressing it, albeit indirectly. As Jonah manages to dim down his resentment of Esther, he begins to think about his mother and the scarf scenes. He may not re-feel that old resentment but he is now thinking about it, perhaps resentful now that these old scenes had this far-reaching emotional effect on him.

This newly developed skill to "listen" to one's associations in real-time, during an emotional episode, provides the patient with a new skill for self-management whereby the patient can control or dim down her occurrent emotion. Within the framework of singular causation, such an experience of self-management effectively comprises an answer to a "what-if-things-had-been-different" question. In other words, the now described associations could be identified as "difference makers" to the emotional episode. Ordinarily, when we are able to identify a difference-maker we infer that we have identified a causal condition to the event that we have managed to alter through this intervention. That is, we can take the effect of "listening" to certain associations can have on one's emotional episode to be showing that those associations were contributing causal factors to that episode.

The experience described in this section cannot be shown to or done for anyone. It can only be described or reported by a subject through the empirical yet non-scientific method of "listening" to one's own associations. I can only appeal to the reader who has undergone psychoanalytic therapy and who is familiar with this experience to regard it as empirical support to the associative explanation in general and for the claim that the episodic nature of an emotional reaction, its temporal duration, allows one to attend to individual associations – which in the first instance occur automatically and below the level of awareness and are present together, blended, condensed.

When a patient realizes that she can self-manage her pathological emotional pattern in this manner, the patient can, through this "internal change" become "thoroughly convinced" that there is indeed a causal and not merely an imaginative connection between her symptom and certain hypothesized nodal emotions. Jonah may not admit or feel that he still

13 On how to understand reasons in the normative sense as considerations that bear on a question see Hieronymi's account, which is very similar to Scanlon's: Pamela Hieronymi, "The Wrong Kind of Reason," *The Journal of Philosophy* 102, no. 9 (2005): 437–457.

resents his mother, but he may nevertheless become convinced that he *must be* resentful of her, and that this old resentment affects his emotional life today in non-desirable ways.

As time goes by, the patient realizes, both through listening to her own voice in analysis and through "listening" to her associations in the midst of some of her emotional episodes that her imagination is quite limited in the places it leads to. Her imagination connects her symptom in real-time to thoughts and emotions that involve recurrent figures, relationships, and memories, which are also familiar from her voiced associations in the analytic situation. The patient gets the hang of her own imagination. She learns how her imagination works and what are its habits or its patterns of association that causally contribute to her symptom. Through the interplay of listening and "listening" one may come to identify the series of nodal emotions that gives rise to one's symptom or at least a part of that series.

Even if the patient is still unable to re-feel and express the nodal emotions in question, a patient that has acquired this new skill of self-management may be tempted to conclude her analysis. Once the series of relevant emotions or emotionally laden memories that comprise the terms in which certain present features have become emotionally salient has been identified through this interplay of listening and "listening" to herself, patient and analyst have deciphered the riddle of the symptom and can construct an etiological narrative.

Jonah can go on with his life with the belief that his relationship with his mother has ruined his life, and manage his symptomatic emotions accordingly. Lear's patient Mr. A (Chapter 3.2), who, say, identified the relevant scene of childhood betrayal, can control his feelings when his girlfriend gets irritated with him at home or when his colleagues compete with him at work. He now knows that these feelings of betrayal are caused only partly because of the contemporary context in which they arise and that those associations to the old scene of betrayal are significant causal factors in his emotional pattern.

At least they are aware of their issues and are able to recognize when these issues cause them to have unreasonable or at least unnecessary troubling emotions. Whenever they experience an episode of their pathological emotional pattern, they can quickly assist in the new skill they have for real-time introspective awareness, and manage their reaction through the identification and description of (some of) its explanatory specifications. The patient can time and again free herself from the nodes that causally contribute to her behavior and dim down the pathological emotional reaction.

Unfortunately, that self-management has to take place time and again, and each time this will ultimately amount to thinking again about those nodal issues. The patient can unplug a nodal emotion by "listening" to its describable aspect and identifying its object and how it or its parts imaginatively connect with fragments of the here-and-now emotionally salient people and things; but she cannot eliminate the nodal emotion or change its place or affective weight within her imaginative–emotional network. These are her nodal emotions and this kind of introspective awareness will not change their potential to cause future occasions of the same troubling emotional pattern.

Alienated from his resentments of his mother, Jonah can regard them and their connection to his recalcitrant resentment of Esther as the doings of some foreign and secret agency within him, whose activities can only be traced after-the-fact through "listening" to and verbalizing them. Even if Jonah is able to "listen" in real-time, during an emotional episode, to words and images from the describable aspect of a nodal emotion, these real-time associations strike or come to his awareness, as if someone else within him is communicating with him.

The patient now *knows very well* that these nodal emotions should not matter in the here-and-now circumstances that only imaginatively or not straightforwardly resemble them, and that belief can be used to control the symptom. *But* these nodal emotions *still* matter anyway, since their enlivenment is not under the patient's control. The patient is responsible for self-managing her symptom through self-awareness, but she cannot be responsible for the operative nodes themselves, since those strike her with no conscious control or intention.

Recall the famous formula of Octave Mannoni: "*Yes, I know very well ... but still.*"[14] In this context the phrase reads as: "*Yes, I know very well* that my emotional symptom is caused by those nodal emotions that are only imaginatively connected to my symptom. *I know* that these nodal emotions are not relevant in the here-and-now situation and indeed I can manage my symptom and control it. *But still* – these nodes have determined my automatic imaginative patterns and thus my emotional life and there is nothing I can do about *that. I* can manage but not change *It.*"

In other words, although *I* rationally disavow the effects of *It*, *It* is just as important as it always was. The nodal emotions are intellectually and introspectively recognized as the causal source of the emotional symptom. Yet the patient sees them as that "pathogen" inside her coming from that foreign *It*, for which her reasonable *I* is not and cannot be responsible, just as she is not responsible for physiological problems with the endocrine system.[15] All *I* can do is "listen" to and recognize *It*, put *It* in its place, until the next time *It* strikes my awareness.

14 Octave Mannoni, "Je sais bien, mais quand même" [1963] in *Clefs Pour L'Imaginaire ou L'autre Scène* (Paris: Editions du Seuil, 1969). That article is mostly about religious and mystical beliefs that persist despite their deliberative disavowal, through the ascription of those beliefs to others. The formula is, however, applicable here as well, and indeed, as Russell Grigg says, in many cases where one avoids responsibility for being unreasonable (personal communication).

15 Freud calls such an emotionally laden memory that causes a symptom "pathogenic memory," all through *Studies on Hysteria*, for example in Breuer and Freud, *Preliminary Communication*, 12.

The "internal change" described in this section consists in the skill to self-manage one's symptoms in real-time through attending or listening to associations. But another "internal change" is required in order to get acquainted with the nodal emotions and not merely be "thoroughly convinced" of their existence. I discuss this second kind of "internal change," the kind that philosophers with an interest in psychoanalysis usually attempt to explain, in the next section.

4. Expressing (hitherto) unconscious emotions

It is almost a cliché to say that bringing the unconscious to consciousness or that de-alienating an emotion consists in expressing that emotion as one's own and taking responsibility for it. But what is the nature of this responsibility and "ownership" and what is the "internal change" that it involves?

Moran, who has been classified as a judgmentalist about emotions in Chapter 1.1, understands such "ownership" in rational terms. That is, the aspect of the mind that is ours as agents and for which we are responsible consists in our deliberative reasoning and its conclusion in a reflectively endorsed mental state. This is not to say that whether reasons are good or bad reasons or whether an inference is valid is a voluntary matter. Whether reasons are good reasons can be judged in reference to the relevant norms (of truth, language use, emotion-fittingness, moral norms etc.). And yet, endorsing a reason as valid is an activity of an agent, not the passive afflictions of a patient. Nobody else but the agent can avow those reasons as *her* reasons to endorse or reject one of her own mental states.

In other words, for Moran, a person asserts herself qua person, qua agent (in a social world) rather than patient, when she articulates and endorses her own reasons to emote (or not), to believe (or not), to act or desire. According to Moran, expressing one's emotion as one's own, rather than merely attributing it to oneself, consists in articulating such endorsed reasons and thereby avowing one's emotion:

> The person might be *told* of her feeling of betrayal, and she may not doubt this. But without her capacity to endorse or withhold endorsement from that attitude, and without the exercise of that capacity making a difference to what she feels, this information may as well be about some other person, or about the voices in her head. From within a purely attributional awareness of herself, she is no more in a position to speak for her feeling than she was before, for she admits no authority over them.[16]

According to Moran's view, verbally expressing an emotion involves looking "out there" to features of the situation the emotion is directed at, and

16 Moran, *Authority and Estrangement*, 93.

rationally deliberating whether or not the situation indeed fits the relevant emotion-type (see 1.1). Expressing an emotion as one's own attitude rather than a state of mind that one passively suffers consists in avowing the emotion as justified. The patient's problem, according to Moran, is that she cannot avow the hypothesized nodal emotions. As Moran says:

> [W]hen [the patient] reflects on the world-directed question itself, whether she has indeed been betrayed by this person, she may find that the answer is no or can't be settled one way or the other ... We might say that the analysand can report on such a belief [the belief that she feels betrayed], but that she does not express it, since although she will describe herself as feeling betrayed she will not in her present state affirm the judgment that this person has in fact betrayed her.[17]

These passages imply that a patient will successfully express her hitherto unconscious emotion if she becomes able to avow it. Taking responsibility for an emotion means, for Moran, to get clear on the reasons for and against it and endorse or reject that emotion according to one's self-aware conclusion of this deliberation. It is when one's emotions become synchronized with one's rational judgment that the emotion is properly "owned," since for Moran, what is properly one's own is what one does or thinks deliberatively and intentionally as a rational agent.

It is in the context of the above passages from Moran's book that Jonathan Lear speaks of pathology of avowal (discussed in Chapter 3.2), and warns against the reliance on rational deliberation and reflective endorsement of an emotion. Rational avowal, Lear says, may cooperate with one's pathology and further entrench an emotion as justified in a way that serves to conceal other emotions that are in fact operative in the person's psychology.[18]

I am not so concerned with the possibility of pathology of avowal in this context. What I find problematic is the very idea that avowal of the sort Moran describes entails an expression of an unconscious emotion at all. If the starting point is an unconscious emotion, that is an emotion that is not currently being affectively experienced, why should avowal make a difference? Claiming that avowal is an expression of a hitherto unconscious emotion amounts to claiming that one would start emoting when one reaches the conclusion that a certain emotion fits the situation under reflection.[19]

As repeatedly argued in this book, judging that I have indeed been betrayed need not involve actually *feeling* betrayed. I can look "out there" at the object of my hypothesized emotion and judge that I have indeed been

17 Moran, *Authority and Estrangement*, 85.

18 Lear, "Avowal and Unfreedom." See also: Jonathan Lear, *A Case for Irony* (Cambridge, MA: Harvard University Press, 2011), Chapter 2, § 5.

19 And Moran seems to claim this in Moran, *Authority and Estrangement*, 57–60. See discussion in Chapter 1.1.

betrayed and even think that I should feel betrayed and yet fail to experience the emotion. What I express in such a case is a rational judgment of fittingness, namely a belief, and that belief need not be accompanied by an emotion, which according to a judgmentalist has intentional content that is the same as that of the belief.

The capacity to avow or disavow an emotion in a manner that may (or may not) affect that emotion accordingly depends on one experiencing and expressing that emotion in the first place. It is only when one actually feels an emotion and is able to verbally express it that one can "step back" from it and assess whether or not one reflectively endorses that emotion as fitting. When it comes to a hypothesized unconscious emotion, it is thus unclear how deliberation that is aimed at an avowal or disavowal would even begin.

Reading Moran's replies to Lear's *A Case for Irony* indicates that Moran does not aim to explain the distinctively psychoanalytic reflective process and how it serves to remove repression.[20] Rather, he offers a more modest diagnosis of what taking responsibility on a hitherto unconscious emotion should entail. His point, as I read it, is exactly that only once repression is removed and one indeed experiences an emotion and is able to verbally express it, one should be able to avow or disavow it. On this reading, taking responsibility on a hitherto unconscious emotion means restoring its reason-sensitivity, where reason-sensitivity in Moran's sense means the alteration of a mental state by virtue of a constitutive and conceptual relation between that mental state and the reasoning about it as explained in Chapter 1.1.

Lear is more interested in how an unconscious emotion becomes available for affective experience in the first place. Lear, as I explained in Chapter 3.2, is a seeing-as conceptualist about emotions, and holds a version of the primal scene account for pathological emotional reactions (a developmental account). He normally speaks mainly of one nodal emotion rather than a primal series of such emotions. Much like early Freud, Lear claims that one should affectively remember the primal scene and express its emotional dimension "by imaginatively re-living the experience, this time with feeling."[21] Similar to early Freud, the kind of catharsis Lear imagines need not be expressed in a great bout of affect. Verbal expression is cathartic enough.[22] Lear describes how this feeling becomes available to the patient:

> It is because she would have held herself responsible, blamed herself, for her [emotion], that [the patient] archaically denied responsibility via repression. But as she is able to cease *holding* herself responsible for her

20 Richard Moran, "Psychoanalysis and the Limits of Reflection," in Lear, *A Case for Irony*, 107–108. See also Moran, "Replies," 469–470.

21 Lear, *Love and Its Place in Nature*, 34.

22 Ibid., 64–64.

> emotions, she is able to *accept* responsibility for them: that is, she is able to acknowledge them as hers. Accepting responsibility is essentially a first-person relation. In accepting responsibility I acknowledge who or what I am.[23]

The move from holding herself and her emotion blameworthy to an emotional stance of acceptance of that attitude is meant to render that hitherto unconscious emotion available for self-aware experience. And yet this process is left under-described. How is the "archaic" repression, as Lear calls it, removed? As long as repression is understood to be this mysterious capacity to render an emotion unconscious or unavailable to self-aware "ownership," the process of removing it remains just as mysterious.

There is indeed a difference between saying "this emotion is coming over me" and "this is how I feel." We can regard an emotion as an experience we suffer as patients, and we can regard it as expressing our own personal affective take on the situation at hand. But I think it is very difficult to pinpoint exactly what this difference is or how one can move from one stance to another. The route to denial of self-involvement seems always open in the case of emotions, due to their phenomenological feature of passivity. Lear does not discuss this fragility of acknowledgment of self-involvement, which haunts analysis at every stage. One must admit that to say that one "owns" an emotion sounds metaphorical.

Although the process through which repression is removed remains mysterious and under-described in Lear's account, I think many will agree that at some point in analysis, the patient becomes able to express a nodal emotion in a way that implicates her qua the person that she is in her social world and her relationships. For Lear, expressing an emotion means getting clear on its intentional content, since he is a conceptualist about emotions. The non-conceptualist version of that aim would be to attend to and verbally describe the here-and-now emotionally salient features of the situation. In other words, much like Moran, Lear's expressive stance involves giving reasons for that occurrent emotion. But unlike Moran, who regards this examination of reasons as deliberation with the aim to either avow or disavow the emotion, Lear speaks of giving reasons for the emotion while withholding any judgment regarding their endorsement as good reasons or their rejection as bad reasons.

As Lear remarks, now that the emotion is expressed, it is indeed available for avowal or disavowal in the manner Moran envisages. He says: "Ironically, once one has accepted responsibility for an emotion, one can, if one wishes, hold oneself responsible for it. Once I accept the emotion as mine," I can ask, "Is this the way I want to be?"[24]

23 Ibid., 66.
24 Ibid., fn. 63.

Lear seems to think that it could be possible in such circumstances to disavow the nodal emotion and that the emotion would accordingly subside, much like Moran suggests, and yet he implies that this is an unlikely scenario.[25] Emotions need not be sensitive to reasons. But we need not be alienated from a recalcitrant emotion. Unlike Moran, Lear does not think that one can own or be responsible for an emotion only if that emotion is responsive to one's rational deliberation in the right way. The patient can still express a recalcitrant emotion as her own and accept that aspect of herself, even if she finds it unjustified or unfitting.

The responsibility for the emotion then becomes the responsibility to be self-aware of this emotion and its describable aspect. No longer repressed, that emotion can be expressed whenever it is enlivened, without being displaced onto various other people and things that only imaginatively relate to its object. In other words, no longer repressed, this emotion will stop serving as the terms in which certain situations become emotionally salient. That is, properly expressed, the hitherto unconscious emotion ceases to be expressed in an imaginatively distorted form that is both baffling and troubling.

Being responsible for an emotion in Lear's sense is revealed to amount to being responsible for its manner of expression. The main goal of analysis, as Lear sees it, is to cure the patient from her symptom and replace it with a new and more productive and joyous form of expression of the same nodal emotion, which has been hitherto expressed through the symptom. As Lear says:

> [T]he anger and disappointment at the dead parent might not go away, even after rational assessment that it is not ultimately warranted, even after analytic therapy. But it might become an occasion for humor, for poetry, for mediation and loss, for taking up moral causes, for writing critical book reviews, for spending more time with one's own children, for reading Shakespeare, for taking up canoeing. The success of therapy does not necessarily depend on the anger's *going away* in the light of rational assessment ... but rather on whether one ceases to be *stuck* with the anger in rigid routines that one does not understand.[26]

Lear proposes a pragmatic vision, whereby therapy is meant to restore one's capacity to enjoy productive activities instead of being trapped in a troubling symptom. But if this shift consists, as Lear suggests, in a shift of the manner in which a very specific nodal emotion is expressed, then this new joyous condition is still haunted by the overemphasis of very few emotions and respectively very few events in one's life. In fact, one's ongoing mental health would from then on depend on one's constant care to make room in

25 Lear, *A Case for Irony*, 70.
26 Lear, *A Case for Irony*, 70–71.

one's life for expressing those nodal emotions in a controlled manner through various intentional actions.

Neglecting the controlled expression of these haunting emotions may result in un-desirable, imaginatively distorted forms of expression, that is, in another or perhaps the same old symptom. If therapy is about controlling the expression of few relatively intense and life-determining emotions, then the result appears to be yet another form of self-management.

The etiological narrative or the primal series of nodal emotions and the symptom stay intact and another new joyous or valued activity now adds a further layer to its temporal stratification. Although the story of suffering has now evolved into a life-affirming story, it is still the same story. This is the patient's story and there is nothing she can do about *that*.[27]

Such a graduate analysand *knows very well* that these few events need not make her life miserable, indeed they can be used as emotional motives to further her flourishing, *but still* those few events have determined not just her past sufferings but her present possibilities for a creative and productive life. Such a graduate patient may not be "stuck" with her symptom, as Lear suggests, but she is still stuck with her nodal emotions and is constantly dealing with their expression. These nodal emotions are as important as they always were and the question regarding the source of this importance haunts Lear's account – as well as the other narrative accounts that trace a pathology back to few specific scenes or memories. Can a few scenes determine one's life options for mental pathology or mental health?

If the primal scene or emotion in Moran's example has occurred in early childhood, then indeed the death of a parent at a young age is emotionally traumatic and we would expect all children to go through extreme emotional turmoil. Perhaps such objective traumas, such as rape or torture or natural disasters, whose affective weight can be attributed to these extreme external circumstances, can only be managed in this manner. But many of the primal scenes that come up in analysis are not so obviously traumatic. In cases like Jonah's or in many other cases from Freud's writings, it is hard to see what makes those scenes or memories so much more emotionally significant than the many other emotional experiences of the patient throughout her life.

The trauma model does not map well on the "neurotic-light" patient I am imagining. In such not-so-traumatic cases, the source of the affective significance of nodal emotions (and indeed of most emotions) cannot be fully ascribed to the external circumstances that triggered them. As I have

27 As Collingwood says about necessity in storytelling, which he sees as analogous to historical narratives: "the whole aim of the novelist is to show the characters acting and the incidents developing in a manner determined by a necessity internal to themselves. The story, if it is a good story, cannot develop otherwise than as it does; the novelist in imagining it cannot imagine it developing except as it does develop" (Collingwood, *The Historical Imagination*, 242). See also Wollheim on the "tyranny of the past," (*The Thread of Life*, 159–161).

stressed through Chapters 3 and 4, the importance of those nodal emotions in one's emotional life appears overemphasized, and psychoanalytic therapy should address that very overemphasis, which is the main source of pathology. An analysis that declares those emotions *the* cause of the patient's symptom and then declares their self-aware controlled expression as the key to the recovered patient's mental health, further serves to overemphasize those few past emotional experiences.

On the associative account, analysis is not just about undoing the condensation and displacement of the symptom and recognizing and expressing hitherto repressed emotions. The repressed emotions themselves are understood to be nodal synthesized emotions. These emotions are "nodal" since they heavily condense many other emotions; they imaginatively synthesize everything that is emotionally conflictual in the patient's life and provide the patient with a dominant model through which she sees the world as emotionally salient. According to the associative account, therapy's aim is to break or loosen the grip of this picture, to undo the affective overemphasis of the nodal emotions by undoing the condensations and displacements that render these emotions so significant in the first place.

In the next section I introduce a different way to understand the kind of emotion expression through verbal description that takes place in analysis. The de-mystified conception of repression explicated in the previous chapter (5.i.4) and the twofold concept of the Freudian unconscious as patterns of inattention and patterns of imaginative association, also allows for a de-mystified and spelled-out understanding of how unconscious emotions may be rendered available to verbal expression and description in the first place. I respectively propose that the responsibility one assumes when making the unconscious conscious or the inattended attended is neither reason-sensitivity in Moran's sense nor emotion ownership in Lear's sense. I will show that this kind of verbal description and self-awareness involves "internal changes" that can gradually undo the condensations and displacements that grant certain synthesized emotions such a dominant role in the patient's present emotional patterns.

5. "Working-through" one's imaginative-emotional network

I will claim in the last section of this chapter that it is misleading to think of analysis as aiming at the exposure of the nodal unconscious emotions that give shape to the symptom imaginative synthesis (condensation). In other words, I will show that undoing the condensations and displacements of the nodal emotions need not grant a major role to the explicit verbal description of the objects of these emotions. But even if this were the purpose of analysis, free association would not reach nodal emotions without obstacle.

According to the associative account, the patient's problem in life is not caused by just one well-individuated emotion that the patient is alienated from, but by an imaginatively interconnected bundle of such unconscious emotions. Many associative routes within the patient's emotional–imaginative network thus lead to the nodal synthesized emotions. But those associative routes pass through many other emotions that are initially blocked by patterns of inattention. Even if we describe free association as having a "direction," as progressing along zigzag lines through many emotions with the purpose of approaching *the* nodal emotions, such a process would go hand in hand with the gradual breaking of patterns of inattention.

In the context of analysis, we may call the encountered patterns of inattention "resistances" that need to be removed in order to continue and free associate until the nodal emotions are enlivened and expressed. But in effect, the patient's habits of inattention or her difficulty to "listen" to and give voice to her associations do not depend on the therapeutic context or aim. That is, although we may describe aversive inattention as "resistance" in the context of the analytic situation, it is not the case that the patient resists under that description. Resistance too is in the realm of non-Anscombian action (described in Chapter 3.4.A).[28] In this section, I consider a moment in an analysis that is already in progress, when a patient overcomes such "resistance" through verbally expressing an incompatible emotion that is en route, so to speak, to the nodal emotions.

Consider a moment in analysis where the patient "listens" to a disturbing passing thought that strikes her, and where the hovering demand to voice associations slows down what would otherwise be an immediate attention deflection. It does not matter much if this emotionally laden thought is a new thought or an old memory, the very fact that it would under normal circumstances be forcefully ignored by the patient qualifies it as "unconscious," since by "unconscious," as stressed in the book, I simply mean inattended to, not-thought-about, unacknowledged. Regarded this way, removing repression is nothing other but resisting the automatic habit of attention deflection once such a thought or emotion strikes one's awareness.

A hitherto inattended emotion has a chance of becoming available to self-aware verbal expression only when the habits of inattention that buffer its enlivenment have already been sufficiently broken. This is how such a thought or emotion can be triggered through free association and strike one's awareness in the first place. Such a thought or emotion can still be ignored or suppressed afresh whenever it surfaces one's awareness through condensation and displacement. The moment I want to describe is exactly the moment where the demand to voice associations suspends what would otherwise be a habitual and unreflective attention deflection. Getting clear on how one breaks this particular habit of inattention will then also serve

28 For the sake of simplicity, I will not discuss the cases where secondary benefit from neurosis may play an additional causal role in sustaining one's patterns of inattention. E.g. Freud, *Inhibitions, Symptoms and Anxiety*, 99.

to clarify how the patient has broken other habits of inattention in such a way that made this particular moment possible in the first place.

As described in the first section of this chapter, such a moment confronts the patient with her aversive reaction to her own association that just came to her. Under normal circumstances, one's aversive attention deflection (as if) spares one from feeling guilty or ashamed, self-disgusted, or anxious about the ignored thought or emotion (see Chapter 3.4). But the suspension of the alienating aversive reaction in analysis, which is often manifested in the patient's hesitance to talk, may give rise to those negative feelings.

Ideally, the patient voices associations despite her aversion and further articulates her initial hesitance and her reasons for keeping silent, which effectively describe her negative feelings about the thought or emotion in question. The analyst is a non-judgmental audience, which helps the patient give voice to her associations. But the patient as listener to her own voice and as "listener" to her associations turns out to be judgmental in her self-directed emotions. Although an aversive emotional reaction is not in the first instance a judgment, verbally expressing it makes it look a judgment, like an appropriateness judgment about the thought or emotion that is the object of the alienating aversion.

Far from "leaving aside all criticism," the patient gives voice to self-criticism, which reveals certain moral and often moralistic expectations the patient has of herself, or other aspects of the patient's self-image that conflict with the voiced thought or emotion. By verbally expressing and voicing her aversive emotions toward an association, the patient effectively expresses an implicit acknowledgment that this association is hers and reflects who she is rather than the "voices in her head."

Why would anyone bother to rationally criticize an emotion that is not of a person qua person? If one genuinely thought of an emotion that came over one as analogous to a tooth ache one would not rationally assess the emotion. If one genuinely thought of an emotion as the result of a criticizable little person within that is not them, why would one feel guilty or ashamed or disgusted with oneself? Whether or not the patient announces her emotional association "with feeling," whether or not the patient accepts her emotion as hers "in the right way" as Lear says when it comes to nodal emotions, the very activity of self-criticism effectively implies this kind of acknowledgement of emotion ownership.

In fact, the very voicing of the association in front of an audience involves the implicit acknowledgment that the association does not just come to the patient, but also comes from the patient. The analytic situation is placed in a second-personal space where people ascribe voiced speech to the person speaking (and not to some other little person within the speaker). The patient not only "listens" to the association that strikes her, but also listens to her own voice pronouncing that association. And this listening at least potentially activates the patient's everyday practice of ascribing thoughts and emotions to the person who voices them. Even the fundamental rule of psychoanalysis to take a judgmental holiday and vocally share free associations implies that although the analyst will not judge us in reference to various notions of appropriateness, the analyst nevertheless assumes that everything we say and how we say it shows something about us, or there would be no need to take such a judgmental holiday.

Furthermore, any such apparently conflictual thought or emotion may be otherwise manifested in our lives outside analysis anyway. If someone we know recognizes this emotion as ours then that person would see us as the source of this emotion and would hold us responsible for having it, whether or not we acknowledge that we have the emotion. If we understand, as Lear does, the responsibility one can have over an emotional attitude in terms of "ownership," then this responsibility does not go away when one turns a blind eye to the emotion. Inasmuch as this describable emotion can be recognized and described by others or impact our relationships, we are in any case responsible for it.

When it comes to the expression of nodal emotions, the ones that comprise the terms of salience that give rise to the symptom, Lear encourages the patient to take responsibility over their manner of expression, starting with the verbal expression of the emotion in question, namely with the description of its object. But the task of verbal expression and description in analysis does not end with the description of the emotional salience of one person or thing from one well-circumscribed situation, whether this is *the* nodal emotion Lear talks about or any other emotion the patient expresses in analysis, long before the expression of nodal emotions is even possible. And there is another kind of responsibility over any emotion expressed in analysis, which goes hand in hand with the special kind of verbal expression that happens in analysis.

Verbally expressing look-alike reasons for an occurrent emotion is as far as one normally gets when one verbally expresses one's emotional reaction *prior* to analysis. In everyday circumstances, one expresses an emotion while addressing a specific person and the very interaction with that person circumscribes the emotion to the here-and-now situation. The kind of "reasons" that are relevant for this emotional interaction are indeed the rationalizations of the emotion, namely the description of the here-and-now emotionally salient object. And those rationalizations, which look like reasons, can be subject to rational criticism with reference to various notions of appropriateness. Even if, according to the associative account, emotions are actually not inherently rationally assessable states, they are nonetheless treated as such in our society, which exerts peer group pressure for emotions to be normatively endorsable.

Analysis provides peculiar circumstances, where giving reasons is regarded on the one hand as rationalizing and on the other hand as a move in free association rather than as a move in rational reflection. That is, analysis regards any voiced thought or emotion that comes to the patient as having been imaginatively triggered by talking about something else and as a further imaginative trigger for further association. The same applies for the reasons voiced in the scenario imagined here, where the patient suspends her aversive reaction to an emotional thought or feeling that struck her (not the nodal emotion that provides the symptomatic terms of salience) and verbally expresses that emotion, its rationalizations and the criticisms against them. All these reasons, both look-alike reasons and reasons in the standard normative sense, are regarded as points of departure for further free association.

In other words, verbally expressing an individuated occurrent emotion does not end with the verbal expression of a detailed propositional attitude. Even if the patient criticizes her rationalizations for this emotion with reference to notions of appropriateness and thereby relates to that hitherto unacknowledged emotion as a propositional attitude, the context of analysis does not respect the integrity of propositions. Whereas ordinary emotional interactions force one to focus on the propositional and inferential character of their expressive speech in sentences, the kind of speaking that occurs in analysis aims to encourage rather than block the imagination's fragmentary and connective operations.

Fragments of the describable aspect of the criticized emotion, various aspects of the object of that emotion, trigger further associations to other emotionally laden thoughts or memories. Rationalizing the initially voiced and criticized emotion, far from serving to individuate the emotion in questions (as it would in normal everyday circumstances), fragments its describable aspect and connects those fragments with various fragments of other emotions. Each such rationalization, in other words, which is effectively a described emotionally salient object, becomes a point of departure for further association. It is no rare occasion that a patient who expresses an occurrent emotion in an analytic session by articulating a propositional attitude with a specific object circumscribed in certain spatio-temporal circumstances, will also express other imaginatively related emotional reactions circumscribed by different spatio-temporal situations within that very analytic session.

This is inevitably an empirical claim, but I am confident that anyone who has gone through psychoanalytic therapy will attest that it is often the case that expressing one emotion in a therapy session comes together with expressing a few more interconnected emotions. Even when talking about a simple emotional reaction the patient had this morning on the bus on the way to the analytic session, other imaginatively related emotions whose objects belong to different spatio-temporal external circumstances will be discussed – within that very session.

The very fact that one emotion "reminds" the patient of other emotions or memories, memories that may trigger in the patient new emotional reactions, demonstrates that these now experienced emotions (whether they echo old reactions or constitute new ones) are both causally and imaginatively connected. That is, verbally expressing emotions out loud demonstrates this wandering from one emotion to the next, a wandering that is presupposed to be not arbitrary but caused by imaginative connections that can be identified and described. In other words, spelling out the imaginative connections between the initially voiced and criticized emotion and the other emotions the patient can now experience and express, effectively exposes what we may call a mini emotional pattern or an associatively interconnected mini-series of emotions.

The verbal expression of the mini-series, its objects, and its imaginative interconnections enables the adding-on of various thematic threads that follow the zigzag lines and run through the emotions of the mini series. Thematic threads comprise an emotional issue, such as: issues with dealing with the anger of others; issues with class consciousness; difficulties in being alone or in company; issues with taking risks; sensitivities about one's looks or sexuality; issues with specific people in certain respects (such as being insecure with that friend, being offensive and mean with a certain colleague, feeling guilty about every little thing with a parent, fearing the envy of certain people and so on). These themes do not comprise rules that somehow determine each temporally indexed emotion in the mini-series. They are not causally operative in the first instance, and their applicability to the imaginative network is just as in flux as the network itself. Themes are concepts that may apply to patterns that are traceable retroactively and that provide a formulation of what troubles the patient or emotionally characterizes her at a certain moment in time.

When a patient verbally expresses one emotion in a psychotherapeutic session, it may be an occasion for the kind of redescription Hacking talks about (see Chapter 4.1). That is, if this is an emotion whose object is from an old memory, it is possible that the current emotional experience has not occurred at the time of the event. And furthermore, the patient's current conceptual capacities as well as endorsed norms, cares and concerns, serve to redescribe that old memory in new ways that may not have been available to that patient in the past. And that redescription may, through fragmentation and association, trigger a new emotional episode.

But there is another form of redescription that may occur in such an analytic session, where not just one but few emotions are described as an imaginatively interconnected mini-series of emotions. Such emotions are not considered in isolation, and one or more of the emotions in the mini-series may have past experiences as their objects. As the patient adds-on thematic threads to the mini-series, as she formulates her issues that can be seen as reflected from the mini-series, those thematic issues shed new light on each of those emotions, now redescribed as instantiating or capturing those particular issues and sensitivities. The past need not be here conceived as a past wound that initiated the issue or the sensitivity. It is just another occasion that captures a certain issue or sensitivity, those things we can be said to be touchy about. In other words, the past event and the current emotional reaction to it is *indicative* of the particular touchy care or concern – it is not its cause.

This described mini-series need not be *the* pattern that involves *the* nodal emotions that developmental and narrative accounts are so focused on, especially since the emotion discussed is not the one the patient came to analysis to dispose of, but just a passing emotional thought that occurred to the patient in this specific session. In fact, in analysis, one discovers that one has many patterns of emotional reaction that have gone so far unnoticed, and some such newly identified mini-patterns may have also been an unnoticed burden on the patient's relationships and social interactions.

One's imaginative–emotional network is not dominated by just one primal series of heavily condensed emotions. The nodal emotions condense entire regions of the patient's emotional–imaginative network, and within such regions it is possible to identify many other mini-series that causally support other mini-patterns of emotional reaction, which the patient did not initially complain about. Such a mini-series may include one nodal emotion of the series whose condensation causes the symptom. Alternatively, some emotions of the mini-series may connect with certain fragments of one (or more) nodal emotion. It is thus possible that certain figures or things that partake in the describable aspect of a nodal emotion that directly imaginatively connects with the symptom will be discussed during such an analytic session, even if that nodal emotion is not expressed as such.

This kind of verbal expression exposes not only look-alike reasons for the individualized emotion under discussion but also what I have been calling explanatory specifications that detail the terms through which the situation under discussion is seen as emotionally salient. Explanatory specifications causally explain the emotion whose verbal expression began this process, as well as the enlivenment or arousal of the other emotions that associatively relate to it. The patient can now see that the emotion she criticized is only partly caused by the circumstances it circumscribes and that it is also caused by those other emotions of hers, by the mini-series of emotions discussed in this particular analytic session.

It is always possible for the patient to declare that mini-series to be a mini-narrative about her past emotional history, over which she has no control. This is her emotional history and this is how her imagination works on that history to produce new emotions, some triggered by new events and situations and others by memories of old ones. The patient cannot go back in time and change her emotional reactions or alternatively the old circumstances to which she now emotionally reacts, and she cannot control the imagination's patterns of association. The patient can always opt to regard emotions as analogous to the operations of mitochondria in cells. Even a patient who feels that emotions are explainable by states that can be brought to attention and are thereby person level phenomena, can always opt to regard emotions as coming from another foreign person within her, such as her past self or her "inner child."

On the other hand, this real-time experience of a mini-series of emotions and the formulation of thematic threads that run through them confronts the patient with emotional issues and sensitivities that are very much alive and present, with no regard to the spatio-temporal index of the scenes or memories discussed. These issues and sensitivities characterize the subject qua person that socially interacts with other persons. At this point, the patient can come to see herself as causally implicated in this mini-pattern.

In other words, the patient can come to acknowledge that the emotion that first seemed to be primarily caused by external circumstances is in fact partly caused by her emotional issues and sensitivities, by her own way of seeing the world as emotionally salient, which in itself is neither the necessary nor the only way to see the world. Although strictly speaking, issues and sensitivities are themes that are added on to the causal imaginative network and are not in themselves causally operative, they are the concepts that the patient will use to describe herself as a person among other persons, and that is the person who is imaginatively associating and effectively sustaining various identifiable patterns. In other words, the responsibility one may come to acknowledge that one has relates to one's involvement in the causal genesis of the emotion under discussion. Although nobody intentionally causes oneself to have an emotional episode that passively strikes one's awareness, when one sees that this emotion reflects one's own issues, one may accept that, to some extent, one is implicated in the formation of one's own emotional reactions.

I cannot say what exactly drives a patient to assume responsibility in this manner. In fact, plausibly, some patients never do. Nothing can force a person to acknowledge that although emotions are passive afflictions, she is nevertheless causally implicated in their formation. Ceasing to hold oneself accountable or blameworthy for an emotion need not encourage one to accept responsibility, as Lear claims. In fact, ceasing to hold oneself blameworthy can lead to a radical renouncement of any responsibility at all.

Perhaps some courage is needed for assuming responsibility for one's self-involvement in one's emotions. Perhaps, in the course of analysis, the patient comes to see the people close to her as exhibiting such patterns themselves and finds herself ascribing to them causal responsibility for their emotional patterns. Analysis makes a new kind of criticism available to the analysand. As she argues with her partner she can accuse him of unfairly "projecting" his own issues on her. Even prior to analysis she may have accused him on occasion that he is "taking out on her" his stress at work, which has nothing to do with her. Perhaps it is again due to the listening to one's own voiced speech in analysis that enables one to see oneself as implicated in the formation of one's emotions in the same manner one would ascribe such implication to others.

Whatever it is that makes the patient assume responsibility for the genesis of the specific emotion she now talks about in analysis, this move involves both disappointment and relief in various interrelated respects.

Especially when it comes to negative emotions such as anger and fear that make other people salient and seen as anger- or fear-provoking, it may be disappointing to find out that these emotions are not entirely the fault of their objects. Even in cases where the emotion under discussion is fitting and justified, giving up on the idea that the world is the sole factor to blame for our emotions, or that our emotions are trustworthy indications about how the world relates to us, leaves us feeling a lot less rational and justified. This may be difficult for a patient who values her rationality as part of her endorsed self-image.

Now in normal circumstances, outside of analysis, when one doubts the justification of one's emotion, one doubts whether one should be going through this emotional episode at all. In fact, this kind of mini-analysis, the unpacking of a condensation of a singular emotional reaction (which is not *the* symptom nor *the* nodal emotion), can occur outside of analysis. The person who is trained in associative reflection and describes her anger at her partner may find herself in real-time unpacking her angry episode to other angers (or maybe guilts or shames) whose objects only imaginatively and not straightforwardly resemble her partner and his behavior in the current situation.

At home, with her partner, she may feel the need to take back an emotional reaction once she realizes that this reaction is largely caused by her own issues and sensitivities. She may apologize to her partner in a way that effectively recounts her unpacking of the initial condensed reaction against him: "I'm sorry, I'm not *really* angry with *you*, I am just frustrated about this issue at work, and I'm also particularly sensitive about this issue, you know what my first boyfriend was like." Outside of analysis it may be inappropriate to let circumstances that do not straightforwardly relate to the here-and-now have this kind of impact on other people.

This mini-analysis in real-time can be used to control and dim down one's emotion. Expressing those other emotions from different contexts and situations effectively shifts one's attention away from the current situation and thereby assists in abandoning one's initial emotional reaction. This form of self-management is more self-aware than the one described in section 3 above, since in this case the operative series of emotions is being directly expressed and acknowledged. Furthermore, this kind of self-management involves acknowledgment of one's own issues and sensitivities due to which one is emotional in the first place (in the broad and loose sense described above, since strictly speaking each reaction is singularly caused by imaginative associations – which are the zigzag lines in one's network, not the thematic threads that can be formulated for them). This kind of self-management cannot be done for others but it can, to a limited extent, be shown to another through the self-explanatory apology of the kind I imagine above. Even people who have not gone through analysis may accept such an apologetic explanation of an unfair emotion. In any case, I appeal to my own as well as to the reader's experiences of such mini self-analysis during an emotional episode for further empirical (but non-scientific) support for the associative account, which regards all emotional attitudes as the condensation and displacement of other emotions.

Such self-management may spare the person who is seen as anger-provoking of the anger that he was initially confronted with, but it is also possible to redescribe the object of the anger and continue to be angry with him. For example, he can now be accused of being insensitive and perhaps even with some justification: "Can't you be more sensitive about my issues? You know very well that saying such things pushes my buttons."

In analysis, however, the analyst is not the ordinary kind of audience to one's expression of one's emotions. In most cases, the emotions expressed do not involve the analyst as a salient object but other people whom the analyst does not even know and has no emotional connection to.[29] Even when the analyst is the object of the patient's emotional reactions in the phenomenon known as transference, which I discuss in the next section, the analyst's non-judgmental attitude should ideally prevent such self-management. In analysis, all emotions enjoy legitimacy for voiced verbal expression and there is ideally no pressure to suppress them or take any of them back in reference to normative notions of appropriateness.[30]

As emphasized in the previous chapter, unpacking a condensed emotional reaction does not show that it was some kind of an illusion and does not render the other emotions revealed in the process more real than the emotional reaction one has initially expressed. Each of these emotions comes with its retroactive rationalizations and explanatory specifications that refer to fragments of other emotions and none of these rationalizations or specifications need to be revoked in analysis. The emotional difficulty to unpack emotions in analysis consists in the acknowledgement that the reality of one's emotions is psychological. This acknowledgement consists in the shift from looking "out there" for reasons to emote in a rationally justified manner to "listening" to one's own private associations as one's subjective causes to emote in an explainable manner.

On the other hand, assuming some responsibility for the causal genesis of an emotion also comes with some relief. Normally, an emotional reaction

29 If the analyst identifies with one of the characters in the patient's life, or if that character links associatively in the analyst's imagination to a character from the analyst's life, then this emotional neutrality may be compromised through the phenomenon of counter-transference. But I here leave that issue aside.

30 As Freud says: "To urge the patient to suppress, renounce or sublimate her instincts the moment she has admitted her erotic transference would be, not an analytic way of dealing with them, but a senseless once." Freud, "Observations on Transference-Love (Further Recommendations on the Technique of Psycho-analysis)" (1915 [1914]), S.E., 12, 159–171, 164. Freud talks about giving the transference emotion "the right to assert itself." Freud, "Remembering, Repeating and Working-Through," S.E., 12, 147–156, 151. The transference emotion needs to be "acquainted" with, rather than managed and pushed aside: Freud, "Remembering, Repeating and Working-Through," 155.

comes with the sense that its object is also its principal cause.[31] This identification of the emotionally salient external circumstances as the primary cause for an emotion is what keeps us in the grip of the emotion. Initially, one feels that one *must* feel the way one does, since all one is doing is being emotionally responsive to a given external situation that one could not have intentionally manufactured and that one can do nothing to change. Assuming responsibility, at least partly, for the causal genesis on this emotion breaks down this *must*. On such occasions, a patient may even explicitly think that another person would react differently to the same situation. Dissolving this *must* provides relief from the initial grip this emotion had on the patient.

Attending to one's emotion in a way that exposes it to be a part of a pattern of emotions that are imaginatively and causally connected, at least partly undoes the displacement that supports this emotion in the first place. The affective weight that in the first instance is ascribed to one set of circumstances from the past or the present is now distributed over the few emotions it "branches out" to. None of the emotions in this mini-series, including the one the patient first expressed, takes up the entire focus of the affective experience. Once the patient assumes responsibility for such a mini-series emotions, she is more concerned with the pattern that emerges from them than with any one of them in particular.

Note also that this assuming of responsibility for the genesis of the emotion now under discussion in analysis, namely the emotion that initially triggered an aversive response that was then made explicit in the form of articulated criticism, does not mean that the patient chose to have that emotion. In fact, exposing the mini-series of emotions in which this initially problematic emotion partakes, which effectively unpacks the condensation that supports it, demonstrates to the patient that in an important respect she is not to be blamed for that emotion. The associations that gave rise to this reaction were created below the level of awareness and the patient does not and cannot control them.

Furthermore, the articulated version of these associations, their identification as similarities etc., which turns them into explanatory specifications, in any case do not qualify as reasons in the standard normative sense. As explained above (6.3), it makes no sense to say of similarities or inversions that they are good or bad and there are no norms in reference to which we could make such judgments. It thus becomes less clear what is criticizable about the emotion whose expression initiated this process.

In other words, the very fact that the initially criticized emotion is now understood as imaginatively caused renders that initial criticism less convincing. The imaginative explainability of emotions makes it possible to become aware of the issues they reflect and to assume responsibility for

31 See introduction to Chapter 1.

them, but without harshly blaming oneself for them. This renders the initial criticism a bit less of a burden, especially given there is nobody actually present in the analytic situation to be hurt or badly influenced by the expression of emotions.

Reflecting imaginatively on one's local mini-pattern also comes with another emotional difficulty. This mini-series of emotions, some of which were hitherto unconscious or unacknowledged, reveals certain cares and concerns that can be added-on to the network as the themes that color its imaginative threads, themes the patient formulates as she provides the aspects in which the various imaginative connections hold. Importantly, these cares and concerns are not judgments about what one wants, needs or values. Unlike the use of the term "care" by the conceptualists described in Chapter 1.3.C, the cares I talk about in this chapter are not psychological entities that can cause psychological phenomena. They are ascribable to a person when examining that person's emotional patterns in a certain period of that person's life. These thematic cares and concerns comprise what we may call one's emotional character that may be apparent to one's intimates who can examine one's emotional behavior, whereas explicitly endorsed cares and concerns, which may in turn be considerations in favor of and guide various intentional actions, comprise one's self-image. Some of these thematic cares and concerns that the patient formulates as a result of exposing mini-series of emotions in analysis probably do not cohere so well with the patient's endorsed cares and concerns, with her self-image.

A patient who likes to think she could never envy her friends since she cares about wholehearted friendships or certain religious moral standards may find it displeasing to discover that she can be ascribed with the care to win a certain competition with a certain friend. A patient who deeply cares about being egalitarian may come to realize that some of her emotions show that she also cares about climbing the social ladder. A patient who deeply cares about her unreserved loyalty to her husband may feel uncomfortable to discover that she also cares about being sexually desired by other men in her life. And so on. Some such tensions have a moral character, some are about the patient's endorsed styles of interactions, such as being cool or elegant or light-hearted, and yet other tensions may be about one's relation to specific people (e.g. How can I be so angry with those I love most? How can I be so insecure with those I don't even respect?).

But the questions about the patient's self-image that come into view (to use one of Lear's favorite expressions[32]) during any given analytic session are often very specific. If a patient discovers that she is competitive and capable of envy on a particular occasion, she is facing a very specific moralistic demand she normally endorses, not an overall realization that she is not a moral person across the board. If a patient discovers that she can be

32 E.g. Lear, *Freud*, 123–124, Lear, *Irony*, 47, 49, 58, 60.

aggressive rather than tolerant and easygoing on certain occasions, she is not thereby discovering that her attempts to cultivate tolerance and patience are a mere sham.

What the patient is giving up on is an all-or-nothing attitude to her values, virtues and styles of interaction in favor of a more complex and qualified understanding of the specific issue discussed. What was before a rigid principle that the person's self-image was wrapped up in is replaced with a more qualified and complex self-ascribed value or virtue or style of interaction. The disappointment and even sadness at the loss of an ideal comes hand in hand with the relief that one need not adhere by that ideal.

It is worthwhile reminding the reader at this point that the neurotic-light patient I am imagining is not a criminal or someone we would normally characterize as evil. When it comes to the moral dimension of such negotiations, the aspect of the patient's self-image that the patient comes to qualify or sometimes reject, usually consists in a specific moralistic demand inherited from the social world. I say "moralistic," since those demands go against certain natural emotions or sexual desires whose expression need not harm anyone (see Chapter 3.4.A.) Coming to terms with natural and relatively harmless aspects of one's cares and concerns is perhaps the greatest source of cathartic relief that comes with expressing a few interconnected emotions.

The patient's self-image includes many very specific endorsed cares and concerns regarding the moral and social realm. Fortunately, not every aspect of the patient's self-image need be on the line at such moments. Only a few or even just one aspect of the patient's self-image come into question on each such occasion. And even then, the realization that one is envious or angry or proud every now and again is itself incremental and gradual, the cumulative result of quite a few such moments in analysis that bring similar issues into view. The patient need not face some terribly traumatic moment of looking in the mirror and discovering that she cannot even recognize herself. Negotiating one's self-image is a long and piecemeal process, a "slow burn" trauma, to use Russell Grigg's deliberately oxymoronic term.[33]

I focus in this section on the unpacking of a certain emotion that comes up in analysis and not of the unpacking of *the* nodal emotion or few such nodal emotions that give shape to the symptom the patient initially came to analysis to cure. This local unpacking of a local condensation induces local "internal changes" in the subject: the release from the grip of the initially criticized emotion; the assuming of responsibility on the genesis of the emotion; and the negotiation of certain aspects of the patient's self-image in reference to the hitherto unacknowledged cares and concerns that can be ascribed to the identified pattern as its add-on thematic stratification. These local internal changes also have more far-ranging effects on the patient's

33 Russell Grigg, "The Place of the Imaginary Ego in Psychoanalysis," *Psychoanalysis Lacan* 1, http://psychoanalysislacan.com/issues/

habits of inattention as well as on the nodal emotions that give shape to her symptom through the imagistic seeing-as relation, that is through their condensation.

This working-through of an emotion, namely unpacking the condensation that causally supports it, relaxes the patient's initial aversive affective reaction to the emotion she was initially hesitant to express. The initial aversive reaction had an individuated emotion or an emotionally laden thought as its object. But once that emotion is unpacked into a mini-series of emotions, the object of the patient's initial aversion is not as individuated as it initially was. In other words, as the object of the initial aversive response "branches out" into a few objects, the initial aversive response loses its grip on its initial object.

This relaxation of aversion together with the acknowledgment of the emotions in the mini-series in question removes this pattern from the unacknowledged and rejected region of the patient's imaginative-emotional network. This removal has a long-term effect. Emotions that would have been ignored due to their association with this hitherto unacknowledged pattern will now be easier to face. If such new emotions or thoughts straightforwardly resemble this newly acknowledged pattern, they would be likely easily "listened" to and acknowledged. Other describable emotions, which prior to this working-through would have been rejected partly because some associations to this mini-pattern, may still be rejected, but the patient's aversion to them will be less intense and perhaps more easily overcome. In other words, the acknowledgement and verbal expression of this mini-series changes, even if only slightly, the patient's patterns of inattention.

Removing this mini-pattern from the unacknowledged part of the patient's emotional–imaginative network, which contains the nodal emotions whose condensation creates the symptom, effectively unblocks certain associative paths that lead to those nodal emotions. As the patient's patterns of attention deflection modify, the associative road to these nodal emotions gradually opens up and they become increasingly more approachable in free association. This process of verbal expression, which gradually exposes parts of the ignored portion of the patient's network, further results in the reduction of the degree of condensation of those nodal emotions. That is to say, inasmuch as those nodal emotions were hitherto associated with the newly exposed mini-pattern, the removal of that pattern from the unacknowledged region of the patient's network unplugs this mini-series from the nodal emotions. The nodal emotions that comprise the terms of salience that cause the symptom the patient initially complained about thereby displace just a little bit less affect than previously.

6. Changing patterns of emotional salience

Working-through one's unacknowledged imaginative-emotional network via the identification and the verbal expression of mini-patterns need not begin at any particular point in this network. Although dissolving the symptom requires undoing the condensation of the relevant nodal emotions, there is no one privileged route for this de-condensation to occur. One may be able to hypothesize nodal emotions that imaginatively connect with the symptom and at some point confront and express them directly, and then slowly work-through the emotions that "radiate" from them.

Or, to take another extreme scenario, one may work-through many emotions that "surround" the nodal emotions without approaching these emotions directly. As the patient works through the surrounding network of emotions that is condensed in a nodal emotion, that emotion becomes gradually increasingly more approachable and less condensed. And the less condensed this nodal emotion is, the less prominent the symptom would be. It could be the case that the patient would reach the nodal emotion and be able to verbally express it only after it has been largely de-condensed. Not so nodal any more, this emotion will have ceased to cause the symptom via seeing-as relations, and its verbal expression would hardly be an affective experience at all.

Verbally expressing a hitherto nodal emotion can, on this scenario, be an after-thought of analysis. That is, on a scenario like this, Jonah may be able to say that he resented his mother for sending him away from hospital, only after his symptoms have already been resolved. The primal scene, on this scenario, would occupy an almost insignificant position in the process of analysis. This is how I read Lacan's phrase: "one does not get better because one remembers. One remembers because one gets better."[34] Lacan's phrase seems to claim that this is always the case. I make no such claims. I only wish to show that this kind of scenario is possible on my account, as well as the therapeutic scenario that grants the identification and verbal expression of nodal emotions a central role in free association. Analysis may also follow other intermediate scenarios that would grant varying degrees of importance to the nodal emotions in the actual process of free association.

Consider the phenomenon of transference, whereby the patient expresses emotional attitudes toward the analyst in analysis. As with any emotional reaction, according to the account I propose, transference emotions are triggered by the here-and-now situation, that is the analytic situation, and are also caused by certain nodal synthesized emotions (that in turn capture the patient's issues and sensitivities). It is often said that the transference experience is when the patient emotionally reacts to the analyst as if the analyst were someone from that patient's life; that the analyst symbolizes, stands for, someone from that patient's life.[35] On the associative and imagistic

34 Jacques Lacan, "The Direction of the Treatment and the Principles of Its Power" [1958], in *Écrits*, trans. Bruce Fink, Héloïse Fink, and Russell Grigg (New-York: Norton, 2006), 521.

35 "the therapist is accepted as symbol – say, of the father": Thomas S. Szasz, "The Concept of Transference," in *Essential Papers in Transference Analysis*, ed. Gregory P. Bauer (Northvale, N.J.: Aronson, 1994), 191.

seeing-as account, conversely, the causal connection between the patient's emotional reactions to people in her life and the patient's reaction to the analyst is not a semantic or a representational relation. As explained in the previous chapter, what causes a here-and-now emotional reaction, whether it is to an analyst or to a waiter, is the bringing to bear (via condensation and displacement) of certain terms (the series of nodal emotions) on the here-and-now.

Outside of analysis, emotional reactions often come with the illusion that their object is not just their causal trigger but also their principal cause qua being an operative reason to emote. But in analysis, especially if the analyst keeps a neutral relation to the patient, as advised by Freud,[36] it becomes more difficult to sustain the emotional reaction as mainly caused and justified by external circumstances, namely by the analyst's behavior. Transference emotions can therefore be more easily recognized as largely caused by the patient's issues and sensitivities (loosely speaking) rather than the patient's emotional reactions outside of analysis. This does not mean that transference stops once it was named and the patient recognized it as such. Transference emotions remain recalcitrant.[37]

Unlike the original emotional symptom that implicates other people in the patient's life and may hurt them and their relationship with the patient, the transference symptom implicates the non-judgmental analyst, who comprises a strange audience for the transference emotions. A normal recipient of an emotional reaction would protest against an unfitting emotion and present the patient with the normative demand to dim it down. The analyst, on the other hand, does not reproach the patient on normative grounds in reference to various notions of appropriateness.

The patient expresses her transference emotions without censorship, but the analyst is a non-cooperative recipient who does not take the patient's verbal expression of her occurrent emotion at face value. That is to say, although the patient treats the analyst as the object and cause of her occurrent emotion, the analyst does not accept or acknowledge this role. Instead, the analyst sees herself or himself as a mere trigger and treats the reaction as largely caused by other emotional issues of the patient and the object of the emotion as dispersed over a few objects from various spatio-temporal circumstances in the patient's emotional history.[38]

The patient is encouraged to continue free associating as she verbally expresses her transference emotions, whereby her affective experience is revealed to involve different people and things and the patient's emotional

36 Freud, "Transference-Love," 164.

37 Freud, "Remembering, Repeating and Working-Through," 155

38 When it comes to transference of a love emotion, for example, Freud urges the analyst not to fool himself that the patient has fallen in love with him due to his irresistible charms. Freud, Transference-Love, 161. "He must treat it as something unreal, as a situation which has to be gone through in treatment and traced back to its unconscious origins": Freud, Transference-Love, 166.

relationships with them, whether in the present or in the past. On the one hand, analysis is a "piece of real life,"[39] inasmuch as all emotions expressed in analysis are considered as real as any other emotion. But on the other hand, transference emotional episodes do not have a strong grip on their object, in the sense that the object remains non-cooperative, and encourages the "branching out" of the patient's attention to different emotionally laden situations from different spatio-temporal contexts. In this sense, analysis is also a "playground."[40] Seeing the analyst as emotionally salient in various ways is no longer a "serious" construal, as Roberts would put it,[41] since the patient's attention is not entirely focused on the analyst qua the object of the emotion. The real-time manifestation of transference emotions allows for an associative inquiry that gradually unpacks the condensation that causally supports them.

Given that analysis itself is the trigger of transference emotions, the nodal emotions that causally contribute to the transference emotions are likely to be the same emotions that give shape to the symptom the patient initially complained about.[42] The transference emotions effectively replace the original symptom. Sometimes that replacement is obvious, as in the case of a woman who falls in love with her analyst and who claims that she is healed from her symptoms.[43] Alternatively, if the symptoms the patient originally complained about persist, they can now be understood in terms of the transference emotions, which are now playing a causal role in sustaining those symptoms.[44] Given that the transference emotions and the symptom both imaginatively connect with the same nodal emotions, they are all now part of the same series. As explained in the previous chapter, the synthesized emotions of such a series are all imaginatively and causally connected. Since the patient is frustrated about her un-cooperated-with transference emotions as well as about their recalcitrance, these emotions qualify as a new symptom, a "transference neurosis."[45] The experience of transference therefore allows for a real-time manifestation of symptomatic emotional episodes that involve the enlivenment of the nodal emotions whose high degree of condensation of many other incompatible and unacknowledged emotions renders them so significant and problematic.

Working-through transference may reveal the nodal emotions that in turn condense and displace many other emotional issues in the patient's life. In

39 Freud, "Remembering, Repeating and Working-Through," 154.

40 Ibid.

41 Roberts, "What an Emotion is," 184.

42 Indeed, Freud claimed that transference emotions "act out" the original emotionally laden memory, whose imaginatively distorted expression caused the symptom in the first place: Freud, "Remembering, Repeating and Working-Through," 150.

43 Freud, "Transference-Love," 162.

44 "we regularly succeed in giving all the symptoms of the illness a new transference meaning": Freud, "Remembering, Repeating and Working-Through," 154.

45 Ibid.

such a scenario, the goal would be to work-through and unpack the nodal emotions to those that "radiate" from it. And yet, we could imagine a scenario where the nodal emotions themselves are not revealed in this process. Instead, other emotions from the patient's unacknowledged network may come into view and be worked-through instead. Unpacking such other emotions, that associatively connect with the transference symptom as well as with those nodal emotions, effectively reduces the condensation of the nodal emotions and gradually unblocks the associative routes that lead to those nodes. Working-through the transference emotions thus need not involve the direct verbal expression of the nodal emotions. In such a scenario, as explained above, the patient can expose and verbally express the regions that "surround" the nodal emotions before approaching them directly.

It does not matter, in other words, whether the patient deals with the nodal emotions (which comprise the terms of salience of the original symptom) or with their imaginative counterpart, namely the transference emotions. As emphasized in this book, the nodal emotions are not in themselves, qua reactions to specific situations from the patient's past, *the* cause for the patient's symptom or the transference neurosis that may replace it during analysis. The affective weight of those nodal emotions and their causal-imaginative effects on the patient's occurrent emotional reactions result from their high degree of condensation of *other* associated emotional issues.

These are the issues that need to be worked-through in analysis. The patient's problem in life is not those nodal emotions as reactions to circumscribed spatio-temporal situations, it is rather the plurality of the patient's unacknowledged emotions and the complexity of the cares and concerns and issues and sensitivities that can be ascribed to the patient. The patient may deal with these issues by verbally expressing and "branching out" the nodal emotions in free association. Or she may deal with them by verbally expressing and "branching out" the transference emotions.

It is this high degree of condensation that makes those nodal emotions the patient's model or imaginative construct through which she sees the world or rather sees certain aspects of present situations as emotionally salient. As the patient works through her emotional network and breaks some of her habits of inattention, the grip of this imaginative picture gradually loosens. A lot less condensed, it is less likely that the imagination would enliven those worked-through nodal emotions. As a result, the patient's patterns of emotional reaction, including (but by no means only) the one she initially complained about, can change. In other words, the terms in which she sees situations as emotionally salient may hopefully be more varied than the relatively few highly condensed synthesized emotions that dominated her life prior to analysis.

This is not to say that one needs or can work-through one's entire imaginative–emotional network or its entire unacknowledged or inattended portion. One's imaginative–emotional network is not just highly rich and complex, it is always in flux, which makes it a moving target for any inquiry. Although the associative account consists in a holistic approach, where emotions are not considered in isolation but rather in imaginatively connected bundles, getting some relief from specific imaginative fixations can be achieved by working-through a few "regions" of such bundles. The end of analysis appears to be a pragmatic matter, a matter of good judgment about the person's emotional well-being.[46]

It is hard to pinpoint what exactly is the notion of emotional well-being that is invoked here. One wants to say that analysis is over when the symptom dissolves. And yet, other symptoms may arise during analysis and previously unnoticed emotional patterns may be declared pathological during analysis. Indeed, one can discover in analysis that one has been burdened by various issues without realizing it due to one's patterns of inattention. As explained in Chapter 5.ii.2, the subject's consideration of certain emotions as pathological is a pragmatic matter, to do with the subject's notions of emotion appropriateness and with her way of managing criticisms by others within her emotional relationships. During analysis, those subjective pragmatic measures are themselves under negotiation and may modify in unpredictable ways.

Although it may seem at first that analysis is aimed at solving the riddle of the initial symptom and at relieving the patient from what she initially complained about, that goal dissipates as analysis progresses. The closer the patient comes to answering her initial question, the less relevant that question becomes. As the initial local symptom becomes better managed or perhaps even just goes away, the patient's rich and complex emotional baggage is slowly revealed. As the patient becomes more self-aware of her emotional patterns, her various issues and sensitivities and their in-flux nature, it becomes difficult to say that there is one or few localized problems or questions to solve.

Prior to analysis the patient is in a grip of a few nodal synthesized emotions in terms of which she sees the world as emotionally salient. Unaware of these nodal synthesized emotions and their implication in patterns of emotional salience, the patient expects reason to convince her of the fittingness or unfittingness of emotional pathology due to which she came to therapy and further expects such conviction to align with her emotional state. As the patient gets better at "listening" to herself she can become aware of the terms in which she sees situations as emotionally salient, where those terms are elements from her various other emotions. Aware of the role past experiences play in seeing the world as emotionally salient, the patient acknowledges that her emotional reactions are not necessitated by external circumstances (unless those are extreme circumstances such as death of a loved one, an earthquake, rape or torture). The initial worries about her emotions' fittingness to external circumstances are

46 Freud, "Analysis Terminable and Interminable" [1937], S.E., 23, 211–253, 249–250.

gradually left behind in favor of an ongoing challenge of negotiating newly formulated and hitherto unacknowledged cares and concerns with her endorsed self-image.

Compare with how Stanley Cavell describes the process of psychoanalytic therapy in connection to his discussion on Wittgenstein's method in the *Investigations*:

> The more one learns, so to speak, the hang of oneself, and mounts one's problems, the less one is able to *say* what one has learned; not because you have *forgotten* what it was, but because nothing you said would seem like an answer or a solution: there is no longer any question or problem which your words would match. You have reached conviction, but not about a proposition; and consistency, but not in a theory. You are different, what you recognize as problems are different, your world is different.[47]

The associative approach does not offer a joyous and productive expression of emotions (Lear), nor a rationally governed life where emotions are, at least when it counts, reason-sensitive (Moran), and certainly not a fine-tuning emotional system that reliably informs us of how external circumstances relate to our endorsed cares and concerns (Prinz). On the account I propose, we may live in relative peace with our emotional lives, but we will always be, to some extent, self-deceived about our emotions and the cares and concerns that can be ascribed to the patterns that we can trace through our emotional experiences. Our emotional lives are complex, in flux and involve many occasions of ambivalence that may give rise to new habits of inattention and sustain some old ones that have not been worked-through in analysis. And we may develop new patterns of emotional reaction that we may suffer from or old patterns may return to haunt us.

In fact, as suggested in Chapter 5.i.4, the capacity to inattend and cultivate habits of inattention is a natural one; it is perhaps one of our basic emotions. Although inattention means that our sense of reality is always partial and compromised, and although it can cause neuroses, it is also a psychologically helpful capacity. Who wants to suffer too harsh truths about themselves and others anyway? If we attended to everything that bothered us, how could we find hope and desire to function and take pleasure in life? As T.S. Eliot says: "Human kind cannot bear too much reality."[48]

Analysis is less about solving problems or curing symptoms than it is about providing tools to cope with one's emotional challenges. Perhaps the most valuable skill that analysis may provide a person who went through it, is the skill to undo condensations during emotional episodes. In contexts

47 Cavell, *Must We Mean What We Say?*, 85–86.
48 T. S. Eliot, *Four Quartets*, (London: Faber & Faber; 2009), 2.

of criticism or self-criticism in reference to various notions of emotion appropriateness, one can perform a mini-analysis in the manner described in the previous section, and provide oneself with both relief and self-understanding. Increasing one's self-awareness of one's emotions cultivates a more forgiving and accepting attitude to oneself (and to others), and may thereby enable one to reduce a bit the frequency of self-deceptive suppression in favor of controlling the public expression of socially objectionable emotions. As Lucy R says to Freud at the end of her analysis: "After all, I can have thoughts and feelings to myself."[49]

49 Freud, Lucy, 121.

Conclusion

The philosophy of emotion has been implicitly governed by a dogma about the role emotions play in our lives. According to the dogma, emotions inform us about our place in the world, about the way the natural and social environment relates to us, to our cares and concerns, including our likes and dislikes, desires, interests, and goals. Emotional salience is, in this view, a matter of tracking core relational themes between our cares and concerns and the external circumstances we encounter. These relations are conceived as the way various situations impinge on one's well-being, qua human organism of a certain social and linguistic niche.

That is, as far as the dogma is concerned, fear tracks all sorts of dangers (e.g. bears, exams), anger tracks wrongs, joy tracks benefits, pride tracks achievements, etc. The tracking is objective, in the sense that an observer from a similar social niche to the emoter would identify the circumstances in which the emotion arose as objectively dangerous or wrongful etc. to that person and her objectively appreciable needs and wants. The causal formation of emotions, according to the *Tracking Dogma*, as we might call it, thus involves some kind of an evaluation of the worldly circumstances confronting the subject.

Philosophers vary as to the extent they demand this tracking system to be sensitive to the dangers and wrongs etc. in our surroundings and to be accurate in its evaluations. But there is wide agreement, that at the very least, emotions *aim* at fittingness, at tracking dangers, wrongs, achievements, benefits, etc. All contemporary philosophers of emotion, in other words, regard emotions as evaluative states of mind. The emotionally salient people and things are taken to be the emotion's intentional object (these are the judgmentalists and seeing-as conceptualists discussed in Chapters 1 and 3) or target (sub-personalists discussed in Chapter 2). According to the *Tracking Dogma*, emotions aim at fitting their intentional objects or targets, which are thereby taken in turn to also be the principal cause of the emotion. The accounts that explicitly talk about evaluations that produce emotions include in their accounts either rational processes (judgmentalism) or law-like causal mechanisms (sub-personalists).

The *Tracking Dogma* comes with a version of the Aristotelian ideal of the Phronimos: The person who has been well brought up and cultivated herself to be a normative member of a certain social and linguistic niche, and who emotes appropriately, with the fitting emotion-type and the fitting intensity under the appropriate circumstances.[1] The *Tracking Dogma* considers this a positive ideal. If emotions aim at tracking core relational themes, should we not all strive for a well-functioning tracking system?

It is true that when we examine people's emotional lives we can notice quite a few patterns of response to typical circumstances that we can judge to be fitting. But many of those patterns are not law-like, that is, we cannot use them to predict how this person will react on any given occasion where the typical circumstances of the pattern are instantiated. I do not always get irritated with the same waiter. Sometimes he amuses me, sometimes I feel compassion for him, and other times I feel indifferent. Indeed, it is quite possible that in a few months I will stop having this pattern altogether, and it is further possible that down the road this pattern will return. As has been shown in this book, any tracking account will have trouble explaining why very similar circumstances, evaluable in the same way as emotion-provoking, sometimes cause an emotional response and sometimes not. In other words, the *Tracking Dogma* inevitably faces the *Emotionality Problem*: A problem that cannot be solved by adding cares and concerns to evaluations. How does it come about that I care enough today but not tomorrow? Each of us can be synoptically ascribed with quite a few patterns of emotional reaction when big enough portions of our emotional history are taken into account. Some of those patterns are widely shared, but most of them are not, if only since most of our emotional reactions occur in ordinary everyday circumstances that concern our intimates and the specific relationships we have with them.

The only kinds of identifiable patterns for which tracking accounts do not face the *Emotionality Problem* are those fitting patterns of response that are also highly predictable. These are the widely shared patterns such as the sadness most of us would feel when our loved one dies, the joy football fans feel when their team wins, the pride most of us feel at our graduation ceremony, and of course the various responses to objects that are so clearly inherited from the evolution of our species such as disgust at vomit, startle from a loud noise, and anger when someone hits us. These predictable and fitting patterns can be ascribed to many people across large populations. The main problem for the *Tracking Dogma* is that these widely shared predictable and fitting patterns of emotional response comprise only a relatively small part of our emotional lives. When considering the emotional history of each person and identifying one person's emotional patterns, some of them are indeed widely shared, but most of them are not, if only since most of our emotional reactions occur in

1 Aristotle, *Nicomachean Ethics*, trans. Terence Irwin, 2nd edn (Indianapolis: Hackett, 1999), 1141b 13–14.

ordinary everyday circumstances that concern our intimates and the specific relationships we have with them.

But the Emotionality Problem is not the only obstacle for the *Tracking Dogma*. As argued in the book, many of the emotional patterns that can be ascribed to us are actually not fitting. We suffer from over-reactions, from emotions that many in our social niche would judge as unfitting, and from emotions that do not fit our endorsed cares and concerns, that we judge to be irrelevant to our well-being. Some of these patterns are quite stable and some are transient. An account of emotion as aiming to track core relational themes within a theory about our well-being cannot begin to explain cases such as these. And all we need to do in order to convince ourselves that these cases are no rare occasion is examine the emotional patterns of our intimates and of our favorite fictional characters, the frequency with which we ascribe people with moods when we think their emotions are not reasonable, and the many expressions in our language used to respond to such unfitting reactions such as: "emotional baggage," "don't shoot the messenger!", "it's time to move on", "touchy!" etc.

Most contemporary accounts do not even bother to provide explanations for this large family of cases. The only exceptions are the developmental accounts discussed in Chapter 3, that lend themselves to the more plausible narrativist account discussed in Chapter 4. Such accounts explain patterns of unfitting reactions in terms of one or a few past emotional experiences. They claim that certain people and things from these past experiences are the true object of the current emotional response. Although the emotional reaction appears inappropriate now, it is in fact fitting to the past experience or memory. Normally, according to these accounts, emotions track dangers and wrongs etc. in the here-and-now, but in some "fringe cases"[2] they track retroactively or in delay. The result is an explanation in the form of a story, where a past event or memory rationalizes a here-and-now emotional episode.

People indeed tell such stories about themselves that are meant to explain their current emotional challenges in terms of past wounds. Yet, such stories often sound like clichés or excuses and are deeply implausible. Why is *this* particular emotionally laden memory or scene so much more important than countless others? Such stories are plausible when the scenes in question are objectively traumatic. These are scenes that would leave a mental scar on anyone, such as rape, torture, natural disaster, the death of a loved one, or alternatively scenes or memories that clearly stand out in one's biography as exceptionally unpleasant. However, most scenes and memories that appear in Freud's case studies, the source and inspiration for the etiological accounts, do not qualify as traumas. In other words, there is nothing objective about most of those scenes and memories for them to be

2 This is the expression Rorty uses to express the supposed rarity of recalcitrant emotions. Rorty, "Explaining Emotions," 103.

emotionally (and retroactively) tracked with such intensity. Although there is thematic affinity between the experiences and memories in question and the current emotional reaction that requires explaining, and although this thematic affinity does not seem arbitrary or contrived, such an explanation cannot be rational, since the importance of those past events and memories cannot be accounted for in terms of an evaluation.

The account offered in this book radically departs from the *Tracking Dogma*. According to the new account, emotions do not have an intrinsic purpose to track anything, they do not relate directly to our well-being, and they involve no evaluations. The account presupposes the minimal evolutionary claim that we are all born "programmed" to emote in certain typical ways in response to certain typical basic objects inherited from the evolution of our species such as bears, heights, snakes, spiders, and caregivers. What is assumed, in other words, is a host of causal co-variances between emotions and basic objects, and not between emotions and superordinate categories such as dangers, benefactors, and other core relational themes understood within a theory of well-being. The account aims to explain how this limited pool of basic objects toward which we emote in predictable and fitting ways in infancy grows to a much bigger pool of objects, toward which we often do not emote in predictable and fitting ways. It further aims to explain how the emotional history of each individual lends itself to thematizing, to the identification of emotional patterns, some very stable and widely shared and many other patterns, some more or less stable and others transient, some fitting and some not. In other words, the account in this book aims not only to explain what the *Tracking Dogma* cannot, but also explain the source of the familiar ascription of core relational themes that pertain to well-being to some of our emotional patterns as well as the source of the familiar thematic affinities that the developmental accounts use for their story-telling.

This account proposes affective processes that are neither rational nor law-like, but result from associative processes of the imagination. This is not to claim, as Hume did, that associations can explain all mental phenomena, but rather that they can explain affective phenomena. The imagination connects present objects and parts of objects, including words qua marks and noises or the associations that are in the wake of those words, to objects and parts of objects from past experiences and memories. The connections are non-conceptual but imagistic (or any other sense modality): similarity, inversion, part–whole, and part–part (of the same whole). These operations of fragmenting and connecting comprise the imagination's ongoing automatic activity below the level of awareness. When enough such connections to certain objects from past emotional experiences accumulate, those past emotions are enlivened together, "condensed," and collectively trigger an affective episode. The subject then often attends to the here-and-now in such a way that certain people and things in the nearby environment become emotionally salient. The affect is thereby "displaced" onto objects in the here-and-now situation. Consequently, the subject can be said to see those here-and-now objects in terms of objects from past emotional experiences.

According to the associative account then, the here-and-now emotionally salient object is not the principal cause of the emotional episode, as it is for the *Tracking Dogma.* It is either merely a trigger, one causal factor among others, or it may just be any other object in the nearby environment to which the subject is attending. Each person's emotional history can thus be seen as an imaginative–emotional network, where each emotional episode imaginatively connects with at least a few other emotional episodes; connections that are both imaginative and causal.

Given that the imagination is a habitual capacity, we can talk about habits of association, habits of emoting in similar ways in typical circumstances. But since the imagination is famously not law-like, these habits may be stable or they may come and go and change over time. And given that the connections in question are not arbitrary but imagistically salient in a way that is sharable with other people, then every person's emotional history lends itself to the identification of patterns, imaginative threads that trace paths in that person's network. And it is further possible to speak about the respects in which these connections hold in conceptual terms, to formulate themes that apply to the threads that run through one's network. And finally, given that aspects of the imagination may be either unoriginal and shared, or original and idiosyncratic, and given that the past experiences of the network includes both infant experiences that are widely shared and further experiences that are particular to the person's biography, some patterns will be widely shared, especially among people of the same social niche that share a great deal of cultural and linguistic references, and some patterns will be personal and particular.

This is how the associative account can explain the existence of many kinds of identifiable patterns, not just the fitting and predictable ones. Some of the thematic threads are those that have been traditionally identified as dangers, wrongs, benefits, benefactors, achievements, and so forth. Other themes can be spoken of in terms of cares and concerns, the ones that the person in question is happy to acknowledge and endorse. But these cares and core relational themes that relate to well-being are not in themselves psychological entities that can be brought to bear on here-and-now situations, as the *Tracking Dogma* suggests. And there is nothing intrinsic about the patterns that the *Tracking Dogma* focuses on that makes them fitting, or about the patterns that Tracking Dogmatists neglect to explain that makes them pathological. Whether a pattern is considered pathological depends on our norms of emotional appropriateness and on what the subject considers to be troubling or disruptive in her work life or the relationships she holds dear.

Unlike the tracking accounts, the associative account does not treat unfitting patterns as an inexplicable remainder. Other themes can be formulated for those patterns as well as for fitting ones, such as aspects of that person's self-image, or the person's issues and sensitivities, some of which are the thematic threads that are used in the kind of storytelling the developmentalists and narrativists construct. But unlike the causal hypotheses of the developmentalists and the narrativists, according to the associative account, none of these themes plays a causal role in the formation of emotions, as they are not written into the associative network that is purely imagistic. They are rather concepts that one can apply to an identified pattern, an identification that is always retroactive, done at a certain point in time. A person's emotional "character," comprised of such themes, is therefore not written in stone, but is both relatively stable and in flux. This relative flexibility of character is implicitly acknowledged every time we are surprised by people's emotional reactions, when we identify with characters that develop over the course of a TV series, when we hope to change ourselves or hope that others will change.

Importantly, the imaginative nature of associations, in particular the fact that they come with a built-in demand for sharability with other people, renders them person level processes. Indeed, they are also available to awareness, in the sense that they can be called to introspective attention. Even if, on the associative account, our character should not be seen as rationally constructed through intentional self-training, this does not mean that this character is merely an object to be described from an observer's perspective. This "character" is better named "personality," a personality that is reflected from our emotionally expressive behavior and that exists in second-personal space (albeit a problematic one, as explained in Chapter 5.i.1.A). Unlike the *Tracking Dogma*, which regards emotions as informing us about the world and our place within it, as objectively relating to our well-being, the associative account regards emotions as indicative of our personality, of our issues and sensitivities, what we are touchy about, expressing our subjective and personal way of seeing the world through the imaginative lens of our experiences and memories.

The associative account does not encounter the *Emotionality Problem*, and can answer the singularity question: What makes a specific individual emote when they do? Each reaction is caused *singularly*, by imaginative associations made at that moment. Except for the biologically programmed reactions to bears, heights, caregivers etc., which can be said to be caused by patterns that go back to infancy and that are inherited from the evolution of our species, most emotional reactions to many other people and things are not caused by patterns. That is, although each reaction can be seen as part of a pattern when considered retroactively, and although the individual past experiences within that pattern were all contributing factors in the formation of the here-and-now emotional reaction, that pattern did not cause this reaction qua pattern. Law-like patterns and patterns of inference are rules that the mind may follow. But associative patterns are not pre-existing rules that the mind follows, but rather a matter of retroactive and synoptic identification.

The either law-like or rational processes proposed by tracking accounts face the problem of reason-sensitivity, namely the requirement of any account of emotion to allow for the commonly known feature of emotions as sometimes dimming down in response to reasoning against them and sometimes not. If a law-like process is said to interact with reasoning through "top-down" feedback (a term that itself still requires elucidation), then once this feedback is achieved, say through repeated reasoning, we would expect emotions to follow the adjusted law-like process and never be recalcitrant, and yet there are recalcitrant emotions, and plausibly all of us suffer from transient recalcitrant patterns. Or, alternatively, if a law-like process is admitted to never interact with reasoning, then we would expect all un-fitting emotions to remain recalcitrant, and yet they are not. And if affective processes were rational, then we would expect emotions to always be sensitive to reasons, and yet they are not.

Associative processes, neither law-like nor rational, do not face this problem. As described in Chapter 5.ii.3, an emotion may dim down as a result of reasoning in two main ways: (1) The first is a genuine dimming down, where reasoning effectively takes away a significant enough associative cause of the emotion. This taking away of the cause is possible not by virtue of a rational connection between the deliberative conclusion and the emotion, but by virtue of the fact that reasoning is done through speaking, even if only through inner speech, and this speaking can have causal-associative effects. (2) The second way for reasoning to influence us may be when it is effectively used as a way of distracting ourselves from the emotionally salient object. We may thus deceive ourselves to think that we have stopped emoting whereas in fact we merely suppressed the expression of our emotion and moved on. If such repeated reasoning apparently succeeds to dispose of an emotional pattern in the long run, it is because we have developed a pattern of inattending to this rejected emotional pattern.

According to the account proposed in this book, inattending to emotions or turning a blind eye to them is common practice. We engage in this self-deceptive activity without self-awareness. Turning a blind eye, in other words, is not an intentional action in Anscombe's sense that it is done under description, and it is not motivated by reasons. After-the-fact, sometimes many years after-the-fact, one can give "reasons" for this suppression, in terms of incompatibility to one's self-image or moral standards. But this reason-giving is retroactive; it is a form of after-the-fact rationalizing. That is, they are only look-alike reasons, not reasons in the standard normative sense. I call this kind of activity that lends itself to retroactive rationalization non-Anscombian action.

Inattention to emotions, the suppression of both their public expression and private acknowledgement, I propose, is itself an emotionally expressive behavior of an emotion I call "alienating aversion." The aspects of one's self-image used to retroactively "rationalize" inattention are nothing other than themes that one can ascribe to the imaginative threads that run through patterns of alienating aversion and plausibly through other aversive patterns (of shame, guilt, and self-disgust).

This use of retroactively ascribable themes as look-alike reasons is familiar from the way we talk about prototypical emotionally expressive behaviors in general. One talks about themes like "danger" to rationalize running away in fear or of "wrongs" to rationalize lashing out in anger. In other words, although the conception of non-Anscombian action is used in this book only in the context of what I call "habits of inattention," it can include all other emotionally expressive behaviors as well. Here too, these are only look-alike reasons, retroactively given to "rationalize" our emotional behavior. Although I cannot defend this claim here, I nevertheless suggest that the realm of non-Anscombian action plausibly includes many emotionally expressive behaviors that are not so prototypical. Arguably, our emotions motivate many of our actions that have traditionally been considered intentional or rationally motivated.

Non-Anscombian actions are associatively caused and since associations come with a built-in demand for their sharability with others and are made at the person level, non-Anscombian actions are person level behaviors. That is to say, we are responsible for these actions, even if not accountable for them (in the sense of blame) as we are in the case of rationally motivated intentional actions. Enlarging the realm of personhood to include not just rational agency but also emotionally expressive agency promises to shed light on the various notions and degrees of responsibility that we can and do ascribe to people. The introduction of the category of non-Anscombian action promises to be fruitful for the philosophy of practical rationality and in particular for the philosophy of action, which engages in the matter of how our actions and interactions relate to reasons and responsibility.

The associative account proposed in this book also comprises a significant advance for the philosophy of psychoanalysis. The affective–associative processes that produce emotional reactions rely on a radically new understanding of the Freudian unconscious, but one that is a good deal more plausible than the mythic or metaphysical unconscious of some of Freud's texts, most of the secondary literature, and popular culture.

On the conception I propose, the unconscious part of one's emotional life is not hidden in some mysterious inaccessible "place" and is not determined by any entity that is somehow separate or different from the person in question (whether a little person within us, biological-cum-metaphysical drives, or mechanisms in the brain). One's "unconscious" mental states often appear right on the surface of one's social behavior. They are there to be recognized and understood by other persons, especially those who know us well. It is a mistake, on my account, to say with Lear that "there are furious people who *sincerely* do not know this about themselves."[3] This

3 Lear, *A Case for Irony*, 57. My Emphasis.

un-knowledge or unawareness is not genuine, but the result of an emotionally expressive self-deceptive activity of inattention.

Unlike other philosophical treatments of the unconscious, the one proposed here takes no recourse to biological-cum-metaphysical drives, mysterious forces, the Id, or notions of censorship and strategic disguise.[4] The novel conception of the Freudian unconscious presented here unpacks the hitherto strange and mystical notion into two kinds of processes, one consisting in the self-deceptive activity of inattention and the other in the "blind" imaginative activity of association. This new understanding of the Freudian unconscious, explicated in ordinary psychological terms and based on the familiar capacities for self-deception and for identifying similarities, inversions, part–whole and part–part relations, promises to liberate the philosophy of psychoanalysis from its relatively marginal position and put it right at the center of philosophical psychology where it belongs.

The philosophy of psychoanalysis is not primarily concerned with explaining emotions or distinctively emotional symptoms, but rather with the explanation of all psychological symptoms. Nevertheless, although I cannot defend this claim here, the associative account has the resources to explain other neurotic symptoms, in particular obsessional neurosis and hysterical symptoms, by regarding them as emotionally expressive behaviors. In fact, and this is again a claim I cannot defend here, the associative account has the resources to explain all affective phenomena, including moods and the object-choices of sexual desire, and further show how affective phenomena causally and imaginatively interrelate.

One of the main novelties of the present account, is that unlike other Freud-inspired accounts, whether for distinctively emotional pathologies or for other neurotic symptoms, it conceives of the causal implication of various emotionally laden past experiences in non-deterministic terms. It is true that one can find in Freud's texts support for the standard deterministic primal scene accounts as well as for the primal memory accounts. Yet, one can *also* find in Freud's original texts moments of doubt, qualification and subtle shifts of emphasis, where Freud hints or gestures toward a different understanding of how one's past influences one's present emotional life. My account takes very seriously these "unofficial" moments in Freud's texts. Freud raised time and again the question of the historical truth of primal scenes.[5] He also fluctuated between treating the past as developmentally significant on the one hand, and as merely mobilized by present conflicts to imaginatively "distort" the expression of those conflicts on the other hand.[6]

4 This does not mean that nothing can be salvaged from these metaphorical and metaphysical terms. But in order to do that, one needs to make sense of them in ordinary psychological terms.

5 Freud, "Construction in Analysis" [1937], S.E., 23, 257–269; Freud, "Historical Truth," in *Moses and Monotheism* (1939 [1934–38]), S.E., 23, 3–137, Section G 127–132; Freud, *An Infantile Neurosis*, S.E., 17, 60.

6 See discussion in Chapter 4.4.

Freud even explicitly analogized primal scenes to the founding myths of nations.[7] And quite early in his career, he analyzed "screen memories" in terms of the condensation and displacement of other emotionally laden memories.[8] Freud also spoke of the "timelessness" of the unconscious and stressed that one's psychology has its own reality.[9]

The crucial and original move I make in Chapter 5 consists in claiming that those emotionally laden memories, traditionally conceived of as "primal" memories that both cause and provide reason for a current emotional pathology, are actually like "screen memories." They acquire their rationally unjustifiable affective weight from their being themselves condensations and displacements of yet *other* emotional experiences. Such memories should not be seen as a part of a narrative or a story of suffering that temporally ends in the here-and-now pathology, but as imaginative constructs, pictures, or models, that imagistically capture a person's emotional baggage – the complex plurality of emotions that this person has not properly expressed or dealt with, and that all together bias that person's way of emotionally attending to various here-and-now people, things, or even just thoughts or imaginings. Indeed, according to the associative account for emotions, all emotionally laden memories can be regarded as screen memories, since they all acquire their affective weight not just from the spatio-temporal circumstances of the memory but from other emotionally laden memories.

The associative explanation for emotional episodes, be they "pathological" or not, does justice to the therapeutic practice that actually deals with very many emotions and does not just focus on one or few "primal" scenes or memories. And it also does justice to the open-endedness of therapy, since it is the only account that explains why our emotional life should not be understood in terms of a story, even if its imaginative nature lends itself to such storytelling. Storytelling is a form of rationalism that the associative account resists.

Finally, and perhaps most importantly, the associative account provides the conceptual foundations for a new defense of psychoanalysis as a therapeutic practice, in the current climate of its marginalization in favor of the growing dominance of cognitive behavioral therapy and psychiatric medical treatments. This marginalization, and at times outright mockery, largely comes from the wrong-headed scientific self-image of many who practice psychoanalysis.

7 Freud, *A Case of Obsessional Neurosis*, 206–209.

8 Freud, "Screen Memories."

9 E.g.: "It will be a long time before [the patient] can take in our proposal that we should equate phantasy and reality and not bother to begin with whether the childhood experiences under examination are the one or the other. Yet this is clearly the only correct attitude to adopt towards these mental productions. They too possess a reality of a sort." Freud, *Introductory Lectures*, Lecture 23, 368.

Many psychoanalysts today continue to insist that psychoanalysis has scientific credence.[10] Some prominent philosophers of psychoanalysis also continue to speak of psychoanalysis as scientific in various ways. Jonathan Lear regards psychoanalysis as a "science of subjectivity."[11] Jim Hopkins regards psychoanalysis as an extension of common-sense psychology, but in a manner that is still reducible to natural science.[12] Indeed, in recent years Hopkins has dedicated his work to show the compatibility of psychoanalysis with neuroscience.[13] Habermas, and to some extent Ricoeur also regard psychoanalysis as science, a social science.[14] Even humanists such as Richard Moran and Robert Pippin talk about the psychoanalytic situation as taking place in a third-personal theoretical space and of psychoanalytic interpretations of a specific person as theoretical claims.[15]

What worries the Freud-bashers as well as the psychoanalysts that continue to resist them is the misleading prejudice that a practice with empirical aims, usually conceived as relieving the patient's initial symptom, must have scientifically verifiable benefits if it is to have any value. But one must admit that the Freud-bashers (e.g. Grünbaum, Crews) are correct. Psychoanalysis is not a scientific practice and there is no way to scientifically verify that it works given a simple means-ends conception of therapeutic practice. As long as psychoanalysts continue to adopt, in one form or another, Freud's misleading self-image as a scientist, their practice will inevitably seem like the claims of astrology or another pseudo-science.

The only way to defend psychoanalysis is to show why and how it is possible to treat people through the non-scientific method of free association. And this task requires regarding the subject not qua organism with a causally-mechanistic brain nor qua self-aware rational agent, but as a person with an associative network of emotions. Such a network is singular and in flux and is therefore not suitable for scientific inquiry, which at the

10 Although I can offer no statistics on this matter, quite a few analysts I speak to hold this view and quite a few psychoanalytic institutes hold what they call "scientific meetings."

11 Lear, *Freud*, 174.

12 Jim Hopkins, "Psychoanalytic and Scientific Reasoning," *British Journal of Psychotherapy* 13, no. 1 (1996): 86–105; Jim Hopkins, "Introduction: Philosophy and Psychoanalysis," in *Philosophical Essays on Freud*, ed. Richard Wollheim and James Hopkins (Cambridge: Cambridge University Press, 1982).

13 E.g. Jim Hopkins, "Psychoanalysis Representation and Neuroscience: The Freudian Unconscious and the Bayesian brain," in *From the Couch to the Lab: Psychoanalysis, Neuroscience and Cognitive Psychology in Dialogue*, ed. A. Fotopolu, D. Pfaff, and M. Conway (Oxford: Oxford University Press, 2012).

14 Jürgen Habermas, *Knowledge and Human Interests*, trans. Jeremy J. Shapiro (Boston: Beacon Press, 1971[1968]). E.g. "Psychoanalysis is relevant to us as the only tangible example of a science incorporating methodical self-reflection": Ibid., 214. Ricoeur says, in reply to Habermas: "To the extent that I take up this critique of the energetic model of the Freudian metapsychology, I accept classing psychoanalysis along with the critical social sciences": Ricoeur, "The Question of Proof," 198.

15 See discussion in Chapter 6.2.

very least demands a more or less stable object – or, rather, a realm of such objects – whose operations are regular enough to be fitting objects of law-like causal explanation and reliable prediction.

The associative account proposed in this book, although focused on distinctive emotional pathologies, nevertheless shows how psychoanalytic therapy is possible, how the kind of speaking that occurs in free association may gradually modify one's habits of inattention and thereby one's patterns of emotional salience, how talking can indeed potentially be a cure. But the cure in question, much like the pathology that the patient initially complains about, depends largely on the subject's own conception of emotional well-being, which is itself a matter for negotiation during analysis.

The fragility of psychoanalysis as a therapeutic practice that cannot "prove" its results does not originate only from this difficulty of defining what a "cure" consists in. Unlike medical cures or pharmaceutical pain relief, psychoanalytic therapy is neither passively consumed by following the doctor's orders nor definitively achieved at a certain point in time. Yet, this fragility is also the strength of psychoanalysis, what we may call its realism, its taking seriously the ongoing challenge of negotiating the gap between one's emotional life and one's endorsed self-image as a civilized and normative member of a certain linguistic and social niche. This is an emotional negotiation that a psychoanalyst can help us navigate if or when we accept that it is ours to conduct.

If we hold a psychoanalytic vision of the human as characterized by pervasive bad faith and a partly blind self-image that is sustained by habits of inattention, then we should reject the ideal of the Phronimos, whose emotional patterns perfectly embed and reflect the norms of his social niche. We should reject this ideal not just because it is out of reach, but also since its harshness encourages further self-deception about our inappropriate emotions, which may in turn cause further pathology.[16] Instead, we should accept that dealing with this gap between emotions and the norms that regulate them comprises an inevitable aspect of the human condition of persons that partake in the social and civilized world. No realistic therapeutic practice that promotes emotional well-being can claim that it can eliminate this gap. On the proposed associative account, the main gain from analysis consists in the acquisition of a new skill for negotiating and managing this gap.

Psychoanalysts who continue to struggle to show that psychoanalysis is a science sell themselves short. Once we adopt the non-reductive or "liberal" naturalistic framework of Macarthur and De Caro as well as Woodward's interventionist framework of singular causation, we can regard both persons and the psychoanalytic therapy they can go through as belonging to the hitherto unacknowledged category of the non-scientific empirical.

16 On how attempting to reason oneself out of behavioral patterns can cause unhappiness see: Lear, *A Case for Irony*, Chapter 2.

Bibliography

Anscombe, G. E. M. *Intention*, 2nd edn. Oxford: Basil Blackwell, 1985 [1963].

Allen, Barry. "The Soul of Knowledge." *History and Theory* 36, no. 1 (1997): 63–82.

Aristotle. *Nicomachean Ethics*. Trans. Terence Irwin, 2nd edn. Indianapolis, IN: Hackett, 1999.

Aristotle. *Rhetoric*, in *The Complete Works 2*. Ed. Jonathan Barnes. Princeton, NJ: Princeton University Press, 1984.

Bach, Kent. "An Analysis of Self-Deception." *Philosophy and Phenomenological Research* 41, no. 3 (1981): 351–371.

Baier, Annette. "What Emotions Are About." *Philosophical Perspectives* 4 (1990): 1–29.

Ben Ze'ev, Aaron. "Emotion Are Not Mere Judgments." *Philosophy and Phenomenological Research* 68, no. 2 (2004): 450–457.

Boyle, Matthew. "Active Belief." *Canadian Journal of Philosophy*, Supplementary Volume 35, "Belief and Agency" (2009): 119–149.

Bower, Gordon H. "Mood and Memory." *American Psychologist* 36, no. 2 (1981): 129–148.

Brady, Michael S. "The Irrationality of Recalcitrant Emotions." *Philosophical Studies* 145, no. 3 (2009): 413–430.

Brady, Michael S. "Recalcitrant Emotions and Visual Illusions." *American Philosophical Quarterly* 44, no. 3 (2007): 273–284.

Brandom, Robert. *Articulating Reason: An Introduction to Inferentialism*. Cambridge, MA: Harvard University Press, 2000.

Calhoun, Cheshire. "Cognitive Emotions?" in *What Is an Emotion? Classical Readings in Philosophical Psychology*. Ed. Cheshire Calhoun and Robert Solomon, 317–342. New York: Oxford University Press, 1984.

Calhoun, Cheshire. "Subjectivity and Emotion," in *Thinking about Feeling*. Ed. Robert Solomon, 107–121. New York: Oxford University Press, 2004.

Carman, Taylor. "First Persons: On Richard Moran's *Authority and Estrangement*." *Inquiry: An Interdisciplinary Journal of Philosophy* 43, no. 3 (2003): 395–408.

Cavell, Marcia. *Becoming a Subject*. Oxford: Clarendon Press, 2006.

Cavell, Stanley. *The Claim of Reason*. Oxford: Oxford University Press, 1979.

Cavell, Stanley. *Must We Mean What We Say?* Cambridge: Cambridge University Press, 1998 [1969].

Cavell, Stanley. *In Quest for the Ordinary: Lines of Skepticism and Romanticism*. Chicago: Chicago University Press, 1988.

Charland, Louis. “Feeling and Representing: Computational Theory and the Modularity of Affect.” *Synthese* 105, no. 3 (1995): 273–301.

Cioffi, Frank. *Freud and the Question of Pseudoscience*. Chicago: Open Court, 1998.

Collins, Arthur W. “Beastly Experience.” *Philosophy and Phenomenological Research* 58, no. 2 (1998): 375–380.

Collingwood, R. G. “The Historical Imagination” [1935], in *The Idea of History*, 231–249. Oxford: Oxford University Press, 1994 [1946].

Collingwood, R. G. *The Principles of Art*. Oxford: Clarendon Press, 1938.

Crews, Frederick, “The Freud Question: An Exchange.” *The New York Review of Books*, December 8, 2011.

Crews, Frederick and Crews, Freda, eds. *The Memory Wars: Freud’s Legacy in Dispute*. London: Granta Books, 1997 [1995].

D’Arms, Justin and Jacobson, Daniel. “The Moralistic Fallacy: On the ‘Appropriateness’ of Emotions.” *Philosophy and Phenomenological Research* 61, no. 1 (2000): 65–90.

D’Arms, Justin and Jacobson, Daniel. “The Significance of Recalcitrant Emotion (or, Anti-quasijudgmentalism),” in *Philosophy and the Emotions*. Ed. Anthony Hatzimoysis, 127–146. Cambridge: Cambridge University Press, 2003.

Davidson, Donald. “Mental Events,” [1970] in *Essays on Actions and Events*. 2nd edn, 207–224. Oxford: Oxford University Press, 2001 [1980].

Davidson, Donald. “Paradoxes of Irrationality,” in *Philosophical Essays on Freud*. Ed. Richard Wollheim and James Hopkins, 289–305. Cambridge: Cambridge University Press, 1982.

Dennett, Daniel. *Darwin’s Dangerous Idea*. New York: Simon & Schuster, 1995.

Deonna, Julien A. and Klaus R. Scherer. “The Case of the Disappearing Intentional Object: Constraints on a Definition of Emotion.” *Emotion Review* 2, no. 44 (2012): 44–52.

Debes, Remy “Neither Here nor There: The Cognitive Nature of Emotion.” *Philosophical Studies* 146, no. 1 (2009): 1–27.

De Sousa, Ronald. “The Rationality of Emotions,” in *Explaining Emotions*. Ed. Amélie Rorty, 127–151. Berkeley: University of California Press, 1980.

De Sousa, Ronald. *The Rationality of Emotion*. Cambridge MA: MIT Press, 1990 [1987].

Diamond, Cora. “Henry James, Moral Philosophers, Moralism.” *The Henry James Review* 18, no. 3 (1997): 243–257.

Döring, Sabine. “Why Be Emotional?” in *The Oxford Handbook of Philosophy of Emotion*. Ed. Peter Goldie, 283–302. Clarendon: Oxford University Press, 2009.

Ekman, Paul. *Emotions Revealed: Recognizing Faces and Feelings to Improve Communication and Emotional Life*. New York: Henry Hold and Co, 2003.

Eliot, T. S. *Four Quartets*. London: Faber & Faber, 2009 [1943].

Fodor, Jerry. *A Theory of Content and Other Essays*. Cambridge, MA: MIT Press, 1990.

Fodor, Jerry. “Meaningful Words without Sense and Other Revolutions.” *3AM Magazine*, October 19, 2012.

Frege, Gottlob. *The Foundations of Arithmetic: The Logico-Mathematical Enquiry into the Concept of Number* [1884]. Trans. J. L. Austin [1950]. Oxford: Basil Blackwell, 1980.

Frege, Gottlob. “The Thought: A Logical Inquiry” [1919] *Mind* 65, no. 259 (1956): 289–311.

Freud, Sigmund. *The Standard Edition of the Complete Psychological Works of Sigmund Freud.* Trans. James Strachey. London: The Hogarth Press, 1995 [1966].

Gardner, Sebastian. *Irrationality and the Philosophy of Psychoanalysis.* Cambridge: Cambridge University Press, 2006 [1993].

Gardner, Sebastian. "The Unconscious," in *The Cambridge Companion to Freud.* Ed. Jerome Neu, 136–160. Cambridge: Cambridge University Press, 1991.

Gendler, Tamar. "Imagination," in *The Stanford Encyclopedia of Philosophy* (Fall 2011 Edition). Ed. Edward N. Zalta. Available at: http://plato.stanford.edu/archives/fall2011/entries/imagination/

Greenspan, Patricia. "A Case of Mixed Feelings: Ambivalence and the Logic of Emotion," in *Explaining Emotions.* Ed. Amélie Rorty, 223–250. Berkeley: University of California Press, 1980.

Greenspan, Patricia. "Emotions, Rationality, and Mind/Body," in *Thinking about Feeling.* Ed. Robert Solomon, 125–134. New York: Oxford University Press, 2004.

Greenspan, Patricia. *Emotions and Reasons.* London: Routledge, 1988.

Greenspan, Patricia. "Learning Emotions and Ethics," in *The Oxford Handbook of Philosophy of Emotion.* Ed. Peter Goldie, 539–560. Clarendon: Oxford University Press, 2009.

Griffiths, Paul E. "The Degeneration of the Cognitive Theory of Emotions." *Philosophical Psychology* 2, no. 3 (1989): 297–313

Griffiths, Paul E. "Is Emotion a Natural Kind?" in *Thinking about Feeling: Contemporary Philosophers on Emotion.* Ed. Robert Solomon, 233–249. New York: Oxford University Press, 2004.

Griffiths, Paul E. "Towards a Machiavellian Theory of Emotional Appraisal," in *Emotion, Evolution and Rationality.* Ed. Dylan Evans and Pierre Cruse, 89–105. Oxford: Oxford University Press, 2004.

Griffiths, Paul E. *What Emotions Really Are: The Problem of Psychological Categories.* Chicago: Chicago University Press, 1998.

Griffiths, Paul and Scarantino, Andréa. "Don't Give Up on Basic Emotions." *Emotion Review* 3, no. 4 (2011): 444–454.

Grigg, Russell. "The Place of the Imaginary Ego in Psychoanalysis." *PsychoanalysisLacan* 1. Available at: http://psychoanalysislacan.com/issues/

Grünbaum, Adolf. *The Foundations of Psychoanalysis: A Philosophical Critique.* Berkeley: University of California Press, 1984.

Hacking, Ian. *Rewriting the Soul: Multiple Personality and the Sciences of Memory.* Princeton, NJ: Princeton University Press, 1995.

Habermas, Jürgen. "The Interpretation of a Case" [1972], in *Philosophy and Psychoanalysis.* Ed. Brian A. Farrell, 43–49. New York : Macmillan College, 1994.

Habermas, Jürgen. *Knowledge and Human Interests.* Trans. Jeremy J. Shapiro. Boston: Beacon Press, 1971 [1968].

Hegel, G. W. F. *Introductory Lectures on Aesthetics.* Trans. Bernard Bosanquet. Ed. Michael Inwood. London: Penguin, 1993.

Hegel, G. W. F. *Hegel's Philosophy of Mind. Being Part Three of the Encyclopaedia of the Philosophical Sciences* [1830]. Trans. W. Wallace. Oxford: Clarendon Press, 1971.

Helm, Bennett W. *Emotional Reason: Deliberation, Motivation, and the Nature of Value.* Cambridge: Cambridge University Press, 2001.

Hieronymi, Pamela. "Controlling Attitudes." *Pacific Philosophical Quarterly* 87 (2006): 45–74.

Hieronymi, Pamela. "Responsibility for Believing." *Synthese* 161, (2008): 357–373.

Hieronymi, Pamela. "The Wrong Kind of Reason." *The Journal of Philosophy* 102, no. 9 (2005): 437–457.

Hopkins, Jim. "Introduction: Philosophy and Psychoanalysis," in *Philosophical Essays on Freud*. Ed. Richard Wollheim and James Hopkins, vii–xlv. Cambridge: Cambridge University Press, 2008.

Hopkins, Jim. "Psychoanalytic and Scientific Reasoning." *British Journal of Psychotherapy* 13, no. 1 (1996): 86–105.

Hopkins, Jim. "Psychoanalysis Representation and Neuroscience: The Freudian Unconscious and the Bayesian Brain," in *From the Couch to the Lab: Psychoanalysis, Neuroscience and Cognitive Psychology in Dialogue*. Ed. A. Fotopolu, D. Pfaff, and M. Conway, 230–265. Oxford: Oxford University Press, 2012.

Hume, David. *A Treatise of Human Nature* [1738]. London: Everyman's Library Press, 1911.

Hutto, D. D. and Myin, E. *Radicalizing Enactivism: Basic Minds without Content*. Cambridge, MA: MIT Press, 2013.

Jones, Karen. "Quick and Smart? Modularity and the Pro-Emotion Consensus." *Canadian Journal of Philosophy* 36, Supplement Volume 32 (2006): 3–27.

Kant, Immanuel. "Anthropology from a Pragmatic Point of View" [1798]. Ed. and trans. Robert B. Louden. Cambridge: Cambridge University Press, 2006.

Kant, Immanuel. *Critique of Judgment* [1790]. Trans. Werner S. Pluhar. Indianapolis, IN: Hackett Publishing Company, 1987.

Klein, Melanie. *Love, Guilt and Reparation and Other Works 1921–1945*. London: Hogarth Press, 1975.

Korsgaard, Christine M. *The Sources of Normativity*. Cambridge: Cambridge University Press, 1996.

Kukkla, Rebecca and Lance, Mark. *Yo and Lo*. Cambridge, MA: Harvard University Press, 2009.

Lacan, Jacques. *Écrits*. Trans. Bruce Fink, Héloïse Fink, and Russell Grigg. New York: Norton, 2006.

Lacan, Jacques. *Le séminaire de Jacques Lacan, Livre V, Les formations de l'inconscient* [1957–1958]. Ed. Jacques-Alain Miller. Paris: Seuil, 1998.

Lakoff, George. *Don't Think of an Elephant: Know Your Values and Frame the Debate*. White River Junction, VT: Chelsea Green Publishing, 2004.

Laplanche, Jean and Pontalis, Jean-Bertrand. *The Language of Psychoanalysis*. Trans. Donald Nicholson-Smith. London: Karnac, 2006 [1973].

Lazarus, Richard S. *Emotion and Adaptation*. New York: Oxford University Press, 1991.

Lear, Jonathan. "Avowal and Unfreedom." *Philosophy and Phenomenological Research* LXIX: 2 (2004): 448–454.

Lear, Jonathan. *A Case for Irony*. Cambridge, MA: Harvard University Press, 2011.

Lear, Jonathan. *Freud*. London: Routledge, 2006.

Lear, Jonathan. *Love and its Place in Nature*. New York: Farrar, Straus & Giroux, 1990.

Lear, Jonathan. "Wisdom Won From Illness: The Psychoanalytic Grasp of Human Being." *International Journal of Psychoanalysis* (2014) 95: 677–693.

Macarthur, David. "Cavell on Skepticism and the Importance of Not-Knowing." *Conversations: The Journal of Cavellian Studies* 2, (2014): 2–23.

Macarthur, David. "Remarks on 'Architecture is a *Gesture*' (Wittgenstein)." *Paragrana* 23, no. 1 (2014): 88–100.

Macarthur, David. "Taking the Human Sciences Seriously," in *Naturalism and Normativity*. Ed. Mario De Caro and David Macarthur, 123–141. New York: Columbia University Press, 2010.

Mackie, J. L. "Causes and Conditions." *American Philosophical Quarterly* 2, no. 2 (1965): 245–264.

Mannoni, Octave "Je sais bien, mais quand même," in *Clefs Pour L'Imaginaire ou L'autre Scène*, 9–33. Paris: Editions du Seuil, 1969 [1963].

Marshall, Graeme. "Overdetermination and the Emotions," in *Explaining Emotions*. Ed. Amélie Rorty, 197–222. Berkeley: University of California Press, 1980.

McDowell, John. *Mind and World*. Cambridge, MA: Harvard University Press, 2004.

Menzies, Peter. "Causal Efficacy of Mental States," in *Physicalism and Mental Causation*. Ed. Sven Walter and Heinz-Dieter Heckmann, 195–223. Charlottesville, VA: Imprint Academic, 2003.

Moran, Richard. "Anscombe on Practical Knowledge," in *Agency and Action*. Ed. J. Hyman and H. Steward, 43–68. Cambridge: Cambridge University Press, 2004.

Moran, Richard. *Authority and Estrangement: An Essay on Self-Knowledge*. Princeton, NJ: Princeton University Press, 2001.

Moran, Richard. "Psychoanalysis and the Limits of Reflection," in *A Case for Irony*. Ed. Jonathan Lear, 103–114. Cambridge, MA: Harvard University Press, 2011.

Moran, Richard. "Replies to Heal, Reginster, Wilson and Lear." *Philosophy and Phenomenological Research* 69, no. 2 (2004): 455–472.

Nagel, Thomas. "Freud's Permanent Revolution." *The New York Review of Books* 41, no. 9, May 12, 1994.

Nussbaum, Martha C. "Emotions as Judgments of Value and Importance," in *Thinking about Feeling*. Ed. Robert Solomon, 183–199. New York: Oxford University Press, 2004.

Nussbaum, Martha C. *Upheavals of Thought: The Intelligence of Emotions*. New York: Cambridge University Press, 2001.

Pippin, Robert B. "Natural and Normative." *Daedelus*, 138, no. 3 (2009): 35–43.

Plato. *The Republic*, in *The Complete Works of Plato*. Ed. John M. Cooper. Indianapolis, IN: Hackett, 1997.

Power, Mick and Dalgleish, Tim. *Cognition and Emotion: From Order to Disorder*, 2nd edn. Hove: Psychology Press, 2008.

Prinz, Jesse J. *Gut Reactions: A Perceptual Theory of Emotion*. New York: Oxford University Press, 2004.

Redding, Paul. "Freud's Theory of Consciousness," in *The Analytic Freud: Philosophy and Psychoanalysis*. Ed. Michael P. Levine, 119–131. London: Routledge, 2000.

Ricoeur, Paul. "Psychoanalysis and the Movement of Contemporary Culture," in *The Conflict of Interpretations: Essays in Hermeneutics*. Ed. Don Ihde, trans. Willis Domingo, 121–159. Evanston, IL: Northwestern University Press: 1974 [1969].

Ricoeur, Paul. "The Question of Proof in Freud's Psychoanalytic Writings," in *The Philosophy of Paul Ricoeur: An Anthology of His Work*. Ed. Charles E. Reagan and David Steward, 184–210. Boston: Beacon Press, 1978.

Roberts, Robert. "Emotions and the Cannons of Evaluation," in *The Oxford Handbook of Philosophy of Emotion*. Ed. Peter Goldie, 561–584. Oxford: Oxford University Press, 2009.

Roberts, Robert. "What an Emotion is: A Sketch." *The Philosophical Review* 97, no. 2 (1988): 183–209.

Robinson, Jenefer. *Deeper than Reason: Emotion and its Role in Literature, Music and Art*. Oxford: Clarendon Press, 2005.

Rorty, Amélie. "Explaining Emotions," in *Explaining Emotions*, 103–126. Berkeley: University of California Press, 1980.

Rorty, Amélie. "Freud on Unconscious Affects, Mourning and the Erotic Mind," in *The Analytic Freud: Philosophy and Psychoanalysis*. Ed. Michael P. Levine, 195–210. London: Routledge, 1999.

Rosch, Eleanor. "Principles of Categorization," in *Cognition and Categorization*. Ed. Eleanor Rosch and Barbara B. Lloyd, 27–48. Hillsdale, NJ: Lawrence Erlbaum Associates, 1978.

Rosch, Eleanor, Mervis, Carolyn, Gray, Wayne, Johnson, David, and Boyes-Braem, Penny. "Basic Objects in Natural Categories." *Cognitive Psychology* 8, (1976): 382–439.

Sartre, Jean-Paul. *Being and Nothingness: An Essay on Phenomenological Ontology*. Trans. Hazel E. Barnes. New York: Philosophical Library, 1956 [1943].

Szasz, Thomas S. "The Concept of Transference," in *Essential Papers in Transference Analysis*. Ed. Gregory P. Bauer, 165–194. Northvale, NJ: Aronson, 1994.

Scanlon, T. M. "Metaphysics and Morals," in *Naturalism and Normativity*. Ed. Mario De Caro and David Macarthur, 173–192. New York: Columbia University Press, 2010.

Scanlon, T. M. *What We Owe to Each Other*. Cambridge, MA: Harvard University Press, 1998.

Shaffer, Jerome. "An Assessment of Emotion." *American Philosophical Quarterly* 20, no. 2 (1983): 161–173.

Solomon, Robert. "Emotions and Choice" [1973], in *Explaining Emotions*. Ed. Amélie Rorty, 251–282. Berkeley: University of California Press, 1980.

Solomon, Robert. "On Emotions as Judgments," in *Not Passion's Slaves: Emotions and Choice*, 92–113. New York: Oxford University Press, 2003.

Steiner, John. "Turning a Blind Eye: The Cover Up For Oedipus," in *Psychoanalysis and Culture: A Kleinian Perspective*. Ed. David Bell, 86–102. London: Duckworth, 1999.

Stevenson, Leslie. "Twelve Conceptions of Imagination." *British Journal of Aesthetics* 43, no. 3 (2003): 238–259.

Symington, Neville. *A Healing Conversation: How Healing Happens*. London: H. Karnac Books, 2006.

Tappolet, Christine. "Emotions, Perceptions, and Emotional Illusions," in *Perceptual Illusions: Philosophical and Psychological Essays*. Ed. Clotilde Calabi, 207–224. London: Palgrave Macmillan, 2012.

Taylor, Charles. "Self-Interpreting Animals," in *Human Agency and Language: Philosophical Papers 1*, 45–76. Cambridge: Cambridge University Press, 1985.

Taylor, Ken. "The Legacy of Freud." Available at: www.philosophytalk.org/community/blog/ken-taylor/2014/02/legacy-freud.
Wittgenstein, Ludwig. *Philosophical Investigations*. Oxford: Blackwell, 2009 [1953].
Wollheim, Richard. *The Mind and Its Depth*. Cambridge, MA: Harvard University Press, 1993.
Wollheim, Richard. *The Thread of Life*. New Haven, CT: Yale University Press, 1999 [1984].
Woodward, James. "A Theory of Singular Causal Explanation." *Erkenntnis* 21, (1984): 231–262.
Woodward, James. "Explanations and Invariance in the Special Sciences." *The British Journal for the Philosophy of Science* 5, no. 2 (2000): 197–254.
Zajonc, Robert. "Feeling and Thinking: Preferences Need No Inferences." *American Psychologist* 35, (1980): 151–175.

Televisionogrophy

"A Nonpartisan Message from Governor Sarah Palin and Senator Hilary Clinton." In *Saturday Night Live*, 34th season (SNL: September 13, 2008).
Angel, Joss Whedon and David Greenwalt, 5 seasons (The WB: October 5, 1999 – May 19, 2004).
Buffy the Vampire Slayer, Joss Whedon, 7 seasons (UPN: March 10, 1997 – May 20, 2003).

Index

For Product Safety Concerns and Information please contact our EU representative GPSR@taylorandfrancis.com Taylor & Francis Verlag GmbH, Kaufingerstraße 24, 80331 München, Germany